CHINESE

CAMBRIDGE LANGUAGE SURVEYS

General editors
S.R. Anderson *(Yale University)*
J. Bresnan *(Stanford University)*
B. Comrie *(Max Planck Institute for Evolutionary Anthropology, Leipzig)*
W. Dressler *(University of Vienna)*
C. Ewen *(University of Leiden)*
R. Lass *(University of Cape Town)*
D. Lightfoot *(University of Maryland)*
P.H. Matthews *(University of Cambridge)*
S. Romaine *(University of Oxford)*
N.V. Smith *(University College, London)*
N. Vincent *(University of Manchester)*

This series offers general accounts of the major language families of the world, with volumes organised either on a purely genetic basis or on a geographical basis, whichever yields the most convenient and intelligible grouping in each case. Each volume compares and contrasts the typological features of the languages it deals with. It also treats the relevant genetic relationships, historical development and sociolinguistic issues arising from their role and use in the world today. The books are intended for linguists from undergraduate level upwards, but no special knowledge of the languages under consideration is assumed. Volumes such as those on Australia, Native North America and the Amazon Basin are also of wider relevance, as the future of the languages and their speakers raises important social and political issues.

Already published
The languages of Australia *R.M.W. Dixon*
The languages of the Soviet Union *Bernard Comrie*
The Mesoamerican Indian languages *Jorge A. Suárez*
The Papuan languages of New Guinea *William A. Foley*
Chinese *Jerry Norman*
The languages of Japan *Masayoshi Shibatani*
Pidgins and Creoles (volume I: Theory and structure; volume II: Reference survey) *John H. Holm*
The Indo-Aryan languages *Colin Masica*
The Celtic languages *edited by Donald MacAulay*
The Romance languages *Rebecca Posner*
The Amazonian languages *edited by R.M.W. Dixon and Alexandra Y. Aikhenvald*
The Korean language *Ho-Min Sohn*
The languages of Native North America *Marianne Mithun*

Further titles in preparation

CHINESE

JERRY NORMAN

Department of Asian Languages and Literature
University of Washington

CAMBRIDGE
UNIVERSITY PRESS

CAMBRIDGE UNIVERSITY PRESS
Cambridge, New York, Melbourne, Madrid, Cape Town, Singapore, São Paulo,
Delhi, Mexico City

Cambridge University Press
The Edinburgh Building, Cambridge CB2 8RU, UK

Published in the United States of America by Cambridge University Press, New York

www.cambridge.org
Information on this title: www.cambridge.org/9780521296533

First published 1988
17th printing 2012

Printed at MPG Books Group, UK

British Library Cataloguning in Publication data
Norman, Jerry
Chinese. – (Cambridge languaue surveys).
I. Title
1. Chinese language
495.1 PL1071

Library of Congress Cataloguing in Publication data
Norman, Jerry, 1936 –
Chinese.
(Cambridge language surveys)
Bibliography.
Includes index.
1. Chinese language – History.
2. Chinese language – Dialects.
3. Chinese language – Writing.
I. Title. II. Series
PL1075.N67 1987 495.1'09 87-6570

ISBN 978-0-521-29653-3 Paperback

CONTENTS

PREFACE

Chinese is only one of a very few contemporary languages whose history is documented in an unbroken tradition extending back to the second millennium BC. At the same time, in its numerous dialectal forms, it has more speakers than any language spoken in the modern world. This vast extension in time and space has imparted to the study of Chinese a complexity hardly equaled elsewhere. In the present book, I have attempted to sketch a general picture of this language in both its synchronic and its diachronic aspects. Due to the limits of space and my own personal background, some areas have been treated in more detail than others; but it is my hope that, despite whatever deficiencies the book may have in this regard, it will serve as a relatively safe introduction to the study of the Chinese language. In writing the book, I have tried to keep in mind both the general linguist as well as the specialist in Chinese studies; I can only hope that both groups will be able to glean some profit from perusing its pages.

I began to work on this book in 1979; the bulk of the writing was done in 1980 and 1981, when I had the good fortune to receive two fellowships, one from the Committee on Chinese Civilization of the American Council of Learned Societies, and the second from the John Simon Guggenheim Memorial Foundation. I am profoundly grateful to both of the organizations for their timely support.

During the course of writing the present book, a number of professional colleagues and friends have read parts of the manuscript and provided me with valuable suggestions. I would like to express especial thanks to Professors Tsulin Mei, of Cornell University, Qiú Xīguī, of Peking University, and William S.-Y. Wang, of the University of California at Berkeley, for their comments and assistance. In addition, I would like to thank Ms Zhāng Huìyīng of the Institute of Linguistics of the Chinese Academy of Social Sciences, who provided me with a number of extremely useful comments on chapters 3–5. My student, Mr Li Ming-kuang, gave me valuable assistance in compiling the bibliography. Finally, I owe a great deal to Professor Eugénie Henderson, who read through the entire manuscript and offered countless excellent suggestions; her frequent words of encouragement were no small help in bringing the book to successful completion. I scarcely need add, I think, that final responsibility for all views expressed, as well as any errors or shortcomings, rests entirely with the author.

MAJOR CHRONOLOGICAL
DIVISIONS OF CHINESE HISTORY

Xià dynasty	Twenty-first to sixteenth centuries BC
Shāng dynasty	Sixteenth to eleventh centuries BC
Western Zhōu dynasty	Eleventh century to 771 BC
Spring and Autumn period (Chūnqiū)	770 to 476 BC
Warring States period (Zhànguó)	475 to 221 BC
Qín dynasty	221 to 207 BC
Western Hàn dynasty	206 BC to AD 24
Eastern Hàn dynasty	AD 25 to 220
Three Kingdoms period (Sānguó)	AD 220 to 265
Western Jìn dynasty	AD 265 to 316
Eastern Jìn dynasty	AD 317 to 420
Nánběicháo (Northern and Southern dynasties)	AD 420 to 589
Súi dynasty	AD 581 to 618
Táng dynasty	AD 618 to 907
Five Dynasties period	AD 907 to 960
Northern Sòng dynasty	AD 960 to 1127
Southern Sòng dynasty	AD 1127 to 1279
Liáo dynasty	AD 916 to 1125
Jīn dynasty	AD 1115 to 1234
Yuán dynasty	AD 1271 to 1368
Míng dynasty	AD 1368 to 1644
Qīng dynasty	AD 1644 to 1911

Note: Although tone marks are given in this table, they are not used for familiar dynasty names in the text.

To the memory of Yuen Ren Chao, 1892–1982

1

Introduction

1.1 The varieties of Chinese

Few language names are as all-encompassing as that of Chinese. It is made to serve at once for the archaic inscriptions of the oracle bones, the literary language of the Zhou dynasty sages, the language of Tang and Song poetry and the early vernacular language of the classical novels, as well as the modern language in both its standard and dialectal forms. And this list is by no means exhaustive. This creates a certain awkwardness when one wants to speak about one of the varieties of Chinese; if ambiguity is to be avoided, it is necessary to employ a complex designation of some sort – Classical Chinese, Literary Chinese, Middle or Ancient Chinese, Early Vernacular Chinese or, in the case of a modern dialect, a geographical designation like Shànghǎi or Fúzhōu dialect. In this book we will examine Chinese in its many diverse aspects and in the process hope to clarify some of their differences and interrelations.

Why have so many disparate historical stages and geographical variants of a linguistic continuum like this been subsumed under a single name? After all, the modern Chinese dialects are really more like a family of languages, and the Chinese of the first millennium BC is at least as different from the modern standard language as Latin is from Italian or French. The explanation is to be found in the profound unity of Chinese culture that has been transmitted in an unbroken line beginning from the third millennium BC and continuing down to the present day. Even in periods of political disunity at various times in the past, the ideal of a single, culturally unified Chinese empire has never been forgotten. The Chinese language, especially in its written form, has always been one of the most powerful symbols of this cultural unity. The aptness of language as a symbol of cultural and even political unity was facilitated by the use of a script that for all practical purposes was independent of any particular phonetic manifestation of their language, allowing the Chinese to look upon the Chinese language as being more uniform and unchanging than it actually was. Such a view was no doubt also reinforced by the use of a literary language which changed but little from century to century and from dynasty to dynasty. When one adds to these considerations the fact that the Chinese throughout most of their history have been conspicuously uninterested in their spoken language, precisely the area where linguistic variation would have been most evident, it is not hard to see why they considered so many linguistically disparate forms to be a single language. In our own nomenclature, we in the West have simply adopted this Chinese idea.

There can be little doubt concerning cultural continuity in Chinese history, but can a similar degree of cultural cohesion be observed over the vast territory of modern China? In a practical sense, the Chinese dialects differ from one another quite dramatically. A speaker of the Peking dialect can no more understand a person speaking Cantonese than an Englishman can understand an Austrian when each employs his native language. Nevertheless, the Cantonese speaker feels a much closer cultural affinity to the Peking native than an Englishman does to an Austrian. In part this can be explained historically; throughout most of Chinese history Canton and Peking have belonged to the same political entity, and have always used the same written language. England and Austria, on the other hand, have not been united politically since the days of the Roman empire. Moreover, after the Renaissance and Reformation, England and Austria lost many of the linguistic, cultural and religious ties which existed in Western Christendom in the Middle Ages; perhaps the most important factor in creating such different cultural entities in Europe was the abandonment of medieval Latin as a common literary language and the adoption of different local languages for political, religious and literary purposes. China did not experience a comparable break with the past until the present century; and when the Chinese began to abandon their old common literary language, they did not sacrifice the country's linguistic unity: they simply replaced the old literary language with a new unified standard based on the dialect of the capital.

There is another factor which may be viewed as a cause of China's continuing linguistic unity. In Europe, since at least the end of the first millennium AD, a large number of literary languages based on local vernaculars arose and in subsequent centuries many of these early written languages became the bases of several of the most important national languages of modern times. Nothing like this seems to have happened in China. The vernacular literary language which began to evolve in the Tang dynasty (AD 618–907) and gradually developed into the vehicle of a flourishing vernacular literature in the Song (AD 960–1279) and Yuan (AD 1271–1368) dynasties was based on a northern variety of spoken Chinese. As far as is known, no comparable written language based on a non-standard dialect (especially the very aberrant dialects of southeastern China) ever developed. Hence, dialectal forms of Chinese generally lack a historical basis on which to build a literary language to compete with the national standard. The present-day standard written language, on the other hand, is a direct continuation and development of the literary vernacular of Song and Yuan times.

This is not to say that non-standard Chinese dialects have never been written; they have. But they have always been the vehicle for certain types of local literature which traditionally have not enjoyed high repute among the Chinese educated classes. There seems to be no case where a non-standard dialect has ever been employed in a written form as the language of administration or even of commerce. Even in periods when China has been disunited, there has never been an attempt to set up a regional literary language based on one of the local dialects. Beginning in the middle of the nineteenth century, Christian missionaries began to write certain local dialects, generally in romanized form, as part of their effort to evangelize the common people of China. A few of these written dialects, especially that of Amoy, enjoyed a certain success among converted Christians, but they have generally been viewed with hostility by Chinese authorities, and are little used nowadays.

Practically speaking, there have been only two forms of written Chinese throughout most of Chinese history: the classical literary language, based on the prose classics of the Late Zhou and Han periods, and the vernacular literary language which first arose during the Tang dynasty. In both cases, the prestige of the established norms was apparently sufficient to block the development of any dialectal or regional competitors.

The notion of a single Chinese language existing in a great number of forms, both written and spoken, has important implications for Chinese linguistics. For one thing, it is very difficult to draw sharp boundaries between the different varieties of the language: the colloquial is permeated with elements taken from the literary language, and many texts written in the literary language clearly betray the influence of the contemporary vernaculars. The current standard language is an amalgam of the popular Peking dialect, loans from the literary language, and even features of other present-day dialects. The Chinese are of course aware of the differences between the modern vernacular-based standard and the older literary language; but they probably do not think of them as two utterly different languages, as the typical foreign observer is prone to do. The poetry of the Tang dynasty can be read and enjoyed by most university graduates in China; the same can scarcely be said of *Beowulf* or even of Chaucer in the English-speaking world.

To study any one of the many different forms of Chinese, it is necessary to possess at least some familiarity with other important varieties of Chinese. In surveying dialects, for example, it is essential to have a good knowledge of the national standard language and, in some cases, of the provincial or local standard as well; lacking such knowledge, the dialectologist will be hard-pressed to distinguish what is genuinely local in the dialect he is studying and what are importations from some type of standard language. The study of older texts is complicated by similar factors; the researcher must be able to distinguish traditional literary elements from vernacular intrusions. Neither of these tasks is entirely straightforward and easy to carry out. The linguist who deals with Chinese is nonetheless constantly faced with the problem of distinguishing different varieties and strains in the particular language he is dealing with.

The history of the Chinese language can be traced back to approximately the middle of the second millennium BC, to the period known historically as the Shang dynasty (sixteenth to eleventh century BC). The texts which survive from that time are divinatory texts inscribed on bone and shell; they tend to be short and formulaic, but there is little doubt that they are written in a language closely related to the far more abundant written records of the succeeding Zhou dynasty, (Zhōu 1956, 129). The Zhou dynasty (eleventh to third century BC) language is preserved in bronze inscriptions and in copious literary texts which have survived down to the present day; the language of these texts is unquestionably ancestral to all later stages of Chinese, including the modern dialects.

At this early period the Chinese language was spoken in a much smaller territory than it is today. Its center was the Yellow River Plain, but even during the Zhou dynasty it had doubtless already begun to spread to some peripheral areas. In subsequent centuries the Chinese (by which I mean Chinese-speaking peoples) were to spread outward, gradually overcoming and assimilating their ethnic neighbors until they would finally occupy the vast territory that they do at the present time.

The language of such well-known Zhou texts as the *Analects* of Confucius and *Mencius* was probably not very different from cultured contemporary speech. The strict distinction between the written language and the vernacular was something that was to develop in later times. The schism between the written literary medium and the spoken vernacular began to develop in the Han dynasty (206 BC–AD 220), but the differences between the two forms of Chinese may still not have been very great. Naturally the gap between what was written and what was spoken increased in direct proportion to the distance from the formative period of the written language: by the Qing dynasty (AD 1644–1911) the difference between the literary language and the popular vernaculars was very great indeed.

Since literary Chinese has been modeled on the language of the first millennium BC, it is very difficult to trace the development of vernacular Chinese in subsequent centuries. Vernacular elements do appear in written sources, to be sure, but they are generally sporadic intrusions into otherwise literary texts. These vernacular elements are chiefly to be found in texts of popular origin such as Buddhist tales, anecdotal collections, and folk poetry. A full-blown vernacular literature began to appear in the Song dynasty and has developed in a direct line down to modern times: it is in this "old vernacular" that most of the great fictional prose of China is written.

Regional dialects have surely existed in China from the most ancient period, but the written record tells us very little about them. The *Fāngyán* of Yáng Xióng (53 BC–AD 18) is an early record of dialect words; unfortunately the Chinese script does not allow us to form any definite idea of how these words were pronounced. Aside from this work, however, there is very little information to be found concerning Chinese dialects right up to modern times. What little there is is sketchy and rarely interpretable in phonetic terms. In the late Ming dynasty (AD 1368–1644) a few dialect dictionaries appeared; but they were chiefly guides to the proper pronunciation of characters found in literary texts, and are rather poor sources for the study of dialectal vocabulary and of no help at all in the study of syntax. It was only with the arrival of Western missionaries and officials that more detailed descriptions of dialects began to appear. These works, valuable as they are, are marred by the fact that their authors were rarely trained linguists. The scientific study of Chinese dialects began with the work of Bernhard Karlgren and Y. R. Chao in the early part of the present century. Karlgren was interested in Chinese dialects only to the degree that they reflected the pronunciation of what he called Ancient Chinese; Chao, on the other hand, was interested in the dialects as subjects worthy of study in themselves. He personally conducted the first scientific survey of the Wú-speaking region, and planned surveys of the entire country. Unfortunately, because of the war with Japan in the 1930s, only a few of these surveys were ever actually completed. The work of Karlgren and Chao nonetheless provided a solid foundation for later work, much of which has been carried out by their students.

The lack of dialectal texts in earlier times indicates that, throughout most of her history, China has had a standard language; this is clearly the case for the written language, but there are numerous indications that it was also the case for the spoken language as well. It especially stands to reason that, during the great periods of imperial consolidation and bureaucratic centralization, there must have been a common spoken medium or *koine* corresponding to the common written language in which the business of government was carried on. The present standard language has its roots in just such a *koine*; it arose in the foreign dynasties of Liao (AD 916–1125), Jin (AD 1115–1234) and Yuan (AD

1271–1368), all of which established their capitals in the region of present-day Peking.

The present work will examine the Chinese language in its many historical and contemporary variants. It is my belief that none of these variants, be it ancient or modern, standard or regional, can be properly understood without reference to the Chinese language viewed as a whole. It is evident to most that the modern language along with all its dialects is fully intelligible only when examined in a historical perspective. I would also contend that earlier stages of Chinese as revealed in written records can often be better understood when examined in the light of modern spoken forms of the language.

1.2 China's linguistic neighbors

In the remainder of this chapter, Chinese will be examined in relation to the languages which are to be found on her periphery. In doing this I will limit myself to those language groups which are actually contiguous to Chinese at the present time; in this way the necessity of discussing the Indo-European languages of India and Iran is eliminated.

To the north of the Chinese-speaking area are found various languages belonging to the Altaic family. This family is composed of several subgroups: Turkic, Mongolian, Tungusic and, according to some, Japanese and Korean (Miller 1971). All these languages are non-tonal and polysyllabic, typologically very unlike Chinese. Grammatical relationships are mainly shown by a set of suffixes. The classic Altaic subgroups – Turkic, Mongolian and Tungusic – all display vowel harmony to varying degrees, and there appear to be vestiges of this in Japanese and Korean also. All these languages employ Subject–Object–Verb word order; indeed, the syntax of all the above-mentioned language groups is so similar that it is often possible to translate from one to another word for word with few, if any, changes of word order. Comparative work on Turkic, Mongolian and Tungusic is well advanced (Ramstedt 1952; 1957; Poppe 1960). A few European Turkologists remain sceptical about the Altaic theory, but among Mongolian and Tungusic specialists, the Altaic affinity is routinely accepted.

The highly complex and diverse Tibeto-Burman family of languages lies to the west and southwest of China. This family is comprised of scores if not hundreds of languages, many of them spoken by small tribal groups. Tibetan and Burmese, the two languages from which the group takes its name, have long written traditions, but the vast majority of these languages have either never been written or have been reduced to written form only in modern times. While the genetic affiliation of these languages to one another is unquestionable, comparative work is still in its infancy. There is no really adequate comparative study of the group as a whole, but work on some of the subgroups has progressed to a high level of sophistication (Matisoff 1970; 1972).

Chinese is considered by most Tibeto-Burmanists and specialists in Chinese to be a rather distant cousin of this group. We will examine this problem in more detail below.

The region south of the Chinese-speaking area is home to several different ethnic groups possessing their own distinctive languages. The Miao-Yao peoples are the northernmost of these groups; at the present time they are found chiefly in western and southern Húnán, northern Guǎngxī, Guǎngdōng, and in a few areas in Yúnnán and Sichuān. Isolated groups of Miaos can also be found in the extreme southwestern corner of Húběi, and ón Hǎinán island. Both Miao and Yao settlements are also encountered in Vietnam, Laos and Thailand, but these are due to rather recent migrations.

While the relationship of the numerous Miao and Yao dialects to one another is not questioned, the wider genetic relationships of Miao-Yao are still very much a matter of controversy. Comparative work on the family by Chang (1947; 1953; 1966), Downer (1963; 1967), Haudricourt (1954c; 1966), and Purnell (1970) will no doubt aid in solving this problem.

The Tai languages taken in the narrow sense form a closely knit group of languages and dialects spoken in the Guǎngxī Zhuang Autonomous Region and Yúnnán, as well as in Vietnam, Laos, Thailand and Burma. This language family is probably the best studied in Southeast Asia from a comparative point of view. F. K. Li's authoritative *Handbook of comparative Tai* (1977) is a crystallization of a lifetime of work on this topic. There is little doubt that Tai is also related to the Kam-Sui and Bê languages, and (perhaps somewhat more distantly) to the poorly known Kelao, Lakkia and Li languages; the still more obscure Lati and Laqua languages of the China–Vietnam border region are also doubtless related in some way.

In 1942 Paul Benedict proposed that Tai and what he termed Kadai (a cover term for the more distant relatives of Tai: Li, Lati, Laqua, and Kelao, etc.) are related genetically to Austronesian, and that the hypothesis of a Sino-Tai relationship, widely held at that time, was invalid. Although the evidence which Benedict gives to support his theory is in some cases very suggestive, his theory has by no means gained universal nor even general acceptance, especially among specialists in Tai and Chinese linguistics. Now that comparative work on both Tai and Austronesian has progressed far beyond what it was at the time of Benedict's original suggestion, the question needs to be re-examined in a careful and systematic way.

Austroasiatic languages are spoken over a vast geographic range: the Munda languages in northwestern India, Khasi in Assam, Palaung-Wa and Mon in Burma, the Mon-Khmer languages in Indo-China, Vietnamese and Muong in Vietnam. At the present time only three languages of this group are indigenous to China, Va, Blang and Benglong, all spoken along the Burmese border in Yúnnán province. Evidence that Austroasiatic languages were once spoken much more widely in China, and may in fact have influenced the development of Chinese in some ways, will be examined below.

Languages of the extremely widespread Austronesian family, which includes such languages as Indonesian, Samoan and Hawaiian, are spoken in the mountainous areas of Táiwān by a number of different tribal groupings. Theories that Austronesian languages were once spoken on the mainland of China are sometimes encountered (Solheim 1964); but such theories are almost always based on archeological or anthropological arguments, and cannot be verified linguistically.

1.3 Typological characteristics of Chinese

Languages basically can be compared in two ways. Their lexicons and morphologies can be compared with a view to determining whether they have a common origin; to prove this sort of genetic relationship, it is essential to show a pattern of recurring regular phonological correspondences in the lexicon. It is also possible to compare languages in order to classify them into phonological, morphological and syntactic types. When this is done, the groupings arrived at frequently cross genetic lines. For example, Modern Chinese and Trique (a Mexican Indian language) are both typologically tonal languages, but it is highly unlikely that a genetic relationship between them could be demonstrated.

In this section some of the general typological features that have often been used to characterize Chinese and other languages in East Asia will be considered. In every case, Chinese shares the features in question with other neighboring languages; this no doubt is in part due to the mutual influence that these languages have exercised on one another historically, and does not necessarily point to any degree of genetic affiliation.

Many of the languages of East Asia, including Chinese, are monosyllabic. This is generally taken to mean that in these languages morphemes are by and large represented by single syllables. Actually there is probably no language in which all morphemes are monosyllables; but in the type of language that we are referring to here, the vast majority of morphemes do in fact consist of single syllables. This is the case with Chinese at all stages of its development. In Modern Chinese there are many polysyllabic *words*, but these almost always consist of strings of monosyllabic morphemes: a word like *diàn-huà* 'telephone' is made up of two morphemes meaning 'electric-speech' respectively: genuinely polysyllabic morphemes like *zhīzhu* 'spider', *dāla* 'hang down', *gēda* 'lump' are decidedly in the minority.

Chinese, along with many other contiguous languages, is a tone language. In languages of this type, each syllable is characterized by a fixed pitch pattern; such pitch movement may be level (neither rising nor falling), or it may be a contour (rising, falling, or some combination of the two). Tones are phonemic, in that they may serve to differentiate meaning just like consonantal and vocalic segments. Standard Chinese has four tones: the first has a high-level pitch, the second is high rising, the third low falling–rising, and the fourth begins at high pitch and falls abruptly; examples of tones are given below:

Tone 1	Tone 2	Tone 3	Tone 4
bā 'eight'	bá 'pull out'	bǎ 'grasp'	bà 'dam'
xī 'tin'	xí 'mat'	xǐ 'wash'	xì 'opera'
liū 'slide'	liú 'flow'	liǔ 'willow'	liù 'six'

Chinese dialects and the other tonal languages of Asia vary greatly in the number of distinct tonal categories which they possess: complicated systems have seven, eight or (rarely) more tones; four or five tones would be considered a fairly simple tonal system. A very few Chinese dialects have only three tones.

Tonal languages are not only extremely widespread throughout Southeast Asia and China, they also show remarkable similarities to one another. Gordon Downer (1963) has shown that the tonal systems of Chinese, Miao-Yao and Tai have developed in almost identical fashion. To these groups we could also add Viet-Muong (Thompson 1976) and Lolo-Burmese (Matisoff 1972); in all these language families, an originally rather small number of tonal contrasts (usually four) has been increased under the influence of features found at the beginning of the syllable, chiefly voicing; occasionally other features of syllable onset, such as aspiration and glottalization, have also led to the formation of new tonal categories. In subsequent chapters we will examine how this has taken place in a number of Chinese dialects. Since at least the time of the *Qièyùn* dictionary (AD 601), the source on which the reconstruction of Middle Chinese is based, Chinese has lacked consonant clusters; but there is strong evidence that in Old Chinese (first millennium BC) a variety of consonant clusters could occur at the beginning of the syllable and perhaps, in a much more limited way, at the end of the syllable as well. The simplification and eventual loss of all consonantal clusters appears to be a tendency affecting most, if not all, East Asian languages. Mon-Khmer, Tai, Miao-Yao, and Lolo-Burmese all exhibit this tendency, although at least some of the languages of each of these groups still keep a certain number of initial clusters. Chinese, taken as a whole, has progressed furthest in this regard. It may be that the age-old contacts between Chinese and Altaic languages spoken to the north of Chinese territory have influenced Chinese along these lines, since Altaic, as far as can be ascertained, has never tolerated any sort of initial consonant combination at the beginning of words (Poppe 1960).

In traditional typological schemes, Chinese has been considered the pre-eminent example of an isolating or analytic language. By this it is meant that in Chinese the word was by and large coterminous with the morpheme, and that grammatical relationships were shown either by word order or by the use of independent grammatical particles, rather than by affixes or by internal changes in the word itself. This is a reasonably accurate way of describing Chinese at all of its historical stages. Modern Chinese dialects have developed a very small number of quasi-suffixes which function as grammatical determinatives, but grammatical relationships are still mostly shown by word order and by particles. In contrast to the complex suffixing languages of the Altaic family, Chinese indeed appears very analytic, and in this it resembles the languages of Southeast Asia, especially those of the Tai, Miao-Yao, Lolo-Burmese, and Viet-Muong groups. Even the Mon-Khmer languages have only very poorly developed affix systems, and may be considered at least mildly analytic.

Another widespread syntactic feature shared by Chinese and the languages of Southeast Asia is the use of measures (or classifiers) with numerals and determinatives. In these languages a numeral or determinative cannot be used alone with a noun: 'three men' in Chinese is *sān-ge rén* where *sān* is the numeral, *ge* the measure, and *rén* the word for 'man'. The order of these elements varies considerably from language to language, but the principle is much the same. Measures have spread to Japanese and Korean under Chinese influence, but in both languages there are still cases in which measures are not obligatory. Even in Chinese it appears that the obligatory use of measures with numerals and determinatives is a relatively late development; the classical language permitted both numerals and determinatives directly before nouns without any intervening element. Unfortunately, we know little about the historical development of this syntactic feature in the other languages where it is found at present.

Word order has come to be considered an important index of typological classification. The relative positions of subject (S), verb (V) and object (O) are a primary feature of any language; in the East Asian area, it neatly divides all languages into two types – those in which the object precedes the verb, and those in which it follows. The Altaic languages and most of the Tibeto-Burman languages have SOV order; Chinese, Tai, Miao-Yao, Viet-Muong, and Mon-Khmer

Table 1.1. Typological traits in Asian languages

	1	2	3	4	5	6	7
Modern Chinese	+	+	+	+	+	+	+
Classical Chinese	+	?	−	+	−	+	+
Thai (Siamese)	+	+	−	+	+	−	+
Li	+	+	−	+	+	−	+
Vietnamese	+	+	+	+	+	−	+
Khmer	−	−	−	+	+	−	+
Miao	+	+	−	+	+	−	+
Yao	+	+	−	+	+	−	+
Written Tibetan	+	−	−	−	−	−	−
Yi (Lolo)	+	+	+	+	+	−	−
Jingpo	−	+	−	+	−	−	−
Malay	−	−	+	−	−	−	+
Rukai (Taiwan)	−	−	+	−	−	+	−
Mongol	−	−	+	−	−	+	−
Manchu	−	−	+	−	−	+	−
Uygur	−	−	+	−	−	+	−
Korean	−	−	+	−	−	+	−
Japanese	−	−	+	−	−	+	−

Features plotted on Table 1.1: (1) morphemes are monosyllabic, (2) the language is tonal, (3) only a single consonant is tolerated at the beginning of a syllable, (4) the language is morphologically and syntactically analytic, (5) the use of measures (classifiers) with numerals is obligatory, (6) the language has adjective–noun order, (7) the language has SVO sentence order. A plus indicates that the feature in question is present, a minus that it is absent.

all have SVO order. In geographic terms the languages to the north, west, and southwest of China are almost all SOV languages, while those to the south and southeast are virtually all SVO languages. It is tempting to think that Chinese, genetically related to the SOV languages of the Tibeto-Burman group, developed its present word order under the influence of some SVO language in prehistoric times.

Another important syntactic feature is the order of adjectives (and modifiers in general) and the nouns to which they refer. Chinese and Altaic both place the adjective before the noun, while almost all the other languages of East Asia place the adjective after the noun which it modifies.

The seven phonological, morphological and syntactic features discussed above are plotted on Table 1.1, for eighteen East Asian languages.[1] The languages are grouped according to their genetic affiliation. Inspection of the table reveals that genetically related languages sometimes belong to quite different typological groups: Vietnamese, for example, typologically resembles Chinese much more than it resembles Khmer, despite the fact that both Vietnamese and Khmer are Austroasiatic languages and neither of them is related to Chinese.

It is also evident that Modern Chinese can be uniquely described in typological terms, at least in the East Asian context: it is the only tonal language that places adjectives and other modifiers before nouns.

Geographically, Chinese is located between the non-tonal, polysyllabic Altaic languages in North Asia and the tonal, monosyllabic languages of Southeast Asia; from the point of view of typology, it also occupies an intermediate position between the languages of these two areas. Adjective–noun order which is found in Chinese, for example, is typical of all the Altaic languages; tonality, on the other hand, is one of the most distinctive characteristics of the Southeast Asian languages. A more profound study of such convergence is necessary before we can begin to speculate about its causes, but one of the factors influencing the presence or absence of certain typological features is clearly geographical proximity. In the past Chinese has almost always been studied in isolation, as if it were never affected by its linguistic neighbors. I believe that such an approach is incorrect; after examining the problem of Chinese genetic links, I will have more to say on this topic.

1.4 The genetic affiliation of Chinese

Although Chinese shows very close typological links to the monosyllabic tonal languages of South China and Southeast Asia, its genealogical roots are to be found elsewhere. Since the nineteenth century some sort of genetic affinity between Chinese and Tibeto-Burman languages has been recognized; such a hypothesis is based on a relatively small number of obvious cognate sets found in Chinese, Tibetan, Burmese and a few other Tibeto-Burman languages. A representative sample of these cognates is given in Table 1.2. Chinese forms are cited in Middle Chinese (MC) and Old Chinese (OC) in F. K. Li's reconstructions (1971); Tibetan and Burmese forms are given in their standard transliterations; Bodo and Trung forms are added to show how these cognates are reflected in more distant, unwritten Tibeto-Burman languages.[2]

The list given in Table 1.2 by itself is virtually sufficient to establish a genetic link between Chinese and the other languages given. The words all represent the sort of fundamental and culturally independent vocabulary that is unlikely to be borrowed from one language to another. The semantic connections are clear and straightforward, and even in this short list recurring phonological regularity is evident: Note the following regular phonological correspondences among the Old Chinese, Tibetan, Burmese and Trung words: a-a-a-a in I, YOU, FIVE, FISH, and NOT: i-i-a-i in WOOD, NAME, YEAR, JOINT, and TWO; i-i-e-i- in DAY and

Table 1.2. Sino-Tibetan comparisons

	MC	OC	WT	WB	Bodo	Trung
'I'	nguo	ngag	nga	ŋa	aŋ	ŋà
'you'	ńźjwo:	njag	—	naŋ	nəŋ	nă
'not'	mju	mjag	ma	ma'	—	mà
'two'	ńźji-	njid	gnyis	hnac	nəy	ă-ni
'three'	sam	səm	gsum	sûm	tam	ă-sə̀m
'five'	nguo:	ngag	lnga	ŋâ	ba	pə́ŋ-ŋà
'six'	ljuk	ljəkw	drug	khrok	—	khlu
'nine'	kjəu:	kjəgw	dgu	kûi	—	də-gə̀
'sun/day'	ńźjet	njit	nyi-ma	ne	—	nì
'tree/wood'	sjen	sjin	shing	sac	—	—
'year'	nien	nin	-ning	hnac	—	ɲiɲ
'name'	mjäng	mjing	ming	ə-mañ	muŋ	—
'eye'	mjuk	mjəkw	mig	myak	megón	miè
'ear'	ńźï:	njəg	rna-ba	na	na:-	ă-nà
'breast'	ńźju:	njug	nu-mu	nui'	—	nuŋ
'joint'	tsiet	tsit	tshigs	ə-chac	—	tsi
'fish'	ngjwo	ngjag	nya	ŋâ	ná	ŋa
'dog'	khiwen:	khwin	khyi	khwe	—	də-gəi
'insect/worm'	bjəu	bjəgw	'bu	pûi	—	bə̀ 'snake'
'bitter'	khuo:	khag	kha	khâ	ká	kha 'salty'
'cold'	ljang	gljang	grang	—	gazaŋ	glaŋ
'kill'	şăt	srat	bsat	sat	—	sat
'die'	si:	sjid	shi-ba	se	təy	ɕi
'poison'	duok	dəkw	dug	tok	—	—

DOG; ə-u-ui-ə in INSECT and NINE: m-m-m-m in NOT and EYE; ŋ-ŋ-ŋ-ŋ in I and FIVE; n-n-n-n in YOU, TWO, DAY, YEAR, EAR, and BREAST; kh-kh-kh-kh in DOG and BITTER; s-s-s-s in THREE, WOOD, and KILL.

A Chinese–Tibeto-Burman affinity is unassailable, yet surprisingly little has been done in the field of Sino-Tibetan linguistic comparison. The phonological correspondences between Chinese and Tibeto-Burman have never been worked out in detail; and until this is done, comparative work cannot really get off the ground. This is not, of course, to say that comparative work cannot be done; indeed, the only way that progress toward the establishment of a more precise statement of the Sino-Tibetan relationship can be made is by the identification of more cognates. It is a two-way street: phonological rules are made on the basis of cognate sets; cognates in turn are in large measure accepted or rejected on the basis of how well they adhere to the rules of phonological correspondence. Sino-Tibetan studies are still at a relatively primitive level; there is not a sufficient number of hard-and-fast cognate sets to work out an overall and general statement of the phonological rules which link the two groups. For the present, work must be concentrated on finding more related words; but this task is made difficult by certain problems both on the Chinese and Tibeto-Burman sides, problems that must be faced head-on if progress in Sino-Tibetan comparison is to be made.

The written record of Chinese goes back several millennia, but, unfortunately for the historical linguist, the Chinese script never gives a precise indication of sound. The older stages of Chinese must be painstakingly reconstructed on the basis of modern dialect forms and certain old documentary sources, especially rhyme dictionaries and ancient poetic collections; this process will be described in some detail in Chapter 2. This means that when we engage in Sino-Tibetan comparative work we are dealing with reconstructions of Chinese which to some degree are based on speculation; this is especially true of Old (or Archaic) Chinese reconstructions which purport to reflect the language of the first millennium BC. All linguistic reconstructions, by their very nature, are subject to revision. No doubt much of the difficulty encountered in Sino-Tibetan comparative work is due to the inadequate reconstructions of Old Chinese which we must employ. Surely one of the most serious drawbacks of these reconstructions is the difficulty of reconstituting Old Chinese initial consonant clusters; there is universal agreement that such clusters existed in Pre-Han (*ante* second century BC) Chinese, but there is no consensus as to their exact nature. Another area about which there is wide disagreement is the Old Chinese vowel system; various schemes, from ones with only two vowels to ones with as many as fourteen, have been proposed. A survey of the various Old Chinese reconstructions presently available will show that there is still a great deal that is unsettled and controversial. In fact, it may well be that Old Chinese by its very nature is a problem for which no unique solution is possible. Despite all these uncertainties, we still know a great deal about Old Chinese; and this information can and should be used in Sino-Tibetan comparison provided that it is used judiciously.

With Middle (or Ancient) Chinese we are on more solid ground, but the reconstruction of this language, which is based on a sixth-century rhyme dictionary, already represents a rather drastically evolved variety of Chinese basically not too different from certain conservative modern southern dialects such as Cantonese, Kèjiā and Mǐn. It lacks consonantal clusters, and its vowel system appears to differ in many ways from that of Old Chinese. All considered, the best strategy to employ in making comparisons between Chinese and Tibeto-Burman languages is to use a consistently worked out reconstruction of Old Chinese, but at all times to keep in mind the Middle Chinese and modern forms on which these reconstructions are ultimately based. Modern dialect words, especially those found in the Mĭn dialects, will, from time to time, also be relevant and useful in this task. What must be cautioned against is an excessive reliance on any one reconstruction of Old Chinese, especially without regard to other, later forms of Chinese.

The most widely accepted classification of the Sino-Tibetan languages is that of Paul Benedict (1972). According to him, this great family or linguistic stock is divided primarily into Chinese (Sinitic) and Tibet-Karen; the latter group is further divided into Karen and Tibeto-Burman. Leaving Karen aside, this implies that any two Tibeto-Burman languages are more closely related to one another than any one of them is to Chinese. The data given in Benedict's *Conspectus* generally bear out this claim; this does not mean, however, that Chinese cannot show an especially close affinity to one or to the other of the Tibeto-Burman languages. In fact, most sinologists who have worked on this problem have at least implicitly taken Tibetan (especially in its archaic written form) to be the closest Tibeto-Burman relative of Chinese. This may in part be due to the fact that Tibetan is lexicographically the best recorded of these languages and at the same time has the oldest written records. Burmese has played only a slightly less important role in Sino-Tibetan comparative research for similar reasons. It may nevertheless turn out that Chinese does have particularly close lexical links to Tibetan.

Sino-Tibetan comparative work also encounters difficulties on the Tibeto-Burman side. Tibeto-Burman is a tremendously diverse and complex language family. Few of the languages possess historical records; even for the ones that have been recorded in modern times, we frequently have only imperfect and fragmentary materials. Although there has been a burgeoning of interest in these languages in recent decades, the majority of them are still only poorly studied. Internal relationships are also unclear. Benedict, in a scheme now widely accepted by experts in the field, divides the Tibeto-Burman languages into seven groups:

1. Tibetan-Kanauri   3. Abor-Miri-Dafla   5. Burmese-Lolo   7. Kuki-Naga
2. Bahing-Vayu   4. Kachin (Jingpo)   6. Bodo-Garo

Of these groupings, Benedict considers numbers one, five, and seven to be 'supergroups', each containing a large number of distinct languages; the other groups are relatively compact, with one of them, (4), consisting of a single language, Kachin or Jingpo. To date no family tree model showing the precise interrelations among these groups has been found acceptable (Matisoff 1978). It is evident that Tibeto-Burman presents the comparativist with a vast, highly diverse, and only partly documented linguistic family whose internal relations are as yet unclear. In view of this, it would be unrealistic to ask that the relationship of Chinese to this family be formulated with any great clarity. It would be a mistake, however, to claim that Chinese–Tibeto-Burman comparison cannot be carried out until all the ins and outs of the Tibeto-Burman languages are completely understood. The history of comparative linguistics shows that larger, more comprehensive comparisons often precede the careful working out of lower-level relationships.

The present is a time of great ferment both in Chinese and in Tibeto-Burman linguistics. New data are constantly being published, as are new and more precise analyses of both the structures and histories of these languages. There is reason to hope that the sort of difficulties alluded to above may be surmounted in the not too distant future, and that the outlines of Sino-Tibetan linguistic history will come to be understood much better than they are at present.

1.5 Chinese in contact with other languages

China is not an island; it is now and always has been surrounded by non-Chinese or, to be more precise, non-Han peoples. A non-Han people is by definition an ethnic group which uses a non-Han language. Today, even those separate ethnic groups who speak some form of Chinese, such as the Manchus, are known to have used different, non-Han languages in the past. Despite the fact that the Chinese have always had non-Chinese-speaking neighbors, there has generally been a strong tendency to view the Chinese as a monolithic ethnic and linguistic entity, highly resistant to any sort of outside cultural or linguistic influence. Such a view has been strengthened by the contrast of several neighboring countries which have absorbed Chinese culture and language on a vast scale. Compared to them, China has indeed seemed like an impermeable nucleus from which cultural and linguistic influences have flowed outward, but which, with a very few minor exceptions, has not been affected by the inflow of foreign elements. There is, to be sure, a good deal of truth in this view. For more than two thousand years China held undisputed cultural pre-eminence in East Asia. It was not only the first literate nation in this part of the world, it also supplied several neighboring peoples with their writing systems. Virtually all the languages spoken on the periphery of China are permeated with Chinese loanwords, while Chinese itself has seemingly remained immune to outside influence. It would be wrong, however, to conclude that Chinese was never influenced by surrounding languages. For one thing, prior to the middle of the second millennium BC, China's cultural superiority was almost certainly not as overwhelming as it was to become later on, and we should not rule out the possibility that in prehistoric times Chinese absorbed foreign elements, perhaps even on a relatively large scale. China's later cultural hegemony in East Asia has been confused with a kind of cultural and linguistic immunity which exempted Chinese from any but the most trivial of outside influences. Widespread acceptance of such a view has no doubt impeded a serious search for foreign influence in Chinese.

The Sino-Tibetan forebears of the Chinese must have come into contact with peoples speaking different and unrelated languages at a very early date. Unfortunately, we do not know when the earliest Sino-Tibetan groups moved into the Yellow River Valley, nor do we know what sort of population they encountered when they arrived there. We can surmise, however, that the Sino-Tibetan dialect which is ancestral to Chinese was influenced in a number of ways by the language (or languages) which they encountered at this early period. Some of the typological differences found between Chinese and Tibeto-Burman may in fact be due to such early linguistic contacts. The fact that only a relatively few Chinese words have been shown to be Sino-Tibetan may indicate that a considerable proportion of the Chinese lexicon is of foreign origin. Some of the words for which Sino-Tibetan etymologies are lacking may go back to languages which have since become extinct; in this case, we of course have no way to trace their origins; in other cases, however, words were borrowed from languages whose descendants still live on along the present periphery of the Chinese-speaking area. Here I would like to examine several words that I think are ancient loanwords from languages whose descendants are still spoken in China, or in countries adjacent to it.

Chinese has two common words for 'dog': *quǎn* (MC *khiwen:*) and *gǒu* (MC *kəu:*).[3] In the spoken language the first of these is obsolete except in a few dialects found in northeastern Fújiàn. Since *quǎn* has a good Sino-Tibetan etymology (see Table 1.2), we may assume that this is the original word for 'dog' in Chinese. Textually *gǒu* appears quite early (in *Mencius* for example), but in pre-Han times it appears that *quǎn* was the primary word. Traditional commentators have attempted to distinguish the two words semantically, but their explanations generally have little basis in linguistic fact. I would like to propose that *gǒu* is an early loanword from a language ancestral to the modern Miao-Yao languages. Purnell (1970) has reconstructed a proto-Miao-Yao form *klu^2B for 'dog'. The relationship of the Yao forms on which this reconstruction is based to Chinese has already been noted by Gordon Downer (1973), but he apparently considered the Chinese word a loan into Yao. But as Haudricourt (1966) has pointed out, the Miao-Yao words in question are certainly related to Spoken Mon *klə* and Written Mon *kluiw* 'dog'; this connection makes Downer's hypothesis seem doubtful, and points to the likelihood that the Chinese borrowed the word from the ancestors of the Miao-Yao at a very early date. After a period during which *gŏu* competed with *quăn*, *gŏu* finally won out as the common word for dog, except for the small area mentioned above.

Another animal name of non-Sino-Tibetan origin is the word for 'tiger', Chinese *hŭ* (MC *xuo:* < OC *xla[*g*]). The relationship of the Old Chinese reconstruction to such Austroasiatic forms as Modern Mon *klaʔ*, Written Mon *kla* and Mundari *kula* is evident (Pinnow 1959, 142). Since the Chinese word occurs in the earliest written records which we possess, it must have been borrowed very early, perhaps in prehistoric times.

The two words discussed above are connected with China's southern neighbors. Another word, meaning 'calf', *dú* (MC *duk* < OC *duk), can be traced to the Altaic languages spoken to China's north; compare the following forms: Mongolian *tuγul*, Manchu *tukšan*, Evenki *tukučən* 'calf', Lamut *tu-* ~ *tuγu-* 'to give birth to a calf'. As in the case of the two examples given above, the attestation of this form in several widely dispersed Altaic languages would seem to preclude the possibility of a loan from Chinese into these languages. Moreover, the livelihood of these northern peoples centers around nomadic herding of one kind or another; it makes more sense to suppose that the agricultural and sedentary Chinese would borrow terms having to do with animal husbandry than the other way around. It is quite possible that the rich Chinese vocabulary having to do with livestock and herding may contain other words of Altaic origin.

The study of ancient linguistic contacts can frequently be elucidated by the study of toponymy. This study is still by and large undeveloped in China, but in one case at least, a toponym provides us with very valuable information concerning the ethnic composition of early China. The ancient name of the Yangtze River was simply *jiāng* (MC *kăng* < OC *krung); in later times this name was extended to mean river in general. The word is clearly related to such Austroasiatic forms as Vietnamese *sông* (< *krong), Written Mon *kruŋ*, Brou *kroung* and Katu *karung*. This form is very important because it supplies strong evidence that Austroasiatic-speaking peoples inhabited southeastern China in earliest historical times. This presence is strongly corroborated by a series of Mĭn dialect words which have unquestionable Austroasiatic connections. The present-day Mĭn-speaking region was a part of the realm of the ancient Yuè people in pre-Han times; T. L. Mei and the present author have shown in an earlier article (Norman and Mei 1976) that the Yuè were an Austroasiatic-speaking people. The common Mĭn word for 'shaman' or 'spirit healer' gives clear indication that the present Mĭn dialects have an Austroasiatic substratum. On the basis of such forms as Fúzhōu *tøiŋ²*, Jiàn'ōu *toŋ³*, and Amoy *taŋ²*, a Proto-Min *dəŋ (or

*duŋ) can be postulated. The cognacy of this form to Vietnamese ʔdoŋ² 'to shamanize, to communicate with spirits', Written Mon *doŋ* 'to dance (as if) under daemonic possession' (Shorto 1962), Santali *dōŋ* 'a kind of dance connected with marriage' and Sora *toŋ-* 'to dance' can scarcely be doubted.

There are a number of words which, although almost certainly of non-Chinese origin, are very difficult to pinpoint etymologically. 'Elephant', Chinese *xiàng* (MC *zjang:*), is clearly to be connected with Proto-Tai *jaŋ C (Li 1977, 168); but related forms are found in Spoken Mon *coiŋ*, Burmese *chaŋ*, as well as in certain Lolo and Karen languages (Benedict 1972). As a result, it is impossible to say in which of these many languages the term originated, if indeed it originated in any of them. It is even possible that it goes back to an extinct language from which a number of Southeast Asian languages inherited it, much as the English word *opossum* comes from an Amerindian language now extinct. The term for 'ivory' or 'tusk', Chinese *yá* (MC *nga* < OC *ngra[g]), presents us with a similar quandary. It is patently related to such Southeast Asian words as Proto-Tai *ŋa (Li 1977, 204), Vietnamese *ngà*, Bahnar *ngəla*, all meaning 'tusk, ivory'. Again, the term is found in two different language families and it is impossible to identify one or the other as the source for the loan into Chinese. Benedict's (1975, 412) attempts to connect the word for 'elephant' with a reconstructed Proto-Austronesian *gadiŋ 'ivory' are unconvincing.

All the words discussed above were taken into Chinese very early, some of them probably in prehistoric times. Chinese continued to borrow foreign elements, though not on a very grand scale. Many later loanwords are associated with items of material culture whose names were borrowed along with the product. A number of such terms originating in Indian or Iranian languages have been identified by such scholars as Friederich Hirth (Hirth and Rockhill 1911) and Berthold Laufer (1919). We cite here several such loans as illustrations:

GRAPE: Chinese *pútao* (MC *buo dâu*, OC *ba*[g] *da*[g]*w*). Laufer (1919, 225) derives this word from a hypothetical Iranian prototype *budāwa, related to Modern Persian *bāda* 'wine'. Actually *bādāwa would appear to be a better and closer reconstruction of the prototype, in light of more recent Old Chinese reconstructions.

JASMINE: Chinese *mòli* (MC *m*[u]*ât li-*). Sanskrit *mallikā*.

SANDALWOOD: Chinese *zhāntán* (MC *tśjän dân*). Sanskrit *candana*. In Modern Chinese the first syllable of this form is generally lost: *tánxiāng* 'sandalwood', where *xiāng* means 'fragrance'.

From the fourth century AD, China's northern border region has been domi-
nated by Altaic-speaking peoples. At various times these peoples invaded and
occupied large areas of northern China. One might expect that the many centuries
of Altaic rule in North China would have led to a large-scale adoption of Altaic
vocabulary by the Chinese. In fact the number of Altaic loanwords from this
period is surprisingly small. It is likely that during the various dynasties when
Altaic-speakers formed the ruling elite numerous loanwords were current in
the Chinese of that time, only to disappear once the dynasty was overthrown
and Chinese rule re-established. In the drama of the Yuan dynasty one can find
many words of Mongolian origin (Zhū 1956); these words were doubtless
understood by the audiences of that time, yet scarcely one of these words has
survived down to modern times. During the Qing dynasty a small but significant
number of Manchu words entered the vernacular of Peking; a few of them still
survive: *sàqimǎ* 'a pastry made of fried noodles, honey and butter' = Manchu
sacima. Others such as *wādan* 'a cloth wrapping' (= Manchu *wadan*) have a
quaint and strongly local flavor, and are probably doomed to disappear in the
long run.

It may be that Altaic has left more of a mark on the grammar of Chinese than
it has on the lexicon. For example, the exclusive/inclusive distinction found in
the first person plural pronouns of the Peking and certain other northern dialects
may be due to an Altaic stimulus. Such a distinction was not found in Old
Chinese, and it begins to appear in North China during the period of Altaic rule.
It is significant in this regard that both Yuan dynasty Mongolian and Manchu
distinguish exclusive and inclusive forms. It may also be that development of
sentence patterns of the SOV type in northern Chinese arose under the influence
of Altaic languages, which show this ordering exclusively.

In general Modern Chinese, in sharp contrast to Japanese, is very resistant to
borrowing foreign terms outright. Most modern terms are purely native creations or calques: television becomes *diànshì* ('electric vision'), laser is *jīguāng*
('intense light'), the communist party is called *gòngchǎndǎng* ('common property
party'), etc. *Tiělù* ('iron road') 'railroad' is an example of a calque based on
French *chemin de fer*. In the early modern period (the end of the nineteenth
century and the first part of the twentieth century) many new terms referring
to modern technology and Western political and economic concepts were first
coined in Japan and then adopted in China. The Japanese employed Chinese
characters, reading them in their own system of pronunciation which had been
borrowed from China a millennium before (Wang 1957, 528ff). When the
Chinese took over these new terms they simply pronounced them in Chinese.
Examples of such terms adopted from Japanese in this way are the following:

Japanese	Chinese	Meaning
kakumei	gémìng	'revolution'
bunka	wénhuà	'culture'
shakai	shèhùi	'society'
kagaku	kēxué	'science'
keitō	xìtŏng	'system'

Although some of these compound terms already existed in early Chinese texts, the Japanese appropriated them to translate new Western concepts; such is the case with the first three terms given above. Others were new creations based on borrowed Chinese morphemes in Japanese; the last two examples are of this type. The latter type of coinage is analogous to new terminology in English created on the basis of Greek and Latin morphemes. Since the Second World War, Chinese and Japanese have more and more gone their own ways. The Japanese increasingly tend to borrow foreign words outright, while the Chinese have begun to create new terms independent of Japanese influence.

Chinese does contain a small number of loanwords from English: *mădá* 'motor', *léidá* 'radar', *mótèr* '(fashion) model', *bàng* 'pound', *xiūkè* 'shock' and *dá* 'dozen' are a few common examples. It sometimes happens that a loanword appears in Chinese, only to disappear once a suitable term created from native elements is coined. An early word for 'telephone' was *délǜfēng*, which represented an attempt to pronounce the English word 'telephone'; this was eventually replaced by a purely Chinese term, *diànhuà*, literally 'electric speech'.

While Chinese has shown considerable resistance to foreign elements, the same cannot be said for most of the languages along China's periphery. Almost all of these languages contain masses of Chinese loanwords. Such loanwords are typically stratified – that is, they have been borrowed at different periods of Chinese history, and consequently exhibit features typical of different stages in the development of Chinese. This material is very valuable for the study of Chinese phonological history, but much of it still remains to be studied systematically.

In Japanese, Korean and Vietnamese, two different types of borrowing are to be found. Like other languages on the margin of China, they have all borrowed individual words from spoken Chinese at various periods in the past, but in addition to this sporadic, item by item absorption of Chinese elements, all three countries at different times borrowed the entire Chinese written language, both graphs and their pronunciations. In the case of pronunciation, each of these nations modified the particular variety of Chinese which they borrowed in accordance with their own speech habits. In succeeding centuries these pronunciations changed further, as each of the languages in question evolved in its own independent fashion. These foreign "dialects" of Chinese often preserve indications of how Chinese characters were pronounced in earlier periods, and provide valuable data for the reconstruction of Middle Chinese, a topic to be dealt with in Chapter 2.

For many centuries, the Japanese, Koreans and Vietnamese employed literary Chinese as their normal vehicle of written expression. The everyday familiarity that the literati of these countries had with literary Chinese influenced their respective languages to a degree that can scarcely be exaggerated. Japanese, Korean and Vietnamese even now are literally inundated with elements of Chinese origin, and all three languages continue to draw on their rich store of Chinese roots in creating new vocabulary. In these areas of the Far East, Chinese has come to play a role analogous to that of Latin and Greek in many European languages. Like Latin in Europe, Chinese continues to exert its influence on the languages in its cultural sphere long after its use as a literary medium has become a thing of the past.

Further reading

Benedict, Paul K. 1972. *Sino-Tibetan: a conspectus*. Cambridge: Cambridge University Press. [A dated, but generally good overview of the Sino-Tibetan language family.]

Bodman, Nicholas C. 1980. Proto-Chinese and Proto-Tibetan: data towards establishing the nature of the relationship. In *Contributions to historical linguistics, issues and materials*, ed. Frans Van Coetsam and Linda R. Waugh. Leiden: E. J. Brill. [The best and most detailed attempt to relate Chinese to Tibeto-Burman in a rigorous and systematic fashion.]

2

The historical phonology of Chinese

2.1 Periodicization of Chinese

In his monumental work, *Études sur la phonologie chinoise* (1915–26), the great Swedish sinologue Bernhard Karlgren divided the long history of Chinese phonology into the following periods:

Proto-Chinese: the period preceding the earliest literary documents
Archaic Chinese: the language of the *Shījīng* (The Book of Poetry), c. 1000 BC
Ancient Chinese: the language of the seventh century AD rhyme dictionary, the *Qièyùn*
Middle Chinese: the language of the Song dynasty rhyme tables
Old Mandarin: the language of the Ming dynasty dictionary, the *Hóngwǔ zhèngyùn*

Few present-day Chinese linguists would agree with this periodicization in all its details. Karlgren's Proto-Chinese is beyond the reach of the historical linguist who limits himself to Chinese materials exclusively, and hence is not a part of Chinese linguistic history proper. His terms "Archaic" and "Ancient Chinese" have now generally been replaced by more conventional and convenient terms "Old Chinese" (for Archaic Chinese) and "Middle Chinese" (for Ancient Chinese); these newer terms have the virtue of being much closer to the usual Chinese terms for these two periods, *shànggǔ hànyǔ* and *zhōnggǔ hànyǔ* respectively. Only a small number of contemporary scholars would consider Karlgren's original Middle Chinese a discrete stage at all; the language of the Song dynasty is better considered an early form of Old Mandarin, a period which lasted until about the beginning of the Ming dynasty. Ming and Early Qing sources generally reflect a stage which can be termed Middle Mandarin, while the nineteenth and twentieth centuries belong to the Modern Mandarin period. The revised scheme sketched here should be considered no more than a working outline. For one thing, the various periods are mostly too long for accurate linguistic description; this is especially true of Old and Middle Chinese, for which some linguists have already proposed revisions.[1]

2.2 Sources of Middle Chinese: the *Qièyùn*

In the present chapter I will limit myself to the three best understood periods of Chinese phonological history: Old and Middle Chinese and Old Mandarin. Since the study of all Chinese historical phonology pivots around the language of the *Qièyùn* dictionary, which for all practical purposes is identical to Middle Chinese, we will begin with a discussion of this most important source.

The *Qièyùn* was compiled in AD 601 by Lù Fǎyán. It is a dictionary of Chinese characters arranged by tone and rhyme. Much ink has been spilled concerning the nature of the language underlying the *Qièyùn*. Before going on to a discussion of these issues, it should be pointed out that the *Qièyùn* (and all other early dictionaries) were not records of a contemporary spoken language or dialect, but rather guides to the proper recitation of literary texts; as such they were concerned only with the reading of Chinese characters, and it would be a serious mistake to regard the *Qièyùn* as a reflection of the contemporary vernacular of any particular place. The proof of this is that it is impossible to identify among the thousands of characters in the dictionary which words had actual currency in the spoken language and which merely represented words which at that time were known only from literary sources, some of which were more than a thousand years old even then. It is also highly probable that at the time of the *Qièyùn*, as now, there existed numerous discrepancies between the reading pronunciations of characters and the actual words of the spoken language. With these reservations in mind, we can see that the real issue concerning the language at the base of the *Qièyùn* is really the question of what regional *reading* pronunciation it was based on.

Karlgren held to the view that the *Qièyùn* represented the language of Chángān, the Sui dynasty capital (1954, 212); others have supposed that it represented an amalgam of regional pronunciations, and was not based on any single contemporary standard. At the present time most people in the field accept the views of the Chinese scholar Zhōu Zǔmó. According to Zhōu (1966), the phonological system of the *Qièyùn* does not reflect the pronunciation of a single region, but represents a compromise between the literary pronunciation of north and south in the late Nanbeichao period (sixth century AD). The most important component was that of the southern dynastic capital of Jīnlíng which, until the reunification of China under the Sui dynasty in AD 581, was the undisputed cultural center of China. Cultured northern pronunciation was best represented by that of Yèxià, capital of several contemporary northern dynasties.

Lù Fǎyán's *Qièyùn* preface tells us that the norms of pronunciation which were adopted in the compilation of the *Qièyùn* were drawn up at a meeting in Chángān at the beginning of the Sui dynasty. Of the eight people present, three were southerners who would naturally have taken the pronunciation of Jīn-líng as their standard. The five northerners all either grew up in Yèxià or had lived there as young men. When Lù Fǎyán spoke of "discussing the discrepancies of north and south" in his preface, it is certain that he was referring to the differences between the learned character pronunciations of Jīnlíng and Yèxià, and not to northern and southern China in general. Since at the time of the meeting none of the participants had resided in Chángān for more than a few years, it is highly unlikely that the *Qièyùn* reflects contemporary Chángān pronunciation.

According to Lù's preface, the two men most influential in setting up the norms on which the *Qièyùn* was to be based were Yán Zhītūi and Xiāo Gāi, both famous scholars of southern origin. It stands to reason that, despite certain accommodations to northern practice as represented by Yèxià, the reading pronunciation of Jīnlíng was the single most influential component of the rhyme dictionary. This thesis is corroborated by other contemporary evidence such as the rhyming practice of late Nanbeichao poets.

The *Qièyùn* turned out to be an extremely successful book; its success can be attributed to its widely based cross-dialectal phonological base and the generally recognized elegance of its standard. Because of this, the *Qièyùn* soon eclipsed its predecessors: of six older rhyme dictionaries mentioned in the *Qièyùn* preface, not a single one survived intact. During the Tang dynasty the *Qièyùn* became the accepted standard of refined literary pronunciation; once it attained this role, it underwent many revisions and enlargements. The editors of these different versions were careful to preserve the original phonological categories of Lù Fǎyán's work; as a result, the *Qièyùn* as it originally issued from the brush of Lù Fǎyán disappeared, but the phonology which it enshrined continued to live on in its later revised versions. Most of the Tang redactions have themselves in turn disappeared, or survive only in fragments. Only one of the Tang revised versions, Wáng Rénxū's *Kānmiù bǔquē qièyùn*, is known in a complete version. The most important redaction was produced early in the Song dynasty; this version, known as the *Guǎngyùn*, was completed in 1011 under the general editorship of Chén Péngnián. A comparison of the *Guǎngyùn* with the earlier *Qièyùn* redactions has shown that it preserves the phonological system of Lù Fǎyán's original book virtually intact. Since the complete Wáng Rénxū version of the *Qièyùn* was not discovered until after the Second World War, all of the early work on the phonology of Middle Chinese was actually based on the *Guǎngyùn*, and the *Guǎngyùn* continues to be used as one of the most important sources for the study of Middle Chinese.

Before proceeding to a discussion of the structure of the *Qièyùn*, it will be

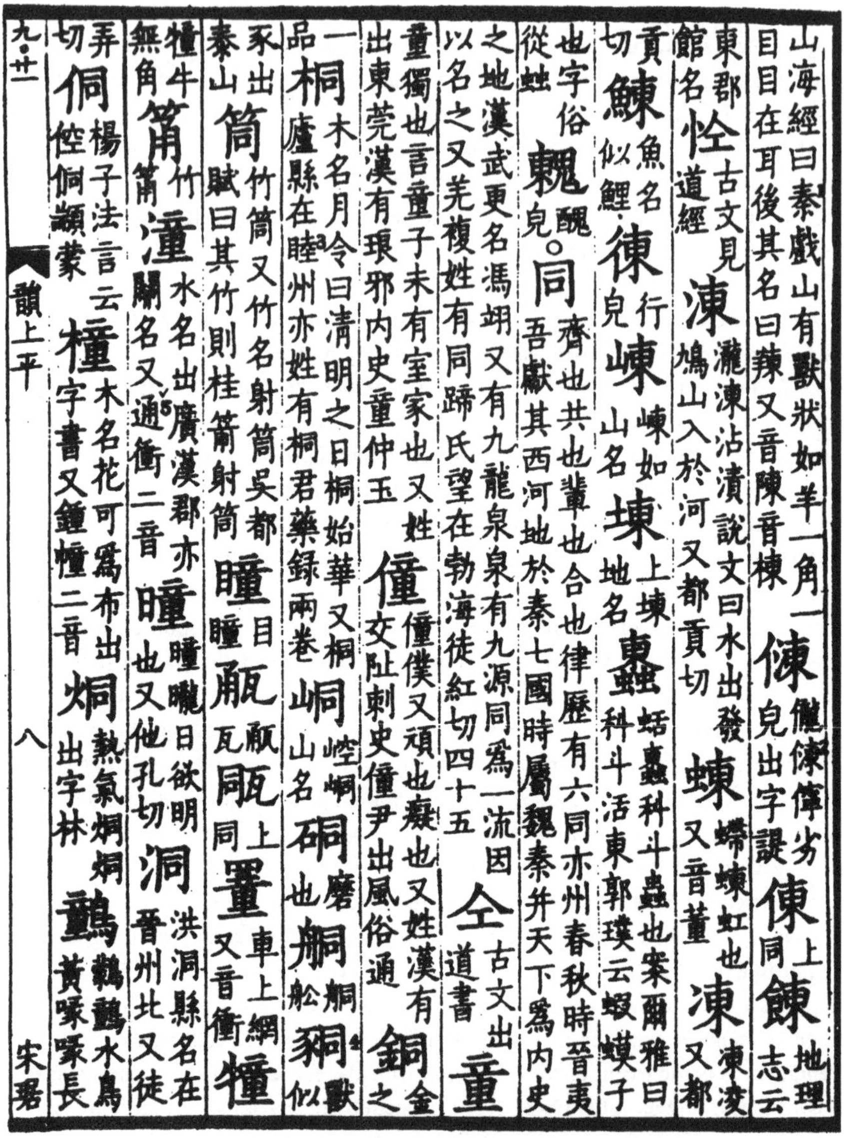
山海經曰秦戲山有獸狀如羊一角一目目在耳後其名曰辣又音陳音棟
倲儱倲儜劣皃出字諟 倲同上 鍊地理志云東郡館名 恮古文見道經 涷瀧涷沾漬說文曰水出發鳩山入於河又都貢切 蝀螮蝀虹也又音董 涷涷凌又都貢切
鯟魚名似鯉 徚行皃 崠崠如山名 埬上埬地名 𧑅蛞𧑅科斗蟲也案爾雅曰科斗活東郭璞云蝦蟆子也字俗從虫
䰤醜皃 ○同齊也共也輩也合也律歷有六同亦州春秋時晉夷吾獻其西河地於秦七國時屬魏秦并天下爲內史之地漢武更名馮翊又有九龍泉泉有九源同爲一流因以名之又羌複姓有同蹄氏望在勃海徒紅切四十五
仝古文出道書 童童獨也言童子未有室家也又姓出東莞漢有琅邪內史童仲玉 僮僮僕又頑也癡也又姓漢有交阯刺史僮尹出風俗通 銅金之一品
桐木名月令曰清明之日桐始華又桐廬縣在睦州亦姓有桐君藥錄兩卷 峒崆峒山名 硐磨也 舸𦨴舸船 㺔獸似豕出秦山
筒竹筒又竹名射筒吳都賦曰其竹則桂箭射筒 瞳目瞳 㼧瓦㼧 㼧同上 罿車上網又音衝 犝犝牛無角
筩竹筩 潼水名出廣漢郡亦關名又通衝二音 曈曈曨日欲明也又他孔切 洞洪洞縣名在晉州北又徒弄切
侗楊子法言云倥侗顓蒙 橦木名花可爲布出字書又鐘幢二音 烔熱氣烔烔出字林 鶇鶇鶇水鳥黃喙喙長
九•廿一 韻上平 八 宋槧

Figure 2.1. A page from the *Guǎngyùn* rhyme dictionary

useful to consider what Lù Fǎyán and his contemporaries understood about the phonology of their language. It is clear that the written graph or character was their point of departure. From the point of view of phonology, the Chinese script is syllabic in that each graph represents a single syllable; hence the notion of syllable was a given quantity. A century or so before the *Qièyùn* was compiled, an important discovery was made: every Chinese syllable belongs to one of four tonal categories (*shēng*); these were called *píng* (level), *shǎng* (rising), *qù* (departing), and *rù* (entering). The meaning of these terms will be examined later in this chapter. It was further understood that syllables could rhyme or not rhyme; by definition syllables that rhyme share the same nuclear vowel and final consonant or offglide. Syllables could also alliterate – that is, they could share the same syllabic onset. Since alliterative syllables that also rhymed might still not be homophonous, there was also at least an implicit understanding that in some cases different elements could occur between the syllable onset and the rhyme proper which could serve to differentiate syllables; this element is what we would now call a medial. In this sort of primitive syllabic phonology, there was clearly no notion of discrete consonantal or vocalic segments, and without such concepts it would be difficult to engage in any very sophisticated phonetic or phonological analysis.

This knowledge did however allow the Chinese to devise a practical means of glossing the pronunciation of characters. One could choose one character which alliterated with the word to be glossed and another with which it shared the same rhyme and medial element, creating a sort of formula from which the pronunciation of the word glossed could be deduced. If, for example, one wished to indicate the pronunciation of a character pronounced *mâk*, two other characters, one beginning with *m-* and the other ending in *-âk*, could be used:

mâk = m(iei) + (k)âk

This method, known in Chinese as *fǎnqiè*, was used by the Chinese for many centuries to record the pronunciation of characters.

The *Qièyùn* and its redactions were all divided into five volumes (*juàn*). The first two contained all the *píng* tone words; each of the remaining volumes was devoted to one of the other tonal categories. Each of the tones was divided into a certain number of rhymes (*yùn*); in many cases rhymes which resembled one another in some way were placed side by side. The first character in each rhyme was used as the name of the rhyme; this character is commonly referred to as the rhyme heading (*yùnmù*, literally 'rhyme eye'). A rhyme contained a number of homophonic groups of characters, each of which was preceded by a dot or circle called a *niǔ* 'button'. The first character of each homophonic group was provided with a *fǎnqiè* formula which gave the pronunciation of all the characters in the group. In the older redactions the *fǎnqiè* formula was X Y Z *fǎn*, where X represents the word glossed, Y the syllabic onset and Z the remainder of the syllable to be glossed. In the *Guǎngyùn* the formula is X Y Z *qiè*. The origin of the terms *fǎn* and *qiè* is not entirely clear.

In modern terminology the consonantal syllabic onset is known as the initial (*shēngmǔ*), and the remainder of the syllable is referred to as the final (*yùnmǔ*). The final can be further analysed into a medial glide (*yùntóu*), main vowel (*yùnfù*) and syllabic ending (*yùnwěi*). The Middle Chinese syllable *sjang* consists of an initial *s*, a medial *j*, a main vowel *a*, and an ending *ng*. In terms of *Qièyùn* phonology, the first (or "upper") *fǎnqiè* character represents the initial, the second (or "lower") *fǎnqiè* character represents the final; the tone is designated twice, once by the volume in which the word occurs and again by the second *fǎnqiè* character which always agrees tonally with the word being glossed.

Since the Chinese at the time of the *Qièyùn* had not analyzed the syllable into discrete vocalic and consonantal segments, it is not surprising that in creating *fǎnqiè* formulas they did not always employ the same first or upper *fǎnqiè* characters; in fact every initial consonant of Middle Chinese is represented by two or more characters; normally the more common the initial, the more characters were used to represent it, and other things being equal, the same can be said of the finals. Fortunately there is still enough system in the *fǎnqiè* formulas to allow scholars (within certain limits) to identify the different initials and finals of Middle Chinese. This type of analysis was first carried out in the nineteenth century by Chén Lǐ; the results of his research are to be found in his famous work, the *Qièyùn kǎo*, published in 1842. His formulation has been corrected and refined by a number of Chinese and foreign linguists, but this sort of analysis at best only tells us that there are so many initial and final categories and which characters are used to represent them in the *fǎnqiè* formulas. Nothing found in the *Qièyùn* or its descendants tells us anything about the phonetic values of these categories. They represent form without substance; the substance must be supplied from elsewhere.

2.3 The Song rhyme tables

Middle Chinese could be reconstructed by comparing the *Qièyùn* initial and final categories with corresponding modern dialect forms; but, in fact, other documentary evidence has been used, for example, the Song dynasty rhyme tables, in Chinese called *děngyùntú*. In these tables the syllables of the *Qièyùn* system are arranged on grids, the initials occupying the horizontal grids and the finals and tones the vertical grids. There is little doubt that the sophisticated phonological theory revealed in these tables is of Indian origin, since the earliest references to this kind of phonology are connected with the names of Buddhist monks. It is not known exactly when this sort of phonological study began in China; the earliest evidence that we have of it is a three-page fragment of a work by a Buddhist monk named Shǒuwēn, about whom we unfortunately know very little.

Zhōu Zǔmó (1966, 502) has concluded that he cannot have lived earlier than the ninth century, and there are certain indications that he may have been somewhat later. Much of the terminology of the later rhyme tables can already be seen in the Shǒuwén fragment, even though the material is not arranged in tabular form as in the later rhyme tables.

The two earliest rhyme tables which have come down to us are the *Yùnjìng* [*Mirror of rhymes*] and the *Qīyīnlüè* [*Summary of the seven sounds*]. Both are Song works which are very closely related to one another structurally, and may well be based on a common prototype. The *Qièyùn zhǐzhǎngtú* and the *Sìshēng děngzǐ* represent later and more evolved examples of rhyme tables. Bernhard Karlgren mistakenly believed that the *Qièyùn zhǐzhǎngtú* was the oldest extant rhyme table, and used it in his work on the reconstruction of Middle Chinese. Virtually all recent work has been based on the *Yùnjìng*. The following discussion is based for the most part on the terminology found in the *Yùnjìng*; in a few cases the terms have been modernized in accordance with linguistic practice in present-day China.

The term *děngyùn*, which is often used to designate the phonology of the rhyme tables, means "classified rhymes." In essence, *děngyùn* refers to an attempt to classify and systematize the phonology of the *Qièyùn* using concepts borrowed from Indian phonological theory. At the time this was done, however, the standard literary pronunciation had already changed considerably; not only had more than two centuries elapsed since the compilation of the *Qièyùn*, but the geographic base of the standard had changed from Jīnlíng along the Lower Yangtze to the region around Chángān, the Tang capital (Pulleyblank 1970). While it would be wrong to exaggerate the differences between the *Qièyùn* and the late Tang standard (they were closely related dialects), there were nevertheless important differences. When the creators of *děngyùn* phonology set about their work, they were faced with the task of reconciling in some fashion two different phonological systems, that of the *Qièyùn* categories and that of the current standard literary pronunciation. We must assume that the categories of *děngyùn* phonology actually refer to the later Tang standard and not to the *Qièyùn* language itself, since the *děngyùn* phonologists would have had no way to know how the standard language of Jīnlíng of some two centuries before was actually pronounced. There was naturally a certain awkwardness in trying to describe one dialect, only imperfectly understood, in terms of a later one; the results, as far as the *Qièyùn* language is concerned, can only be accepted with considerable reservation. The *děngyùn* phonology tells us much more about the later Tang standard than it does about the *Qièyùn* language, but, even in this area, it must be approached with caution. It seems doubtful to me that the late Tang literary pronunciation can be reconstructed solely on the basis of the rhyme tables without reference to other contemporary evidence. I also suspect that the highly formalized nature of *děngyùn* phonology led to artificial distinctions in some cases; the lingering influence of Indian and perhaps even Tibetan models must also be taken into account when dealing with the rhyme table categories. Now let us examine these categories, first the initials and then the finals.

The preface to the *Yùnjìng* recognizes thirty-six initials, each named by an example of itself: the initial *t-* is called *duān* (MC *tuân*), a word which began with *t* in Middle Chinese. The Shǒuwēn fragments have a list of only thirty initials; this no doubt represents an earlier version of the initials, which was perhaps produced under Tibetan influence, since the thirty initials correspond in number exactly to the thirty initials of Classical Tibetan. Neither the thirty nor the thirty-six initials, however, correspond exactly to the initials of the *Qièyùn*; this is one of the most evident differences between the two systems.

The primary division of the initials is into *qīng* 'clear' and *zhuó* 'muddy'. *Qīng* designates the voiceless initials; the *qīng* initials are further divided into *quánqīng* 'completely clear', the voiceless unaspirated initials, and *cìqīng* 'secondarily clear', the voiceless aspirated initials. *Quánzhuó* 'completely muddy' refers to the voiced obstruents (stops, affricates and fricatives); there is evidence that in the late Tang standard language the *quánzhuó* initials were pronounced as voiced aspirates or murmured stops, much like their descendants in certain contemporary Wú dialects.[2] The *cìzhuó* or 'secondarily muddy' initials are the voiced sonorants.

The *Yùnjìng* and other rhyme tables generally recognized five positions of articulation for the initials:

(1) *chún* 'labial'. The *Qièyùn* had only bilabials; by the time of the rhyme tables, however, some bilabials had become labiodentals; in the rhyme table terminology the former are called *zhòngchún* 'heavy labials' and the latter *qīngchún* 'light labials'.

(2) *shé* 'linguals'. These initials are divided into *shétóu* 'apicals' (*t, th, d*) and *shéshàng* 'laminals'. Karlgren thought the latter class of initials was palatalized (*t', t'h, d'h*); most present-day scholars follow Luó Chángpéi (1931) in considering them retroflex stops (*ṭ, ṭh, ḍ*).

(3) *yá* ('velars'). The term *yá* literally means 'large tooth', and the conventional explanation for this term is that the velars are produced in the vicinity of the back molars. Roy Miller (1975) has pointed out that the term was no doubt influenced by the tendency of the *děngyùn* phonologists to choose words which exemplified the categories to which they referred; in Middle Chinese *yá* was *nga*, beginning with the velar nasal.

(4) *chǐ* 'dentals'. *Chǐ* refers to the front teeth, as opposed to the back teeth, called *yá*. Into this category were placed the various sibilant initials, divided into two classes: the *chǐtóu* 'alveolars' which included the plain sibilants (*ts, tsh, dz*, etc.) and the *zhèngchǐ* 'dentals proper' comprising the alveo-palatals or, according to some (Pulleyblank 1970), retroflex sibilants. The *zhèngchǐ* initials actually represent the merger of two contrasting sets of initials in the *Qièyùn*, one having a prepalatal articulation and the other a retroflex articulation.

(5) *hóu* 'gutturals'. This series contains four initials whose reconstruction has been controversial. Karlgren proposed that they were glottal stop for the initial *yǐng*, *x* for *xiǎo*, *ɣ* for *xiá*, and *ø* [zero] for *yù*. If one were to take the name of the group seriously, a reconstruction of *h* for *xiǎo* and *ɦ* for *xiá* would make better sense, but such an argument is by no means conclusive.

The rhyme table treatment of the initials implies that the initial consonants were viewed as discrete phonological units which could be analyzed apart from the rest of the syllable; yet, despite the fact that the *děngyùn* phonology was created under strong Indian influence, the finals were not subjected to the same sort of segmentation and analysis. All the categories applied to the finals in effect refer to the finals as a whole. As a result, it is very difficult to say, for example, how many vowel phonemes are implied in this sort of analysis. The vagueness of the categories applied to the finals has led to many different interpretations, and indeed this remains one of the least satisfactory areas in the study of Middle Chinese phonology. With this in mind, let us examine the rhyme table categories that are used to describe the finals.

The division of all syllables into the four tones was taken over intact from *Qièyùn*. All syllables were further divided into two general categories called *inner* (*nèi*) and *outer* (*wài*). It seems likely that these terms were taken from the Indian phonological terms *ābhyantara* 'internal' and *bāhya* 'external'; the first term refers to sounds that in some sense are produced within the mouth, and the second to sounds produced somewhere outside the mouth (Allen 1953, 22). As applied to vowels, the low vowel *a* was 'external' because it was considered a neutral vowel in that it involved no special articulatory effort in the mouth (Allen 1953, 59). There is general agreement among Chinese linguists that in the rhyme tables the *wài* or 'outer' finals contained low or open vowels, while the *nèi* or 'inner' finals contained high or close vowels; in general this explanation is close to the Indian concept, even if not entirely the same. Pulleyblank (1970) has gone so far as to propose that the *děngyùn* phonology is based on a two-way vocalic distinction of *a* versus *ə*; in his analysis *wài* finals have *a* as their main vowel and *nèi* finals all have *ə* as their main vowel. In the *Sìshēng děngzǐ*, one of the later rhyme tables,

Table 2.1. The four divisions (*Děng*)

Division	Volpicelli	Schaank	Karlgren	Pulleyblank
I	kou	kau	kâu	kau
II	kau	kyau	kau	kjau
III	keu	kyiau	ki̯äu	kiau
IV	kiu	kiau	kieu	kjiau

all rhymes are classified into sixteen *shè* or groups; each *shè* consists of all the *nèi* or *wài* rhymes which have the same final consonant or offglide. Thus all the rhymes ending in *m* will be placed into two *shè*, one of the *nèi* category and another of the *wài* category.

Another two-way categorization is that of *kāi* 'open' and *hé* 'closed'. Karlgren explained this distinction as referring to the presence or absence of a rounded medial in the syllable; although not actually wrong, this description of the *kāi/hé* distinction is somewhat misleading. As pointed out above, the *děngyùn* phonologists did not operate with the idea of discrete segments when analyzing finals, and so could not have been describing a medial which is a segmental category. It is better to view this distinction as a feature of syllable onset. In most modern dialects, syllables in which a round medial such as -*u*- or -*y*- occurs are visibly rounded throughout the articulation of the initial. I think that it was the simple observation of the different lip gestures made when a speaker said syllables like *kan* and *kwan* that lay at the root of the *kāi/hé* distinction.

Of all the *děngyùn* categories, none is so difficult to interpret as the term *děng*, which Karlgren translates as 'division' and others have preferred to call 'grade.' In the *Yùnjìng* each of the four tones on a table is divided into four *děng*. Sometimes the *děng* are occupied by the same *Qièyùn* rhyme, but at other times by two, three or four different rhymes. There is general agreement that syllables placed in the third division had some sort of palatal medial, and that first-division words lacked any such palatal element. Beyond this, theories vary concerning the other divisions. M. Z. Volpicelli (1896) thought that the four divisions represented four different main vowels; S. H. Schaank (1897–8) and Pulleyblank (1971) share the view that the four divisions represent different medials preceding the same main vowel. Karlgren chose a position between these two. Table 2.1 shows the interpretations of the four above-mentioned scholars for the syllables with velar initials found in table 25 of the *Yùnjìng* (see Figure 2.2).

The way one reconstructs the divisions depends in large degree on how one perceives the rhyme tables. Volpicelli and Schaank tried to reconstruct "Ancient Chinese" by using only the rhyme tables found at the front of the eighteenth-

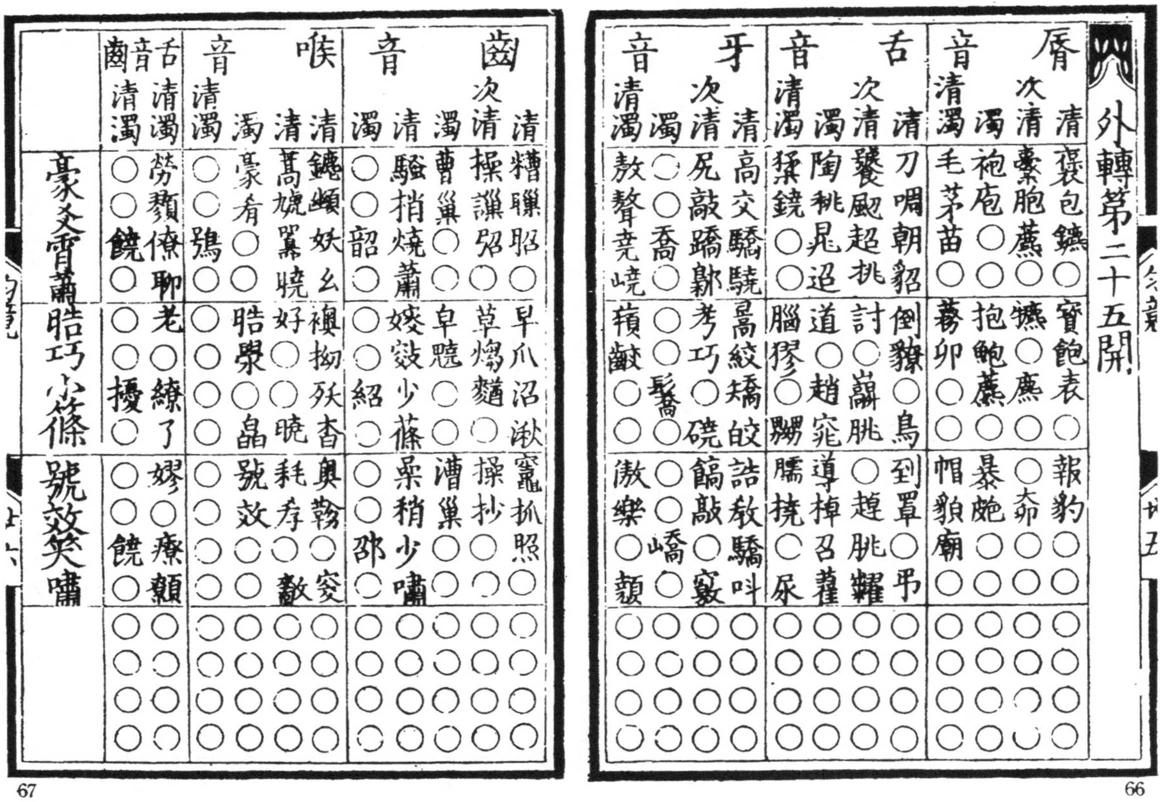

Figure 2.2. Table 25 of the *Yunjing* rhyme tables

century *Kāngxī* dictionary; they neglected the categories of the *Qièyùn* almost entirely. Karlgren took the rhyme tables as a sort of key to the *Qièyùn*. More recently Pulleyblank has insisted that the early rhyme tables are not in fact "keys" to the *Qièyùn* at all, but represent a conscious and systematic attempt to describe the standard language of the late Tang dynasty. The view that the rhyme tables are a key to the *Qièyùn* implies that the *Qièyùn* categories cannot be interpreted apart from these tables, and this attitude in some cases leads to errors in the interpretation of the *Qièyùn* categories. If Pulleyblank's view or some related version of it is accepted, then one is free to reconstruct the *Qièyùn* phonological system in its own terms, freed from the fetters of these Song dynasty "keys". To the present author it seems that the question of the nature of these tables is still moot, and that consequently it is difficult to accept any of the existing interpretations without some reservation. Be that as it may, the rhyme tables have nonetheless played a very important role in the reconstruction of Middle Chinese.

2.4   The methodology of Middle Chinese reconstruction

In his *Compendium of Phonetics in Ancient and Archaic Chinese* (1954) Karlgren gives a succinct description of the methodology used in reconstructing Middle Chinese. Karlgren considered Middle Chinese to be the language reflected in the categories of the *Qièyùn* as they have come down to us in its various redactions. The *Qièyùn* categories in most cases are interpreted in light of the rhyme tables; even though Karlgren admitted that the *Qièyùn zhǐzhǎngtú* was based on a later stage of Chinese, he felt that it was still useful in interpreting the *Qièyùn*, since it was much closer to it in time than the modern dialects. Second in importance to the rhyme tables were the so-called Sinoxenic dialects (a term created by Samuel Martin to refer to the systems of pronouncing Chinese characters in Japan, Korea and Vietnam). In all three of these countries Chinese has been studied and used extensively for many centuries, and each country has its own distinctive manner of reading Chinese texts aloud. Karlgren, while recognizing that these foreign dialects were "corrupt" in some respects, considered that they were of paramount importance in reconstructing the language of the *Qièyùn*. Third in importance in Karlgren's view were the native Chinese dialects.

The entire process of reconstructing Middle Chinese was of course vastly complicated, but some simple examples will suffice to illustrate the principles which were employed. A comparative study of the *Guǎngyùn fǎnqiè* formulas reveals that there was a distinct initial consonant in the language represented by eight *fǎnqiè* upper characters pronounced (in Modern Chinese) *tā, tuō, tǔ, tù, tōng, tiān, tái* and *tāng*; this initial corresponds to the rhyme table initial *tòu*, and *tòu* is one of the *shétóu* sounds. Each of the *shétóu* sounds corresponds to a distinctive

Table 2.2. Dialectal reflexes of the Shétóu initials

	Peking	Sūzhōu	Xiàmèn	Guǎngzhōu	Kanon	Sino Vietnamese	Sino-Korean
duān 端							
多	tuo¹	təu¹	to¹	to¹	ta	ʔda¹	ta
刀	tau¹	tæ¹	to¹	tou¹	to	ʔdao¹	to
短	tuan³	tø³	tuan³	tyn³	tan	ʔdoan³	tān
tòu 透							
他	t'a¹	t'ɒ¹	t'a¹	t'a¹	ta	tha¹	t'a
天	t'ien¹	t'iɪ¹	t'ien¹	t'in¹	ten	thien¹	ch'ŏn
铁	t'ie³	t'iəʔ⁷	t'iet⁷	t'it⁷	tetsu	thiet⁷	ch'ŏl
dìng 定							
弟	ti⁵	di⁶	ti⁶	tai⁶	tei	ʔde⁶	che
头	t'ou²	dɤ²	t'ɔ²	t'au²	tō	ʔdəu²	tu
豆	tou⁵	dɤ⁶	tɔ⁶	tau⁶	tō	ʔdao⁶	tu
ní 泥							
内	nei⁵	nE⁶	lui⁶	noi⁶	dai	noi⁶	nae
年	nien²	niɪ²	lian²	nin²	nen	nien²	yŏn
农	nuŋ²	noŋ²	loŋ²	nuŋ²	nō	noŋ²	nong

set of *fǎnqiè* upper characters in the *Guǎngyùn*. The only way phonetic substance can be given to these categories is by comparing them to actual pronunciations in modern Chinese dialects and in the Sinoxenic dialects of Japan, Korea and Vietnam. Table 2.2 gives the readings of several common characters from each of the *shétóu* initials in several Chinese and Sinoxenic dialects. A glance at the table shows that a large majority of the forms are either dental or alveolar stops and nasals. The initial *ní* may be safely reconstructed as a nasal on the basis of the forms given. The initials *duān* and *tòu* are voiceless dental (or alveolar) stops in all the dialects; with the exception of Kanon, which has merged the two series. The remaining dialects have an unaspirated stop for *duān* and an aspirated stop for *tòu*; it is reasonable to suppose that Middle Chinese possessed the same sort of contrast. The only dialect which clearly distinguishes the initial *dìng* from *duān* and *tòu* is Sūzhōu in which *dìng* corresponds to a voiced stop contrasting with the voiceless correspondences for *duān* and *tòu*. Provisionally at least, the initial *dìng* can be considered some kind of voiced dental stop in Middle Chinese. Karlgren argued that *dìng* and the other *quánzhuó* initials were voiced aspirates, whereas the present consensus is that at the time of the *Qièyùn* they were voiced unaspirated stops. Once one set of the rhyme table initials has been reconstructed, the meaning of the terms *quánqīng*, *cìqīng*, *quánzhuó* and *cìzhuó*

Table 2.3. Middle Chinese initials

Bilabials	p	ph	b	m		
Dentals	t	th	d	nl		
Sibilants	ts	tsh	dz		s	z
Retroflexes	ṭ	ṭh	ḍ			
Retroflex sibilants	tṣ	tṣh	dẓ		ṣ	ẓ
Palatal sibilants	tś	tśh	dź	nź	ś	ź
Velars	k	kh	g	ng	x	
Glottals	· (ʔ)				j	∅ (zero)

Table 2.4. The four divisions in the dialects

Division	I	II	III	IV
dialect	高	交	骄	叫
Peking	kau	tɕiau	tɕiau	tɕiau
Sūzhōu	kæ	kæ	tɕiæ	tɕiæ
Xiàmén	ko	kau	kiau	kiau
Guǎngzhōu	kou	kaau	kiu	kiu
Kanon	kau	kau	keu	keu
Sino-Vietnamese	cao	giao	kiêu	kiêu
Sino-Korean	ko	kyo	kyo	kyo

becomes clear, and this information can then be applied to other sets of initials. The above example illustrates in a very simple way how the *Qièyùn* and rhyme table categories, which viewed in isolation were just so many abstract formulas, were given phonetic substance by comparing them with corresponding words in the Modern Chinese dialects and Sinoxenic reading systems. Table 2.3 shows the inventory of Middle Chinese initials as reconstructed by Karlgren and modified by F. K. Li (1971).

The reconstruction of the finals was carried out in similar fashion: the *děngyùn* categories which were applied to the finals were compared with actual dialect forms, and reconstructed values were postulated. In the case of the finals, however, the rhyme tables do not actually distinguish all the different and distinct rhymes of the *Qièyùn*, so that even after all the rhyme table distinctions are reconstituted, there still remain a considerable number of *Qièyùn* categories which must be dealt with if all the Middle Chinese rhymes are to be distinguished. As indicated above, the most difficult of the rhyme table categories applied to the finals is the notion of *děng* or 'division'. In Table 2.4 the actual pronunciation of a representative sample of words from table 25 of the *Yùnjìng* is shown. (The examples for divisions I, II and III are *píng* tone; a *qù* tone word is used to exemplify the fourth division, since it is a more common word than the corresponding *píng* tone form.) Each of the words is in a different division; they all share the same initial and offglide, so the significance of *děng* must be sought in the remainder of the syllable – in either the medial or the main vowel, or perhaps in both simultaneously.

Using the forms in Table 2.4 as examples, we can now outline the main lines of Karlgren's thinking concerning the reconstruction of the four divisions: (1) The offglide in all the forms is *u*. (2) The main vowels in divisions I and II must be some sort of low vowel like *a*. (3) The four divisions differ not only in the presence or absence of a medial *i*, but also in having several different main vowels in several of the dialects (Xiàmén, Guǎngzhōu, Sino-Vietnamese); hence the divisions differed both by medial and main vowel. (4) Division I is clearly the least palatalized; a low back *â* [ɑ] is postulated as the main vowel. (5) Division II causes palatalization of the preceding velar in some dialects but not in others; this would make sense only if it had some sort of front vowel without an intervening medial *i* (which, as we will see below, is the distinguishing characteristic of divisions III and IV). A low front vowel *a* [a] is reconstructed as the main vowel of this division. (6) Divisions III and IV clearly both had a palatal medial of some sort; and, judging from Kanon and Sino-Vietnamese, the nucleus was some kind of mid vowel. (7) The most difficult question to answer is how the third and fourth divisions differed from one another; in the present sample all the dialects have merged them. To resolve this problem, Karlgren had recourse to Sino-Korean where, in a few cases (not illustrated in Table 2.4), fourth-division words have a medial *y* where the corresponding third-division words lack this medial: *jiàn* 'to see', a fourth division word, is *kyŏn* [kjən] in Sino-Korean, where *jiàn* 'to construct', a third division word, is *kŏn* [kən]. On the basis of cases like this, Karlgren concluded that the fourth division had a longer and more vocalic medial *i*, as opposed to a shorter, more consonantal *i̯* in the third division. The stronger and more vocalic *i* survives in Sino-Korean (in some cases at least), whereas the weaker and more consonantal third-division medial *i̯* drops out. Finally, since third- and fourth-division finals are different rhymes in the *Qièyùn*, they must be reconstructed with different main vowels in order to preserve the rhyme distinction. Karlgren proposed that the fourth division had a more strongly palatal *e* [e] as its main vowel, which matched its strongly palatal medial *i*; by similar reasoning, then, the third division had a somewhat less palatal main vowel to match its more weakly palatal medial; Karlgren reconstructed this vowel as *ä* [ɛ]. As a result of this analysis we arrive at the following Middle Chinese forms:

Division	I	II	III	IV
Reconstruction	kâu	kau	kįäu	kieu

A solution to the problem of the nature of the *děng* was of course an immense help in reconstructing the *Qièyùn* finals, but it did not solve all the problems by any means. Although one could easily classify all the *Qièyùn* rhymes as to division, in some cases the *Qièyùn zhǐzhǎngtú* treated distinct *Qièyùn* rhymes as if they were identical; such rhymes had doubtless merged at an early date, and it was difficult to find evidence for distinguishing them. Generally Karlgren found his solution to this problem in marginal distinctions maintained in one or more of the native or foreign dialects which he relied upon. In two cases he was unable to find any evidence for distinguishing two important *Qièyùn* rhymes; in one case he reconstructed two separate rhymes as *i*; F. K. Li (1971) has proposed that these two rhymes be distinguished as *i* versus *ï*, on the basis of their separate origins in Old Chinese. Likewise, Karlgren has reconstructed two distinct *Qièyùn* rhymes both as *ai*; Li distinguishes them as *ai* and *aï*.

Karlgren's Middle Chinese vowel system is highly complex; it consists of sixteen distinct vowels and four medials, two of which can also function as offglides; his medials are *i*, *į*, *u* and *w*; the difference between *i* and *į* is discussed above; *u*, in contrast to *w*, is used when the *kāi* and *hé* variants of a final are put into different *Qièyùn* (or *Guǎngyùn*) rhymes. Since his transcriptional system is a bit strange to most modern linguists (it was based on J. A. Lundell's Swedish dialect alphabet), we will examine all his vowels and medials, describing the phonetic interpretation of each and listing the finals in which each occurs. Bracketed symbols are taken from the International Phonetic Alphabet.

(1) *i*. A high front unrounded vowel, [i]: (*j*)*i*, (*j*)*wi*. The first of these two finals actually represents two contrasting rhymes, as we pointed out above. Karlgren writes these finals with the *j* after labials, velars and gutturals; otherwise he generally omits the *j*.

(2) *e*. An upper mid, front unrounded vowel, [e]: *iei*, *iwei*, *ieu*, *iem*, *iep*, *ien*, *iwen*, *iet*, *iwet*, *ieng*, *iweng*, *iek*, *iwek*.

(3) *ě*. A shorter variety of vowel (2): *įěu*, *įěn*, *įwěn*, *įět*, *įwět*.

(4) *ę*. Karlgren writes this [e] when it functions as a glide and the preceding or following *i* is to be taken as the main vowel of the final: (*j*)*ęi*, (*j*)*węi*, (*j*)*ię*, (*j*)*wię*.

(5) *ä*. A lower mid, front unrounded vowel, [ɛ]: *įäi*, *įwäi*, *įäu*, *įäm*, *įäp*, *įän*, *įwän*, *įät*, *įwät*, *įäng*, *įwäng*, *įäk*.

(6) *ɛ*. A front unrounded vowel somewhat lower than vowel (5), [æ]: *įɛn*, *įɛt*, *ɛng*, *wɛng*, *ɛk*, *wɛk*.

(7) *a*. A low front unrounded vowel, [a]: *a, wa, i̯a, ai, aï, wai, waï, au, am, ap, an, wan, at, wat, i̯ang, i̯wang, i̯ak, i̯wak*.

(8) *ă*. A shorter variety of vowel (7): *ăi, wăi, ăm, ăp, ăn, wăn, ăt, wăt*.

(9) *ə*. A mid, central unrounded vowel, [ə]: *i̯əm, i̯əp, ən, uən, uət, i̯ən, i̯uən, i̯ət, i̯uət, əng, wəng, i̯əng*.

(10) *ə̯*. A short (non-syllabic) variety of vowel (9): *ə̯u, i̯ə̯u* – in these finals *u* is to be taken as the main vowel.

(11) *ɐ*. A lower mid to low unrounded central vowel, [ɐ]: *i̯ɐi, i̯wɐi, i̯ɐm, i̯wɐm, i̯ɐp, i̯wɐp, i̯ɐn, i̯wɐn, i̯ɐt, i̯wɐt, ɐng, wɐng, i̯ɐng, i̯wɐng, ɐk, wɐk, i̯ɐk*.

(12) *u*. A high back rounded vowel, [u]: *i̯u, ung, i̯ung, uk, i̯uk*.

(13) *o*. An upper mid, back rounded vowel, [o]: *uo, i̯wo, uong, i̯wong, uok, i̯wok*.

(14) *å*. A lower mid, back rounded vowel, [ɔ]: *ång, åk*.

(15) *â*. A low back, unrounded vowel, [ɑ]: *â, uâ, i̯â, i̯wâ, âi, uâi, âu, âm, âp, ân, uân, ât, uât, âng, wâng, âk, wâk*.

(16) *ậ*. A shorter variety of vowel (15): *ậi, uậi, ậm, ập*.

The four medials may be described as follows:

(1) *i̯*. A short, consonantal palatal onglide, [j]. F. K. Li uses the I P A symbol given here for this medial, a practice which we shall also follow hereafter.

(2) *i*. A palatal glide, longer and more vocalic than medial (1). It also occurs as an offglide.

(3) *w*. A short back rounded medial, [w].

(4) *u*. A back rounded medial, longer and more vocalic than medial (3).

Karlgren's reconstruction of the Middle Chinese finals has been criticized by a number of scholars. Y. R. Chao (1941) examined his system with a view to determining its contrastive elements; in the process he proposed several revisions in the system, some of which were subsequently accepted by Karlgren. Samuel Martin (1953) made a thoroughgoing phonemic analysis of Karlgren's reconstruction, reducing the number of vocalic contrasts to six. Martin treated Karlgren's reconstruction, along with Chao's revisions of it, as a valid phonetic reconstruction of Middle Chinese; his resulting phonemicization, while interesting from the point of view of phonological analysis, did little to advance our knowledge of Middle Chinese itself. Lǐ Róng (1952) and Dǒng Tónghé (1954) subjected Karlgren's reconstruction to a more searching examination, producing in the process fairly drastic revisions of it. Tōdō Akiyasu (1957), taking into account the work of the above-mentioned scholars as well as that of several Japanese predecessors, proposed an even more drastically revised version of Middle Chinese. In 1962 Edwin Pulleyblank, as a preliminary step toward re-examining the problem of Old Chinese, proposed his own revised reconstruction of Middle Chinese (Pulleyblank 1962a; 1962b). Although all the aforementioned revisions differ from Karlgren's original reconstruction in many important ways, both in interpretation and in substance, from a methodological point of view these revisions depart little (if at all) from Karlgren's views. The differences come about because of a refinement of technique: a closer examination of the sources reveals more distinctions than Karlgren posited; more and better information relevant to reconstructing some of the more difficult contrasts has come to light; the Chinese transcriptions of Buddhist names and terms and Chinese words transcribed in alphabetic scripts (Tibetan, Brahmi, Uygur) have also thrown some light on problems of reconstruction. Such material can be employed, however, without questioning Karlgren's basic methodology. All the reconstructions and revisions of Middle Chinese published up until the present can and should be viewed as products of a single methodological tradition going back to the original work of Bernhard Karlgren and his predecessors.

Pulleyblank (1970) and Miller (1975) have both raised serious questions concerning this traditional methodology. Pulleyblank for the first time rejects the direct relevance of the rhyme table categories to the reconstruction of the *Qièyùn* language; this is because the earliest rhyme tables are based on another dialect, two centuries later in time and based on different geographic standards. In Pulleyblank's view this later form of Chinese should be first reconstructed independently, and only then be used along with other data to reconstruct the categories of the *Qièyùn* language. Miller's objections to the methodology outlined here are much more radical; he describes it as a "highly eclectic, pick-and-choose system" that brings together elements of the traditional historical comparative method with purely intuitive and, at times, arbitrary processes. He finds traditional Chinese linguistic terminology rife with terms chosen for their exemplary function, and even tainted in many cases by philosophical or mystical speculation. As a result, Miller sees little value in most of the reconstructions produced before 1975. While I do not subscribe to this criticism in all its details, I think that Miller's criticism can be accounted useful if it leads to a sober re-examination of the whole question of historical reconstruction in Chinese. It indeed seems that Karlgren's approach to this topic has pretty much run its course; pursued further, it can only lead to an unending process of juggling and rejuggling of the same old elements, without any really new insights into the historical process. If Chinese historical linguistics is to be rescued from scholasticism, a thoroughgoing re-evaluation of basic assumptions about methodology is essential. Although it is well beyond the scope of a book of this type to carry out such a re-evaluation, I will offer a few preliminary thoughts on the subject. The *Qièyùn* itself must be viewed as the primary source for Middle Chinese, the stable core to which other bodies of information are referred; despite disclaimers to the contrary, Karlgren's reconstruction of "Ancient" Chinese is in its essence a reconstruction of the rhyme table categories. The *Qièyùn* is the basic datum, and the rhyme tables are interpretations of this datum based on later and geographically disparate dialects. We are under no compulsion to accept such interpretations; they are no more than one other type of evidence, to be judged along with other equally valuable types such as modern dialect forms, ancient transcriptions and Sinoxenic readings. The value attributed them because of their early date is offset by the fact that their meaning is anything but clear, and consequently any interpretation of them is of necessity speculative. The native Chinese dialects should take precedence over the Sinoxenic materials: the latter are loanwords taken into a foreign medium, and subject to the internal historical processes of that medium. The Sinoxenic material needs to be studied much more thoroughly before being used to interpret the earlier stages of Chinese. The Chinese dialects are the organic, autochthonous descendants of Middle Chinese, and clearly should be the primary data on which any reconstruction of earlier stages of the language is based. More account needs to be taken of the rich stock of Chinese loanwords in neighboring languages such as Vietnamese, the various Tai languages, Miao-Yao and perhaps others as well. Ancient transcriptional evidence, Buddhist as well as other types, needs to be studied more systematically. Finally there should be a more conscious and rigorous approach to methodology; we should know precisely what we are doing at every stage of the reconstructive process.

Another aspect of Chinese historical linguistics that demands more attention is the distinction between the literary and popular components of the various historical and modern stages of the language. Popular forms are those elements of a language that go back in an unbroken line to the protolanguage; literary elements are words or expressions which at some point ceased to be living words in the spoken language. Such literary elements survive in the texts, and are frequently reintroduced into the spoken language. Note that this distinction is not the same as that of colloquial versus literary which one often encounters in works on Chinese dialects; this distinction refers to contemporary usage, while the popular/literary distinction refers to be historical status of the elements in question. A word which is literary in the historical linguistic sense may be colloquial in that it is employed as an everyday word in the spoken language, just as in English many Latin words (clearly of literary origin in the historical sense) are perfectly good everyday colloquial words. A great majority of the words in the *Qièyùn* do not actually reflect the spoken language of the time it was written, but are reading pronunciations of words encountered in texts. In some cases, of course, these reading pronunciations actually coincided with popular spoken forms, but unfortunately the *Qièyùn* makes no distinction between the two types of elements. Chinese historical phonology hitherto has been the study of the development of the various stages of the literary language as codified in traditional dictionaries. Certainly another approach is possible: the reconstruction of the ancestor of the spoken (popular) forms of Chinese, working backward from the present spoken dialects. One important benefit of this approach would be to establish a core of words which has evolved organically from the ancestral form of Chinese down to the present day; in doing this, we would escape from much of the artificiality which plagues the traditional approach. In the process of studying the evolution of spoken Chinese one could integrate much valuable data on the spoken language preserved in historical texts, an area still largely unexplored. An added advantage of this approach would be to give us a better appreciation and better control of the purely literary monuments of Chinese linguistic history.

2.5 The reconstruction of Old Chinese

The reconstruction of Old Chinese, unlike that of Middle Chinese which is essentially the phonological interpretation of a single source, is based on several different bodies of data. Historically, the study of Old Chinese phonology began about 400 years ago with the work of the Fukienese scholar Chén Dì (1541–1617). Prior to Chén's time, the Chinese lacked any notion of historical change in language; when they encountered discrepancies in the rhymes of verse from different historical eras, they attributed it to the rhyming laxity of ancient poets, or, to put it in another way, they attributed changes in rhyming practice to a gradual development of more strict prosodic standards, rather than to a change in the language itself. It was Chén Dì's great accomplishment to see that these discrepancies were due to phonological change, and not to a sort of loose attitude concerning rhyme on the part of ancient versifiers. He epitomized his new view in a motto to which few modern linguists could take exception: "It is a natural principle that the script and the sounds of language differ according to time and place." The most important implication of this view was that the language of the ancient poets of the first millennium BC formed a unified and internally consistent system, and the rhymes of this ancient verse could be used to study ancient phonology in a rigorous manner.

The most important corpus of ancient poetry was the *Shījīng* [*Classic of poetry*], a collection of 305 anonymous poems brought together in the sixth century BC. The contents are compositions of different periods, the early and late pieces differing by as much as 500 years. Despite this disparity of age, the poems of the

Shījīng in general display a consistent pattern of rhyming. When *Shījīng* rhymes were compared to those of the *Qièyùn*, it was immediately evident that the languages of these two sources differed in many important ways. In the beginning, the study of Old Chinese phonology (called *gǔyīn* 'ancient sounds' by the Qing dynasty phonologists) consisted in comparing the *Qièyùn* rhymes with those of the *Shījīng*, and trying to determine on this basis what the rhyming system of the *Shījīng* was. The words that could rhyme together in the *Shījīng* were placed together in rhyme groups, called *yùnbù* in Chinese; all the characters which belonged to the same *yùnbù* could potentially rhyme together. The characters of a single rhyme group bore a definite relationship to the rhymes of the *Qièyùn* and vice versa; for example, the rhyme *táng* of the *Qièyùn* belongs in its entirety to the *yáng* rhyme group of Old Chinese; in other cases, however, a single *Qièyùn* rhyme would be divided among several Old Chinese rhyme groups.

During the Qing dynasty a number of outstanding scholars, using the principle of historical change propounded by Chén Dì, subjected the rhyming system of the *Shījīng* to a rigorous analysis. Two early phonologists, Gù Yánwǔ (1613–82) and Jiāng Yǒng (1681–1726) laid the foundations of the brilliant accomplishments of the late eighteenth and early nineteenth centuries. Both men made important discoveries, essential to further development of the field; it is to Gù Yánwǔ that we owe the important principle that the Old Chinese rhyme groups could be composed of more than one *Qièyùn* rhyme; he, for example, divided the *Qièyùn* rhyme *má* between two different Old Chinese groups, *yú* and *gē*. He also observed that in the *Shījīng*, *rù* tone words (those which ended in *p*, *t* and *k* in Middle Chinese) in some cases rhymed with open syllables, so that *rù* tone words sometimes had to be placed together with non-*rù* words in the same Old Chinese rhyme group. Jiāng Yǒng refined Gù's analysis, distinguishing more rhyme groups in the process.

The greatest Qing philologist was undoubtedly Duàn Yùcái (1735–1815). Building upon the work of his predecessors, he carried the analysis of Old Chinese phonology to new heights. Before Duàn, the *Shījīng* was virtually the sole source used in the study of Old Chinese. Duàn was the first one to understand the great importance of the Chinese script to the study of the Chinese phonology of the first millennium BC. More than 80 per cent of the graphs recorded in the Hàn dynasty dictionary *Shuōwén jiězì* are phonetically based, consisting of a semantic and a phonetic component. Such characters in Chinese are called *xiéshēngzì*, usually translated into English as 'phonetic compound characters'. Table 2.5 shows a few examples of this kind of graph; readings are given in Middle Chinese and the semantic and phonetic components are identified.

Duàn observed that characters which shared the same phonetic component, as

Table 2.5. Phonetic compound characters (*xiéshēngzì*)

Phonetic compound	Semantic component	Phonetic component
狐 ɣwa 'fox'	犭 'dog'	瓜 kwa
枫 pjung 'maple'	木 'tree'	风 pjung
伯 pɒk 'eldest'	亻 'person'	白 bɒk
湖 ɣuo 'lake'	氵 'water'	胡 ɣuo
纺 phjwang 'spin'	纟 'silk'	方 pjwang
雞 kiei 'chicken'	隹 'bird'	奚 ɣiei

a general rule, could rhyme in the system revealed in the *Shījīng*. This was a discovery of the utmost importance, because until this time only those characters which actually occurred as rhymes in the *Shījīng* (or other ancient verse) could be placed in one of the rhyme groups; now it would be possible to classify virtually every character in the language into its proper category. Another of Duàn's contributions was for the first time to arrange his rhyme groups according to their phonological proximity to one another, this for the most part being determined by cases of irregular cross-rhyming or exceptional use of phonetic components in the script. Two other Qing philologists, both contemporaries of Duàn Yùcái, Kǒng Guǎngsēn (1752–86) and Wáng Niànsūn (1744–1832), proposed further refinements in the system of Old Chinese rhyme groups. The accomplishments of these Qing dynasty scholars were finally summed up in a definitive way by Jiāng Yǒugào, an otherwise rather obscure person who died in 1851. Jiāng's system of Old Chinese rhyme groups, with a few minor adjustments made by later scholars, is essentially the scheme on which modern reconstructions of the Old Chinese rhymes are made.

Qing philologists were almost exclusively interested in the problem of Old Chinese rhymes. The only exception is Qián Dàxīn (1727–86), who made two lasting discoveries concerning Old Chinese initials – that Old Chinese had no dentilabials, nor laminals (*shéshàngyīn*). Apart from the solo efforts of Qián, the reconstruction of the initials has almost entirely been the work of twentieth-century scholars following the lead of Bernhard Karlgren. Obviously the rhymes found in ancient verse tell us nothing concerning initials; virtually the sole source of information on this subject is the phonetic compound characters mentioned above. Karlgren, beginning with the *Analytic dictionary* published in 1923, used this material to create hypotheses about the Old Chinese initials. One of the methodological principles he laid down, which has guided all subsequent research on this subject, is that the initials of all the words in a single phonetic series (a set of characters all of which share a common phonetic element) have a single point of articulation. When a phonetic series fails to satisfy this condition, Karlgren posited compound or cluster initials. This line of reasoning enabled him to make a most significant discovery – that, whereas Middle Chinese tolerated only simple consonant initials, Old Chinese possessed cluster initials. At the present time, while no-one doubts the existence of initial consonantal clusters in Old Chinese, there is considerable controversy concerning their precise reconstruction.

The first complete reconstruction of Old Chinese was produced by Karlgren and published in definitive form in his 1940 work, "Grammata serica." As in the case of Middle Chinese, both the rhyme groups and the evidence for initials were abstract entities, in themselves devoid of any phonological substance. In order to make actual reconstructions, Karlgren had no recourse but to compare these categories to his reconstructed Middle Chinese; thus Old Chinese is a reconstruction based on another reconstruction, a kind of second-degree abstraction. Not surprisingly, in light of the highly hypothetical nature of Old Chinese, Karlgren's reconstruction has elicited no small amount of criticism. His earliest and perhaps most vociferous critic was the Chinese linguist, Dǒng Tónghé (1948a), who published his criticisms of Karlgren along with his own reconstruction in "Shànggǔ yīnyùn biǎogǎo" [Draft table of Old Chinese phonology]. After Dǒng, Wáng Lì, another prominent Chinese linguist, proposed a new and quite different reconstruction of Old Chinese in his book, *Hànyǔ shǐgǎo* [*A draft history of Chinese*], in 1957. In the late 1950s and early 1960s, Sergei Yakhontov, a Soviet sinologist, published a number of highly original articles on the topic of Old Chinese reconstruction. At almost the same time Edwin Pulleyblank (1962a; 1962b) entered the lists with a formidable array of new approaches and ideas concerning the nature of Old Chinese. By this time, it is safe to say, Karlgren's Old Chinese reconstruction was no longer considered viable by serious linguists interested in Old Chinese.

F. K. Li's 1971 article, "Shànggǔyīn yánjiū" [Studies on Archaic Chinese phonology] at the present time presents the most complete, up-to-date and internally consistent reconstruction of Old Chinese. Although Li has not produced a dictionary of the order of Karlgren's 1940 "Grammata serica," which gives his reconstruction of a large body of the Old Chinese lexicon, he has presented his ideas in a sufficiently systematic and complete form to allow others familiar with the data to produce reasonably accurate reconstructions in his system. Neither Yakhontov's nor Pulleyblank's published work on Old Chinese has yet reached this degree of completeness, and it would consequently be very difficult for any one other than the creators of these reconstructions to employ them.

Let us now sketch the main features of Li's Old Chinese as presented in his

Table 2.6. The Old Chinese initials

p	ph	b	m			
t	th	d	n	l	r	
ts	tsh	dz				s
k	kh	g	ng			
kw	khw	gw	ngw			
ʔ						h
ʔw						hw

Table 2.7. The evolution of Old Chinese initials

1. 龙	ljwong	*ljung
聋	lung	*lung
庞	bång	*brung
宠	tśhjwong	*hljung
2. 余	jiwo	*rag
途	duo	*dag
除	djwo	*drjag
徐	zjwo	*rjag

1971 article and subsequently revised in 1976. Table 2.6 shows that his inventory of Old Chinese initials is much simpler than that of Middle Chinese.

In reconstructing the Old Chinese initial system, Li follows Karlgren's hypothesis that the initials of all the words in a single phonetic series (a set of characters all of which share a common phonetic element) have a single point of articulation. In many cases this entails reconstructing consonant clusters of various shapes for Old Chinese. The examples in Table 2.7 illustrates this principle in the case of two relatively complicated phonetic series.

In both of the cases illustrated in this table, all the initials of the Old Chinese forms have a common point of articulation, either *l* or *r* in the first set, either *d* or *r* in the second set. The forms given in the table also demonstrate how most of the complexity found in the Middle Chinese initials is brought about by the action of various medials, of which Li recognizes three: a palatal *j*, a retroflex *r*, and *l*; *j* caused the palatalization of preceding dental: *$tj > tś$, *$dj > ź$. The combination of *rj* brought about the palatalization even of velar and glottal initials: *$krj > tś$, *$hrj > ś$, etc. The effects of medial *r* are far-reaching; on the one hand, it produces the two series of retroflex initials found in Middle Chinese: *$tr > ṭ$, *$tshr > ṭsh$, etc. Below we will see that it also affects vocalic development. In Li's scheme medial *l* simply disappears, leaving no effect on either the initial or the vowel: *$klau > kâu$.

In addition to the medials, Li also reconstructs two consonantal prefixes: *h* and *s*. Strictly speaking, *h* indicates only that the following nasal or liquid is voiceless; *s*, which can precede almost all of the consonants, remains as *s* in Middle Chinese: **smang > sâng*, **shwit > siwet*. Of the clusters consisting of *h* plus a nasal or liquid, **hm* becomes *x*, **hn* becomes *th*, and **hng* becomes *x*.

Li's Old Chinese has a rich inventory of final consonants; in addition to the six final consonants posited for Middle Chinese which he also posits for Old Chinese, he also proposes that Old Chinese had labiovelar endings, and following Karlgren he reconstructs a series of voiced final stops: the reconstruction of these voiced finals is based on the fact that many open syllables of Middle Chinese occur in Old Chinese phonetic compound series with words ending in stops; occasional rhymes between Middle Chinese open and *rù shēng* words (those ending in *p*, *t* and *k*) are also found in the *Shījīng*. Finally, Li proposes that the rhyme group *gē* ended in *r*. The result of adding all these new final consonants is that Old Chinese has no open syllables, an unusual situation to be sure, but one that Li considers a logical and even necessary outcome of a consistent analysis of the evidence.

The rich array of initials, medials and final consonants which Li constructs allows him to posit a simple vowel system of only four contrasting elements:

i   u

ə

a

Each of the Old Chinese rhyme groups has a single vowel and final consonant. The *yáng* groups, those that end in a nasal, have only a single final consonant; the *yīn* groups, those with non-nasal endings, usually have both voiceless and voiced endings. This situation is illustrated in Table 2.8, where the traditional rhyme groups along with Li's reconstructions are given.

As in the case of the initials, the complexities of the Middle Chinese vowel system are mostly the result of the Old Chinese medials. The medial *j* frequently palatalizes the following vowel: **djan > źjän*, **ljar > lje*, **kjagw > kjäu*, etc.; medial *r* tends to centralize or front the vowels it precedes: **sran > ṣăn*, **krak > kɒk*, **pruk > påk*, etc. The loss of medial *l* leaves no effect on the vowel: *klak > kâk*. Another factor in the development of the Middle Chinese vowels is the action of final labiovelars on a preceding schwa: **kəkw > kuok*, **tjəngw > tśjung*.

In Li's Old Chinese, complex consonantal initials are abundant, while the number of vocalic elements is comparatively small. This situation is quite different from that in Middle Chinese, where one finds no initial consonant clusters but a plethora of distinct vowels instead. This sort of development is very much in line

Table 2.8. Old Chinese rhymes

1. 之 ək, əg		13. 蒸 əng
2. 幽 əkw, əgw		14. 中 əngw
3. 宵 akw, agw		—
4. 侯 uk, ug		15. 东 ung
5. 鱼 ak, ag		16. 阳 ang
6. 支 ik, ig		17. 耕 ing
7. 歌 ar		—
8. 祭 at, ad		18. 元 an
9. 脂 it, id		19. 真 in
10. 微 ət, əd		20. 文 ən
11. 缉 əp		21. 侵 əm
12. 叶 ap		22. 谈 am

with the sort of typological drift described for the monosyllabic tonal languages of Asia in Chapter 1. But while it is possible to view Li's and others' Old Chinese reconstructions as realistic in this general typological sense, it would be a mistake to adopt a strictly realistic view of the details. For the present, at least, it is best to consider the various Old Chinese reconstructions which have been proposed as convenient but highly hypothetical phonological summaries of what is known of Old Chinese from the sources described above. Different reconstructions can only be judged on the basis of how consistently and simply they summarize these data. In the view of the present author, F. K. Li's reconstruction meets these criteria best at the present time.[3]

2.6 Old Mandarin

After the end of the Tang dynasty, China's political center of gravity moved eastward. The Song capital was Kāifēng, a city located on the North China Plain in the province of Hénán. From the twelfth to the fourteenth centuries North China fell under the foreign rule of first the Jurchens and then the Mongols. The two dynasties ruled over by these Altaic overlords had their capital in the vicinity of present-day Peking. Quite naturally, a new common spoken language arose which reflected these new political realities; this new koine, based on the lowland dialects of northeastern China, differed quite radically from the late Tang common language, which was in essence a northwestern dialect. It was precisely during the Jurchen and Mongol periods that a new vernacular literature, almost entirely popular in origin, arose. Among the new genres which appeared at this time was a new verse (or song) form called the *qǔ* or *sǎnqǔ*. Unlike more formal types of poetry, which were rhymed according to much earlier norms, this new form of verse was rhymed according to current vernacular pronunciation. In the early fourteenth century, a writer of *qǔ*, Zhōu Déqīng, codified the rhymes of *qǔ* in a small book which he called the *Zhōngyuán yīnyùn* [*Rhymes of the central plain*]. Zhōu classified almost 6,000 characters into nineteen rhymes, each of which was named by a pair of characters which exemplified the rhyme in question. The rhymes were subdivided into groups of homophonous characters, but unlike earlier rhyme books, the *Zhōngyuán yīnyùn* did not employ *fǎnqiè* formulas. Despite this rather austere format, it is still relatively easy to reconstruct the phonological system of the *Zhōngyuán yīnyùn* by comparing its categories with those of present-day Mandarin dialects, with an occasional backward glance to the *Qièyùn* language. In fact reconstructions have been made by a number of scholars (Zhào 1936; Lù 1946; Dǒng 1954; Tōdō 1957; Stimson 1966). Although there are disagreements and discrepancies among all these reconstructions, they generally reflect different views of phonemic interpretation and not matters of real substance.

When viewed in the light of Chinese phonological history, the *Zhōngyuán yīnyùn* presents a very modern aspect. The voiced obstruents of the *Qièyùn* language have already evolved into voiceless stops and affricates; the pattern of development – aspirates in the *píng* tone and unaspirated stops in the other tones – is identical to that found in a majority of modern Mandarin dialects. Another feature which reminds us of modern Mandarin dialects is the total loss of the entering tone category. Perhaps the most striking difference between the *Zhōngyuán yīnyùn* and present-day northern Chinese is its retention of final *m*, which has merged with final *n* in the modern northern dialects.

One of the most interesting things about Zhōu Déqīng's book is its almost complete break with tradition. We have seen above how the *Qièyùn* system was retained in its many revisions, even though the phonology enshrined in it no longer reflected contemporary usage. Chinese works on phonology have generally lagged far behind actual developments in the spoken language; this conservative lag often makes it quite difficult for us to date particular phonological changes with precision. The *Zhōngyuán yīnyùn* is probably the single most important exception to this tendency; Zhōu Déqīng pretty well ignored the tradition found in the rhyme books and tables and went directly to real current pronunciation when he established his phonological categories. One of the effects of Jurchen and Mongol rule in China had been to weaken the fetters of tradition; the old self-contained world of the Chinese was opened to new influences of all kinds. Culturally this was reflected in new forms of music and in a literature based on the popular vernacular; and it is in this context that Zhōu's achieve-

Table 2.9. *Zhōngyuán yīnyùn* initials

Labials	p	pʻ	m		f	v
Dentals	t	tʻ	n	l		
Dental sibilants	ts	tsʻ			s	
Alveopalatals	tʃ	tʃʻ			ʃ	ʒ
Velars	k	kʻ	ŋ		x	
Glottals	ʔ					

Table 2.10. *Zhōngyuán yīnyùn* finals

ï		a		o	ai	ei	ɑu	au	ou	iu
i		ia	ie	io	iai	iei		iau	iou	
u		ua		uo	uai	uei		uau		
			ye							
an	on	ən			aŋ	əŋ	uŋ	am	əm	
ian		iən	ien		iaŋ	iəŋ	iuŋ	iam	iəm	iem
uan		uən			uaŋ	uəŋ				
		yən	yen			yəŋ				

ment is to be seen. His break from tradition is closely related to other social developments which favored popular culture over that of the old literary class, and innovation over a rigid adherence to traditional norms.

Tables 2.9 and 2.10 show the initials and finals of the *Zhōngyuán yīnyùn* as reconstructed by Dǒng Tónghé (1954).

Another highly interesting source of information on Old Mandarin is the material written in the 'Phags-pa alphabet. This alphabet was created by the Tibetan lama, 'Phags-pa, at the behest of Emperor Khubilai in 1260, as a new Mongolian script which was apparently intended to replace the older Uygur alphabet which had been used for writing Mongolian up until that time. 'Phags-pa's new script, which for the most part was simply a vertically written adaptation of the Tibetan alphabet, was used not only for Mongolian but also for the writing of Chinese and other languages of the Mongol empire. A number of Chinese 'Phags-pa sources have survived. These mostly consist of inscriptions, but there are also several editions of the *Bǎi jiā xìng* (a listing of common Chinese surnames), and a short rhyme book, the *Měnggǔ zìyùn*. These various sources have been studied by Dragunov (1930), Luó (1963), Luó and Cài (1959) and Hashimoto (1967). Although the language revealed in the 'Phags-pa materials is close to that of the *Zhōngyuán yīnyùn* in many ways, there are a number of puzzling differences. Unlike the *Zhōngyuán yīnyùn*, in which there is only a two-way contrast of stops and affricates (voiceless aspirated versus voiceless unaspirated), the language written in 'Phags-pa script in most cases retains the older three-way distinction as found in the *Qièyùn* and the rhyme tables. Moreover, when we transcribe the three series using the standard transliteration values attached to the corresponding letters in the Tibetan alphabet, it turns out that the Middle Chinese voiced stops are written with the Tibetan voiceless unaspirated series. This situation, so startling at first sight, can be readily understood if only we remember that the 'Phags-pa script was devised for writing Mongolian and only secondarily applied to Chinese. Middle Mongolian had only a two-way contrast of stops, one of which was lenis and unaspirated, the other fortis and aspirated; the first of these series was written with the Tibetan letters representing *b*, *d*, *g*, while the second was transcribed with the Tibetan aspirates *ph*, *th*, *kh*. The two series were phonetically very close to the two series of stops in Old Mandarin as recorded in the *Zhōngyuán yīnyùn*; and quite naturally, when Chinese came to be written in the 'Phags-pa script, the corresponding Mongolian letters were used to write the Chinese stops: *b* was used for Chinese voiceless unaspirated [p], *ph* was used for [p'], etc.

When the 'Phags-pa alphabet was applied to writing Chinese, a certain number of artificial distinctions were made under the influence of rhyme table phonology. One possible explanation for this is that since tones were not indicated in 'Phags-pa spelling, the framers of the new orthography felt that too few syllabic distinctions were being made, and remedied this deficiency by resuscitating distinctions found in the rhyme tables which no longer actually existed in the spoken language. The third series of consonants (the old Middle Chinese voiced or "muddy" stops), which had already disappeared in the northern dialects of that time, could only be written with the one series of stops that remained in the Tibetan alphabet, namely the voiceless unaspirated stops: *p*, *t*, *k*. This method of transcription would be difficult to understand only if we assumed on the one hand that the Chinese of the 'Phags-pa sources was in all respects a faithful representation of some contemporary Chinese dialect, and on the other hand that those who devised the Chinese method of transcription knew both how Middle Chinese and seventh-century Tibetan (the period when the Tibetan orthography was first fixed) were pronounced. Since all three of these assumptions are highly doubtful, we must conclude that the problematic 'Phags-pa transcription of the Chinese stops is purely an artificial device, and that it tells us nothing about the actual pronunciation of Yuán dynasty Chinese. However, despite a certain amount of artificiality, the Chinese 'Phags-pa sources, if treated critically, can tell us a great deal about the pronunciation of northern Chinese during the Yuán dynasty. This is especially true in the case of the finals.

Table 2.11. Old Mandarin from the *Zhōngyuán yīnyùn* (ZY) and
'Phags-pa script (PP)

	ZY	PP		ZY	PP
百	pai	bay	郑	tʃiəŋ	čiŋ
家	kia	gya	王	uaŋ	·ɥaŋ
姓	siəŋ	siŋ	冯	fuŋ	hɥuŋ
蒙	muŋ	muŋ	陈	tʃ'iən	čin
古	ku	gu	褚	tʃ'iu	č'eu
文	vən	vun	卫	uei	·uė
赵	tʃiau	čėv	蒋	tsiaŋ	jyaŋ
钱	ts'ien	jėn	沈	ʃiəm	šim
孙	suən	sun	韩	xan	ɣan
李	li	li	杨	iaŋ	yaŋ

At the present time there are many unsolved questions concerning Old Mandarin, not the least of which is the precise relationship between the language of
the *Zhōngyuán yīnyùn* and the 'Phags-pa materials. An idea of the differences
between the two sources can be obtained from Table 2.11.[4]

2.7 Tonal development

Although the Modern Chinese dialects are all tonal, this was not necessarily
always the case. Studies in recent years have shown that some present-day tonal
languages like Vietnamese are derived from non-tonal ancestral languages. Before
examining the question of whether Old Chinese had tones or not, it will be
necessary to examine the situation in Middle Chinese, since, as we have seen
above, Old Chinese is essentially a backward projection of the categories found
in Middle Chinese.

From the *Qièyùn* we know that Middle Chinese possessed four tonal categories. The entering tone (*rùshēng*) consisted of all syllables which ended in one
of the three stops *p*, *t* and *k*. In the past it was generally assumed that the other
Qièyùn tones, like their modern descendants, ended in vowels or nasals, and
differed from one another in possessing contrasting pitch contours. In the *Études*
for example, Karlgren viewed the traditional names of the *Qièyùn* tones as descriptive terms, and interpreted the four tones as follows: *píng* 'level and non-abrupt',
shǎng 'rising and non-abrupt', *qù* '(probably) falling and non-abrupt', *rù* 'abrupt
– that is, ending in a stop'. There are two difficulties with this kind of facile
interpretation. The first is that the traditional names of the tones (like so many
traditional phonological terms) exemplify the categories to which they refer; hence
we cannot be certain that they were chosen primarily for their descriptive func-

tion. The second difficulty is that, unlike the interpretations given to the initial
and final categories of the *Qièyùn* language, Karlgren's tonal scheme cannot be
verified by reference to actual phonetic values in Modern Chinese dialects or in
the Sinoxenic materials which, with the exception of Sino-Vietnamese, do not
preserve tonal values anyway. An examination of the actual pronunciation of
tonal categories in modern dialects shows a bewildering variety of values for
every one of the Middle Chinese categories; and most linguists who have examined
the problem have concluded that, while the evolution of tonal categories as categories is quite clear, it is impossible to reconstruct the phonetic values of these
categories on the basis of modern pronunciation, at least not with the techniques
presently available to us. It is possible to trace the development of any of the
tonal categories into any modern dialect with great exactitude as long as one
limits oneself to the splits and mergers of the categories themselves and does not
attempt to describe exactly what happened phonetically.

Probably the single most important factor in the development of the *Qièyùn*
tonal categories to those of modern dialects was the development of tonal register. Register refers to the effects of initial consonants on the tones of the syllables
in which they occur; typically, voiced initials condition a lower pitch and voiceless initials a higher pitch. If voicing is subsequently lost as a distinctive element
in a tonal language, as is frequently the case, then these register distinctions
become phonemic. At some point in the history of Chinese, the primary four-
way tonal contrast of Middle Chinese was affected by initial consonants in this
way: syllables with voiced initials began to be pronounced at a lower pitch than
those which had voiceless initials; in this way each of the original tonal categories split into two registers. As long as the voicing of the initials persisted, such
splits were merely allophonic; but when voicing was lost as a distinctive feature
of a dialect's phonological system, these splits became phonemic. At this stage
a new eight-term tonal system was created. Since most Modern Chinese dialects derive from such a primitive eight-tone system, Karlgren believed that a
register distinction already existed at the time of the *Qièyùn*. If it did, it was
clearly not phonemic, since voicing was without any doubt an element present in the distinctive feature system of the *Qièyùn* language. But while it is
difficult to determine whether a non-phonemic register had developed by the
time of the *Qièyùn*, it is certain that the original tonal categories had split into
two registers by the late Tang; a description of a Chinese dialect by the ninth-
century Japanese monk Annen alludes to such a split in unmistakable terms (Mei
1970).

The Chinese have traditionally referred to these two registers as *yīn* and *yáng*;
yīn is applied to the higher or upper register associated with Middle Chinese

Table 2.12. The traditional eight tonal categories

Initial class	Tonal category			
	píng	*shǎng*	*qù*	*rù*
Voiceless	1. *yīnpíng*	3. *yīnshǎng*	5. *yīnqù*	7. *yīnrù*
	'upper level'	'upper rising'	'upper departing'	'upper entering'
Voiced	2. *yángpíng*	4. *yángshǎng*	6. *yángqù*	8. *yángrù*
	'lower level'	'lower rising'	'lower departing'	'lower entering'

voiceless initials, and *yáng* is applied to the lower register conditioned by the Middle Chinese voiced initials. One complicating factor in this scheme is that sonorant initials (nasals, laterals and semivowels) sometimes condition the same tonal changes as the voiced obstruents, and sometimes condition the same changes as the voiceless initials, depending on the tonal category. Table 2.12 shows the eight traditional categories with their Chinese and English names; some linguists refer to these categories by the numbers given here. Hereafter we will adopt this numerical scheme in referring to the tonal categories in modern dialects. We will see in later chapters that only a few dialects preserve this eight-term system intact; in most cases the modern dialects have merged one or more of these categories; more rarely, one of the categories has split.

While the register distinction described here is a relatively late development in the history of Chinese, the *Qièyùn* distinction of *píng*, *shǎng*, *qù* and *rù* would seem to be very ancient. Even if the *rù* tone is reinterpreted as a non-tonal distinction, as some would have it, the other three categories remain as apparently irreducible terms in the phonological system. Such a view of the four tones of Middle Chinese was implicitly accepted by almost all the early linguists who concerned themselves with the development of Chinese. Some like Henri Maspero (1912) went so far as to propose that tone is an inherent feature of languages and cannot be derived from non-tonal elements; a corollary of this view was that tonal languages could not be genetically related to languages which lacked tone.

The hypothesis that tone is an inherent and unchanging feature of some language families was definitively refuted by André Haudricourt in his article "De l'origine des tons en vietnamien" (1954a). It had long been recognized that the basic vocabulary of Vietnamese showed close links to that of Mon-Khmer and the other Austroasiatic languages. The Mon-Khmer languages are basically non-tonal, while Vietnamese possesses a complex array of tones similar to that found in Chinese and the Tai languages. This apparent contradiction led many to vacil-

Table 2.13. Vietnamese tones

Register	Tonal category			
	A	B	C	D
Upper	1. ngang	3. sắc	5. hỏi	7. sắc
Lower	2. huyền	4. nạng	6. ngã	8. nạng

late about the genetic affiliation of Vietnamese: was it an Austroasiatic language, as its basic vocabulary suggested, or was it related to Tai and Chinese, as its tonal system would seem to indicate? If it were to be linked genetically to Austroasiatic, then it would be necessary to explain how its tonal system developed from a protolanguage which demonstrably lacked tones.

Viewed in Chinese terms, Vietnamese has eight tones. Maspero in 1912 had already demonstrated that these eight tones belonged to two different registers similar to those described for Chinese above. The Vietnamese tones (identified by their traditional native names in Table 2.13) can be plotted using the same scheme as that used for Chinese. Tonal categories A, B and C correspond to the traditional Chinese categories *píng*, *shǎng* and *qù* respectively. Category D, like the Chinese *rù* tone, consists of all syllables which ended in a stop (p, t, c, k, ch in Vietnamese orthography). The register distinction is derived from the influence of different types of initials on the tone: the upper register comes from original voiceless initials and the lower register derives from original voiced initials. At a later stage voiceless and voiced initials merged, producing the present-day situation in which each of the original tonal categories is split into two contrasting registers. Of the original tonal categories, the origin of D is quite clear: it consists of all syllables which ended in stops. In comparing Vietnamese words with their Austroasiatic cognates, Haudricourt observed that Vietnamese words of category C (*hỏi–ngã*) frequently correspond to cognate words ending in *-h* or *-s* in other languages:

	Vietnamese	Mon	Mnong
'seven'	bảy	tpah	poh
'nose'	mũi	muh	mŭh
'root'	rễ	rэh	ries

Likewise, in the case of category B (*sắc–nạng*), he noticed that Vietnamese words belonging to these tones were often related to words in Khmu and Riang (two related Mon-Khmer languages) which end in a glottal stop.

	Vietnamese	Khmu	Riang
'leaf'	lá	hlaʔ	laʔ
'rice'	gạo	rənkoʔ	koʔ
'fish'	cá	kaʔ	—
'dog'	chó	soʔ	soʔ
'louse'	chí	—	siʔ

On the basis of this evidence, Haudricourt proposed that Vietnamese words of category C derive from a final *h* that was subsequently lost in Vietnamese, and that words of category B derive from forms which formerly ended in glottal stop.

If Vietnamese, which has as complicated a set of tones as any conservative Chinese dialect, can be shown to descend from an atonal protolanguage, then what about Chinese itself? In the same year that Haudricourt published his article on Vietnamese tones, he turned his attention to the problem of Chinese. Noticing that in the earliest layer of Chinese loanwords in Vietnamese the Chinese departing tone corresponds regularly to the Vietnamese *hỏi–ngã* (category C) tone, he proposed that the two tonal categories had the same origin – they are both the result of the loss of an original final *h*, which in turn derives from a still earlier *s* (Haudricourt 1954b). This idea was subsequently adopted by Sergei Yakhontov (1960; 1965) and Edwin Pulleyblank (1962b). Pulleyblank strengthened the theory considerably by citing evidence for a final -*s* in early Chinese transcriptions of foreign words. We will see in Chapter 4 that the final *s* postulated for Chinese departing tone words plays an important role in early Chinese grammar.

Haudricourt himself did not carry the analogy between Chinese and Vietnamese tonal development to its logical conclusion, but Pulleyblank in the article cited above suggested the possibility that the Old Chinese rising tone, like the corresponding *sắc–nặng* tones of Vietnamese, might also have derived from a glottal stop. Later, Mei Tsu-lin (1970), arguing from modern dialect data and early transcriptions of Sanskrit words, showed that there is a strong probability that the rising tone does in fact originate from a glottal stop.

If the rising tone can be derived from such a glottal segment and the departing tone from a final *s*, then Old Chinese was in effect a toneless language. The *ping* tone was the unmarked category consisting of those syllables which ended in plain vowels or other voiced segments, and the entering tone, as we have seen, was distinguished by its stop endings. It turns out then that the "tones" of Old Chinese may not have been tones at all, or at least not what we normally think of as tones; rather, these four categories were distinguished by the manner of articulation of the elements at the end of the syllable:

píng	*shǎng*	*qù*	*rù*
pa[g]	pa-ʔ	pa-s	pak
pang	pang-ʔ	pang-s	kap
pan	pan-ʔ	pat-s	pat

I find this theory of tonogenesis very attractive, but it must be admitted that in its present form it is overly schematic. In the case of the departing tone, for example, showing that some of the words in this category originally had a final *s* does not necessarily mean that *all* departing words ended in *s* in Old Chinese; tones, like other phonological elements, may have complex origins. Moreover, real evidence has never been adduced that *s* could follow a nasal either in the Austroasiatic materials or in the ancient transcriptions. Perhaps considerations of this kind explain the reluctance of native Chinese linguists like F. K. Li (1971) to accept the theory as it now stands.

If Old Chinese was a toneless language, as the above arguments suggest, the question of when tones developed naturally arises. Pulleyblank (1978) suggests that tones may have developed rather late; he proposes that since there is documentary evidence that final *s* in certain rhymes persisted down to the sixth century AD, and that glottality still survives as a feature of the rising tone in several modern dialects, one is justified in retaining ʔ and *h* (<*s*) as markers of the rising and departing tones respectively for the *Qièyùn* language, even while allowing that associated features of pitch and contour may have already been present. By the ninth century the Japanese monk Annen, however, clearly describes a tonal system based on pitch and contour which already distinguished two registers, a system which in general outline is very like that found in a number of modern southeastern dialects.

Further reading

Chao, Yuen Ren 1941. Distinctions within Ancient Chinese. *Harvard Journal of Asiatic Studies* 5, 303–22. [An excellent exposition of the categories of Middle Chinese in terms of structural phonemic theory.]

Karlgren, Bernhard 1954. Compendium of phonetics in Ancient and Archaic Chinese. *Bulletin of the Museum of Far Eastern Antiquities* 26; 211–367. [A concise but at times opaque description of Karlgren's methodology for reconstructing Ancient (Middle) and Archaic (Old) Chinese.]

Tōdō, Akiyasu 1957. *Chūgokugo oninron.* Tokyo: Konan Shoin. [Tōdō's book is a brief but comprehensive treatment of Chinese historical phonology. (Japanese)]

Yakhontov, S. E. 1965. *Drevnekitajskij jazyk.* Moscow: Nauka. [The first part of this short book presents a sketch of Yakhontov's ideas on Old Chinese. (Russian)]

3

The Chinese script

3.1 The beginnings of Chinese writing[1]

The Chinese script appears as a fully developed writing system in the late Shang dynasty (fourteenth to eleventh centuries BC). From this period we have copious examples of the script inscribed or written on bones and tortoise shells, for the most part in the form of short divinatory texts. From the same period there also exist a number of inscriptions on bronze vessels of various sorts. The former type of graphic record is referred to as the oracle bone script while the latter is commonly known as the bronze script. The script of this period is already a fully developed writing system, capable of recording the contemporary Chinese language in a complete and unambiguous manner. The maturity of this early script has suggested to many scholars that it must have passed through a fairly long period of development before reaching this stage, but the few examples of writing which precede the fourteenth century are unfortunately too sparse to allow any sort of reconstruction of this development.[2] On the basis of available evidence, however, it would not be unreasonable to assume that Chinese writing began sometime in the early Shang or even somewhat earlier in the late Xia dynasty or approximately in the seventeenth century BC (Qiú 1978, 169).

From the very beginning the Chinese writing system has basically been morphemic: that is, almost every graph represents a single morpheme. Since the overwhelming majority of Old Chinese morphemes were monosyllables, this means that, at the phonological level, every graph represents a single syllable. The Chinese script differs from purely syllabic scripts (like Japanese *kana*) in that homophonous syllables are represented by different graphs when they have different meanings. For example, *shǒu* 'head' (MC *śjəu:*, OC **hrjəgwx*) and *shǒu* 'hand' (MC *śjəu:*, OC **hrjəgwx*) are represented by different graphs, even though they are homophonous as far back as they can be traced.[3]

The earliest Chinese writing shows that it had a basically pictographic origin. At the earliest stages of its development, it is quite clear that the chief device for creating graphs was to draw a picture of what was to be represented. Examples

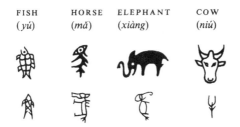

Figure 3.1. Pictographs in early Chinese writing

Figure 3.2. The graph for *quǎn* 'dog'

of this sort of graph are shown in Figure 3.1. The more truly representational a graph is, the more difficult and time-consuming it is to depict. There is a natural tendency for such graphs to become progressively simplified and stylized as a writing system matures and becomes more widely used. As a result, pictographs gradually tend to lose their obvious pictorial quality. The graph for *quǎn* 'dog' shown in Figure 3.2 can serve as a good illustration of this sort of development.

Not all the elements of language could be easily represented in pictorial form. Faced with this problem, the early creators of the Chinese script resorted to various other devices. One was to use a more abstract representation; for example, to write *shàng* 'above' they drew a horizontal line and placed another shorter horizontal line above it (see Table 3.1 below); *xià* 'below' was written similarly, but with a short line below a longer horizontal line. The word *wéi* 'surround' was written by depicting four small graphs for 'foot' around an empty square, probably representing a walled city. In all these cases the graphic representations are linked directly to their corresponding morphemes without any reference to the sound or pronunciation of the word in question. But these devices also proved inadequate to represent early Chinese in a complete fashion. Ultimately, as in all fully developed writing systems, the pronunciation of elements to be written had to be taken into account. One way to do this was to use the *rebus* principle, that is, to employ a pictograph or other non-phonetic representational graph for its sound value alone; for example, the word *lái* 'come' would be difficult to represent relying on the pictographic or other purely representational devices. One solution to this problem was to borrow the graph for a homophone or a near-homophone. In this particular case a pictograph representing *lái* 'wheat' was chosen; in the subsequent history of the language this word for 'wheat' became obsolete and the graph in question now survives only in its "borrowed" sense of 'come'.[4] Grammatical elements were particularly hard to represent in pictorial form; as a result, virtually all the early graphs for such elements are based on this "phonetic borrowing" principle.

In addition to the types of characters described above, a very small number of early graphs were apparently purely arbitrary signs bearing no representational or phonetic relationship to the word depicted. An example of this sort of graph is that for *wǔ* 'five' which is written with an X, or the word for *qī* 'seven', written with a simple cross.

In early China another device for character formation was developed which in subsequent centuries was to become progressively more important: this was the device of phonetic compounding. A character of this type consists of a semantic element combined with a second element used to indicate the pronunciation of the new graph; for example, the word *láng* 'wolf' was written with the graph for *quǎn* 'dog' on the left and a graph pronounced *liáng* (meaning 'good') on the right. The phonetic element here is generally used for its sound value alone, independent of its meaning. The original impetus for creating characters of this type may have been the need to distinguish graphs that looked alike and could easily be confused. The numerous characters for types of birds, for example, could be distinguished more clearly if such phonetic elements were added to them. Another impetus was probably the increased borrowing of simple graphs for their phonetic values to write words otherwise difficult to depict. As this device was used more and more, the danger of ambiguity and confusion undoubtedly increased. This ambiguity could be resolved by adding semantic indicators. An example of this is the very early use of the pictograph for *jī* 'winnowing basket' for the word *qí*, a modal particle denoting probability or futurity; since the grammatical word *qí* had a much higher textual frequency than *jī*, the graph *zhú* 'bamboo' was eventually added to *jī* to distinguish it from *qí*.[5] The Shang script then contained characters of two basic types; one type was semantically representational without any indication of the pronunciation of the words represented, and the other type was in some fashion tied to the pronunciation of the words. In both cases it is essential to keep in mind that the individual graphs or characters of the Shang writing system represented specific words in the Shang language, each of which had its own semantic and phonological characteristics. The notion which is sometimes encountered that Chinese characters in some platonic fashion directly represent ideas rather than specific Chinese words is patently

Table 3.1. Examples of Shang dynasty characters

1. ⊙ (日, ńźjet/*njit) 'sun'	4. ⸗ (上, źjang-/*djangh) 'above'
2. 𣲖 (休, xjəu/*xjəgw) 'rest'	5. 𠀉 (其, gï/*gjəg) 'modal particle'
3. 来 (來, lậi/*ləg) 'come'	6. 𪚥 (鸡, kiei/*kig) 'chicken'

absurd, and leads to gross misunderstandings concerning both the Chinese script and the nature of writing in general. For this reason, the term ideograph, which has often been used to refer to Chinese characters, is best avoided. Chinese characters represent Chinese words, and an understanding of the semantic and phonological make-up of these words is essential to an understanding of how the Chinese writing system works.

The characters in Table 3.1 illustrate some of the various categories of Shang graphs. Following each graph, in parentheses, the modern form of the graph along with its Middle Chinese reading and F. K. Li's Old Chinese reconstruction are given. Example 1 in Table 3.1 is a clear example of an original pictograph; it is the picture of the sun. Example 2 shows the character *rén* 'person' next to *mù* 'tree'; the conjunction of these two elements is used to express the word *xiū* 'to rest' since presumably people often rest in the shade of a tree. Example 3 is the word *lái* 'come' alluded to above; in origin a pictograph for a word meaning 'wheat', it was borrowed to write *lái*, which at that time was either a homophone or a near-homophone. Graph 4 is an abstract relational character; it is the word *shàng* 'above', showing one horizontal stroke above another. Example 5 shows the word *qí* whose origin was described above. The last graph shown is that for *jī* 'chicken'; this word was also written with a simple pictograph, but here a phonetic element *yiei/*gig* is added at the left of the pictograph to indicate its pronunciation; at the same time, the original pictograph has been somewhat simplified.

Whereas in the Shang dynasty the major sources for the study of the script are the oracle bones and shells, in the Western Zhou dynasty (eleventh century to 771 BC) and the Spring and Autumn period (770–476 BC) the chief sources are bronze inscriptions. These inscriptions, found on bronze vessels of various shapes and functions, range from a few characters up to several hundred. The script of this period in its basic structure and style is very similar to that of the late Shang, and is clearly derived from it. It shows a general tendency toward

Table 3.2. *Graphic development in Western Zhou and the Spring and Autumn periods*

Modern graph	Early Western Zhou	Late Western Zhou	Spring and Autumn period
tiān 'sky'	〔graph〕	〔graph〕 〔graph〕	〔graph〕 〔graph〕
bèi 'shell'	〔graph〕	〔graph〕 〔graph〕	〔graph〕
huǒ 'fire'	〔graph〕	〔graph〕 〔graph〕	〔graph〕 〔graph〕
mǎ 'horse'	〔graph〕	〔graph〕 〔graph〕	〔graph〕

a greater linearity and regularity of form, as can be seen in Table 3.2. This tendency becomes even more pronounced in the Spring and Autumn period.[6]

From these representative examples it is obvious that the script, as it matured, became simpler, and progressively began to lose some of its pictographic quality. This was due to the growing importance and use of writing as society became more complex, and to a need to simplify and rationalize the linear structure of the graphs as their use became ever more prevalent. In general a tendency to straighten out the strokes and to convert earlier rounded strokes to sharper angles can also be observed.

In the era after the Spring and Autumn period, the use of the script spread to virtually all levels of society; this popularization of writing led to the development of many drastically simplified graphs, accelerating the movement away from obvious pictographic forms even more, and indeed imparted a wholly new visual aspect to the script. This development of what one might call (after similar developments in Ancient Egypt) "demotic" forms of the script was especially widespread in the states of eastern China. The script of the western state of Qín, by way of contrast, generally tended to preserve the earlier pictorial aspect of the script more faithfully. The main tendency observable in the Warring States period (475–222 BC) is a further development toward simplification, although here and there some examples of greater elaboration can also be observed. No doubt chiefly as a consequence of political fragmentation, a growing diversity among the scripts of the various states and regions can also be observed; thus, on the eve of the first great imperial consolidation under Qín Shǐ Huáng in 221 BC, the Chinese script in the course of its history of over a millennium had evolved far away from its primitive pictorial roots and, owing to the centrifugal forces created by political disunity, was undergoing a process of rapid diversification.

3.2 Codification of the script under the Qin dynasty

The Qin dynasty is a great watershed in the history of Chinese script. The two or three centuries preceding the unification of the entire country under Qín Shǐ Huáng saw a rapid development of writing in virtually all areas of the country. Not only did the script develop steadily toward a simpler and less pictographic form, it took on markedly different forms in the different independent principalities of the Warring States period. The new Qin empire, as a part of a policy of standardization of such things as weights and measures, currency and legal statutes, also put into effect a policy of script reform. In practical terms, this meant that they made the use of the Qin script mandatory throughout the empire, and as a result the various local scripts which had been in use up to that time fell into disuse. It is the Qin script, then, that is ancestral to all later forms of Chinese writing. As pointed out in the preceding section, the writing system of the old (pre-imperial) Qin state tended to be considerably more conservative than that of the states of eastern China; this means that by definitively adopting the Qin script forms, China preserved the maximum degree of continuity with the past.

The script which was adopted under the Qin dynasty existed in two different forms, a more complex standard form and a simplified demotic form. The former script is known as *zhuànshū* or 'seal script' from its widespread use on seals. The Qin seal script is directly descended from the bronze inscriptional script of the late Western Zhou dynasty (see above). In the course of its development the seal script had taken on a more regular and balanced appearance without, however, changing to such a degree that its ultimate pictographic origins became totally obscured. Traditionally the invention of the Qin seal script has been attributed to the Qin Prime Minister Lǐ Sī (*ob.* 208 BC), but modern research has shown that the Qin seal script in its essential details was already in existence before the Qin dynasty; it is of course possible that Lǐ Sī played some role in standardizing the official form of this script.

More important than the seal script in the subsequent history of Chinese writing was the second variety of script used during the Qin dynasty. This latter demotic form of writing came to be known as *lìshū* 'clerical script' from its association with various types of clerks employed by the government. In origin it was nothing more than an organic continuation of the old Qin state's demotic script. The clerical script in its graphic form was highly evolved, and represented a much simplified version of the standard seal script.

3.3 The varieties of ancient script and its nomenclature

The forms of Chinese writing used up until the end of the Qin dynasty are referred to as *gǔwénzì* 'ancient script'. Since the script up to this time underwent many transformations, it will be useful at this point to list and explain what the major types of ancient script were.

(1) Shang dynasty script. The representative script of this period is *jiǎgǔwén* 'the oracle bone script'. This is the earliest variety of script known to us in purely chronological terms. It appears inscribed (or occasionally written with a brush) on bones and shells. The texts are almost always of a divinatory or oracular nature. Although most examples of this script are from the Shang dynasty, recently some Zhou dynasty *jiǎgǔwén* has been discovered. Inscriptions on bronze vessels, referred to in Chinese as *jīnwén*, are also found from the late Shang dynasty. Shang dynasty bronze inscriptions are generally very short, consisting of only a few characters. Chinese scholars believe that the writing brush (*máobǐ*) was already used at this period; unfortunately, the materials on which the writing brush was employed were mostly perishable, and very few examples of actual brush writing have come down to us. The bronze inscriptional script, however, preserves a style of script closely modeled on brush-writing techniques. *Jiǎgǔwén*, on the other hand, being incised on various hard materials with some sort of sharp tool, presents a more angular and linearized style of writing.

(2) Western Zhou and Chunqiu periods. This era saw a great flowering of bronze vessel production. Many of these vessels were cast with long inscriptions, numbering in hundreds of characters in some cases. *Jīnwén* consequently has come to be considered the representative script of this period. Early Western Zhou bronze script is quite similar to that found on vessels dating from the Shang. Subsequently it shows a tendency toward greater regularity, as well as a further development in the direction of sharper angles and thinner lines.

In connection with the bronze script, another sort of writing called *zhòuwén* 'Zhòu script' (sometimes also called *dàzhuàn* 'great seal') should be mentioned. According to the Han dynasty dictionary *Shuōwén jiězì*, it is said to have been invented by an official historiographer named Zhòu. Although some controversy still surrounds the origin of this script form, recent scholarship tends to identify it as basically the same as Western Zhou bronze script.

(3) Script of the Six States period. This term (*liùguó wénzì* in Chinese) is used to refer to the scripts of the various independent principalities of eastern China during the Warring States period. This script, which existed in many local varia-

tions, is known from a number of sources, the most important of which are bronze vessels and texts written on bamboo strips and silk. The *Shuōwén jiězì*, in addition to *zhòuwén*, also preserves another form of writing which it refers to as *gǔwén* 'the ancient script'. Its immediate origin was from a corpus of pre-Qin texts discovered in the Han dynasty; these texts were written in a type of script which was clearly in use some time prior to the Qin dynasty. A comparison with various graphic materials predating the Qin period shows it to have close links with the script of eastern China in the Warring States period.

(4) Seal script, *zhuànshū*. This script is also frequently referred to as *xiǎozhuàn* 'the small seal' to distinguish it from the so-called *dàzhuàn* 'the great seal' which is an alternate designation of the *zhòuwén* mentioned above in connection with the Western Zhou bronze script. *Zhuànshū* is the official and more formal variety of Qin dynasty script. It is the basic script described in the Han dynasty graphic dictionary *Shuōwén jiězì*.

To give the reader an idea of Chinese script evolution up until the beginning of the Han dynasty, the development of twelve characters is traced in Table 3.3. An example of each character is given in its Shang oracle bone, Zhou bronze, Warring States, seal and clerical forms.[7]

3.4 Developments in the Han dynasty

With the end of the Qin dynasty and the beginning of Han, the period of the ancient script effectively came to an end. During the Han dynasty the demotic clerical script became the official form of writing employed for all purposes, including inscriptions. In the early Western Han (206 BC–AD 24) the clerical script was, as one might expect, still very similar to the clerical script of the Qin dynasty; but by the first century BC a new form of this script begins to appear, characterized by a rather more undulant and regular style of brushwork. This new, modified script form which, like the earlier Qin script, was mainly a creation of the clerks and lower-level officials of the government chanceries, quickly spread to all levels of society and became the standard Han form of writing. This somewhat more evolved Han version of *lìshū* is the classic form of the clerical script, and is still widely practised by modern calligraphers.[8]

The transition from the seal script to the clerical script and the subsequent universal adoption of the clerical script in the Han dynasty probably represents the most important transition in the entire history of Chinese writing. It marks the change from the ancient form of writing in which, despite a progressive tendency toward a more stylized and abstract representation, the essentially pictographic roots of the script could still be discerned, to a more purely con-

Table 3.3. Development of the Chinese script

	Shang bone script	Zhou bronze script	Warring States script	Seal script	Clerical script (Han)
1. 'child'					子
2. 'cloud'				雲	雲
3. 'water'					水
4. 'year'					年
5. 'silk'					絲
6. 'be born'					生
7. 'eye'					目
8. 'fruit'					果
9. 'tripod'					鼎
10. 'deer'					鹿
11. 'wise'					聖
12. 'buy'					買

ventionalized form of writing. This change took several forms. In the clerical script, all attempts to preserve the pictorial nature of graphs are abandoned and convenience becomes the overriding principle. Rounded and circular strokes are straightened out and linearized to make graphs easier to write: the graph for sun, for example, in *zhuànshū* was a circle with a short horizontal line through it; now it becomes a small square crossed by a short horizontal stroke, thereby losing its earlier pictorial aspect. Character components are simplified and consolidated; a number of components, distinct in the seal script, are merged, and commonly recurring components are given variant shapes depending on what position they occupy in the whole graph. The overall impression one gets is of a drastically pruned version of the more ancient script forms. The clerical script in its classical Han form is already well on its way to becoming *kǎishū*, the 'standard' script still in use today. For a contemporary person, it takes specialized training and a great deal of practice to read a text written in seal script, whereas the clerical script can for the most part be read by anyone who has a good knowledge of the standard modern script.

The other important development in the history of Chinese writing which took place at this time is the emergence of the cursive script. The roots of this development can already be observed in the Qin demotic script, where some individual characters are written in an especially flowing and abbreviated fashion strongly reminiscent of the later cursive forms. A fully-fledged independent cursive script does not seem to have come into being, however, until the latter part of the first century BC, only shortly after the mature development of the classical Han clerical script. Both these scripts, the clerical and the cursive,[9] were widely used during the Han dynasty; the former being the formal and official script, with the latter serving chiefly as an auxiliary and informal means of writing drafts and letters. The Han cursive was developed on the basis of the older, early Han clerical script rather than the more fully developed mature classical form of this script. It was a radically simplified system of writing, in which strokes were freely joined together in order to obtain maximum speed and convenience.

The Han dynasty also saw the beginnings of the systematic study of the Chinese script. With the appearance of Xǔ Shèn's dictionary, the *Shuōwén jiězì*, China possessed for the first time a systematically elaborated theory of script development and analysis. Even when one takes into account shortcomings attributable to contemporary cosmological speculation, Xǔ Shèn's work remains a remarkable accomplishment, whose principles were to guide graphic analysis for almost two millennia, and whose relevance to contemporary research in this area is still considerable.

Xǔ Shèn based his analysis of Chinese characters on the small seal script, this being the oldest variety of writing known to most of his contemporaries. Where older forms such as *zhòuwén* or *gǔwén* (see section 3.2) were known, and differed appreciably from the seal forms, they were also given and analyzed. Xǔ Shèn divided all graphs into two broad categories – *wén* or simple non-composite graphs, and *zì*, composite graphs. The title of his dictionary reflects this important division, *shuōwén jiězì* meaning something like 'explanations of simple graphs and analyses of composite graphs'. *Wén* cannot be broken down into smaller components; *zì*, on the other hand, consist of two or more components which themselves are generally *wén*. Xǔ further classified all characters into six categories which he called *liùshū* 'the six principles of writing'.[10] Of the six categories, only four are concerned directly with the structure of graphs. The first two, *zhǐshì* and *xiàngxíng*, refer to simple graphs (*wén*) and are non-phonetic in nature. *Zhǐshì* graphs are non-pictorial, often rather abstract representations of words; words belonging to this category generally do not refer to physical objects but to various relational and abstract concepts; examples are the graphs for numerals, position words ('above', 'below') and certain other words difficult to depict in a more concrete form. The number of such graphs is small, and this process of graphic formation ceased being productive at a very early date. *Xiàng-xíng* graphs are pictographs; in one sense or another they are visual representations of the things denoted by the words they stand for. This category of graphs is much larger than the *zhǐshì* category, but it too ceased to be productive at a relatively early date in the history of graphic development.

The overwhelming majority of Chinese characters belong to the *zì* or composite graph category; *zì* in turn consist of two basic types, *huìyì* and *xíngshēng*.[11] The former category is non-phonetic: a *huìyì* ('joined meanings') character generally has two graphic components whose meanings taken together suggest another word; for example, according to Xǔ Shèn, *wǔ*, the word for 'military' consists of two simple graphs, one meaning 'dagger-ax' and one meaning 'to stop' – the composite notion 'stop dagger-axes' suggests the word *wǔ* 'military'. *Huìyì* characters form a fairly large category; the process, although not nearly as productive as the *xíngshēng* process, has continued to be employed in the formation of new characters throughout Chinese history and is still used today.

Xíngshēng, phonetic compounds, formed by far the largest category of graphs in Xǔ Shèn's time, as they still do today.[12] A *xíngshēng* character consists of two elements, one of which gives a clue to the semantic category of the word represented and the other a clue to its sound; Xǔ Shèn cites as an example of this category the word *hé* (OC **gar*) 'the Yellow River' which consists of the graph for 'water' on the left and a graph pronounced *kě* (OC **kharx*) on the right; this right-side component is used to suggest the pronunciation of the new composite graph. In modern nomenclature the semantic component is referred to as the *signific* and the part which concerns the character's sound is called the *phonetic*. Phonetics only occasionally coincide perfectly with the pronunciation of the composite graph in which they are used; nonetheless, the parameters of phonetic usage are sufficiently narrow to prove valuable information about the phonological make-up of Han and pre-Han Chinese (see section 2.5). The category of phonetic compounds has remained the most productive process of graphic formation for more than two millennia.

The remaining two categories of the *liùshū* classification strictly speaking do not refer to graphic structure. *Jiǎjiè* or 'loan characters' are graphs originally devised to write one word which later are borrowed to represent the sound of another, often totally unrelated word. This process has already been described in the previous section. The meaning of the category called *zhuǎnzhù* has been debated by Chinese scholars for many centuries, but its precise significance is still controversial.

The *Shuōwén jiězì* contains 9,353 characters (Liú 1963). Xǔ arranged these characters under 540 radicals or graphic classifiers. These radicals are elements which a number of characters have in common, and which can thus be used as a means of classifying those characters' graphic shapes; frequently they correspond to the characters' significs, but this is not necessarily always the case. By placing all characters under one of his 540 radicals, Xǔ Shèn showed that the great majority of Chinese characters were not purely arbitrary graphic symbols bearing no clear-cut relationship to one another but were rather made up of a relatively small number of components, and that, by using his radical system, characters could be arranged in a reasonably logical fashion.

In his definitions of individual graphs, Xǔ Shèn took into account the fact that every character had a shape (*xíng*), a meaning (*yì*) and a sound or pronunciation (*shēng*). A typical entry in his dictionary will refer to one or more of these three concepts. For example, the word *shuō* 'relate, explain' which occurs in the title of Xu's dictionary is defined thus:

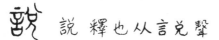

First of all, the small seal form of the graph is given; next is the meaning: *shuō* means 'to explain'. The next phrase explains the graphic form: "it (*shuō*) is from *yán* with *duì* as its phonetic." *Yán* 'to speak' is the signific, and is also the radical under which the word *shuō* is classified. In terms of the modern language, it is hard to see how *duì* could be phonetic in a word pronounced *shuō*, but this is simply because almost two millennia of phonological change have obscured the original similarity of the two sounds. In F. K. Li's reconstruction of Old Chinese, *shuō* is *hrjuat and *duì* is *duadh; in these forms the original similarity in sound is much more evident. The graphic shape of the two components of *shuō* (*yán* and *duì*) are explained under their respective entries elsewhere in the dictionary.

3.5 Post-Han developments in the script
The standard form of the script called *kǎishū* which is still in use at the present time began to take form in the latter part of the Han dynasty. *Kǎishū* represents a further evolution toward a more regular and convenient form of writing in which the smooth, wavelike strokes of the clerical script are transformed into straighter lines and sharper angles. In its evolution it was also no doubt influ-

enced by new writing techniques developed in conjunction with cursive forms of writing. Forms transitional between the classical clerical script and the new standard script are to be found already in certain late Han sources, but a fully mature *kǎishū* does not appear until about the time of the famous Eastern Jin calligrapher Wáng Xīzhī (AD 321–79). By the Nanbeichao period, *kǎishū* emerges as the standard form of the Chinese script and replaces the clerical script for all ordinary purposes. It is this form of writing that has been in unbroken use since that time, and which forms the basis of all modern forms of writing in China.

Cursive forms of the Chinese script (*cǎoshū*) began to develop as early as the third century BC as indicated above. These early forms of cursive were closely associated with the evolving clerical script, and in their mature form came later to be known as *zhāngcǎo* 'regulated cursive'. In the century after the fall of the Eastern Han dynasty, as the new standard script (*kǎishū*) was taking form, the classical form of the cursive script (the so-called *jīncǎo* 'modern cursive') was also developing. In this cursive form, older elements reminiscent of the clerical script were eliminated and further simplifications and abbreviations were adopted and a number of characters were given wholly different graphic forms; in general, *jīncǎo* has more connected strokes than the older cursive forms, giving it an even more flowing appearance. The extreme simplification effected by this script made it difficult to read, and thus reduced its practicality. This is undoubtedly the reason why another form of writing intermediate between *cǎoshū* and *kǎishū* became popular. This script, called *xíngshū* 'running script', while adopting many of the features of cursive writing, remains in its basic outlines much closer to *kǎishū*, making it more useful to the average person as a means of drafting documents and writing personal letters.[13] Forms of writing very close in spirit to the running script can already be seen in materials from the late Eastern Han dynasty and it seems to have been formed in tandem with the standard script. In comparison to both *kǎishū* and *cǎoshu*, *xíngshū* is much less codified; at the hands of some writers it comes close to *cǎoshū* while for others it remains much closer to standard forms.

By the Tang dynasty *kǎishū* and *xíngshū* had become the two prevalent scripts; if the small seal and clerical scripts survived at all, it was as a form of specialized historical knowledge. Examples of the various types of script discussed in this section and the preceding section are shown in Table 3.4.

3.6 The number of Chinese characters

After the Han dynasty the overall number of Chinese characters greatly proliferated as the script became ever more widely used. There were a number of

Table 3.4. Varieties of Chinese script

Zhuànshū	Lìshū	Kǎishū	Zhāngcǎo	Cǎoshū

reasons for this. In earlier forms of the script it was quite common to use the same graph to represent two or more words which, although frequently close in both sound and meaning, carried the possibility of confusion. At an early date, such words began to be differentiated, generally by means of adding an extra semantic or phonetic component. Some examples of this process were given in section 3.1. In the centuries following unification under the Qin dynasty, an ever increasing number of new characters were created on the basis of the principle which required that each word have its own separate graphic representation.[14] It is estimated that at the end of the Shang dynasty there were between 4,000 and 5,000 separate graphs in common use; the *Shuōwén jiězì* in the Eastern Han contained 9,353 different characters; by the Northern Song dynasty (AD 960–1127) the rhyme dictionary *Jíyùn* was able to bring together a grand total of 53,525 characters.

How is this tremendous increase in the number of characters to be explained? There were several different factors involved. One important reason for the great

Table 3.5. Number of characters in Chinese dictionaries

Date (AD)	Dynasty or period	Name of dictionary	Number of characters
100	Eastern Han	*Shuōwén jiězì*	9,353
6th c.	Liang	*Yùpiān*	12,158
601	Sui	*Qièyùn*	16,917
1011	Northern Song	*Guǎngyùn*	26,194
1039	Northern Song	*Jíyùn*	53,525
1615	Ming	*Zìhuì*	33,179
1716	Qing	*Kāngxī zìdiǎn*	47,035
1916	Minguo	*Zhōnghuá dà zìdiǎn*	48,000

multiplication in the number of graphs was the cumulative nature of the Chinese literary tradition: graphs used to write ancient texts were always preserved and included in dictionaries even when the words they represented had long since passed out of real usage. Thus, as the corpus of Chinese literature increased over time, the number of characters naturally also rose. As the quantity of literature increased, new words continued to enter the language; some of these words came from the vernacular language; in other cases dialectal and even foreign words were incorporated in the language. New proper names, both of places and people, also progressively enriched the total graphic inventory. Another very important factor in the proliferation of characters was the coining of variant ways to write the same word; these variants of a single word (sometimes referred to as allographs) often coexist, and were used over long periods of time because of the lack of any strict policy of standardization. An idea of the number of Chinese characters found in representative dictionaries at different periods can be seen from Table 3.5.[15]

Up until the present time the dictionary with the largest number of characters is the *Jíyùn* compiled by Dīng Dù (AD 990–1053) and a group of assisting scholars in the Song dynasty. It is very clear in the case of this dictionary that the reason for this extraordinarily large number of characters is the inclusion of large numbers of variant ways of writing one and the same word. But even when allowance is made for this, it is undeniable that the total number of Chinese characters in existence is staggering.

In face of these large figures for the overall number of characters, it is natural to ask how many characters are in ordinary use. Surely no-one could remember tens of thousands of different graphs, nor would one need such a large number for recording almost any conceivable stage of the language. As pointed out in the beginning of this chapter, a Chinese character generally represents a single mor-

pheme; although the number of words in a language with a well-developed literature may be quite large, numbering in some cases hundreds of thousands, the
number of morphemes (especially native, non-borrowed morphemes) is much
smaller, numbering generally in the thousands. This would suggest that the number of characters needed to write any one synchronic stage of Chinese should
number thousands rather than tens of thousands, and this would in fact appear to
be the case. A number of statistical studies all bear this out. The Thirteen Confucian Classics (*Shísān jīng*), which cover a period of almost a millennium from
the Zhou dynasty down to early Han, contain a total of 6,544 different characters
(Qián 1980); this number is actually on the high side, since the period during
which the Thirteen Classics were written is very long, and moreover one of the
works contained in the collection is the *Ěryǎ*, a dictionary which contains large
numbers of strange and little used characters. The *Shuōwén jiězì*, as indicated
earlier, contains almost 10,000 characters, but it is doubtful that all the words it
contains were still in common use at the time of its compilation. Modern studies
bring us closer to the actual number of characters needed by an ordinary literate
person. In a study done by the Institute of Psychology of the Academy of Sciences
in the 1960s, it was determined that the average college-educated Chinese person
who is not an expert in the fields of Chinese literature or Chinese history knew
between 3,500 and 4,000 characters. A frequency study of the four-volume edition of Chairman Máo Zédōng's *Collected Works* discovered a total of only
2,981 different characters (Zhāng 1980, 196). It is estimated that the average
printing shop stocks about 6,000 different characters (Guān and Tián 1981).

Another way to approach this problem would be to examine how many characters occur in some specific number of compounds. Guān and Tián, in a preliminary survey of this kind found that in the *Xiàndài hànyǔ cídiǎn* (see section
7.9), 1,972 characters occur in five or more combinations, and that 1,094 occur
in two to four combinations for a total of 3,066. This comes close to representing the number of characters an average reader would have to know to read
most modern prose. A few characters for grammatical morphemes, personal and
place names, and colloquial words which are of a high frequency but which
do not themselves enter into lexical combinations should probably be added to
this number to arrive at a more realistic figure. All these statistics suggest that
an ordinary literate Chinese person knows and uses somewhere between 3,000
and 4,000 Chinese characters. Specialists in classical literature or history would
naturally know more, since they regularly deal with ancient texts containing
numerous characters no longer used in modern Chinese; but even in the case of
such people as these, it is doubtful if their active character vocabulary would
exceed 5,000 or 6,000.

3.7   The adaptability of the Chinese script

Alphabetic writing can easily be adapted to various different languages; the Latin alphabet has been used to write hundreds of different languages; the Cyrillic and Arabic scripts have likewise been adapted to use for scores of languages. A logographic script, on the other hand, would seem to be much more closely wedded to the language for which it was initially invented. This is especially clear in the case of the large category of *xíngshēng* characters in which one of the elements represents the sound of the word being written. When one applies a character of this category to an unrelated word in another language, the relationship between graph and word becomes purely arbitrary. Not only is this the case when Chinese characters are used to write unrelated languages, it is to some extent also the case when characters developed to write the Chinese of the second millennium BC are employed to write later stages of the same language. Phonological changes in the language have made the phonological principle underlying many *xíngshēng* characters appear quite arbitrary to speakers of later forms of the language.

Nowadays essentially the same characters are used to write the classical language and the modern standard language based on the contemporary Peking dialect; yet these two languages are drastically different in almost every respect. The question arises then as to how the same script has been adapted to write quite different languages.

There is one respect in which the relationship between graph and word has not changed throughout the history of written Chinese: every graph continues to correspond to a single syllable. The morphemes of the modern language, however, cannot all be matched in a one-to-one fashion with those of the classical language. This raises the problem of how to write words in the modern language which have no known or obvious correspondences in the earlier classical language. It should be remembered that adapting the traditional script to the writing of Modern Chinese has for the most part not been a conscious, well-planned process. It has been rather the work of innumerable anonymous writers over many centuries; it has also been something like a trial-and-error process, in that certain words have been written a number of different ways before a single accepted manner of writing has been settled on.

In this process of graphic adaptation, a number of principles can be observed. Whenever possible, the same etymon is written with the same character; the modern word *shuǐ* 'water' is etymologically the same as the Old Chinese word for 'water' (**hrjədx* in F. K. Li's reconstruction) and so a single graph can be used for both the modern and the ancient forms. In actuality, the great majority of words in modern Chinese can be written in this way, but there are a significant number, many of them very high-frequency words, which cannot. Where there is no traditional character available, two devices have been used for representing modern words: frequently new characters have been created, generally on the basis of the *xíngshēng* and *huìyì* principles; in some other cases an unrelated traditional character has been used, confusing in the process the etymological roots of the word thus written. In a number of other cases, new graphs have been devised for words for which there is an ancient etymon; the adoption of a simpler graph has usually been the reason for such substitutions.

Table 3.6 contains a list of graphs which illustrate some of the processes that have been employed in adapting the traditional script to writing the modern language. Explanations are given in the notes to the table. All these examples demonstrate that the Chinese writing system, far from being a static, fossilized form of writing, can be readily adapted to write various forms of Chinese, and in fact has been undergoing a constant process of adaptation throughout its history. This versatility is probably one reason for its tenacity which seems surprising to most non-Chinese in view of the writing system's incredible complexity.

In addition to the standard stock of Chinese characters used to write the classical and modern standard languages, there are also a considerable number of dialectal characters. Such characters have been coined to write words peculiar to various dialects and are used to record folk verse, dramatic texts, dialogue in local stories and other types of local literature. As in the examples from Table 3.6, most of these characters are based on the *xíngshēng* and *huìyì* principles. A few examples of dialectal characters are shown in Table 3.7. The first Sūzhōu character represents a fusion of two morphemes, $f\partial \textit{P}^7$ 'not' and $z\partial n^2$ 'once, at some point in the past'. The graph is composed of the character conventionally used for $f\partial \textit{P}^7$ on the left and $z\partial n^2$ on the right. The second Sūzhōu character is used to write the word li^1 'he, she'. Although such a character exists in the early lexical sources, it is not attested with this meaning; it consists of the 'man' radical on the left and a phonetic element (pronounced li^3 in Sūzhōu) at the right.

The Fúzhōu negative η^6 is written with the 'man' radical on the left and the common negative *bù* on the right. In Fúzhōu the 'man' radical is frequently used to make new characters for dialect words; this particular character would not seem to be either a *xíngshēng* or *huìyì* character, since it contains no phonetic element and its meaning cannot be considered as derived in any sense from 'man' and 'not'; nor indeed does it seem to belong to any of the other six traditional graphic categories. The second Fúzhōu character, on the other hand, is a typical *xíngshēng* form: the left-hand component is pronounced tai^2 and the right-hand component is the 'knife' radical.

In Guǎngzhōu the 'mouth' radical is frequently employed for writing colloquial dialect characters; this is the case with the first of the Guǎngzhōu characters shown in Table 3.7; the right-hand component in the character is phonetic,

Table 3.6. Adaptation of characters in writing the modern language

Modern character	Modern pronunciation	Meaning	Guǎngyùn reading
1. 筷	kuài	'chopstick'	—
2. 趕	gǎn	'overtake'	—
3. 找	zhǎo	'search for'	—
4. 另	lìng	'another'	—
別	bié	'another'	pjät
5. 不	bù	'not'	pjəu
6. 吃(喫)	chī	'eat'	kjət (khiek)
7. 喝(欲)	hē	'drink'	xât (xâp)
8. 歪(䘌)	wāi	'askew'	— (xwai)
9. 汆(爨)	cuān	'parboil'	— (tshuân)
10. 饺(角)	jiǎo	'dumpling'	— (kåk)

1. The old word for 'chopstick' is *zhù* (MC *ḍjwo-*), still used in some conservative southern dialects. According to a Ming dynasty work by Lù Róng, the word *zhù* was tabooed on boats because it was homophonous with another word pronounced *zhù* meaning 'stop'; it was replaced by a word of opposite meaning *kuài* '(go) fast'. From here, this taboo replacement has spread to most modern Chinese dialects. For the new meaning of 'chopsticks', a bamboo radical was added to the top of the traditional character meaning 'fast'.[16]

2. The word *gǎn* 'pursue, overtake' is not found in early dictionaries such as the *Guǎngyùn* and *Jíyùn*. It consists of a radical *zǒu* 'to run' and a phonetic pronounced *hàn*.

3. This character apparently first occurs in the Ming dynasty in the sense given here. It consists of two elements, the hand radical on the left and a second component *gē* 'dagger-ax' on the right. It can be explained neither as a *xíngshēng* nor as a *huìyì* character; its apparently purely arbitrary nature is a puzzle.

4. The character *lìng* 'another' would appear to be an abbreviation of another word, *bié*, which is very close in meaning.

5. *Bù* is the common negative used before verbs and adjectives. The pronunciation *bù*, however, does not correspond to the Middle Chinese readings found in the *Guǎngyùn*. The reading given in Table 3.6 would regularly yield **fōu* or **fū* rather than *bù*; but since the character given is the most common negative in classical texts, it has been borrowed to write the corresponding common negative in the modern language. Modern *bù* should go back to a Middle Chinese **puət*, which is not attested in the early lexical sources.

6. The very common verb *chī* is written with the character given here, to which it corresponds neither phonologically nor semantically. A Middle Chinese *kjət* would give a modern pronunciation *ji*; in the *Guǎngyùn* this character is glossed as 'to stutter'. In fact the etymology of the modern word *chī* 'to eat' is quite puzzling; it has regular correspondences in a great many dialects (including non-Mandarin dialects), but so far no-one has been able to connect it convincingly to any character in the early dictionaries. The character given in parentheses was formerly used to write the same word, but,

Table 3.7. Dialectal characters

Dialect	Character	Pronunciation	Meaning
1. Sūzhōu	嚜	fən^1	'not yet'
2.	伹	li^1	'he, she'
3. Fúzhōu	伓	ŋ^6	'not'
4.	刣	thai^2	'kill'
5. Guǎngzhoū	唔	m^2	'not'
6.	劏	thɔŋ^1	'slaughter'

pronounced η^2. (The apparent discrepancy in sound can be explained by two factors: m^2 'not' is the only etymological syllabic m in the language; moreover, there been a tendency in recent times for a number of words pronounced as syllabic η to shift to syllabic m – the word for 'five', which is pronounced both as η^4 and m^4, is an example of this.) The second character for $th\mathit{ɔ}\eta^1$ is, like its Fúzhōu counterpart, a *xíngshēng* graph; the left-hand component is pronounced $t\mathit{ɔ}\eta^1$, and the right-hand component is the 'knife' radical.

Notes to Table 3.6. (*cont.*)

although it is glossed by the *Guǎngyùn* as meaning 'to eat', it cannot be reconciled phonologically with the modern word *chī*.

7. The character now used to write *hē* 'to drink' is etymologically incorrect; in the *Guǎngyùn* it is defined only as 'to scold, to reprove'. The etymologically correct character is the one in parentheses, defined in the *Guǎngyùn* as 'to drink in large quantity'. It is quite possible that the use of the first character is influenced by *kě* 'thirsty', which contains the same phonetic component.

8. The original character for *wāi* 'askew' (shown in parentheses) is of the *xíngshēng* type; it has now been replaced by a later graph consisting of the negative *bù* on top of *zhèng* 'upright'. The phonetic portion of the original character is rather rare and probably unknown to most people; the structure of the later *huìyì* form is immediately clear to anyone even with an elementary knowledge of Chinese characters, and this no doubt accounts for its prevailing over its rival.

9. The verb *cuān*, which means to plunge something into boiling water for a short time to cook it lightly, is now written with this *huìyì* character, which consists of the graph for 'to enter' above the graph for 'water'. It replaces the extraordinarily complex, but etymologically more correct, thirty-two-stroke character shown in parentheses.

10. The character used to write *jiǎozi* 'a sort of boiled, meat-filled dumpling' is written with this *xíngshēng* character, which consists of the food radical on the left with a phonetic element *jiāo* on the right. In origin the word *jiǎozi* is nothing more than the word *jiǎo* 'horn' shown in parentheses; *jiǎozi* were originally named for their horn-like shape, but the etymological sense was lost at some point and the need for a new character specifically for this word was felt.

More important than the use of Chinese graphs for writing dialectal words in China is the large-scale adoption of the Chinese writing system in Korea, Japan and Vietnam. Since medieval times, Chinese characters have been the basis of the writing systems in these countries. In all three countries classical Chinese became the official written language, much as Latin was in pre-modern Europe. As long as these foreign peoples used the Chinese script to write literary Chinese no problem arose, but once the idea of writing was introduced, it was only natural for them to want to devise ways of writing their own native languages. There are really only three ways a morphemic script like the Chinese script can be adapted to writing an unrelated language. The graphs can be borrowed to write their semantic analogues; for example, the Chinese graph for *shuǐ* 'water' could be borrowed to write Korean *mǔl* 'water'. Another way is to use the characters for their sound values alone; in this way the graphs cease being morphemic and become syllabograms. A Chinese character pronounced *ko*, for example, could be employed to write the syllable *ko* in Japanese irrespective of its meaning. A third way would be to fashion new characters using the *xíngshēng* or *huìyì* principles. In actuality all these processes have been employed at one time or another in the three countries where Chinese characters were adopted.

The first two methods were widely used in early Korea and Japan. In Japan the phonetic use of characters to represent syllables eventually resulted in the development of two syllabaries (called *kana* in Japanese) based on simplified forms of Chinese characters. Modern Japanese orthography is a mixed script, employing syllabic writing for grammatical particles and suffixes, and Chinese characters for most nouns and verbs. As a general rule Chinese loanwords (of which there are many thousands) are written with Chinese characters. After the Second World War, the number of Chinese characters to be used was limited by law to a list of 1,850. Words that had formerly been written with characters which were not on this list had to be written in the *kana* syllabaries. In addition to this limitation on the total number of Chinese characters, a number of difficult graphs were simplified in form and put into use. This script reform undoubtedly gave an impetus to the script reforms that were inaugurated in China in the following decade.

Although there would not be any particular difficulty in writing Japanese in an alphabetic system (or even in one of the native syllabaries), and the advantages gained in convenience and speed, especially in this increasingly mechanized and computerized age, would be many, Chinese characters are viewed by a majority of the Japanese as such an integral part of the native culture that there seems to be little likelihood that characters will be abandoned, at least in the foreseeable future (Miller 1967, 134).

The use of Chinese characters has had a rather different fate in the two other countries where they enjoyed official status for many centuries. The native Korean alphabet *hangŭl*, invented in the fifteenth century, has increasingly come to replace Chinese characters since the Second World War. Before this time, Korean was generally written in a mixed orthography, native Korean words being written in *hangŭl* and Chinese loanwords in Chinese characters. This mixed style still survives in South Korea. In North Korea, on the other hand, characters have been abandoned altogether and only the Korean alphabet is used; even in South Korea, there appears to be a tendency toward greater use of the native alphabet at the expense of Chinese characters, so at present the prospects for the long-term survival of Chinese characters in Korea are rather doubtful.

In Vietnam, as in Korea and Japan, classical Chinese was the official language of the court and administration up until the present century. Alongside this official scholarly language there developed a sort of popular Vietnamese writing system known as *chữ nôm* which, like the Chinese script, was morphemic, representing each individual morpheme with a separate graph. In some cases Chinese characters were used unchanged either for meaning or for sound; but the majority of graphs in the *chữ nôm* script were newly created characters mostly of the *xíngshēng* type. This adaptation of Chinese writing to the unrelated Vietnamese language never seems to have played an important role in Vietnam. It was an alphabetic system, based on the Latin alphabet, invented by Roman Catholic missionaries in the seventeenth century that was eventually to win out over both character systems; as a result, today almost no-one in Vietnam is able to read *chữ nôm* and very few people (except for some ethnic Chinese) are able to read traditional Chinese characters. The latinized writing system (called *quốc ngữ*) has for all intents and purposes become the only writing system employed to write Vietnamese (Thompson 1965).

Perhaps in the long run Chinese characters will survive only in China itself and in Japan; at least at present in these two countries, there are few signs of any impending reform that would do away with Chinese characters altogether.

3.8 Recent developments in the Chinese writing system[17]

The Chinese script has been changing throughout its history; in certain periods like the Qin and Han dynasties it underwent large-scale revision, which gave it a wholly new aspect. From the Tang dynasty down to the beginning of the twentieth century, on the other hand, the official script changed very little. In the Ming and Qing dynasties there developed a very strong conservative attitude toward the writing system which was opposed to virtually any innovation, especially to acceptance of simplified or so-called popular (*súti*) graphic forms. Despite this generally conservative and non-innovative orientation toward the script from the Tang dynasty on, a large number of popular simplified characters were created and used widely among the common people for writing such things as account books, pawn tickets, medicinal prescriptions, operatic scripts and certain forms of vernacular literature. Even members of the literati employed these non-official but convenient forms in personal correspondence and for copying materials for private use; such characters were strictly banned, however, for any public or official use. As part of the general reform movement of the early twentieth century, the reform and simplification of the traditional script occupied an important place. There was a widespread desire on the part of concerned individuals that the Chinese script should be simplified, and it was felt that one of the most practical ways to effect this was to accept the many simplified characters already current as official forms suitable for use in printing. In 1935 the Nationalist government actually promulgated a list of 324 simplified characters for official use but, due to conservative opposition, support for the reform was withdrawn in the following year. After 1949, the government of the People's Republic of China took a strong stand in favor of script reform; this culminated in the issuance of a list of 515 simplified characters in 1956 (Chén 1956). This list contained many simplified forms which had been in unofficial use for many centuries, and at the same time a number of newly created abbreviated forms were introduced. In the previous year, the government had decreed that henceforth Chinese should be written horizontally from left to right on the model of European languages, thus bringing to an end the old pattern of vertical writing starting on the right-hand side of the page. (In practice, classical literature, history and some modern works on historical and archeological topics are still printed in the old way.)

In 1964 a further list of more than 2,000 simplified characters, many of them resulting from the simplification of common radicals and phonetic components, was put into effect. While this process of script reform was probably not as drastic as the switch from seal script to the clerical script in the Han dynasty, it does represent a thoroughgoing reformation of the way in which Chinese is written.

Ten simplified characters currently in official use, along with their former non-simplified forms, are given in Table 3.8. In the notes to the table, the various principles employed in their formation are explained.[18]

At the present time in China one can observe a large number of simplified characters in widespread use which have still not received official approval. They are widely used in personal correspondence; they may also be observed on street signs, wall slogans, and in various kinds of handwritten materials. A few of these unofficial but commonly used characters are shown in Table 3.9. Full forms of characters are shown in parentheses after the simplified forms.

Table 3.8. Structure of simplified characters

1. 云 (雲)	yún 'cloud'	6. 洁 (潔)	jié 'clean'
2. 礼 (禮)	lǐ 'ritual'	7. 里 (裏)	lǐ 'inside'
3. 后 (後)	hòu 'behind'	8. 扑 (撲)	pū 'pounce'
4. 医 (醫)	yī 'doctor'	9. 历 (歷)	lì 'undergo'
5. 门 (門)	mén 'door'	10. 让 (讓)	ràng 'allow'

1. The simplified character is actually the original character for 'cloud'. Very early it was borrowed to write a homophonous word *yún* 'to say'; to keep the two graphs distinct, a 'rain' radical was added to the top of the original graph to form a new unambiguous graph for 'cloud'. In Modern Chinese the old word for 'to say' is obsolete, so the graph can be restored to its original use.

2. Both characters, the simplified and complex forms, have existed from ancient times; both forms are given, for example, in the *Shuōwén jiézì* where the simpler form is already identified as the "ancient (*gǔwén*) form"! The more complex form has been eliminated in favor of the simpler one.

3. The simplified character usually has the meaning of 'empress'; it has been homophonous with the word for 'behind' as far back as we know; moreover, there are already examples of the simpler form being used in the *Lǐjì* (*The Book of Rites*) which is a Han dynasty compilation. The use of the simplified character is based on this and other ancient precedents.

4. The simpler form makes official a character already well established in popular usage. The simplified graph occurs in the *Suōwén jiézì* in the meaning of 'quiver'. Some scholars have suggested that it may also have been used for the pouch in which doctors carried acupuncture materials, but there is no real evidence for such a view.

5. The simplified form of *mén* 'door' is based on its cursive form. A fairly large number of modern simplified graphs have been created by regularizing cursive forms for use in printing.

6. This is a newly created *xíngshēng* character; it consists of the 'water' radical on the left and a phonetic element on the right. The right-hand element, when pronounced alone, is *jí*, but is pronounced *jié* when it occurs in the common word *jié* 'to connect'; the latter character differs from *jié* 'clean' only in having the 'silk' radical on the left.

7. The less complex form originally means 'a Chinese mile' (about one third of an English mile); it is homophonous with the word for 'inside'. The substitution of *lǐ* 'mile' for *lǐ* 'inside' can already be found in many pre-modern novels. This is a case of a simplified character being identical with an already existing character still in common use; the difference in meaning and the different contexts in which the two words are likely to occur will normally ensure that no confusion will result.

8. These two characters were originally homophonous; the first means 'to pounce on, to attack' whereas the second one is glossed as 'to hit lightly'. It seems likely that the two characters were originally a single morpheme, so the simpler graph has been retained for both meanings.

9. The new form for *lì* 'undergo' represents the official adoption of a popular graph already well established in usage. The simplified form is a *xíngshēng* character with the graph *lì* 'strength' (written inside the 'cliff' radical) as its phonetic.

Table 3.9. Unofficial simplified characters

1. 歺(餐)	cān 'meal'		6. 初(稻)	dào 'rice plant'
2. 尸(展)	zhǎn 'unfold'		7. 袄(褲)	kù 'trousers'
3. 仅(信)	xìn 'letter'		8. 氿(酒)	jiǔ 'wine'
4. 娃(鞋)	xié 'shoe'		9. 付(副)	fù 'deputy'
5. 宀(家)	jiā 'home'		10. 砧(建)	jiàn 'construct'

There have been several movements in China in the twentieth century which have advocated the out-and-out abolition of the traditional script and its replacement with some sort of alphabetic writing (see section 10.4). Although some minor steps have been taken in this direction, the position of Chinese characters in Chinese society seems scarcely to have been shaken. Perhaps they play such an important role in Chinese cultural identity that it would take an almost super-human effort to dislodge them after almost 4,000 years of hegemony.

Further reading

Boltz, William G. 1986. Early Chinese writing. *World Archeology* 17, 420–36. [An excellent introduction to the problem of the origin of writing in China.]

Chén Guāngyáo 1956. *Jiǎnhuà hànzì zìtǐ shuōmíng*. Peking: Zhōnghuá Shūjú. [A clear exposition of the principles used in contemporary script reform.]

Lǐ Xiàodìng 1977. *Hànzì shǐhuà*. Taibei: Liánjīng Chūbǎn Shìyè Gōngsī. [A general introduction to the origin and development of the Chinese script.]

Lǐ Xuéqín 1985. *Gǔ wénzìxué chūjiē*. Peking: Zhōnghuá Shūjú. [An excellent guide to recent developments in Chinese epigraphy.]

Liáng Dōnghàn 1959. *Hànzì de jiégòu jí qí liúbiàn*. Shanghai: Jiàoyù Chūbǎnshè. [A useful general discussion of all aspects of the Chinese writing system.]

Notes to Table 3.8. (*cont.*)

10. The simplified form of *ràng* 'to allow' illustrates several interesting points. First of all, it is a newly created *xíngshēng* character consisting of the 'speech' radical on the left and a phonetic element on the right. The radical itself is a simplified component based on its cursive form, and is used in its simplified form whenever it occurs as the left-hand component in a character. The phonetic, pronounced *shàng*, is at first sight rather puzzling, since the alternation of words beginning with *sh* and *r* in a single phonetic series is unusual. The explanation for this rather odd usage probably lies in the character's dialectal origin; in certain Wú dialects the literary readings of *ràng* and *shàng* are the same. (In the Sūzhōu dialect, for example, both are pronounced *zaŋ*[6].) Although this particular simplified character is probably of regional origin, its extreme simplicity no doubt led to its being adopted in other regions of China, and finally to its acceptance as an officially sanctioned simplified character.

4

The classical and literary Languages

4.1 Classical and literary Chinese

Classical Chinese is a conventional way of referring to the written form of Old Chinese, the language of the period from the end of the Spring and Autumn period down to the end of the Han dynasty. The major prose works of this period, works like the *Lúnyǔ* (*Confucian Analects*), the *Mèngzǐ* (*Mencius*), the *Zuǒzhuàn* and Sīmǎ Qiān's *Shǐjì*, served as models to writers of later ages. The language of these works is by no means absolutely uniform; nonetheless, it is sufficiently similar in its basic grammatical and lexical structure to be viewed as a single language for most purposes. Works dating from before the fifth century BC are written in Preclassical Chinese. This language differed considerably from that of the classical age and rarely served as model to later writers.

Classical Chinese was almost certainly based on the vernacular language of the period in which it was produced; but, being a literary language, it undoubtedly differed from the everyday colloquial in many ways, just as present-day written English differs from the English spoken by most native speakers. Like most literary languages, Classical Chinese here and there revealed local and temporal variations; these variations were not, however, so great as to be termed different dialects in any meaningful sense of the term. In the Postclassical period, writers continued to model their prose on this early literary language, and the written languages thus began to take on an archaic aspect as the spoken language underwent a very different and by and large independent development. Thus Classical Chinese came to play a role in China analogous to that played by Latin in Western Europe; it became a purely written vehicle, used alongside related but historically more evolved spoken varieties of the same language. It is not surprising that, in such a situation, the two differing forms of Chinese, the literary and the vernacular, should influence one another. In the case of the written language, this meant that, although most writers consciously imitated Classical models, their writing was nonetheless colored to some degree by their variety of spoken Chinese. Thus, Postclassical literary Chinese, sometimes viewed as a timeless imitation of earlier models, often betrays its age by means of such vernacular intrusions. Some features of this type will be discussed in Chapter 5.

Some early Western students of Classical Chinese came to the startling conclusion that Classical Chinese had no grammar. If that were true, this chapter could be conveniently dispensed with; but what most of these people seem to have meant was that Chinese had no morphology, and because of their Western classical education, they naturally equated grammar with the study of morphology. Nowadays no-one would claim (seriously at least) that any stage of the Chinese language lacked grammar. By definition, any language is a structured symbolic system, which is no more than another way of saying that it is a grammatical system.

In the virtual absence of morphology, grammatical processes in Classical Chinese are almost totally syntactic. The classification of words into major paradigmatic classes plays an important role, since very often the interpretation of the structure of a string of words depends on their class membership. A noun following a verb, for example, will normally be interpreted as a verb–object construction, although certain other interpretations are also possible, depending on the phrase's syntactic position and the general semantic context. In languages that lack morphological marking of grammatical relationships, word order is by necessity one of the major processes by which such relationships are shown. The use of particles and other grammatical morphemes (prepositions, pronouns, auxiliary verbs, etc.) also plays an important role in the mapping out of grammatical relationships. In the following sections some of the more important features of Classical Chinese grammar will be outlined.

4.2 Morphemes and words

Old Chinese morphemes are almost entirely monosyllabic; moreover, most words are also monomorphemic. Not only is there a total lack of grammatical morphology, but even derivational morphology is very scant. In typological terms, Classical Chinese is an almost perfect example of an isolating language.

Despite its isolating character, there were a few derivational processes in Classical Chinese, although none was fully productive; they may represent vestiges of an older stage in which such processes were more important.

What is called "derivation by tone change" has been studied by Downer (1959), Chou (1962) and Mei (1980). In this process, pairs of semantically related words differ by tonal category, one of the pair (considered to be the derived member) in the departing tone, and the other in one of the three remaining tonal categories. As seen in Chapter 2, some scholars believe that the departing tone derived from an original final *s (cf. section 2.7); if this is the case, then this process, rather

Table 4.1. Derivation by tone change

dâk/*dak 'to measure'	duo-/*dagh 'measure'
γɐng/*grang 'to walk, to behave'	γɐng-/*grangh 'behavior'
djwän/*drjuan 'to transmit'	djwän-/*drjuanh 'a record'
ljang/*ljang 'to measure'	ljang-/*ljangh 'quantity'
źjang:/*djangx 'to ascend'	źjang-*djangh 'top, above'
jiäm/*ram 'salt'	jiäm-/*ramh 'to salt'
kâu/*kagw 'grease'	kâu-/*kagwh 'to grease'
dien/*din 'field'	dien-/*dinh 'to work fields'
ʔak/*ʔak 'to be evil'	ʔuo-/*ʔagh 'to hate, to deem evil'
tâp/*təp 'to reply (to a greeting)'	tuâi-/*təbh 'to reply (to a person)'

Table 4.2. Derivation by manner of articulation

kien-/*kinh 'to see'	γien-/*ginh 'to be seen'
kiei/*kid 'to tie'	γiei/*gid 'to be attached'
puâi-/*pəgh 'back'	buâi-/*bəgh 'to turn the back on'
pjuən/*pən 'to divide'	bjuən-/*bənh 'a share'
tsâng-/*tsangh 'to bury'	dzâng-/*dzangh 'a grave'

than being one of tonal change, actually represents an ancient suffix. The relationship between such tonally derived pairs is not always the same; some common types are verb–noun, noun–verb, and intransitive–transitive. Example of this process are shown in Table 4.1. For each word the Middle Chinese and F. K. Li's Old Chinese readings are given.

In another derivational process, there is an alternation between an unaspirated voiceless initial and a second form with a voiced initial. The relationship in this case is usually that of a transitive verb to a neutral or intransitive verb; in some cases the derived member of the pair is a deverbal noun. Some typical examples of this process are shown in Table 4.2.[1]

There are a number of cases of bimorphemic syllables in Old Chinese; these result from the fusion of two syllables, the second of which is usually an unstressed pronoun or demonstrative. Two common negatives are considered to represent a fusion of a negative plus the third-person objective pronoun *zhī* (MC *tśï*, OC *tjəg): *fú* (MC *pjuət*, OC *pjət*) is a fusion of *bù* (MC *pjəu*, OC *pjəg*) 'not' and *zhī* 'him, her, it'. Syntactically this makes perfect sense, since object pronouns regularly occur between the negative and the verb in Old Chinese. In most Classical Chinese texts such an interpretation of *fú* works very well; it is used with transitive verbs without any further indication of an object (Dīng 1935). A similar case is presented by the negative imperative marker *wù* (MC *mjuət*, OC *mjət*), which is considered by many to be a fusion of *wú* (MC *mju*, OC **mjag*) 'negative imperative' plus the same pronoun *zhī* mentioned above. This explanation does not apply to Preclassical texts, where both *fú* and *wù* are frequently used where there is no reason to assume the underlying presence of a third-person objective pronoun. Moreover, in Postclassical Chinese the distinction between *bù* and *fú*, on the one hand, and *wú* and *wù*, on the other, becomes blurred.

The fusion words *yān* and *rán* present another sort of problem. *Yān* (MC *jän*, OC **gwjan*) is commonly thought to be a fusion of the preposition *yú* (MC *ju*, OC **gwjag*) and a pronominal or demonstrative element having an initial **n*. In like manner, *rán* (MC *ńźjän*, OC **njan*) is viewed as a fusion of *rú* (MC *ńźjwo*, OC **njag*) 'like' plus the same second element as that found in *yān*. But what was this second element? In the case of *fú* and *wù* the second element of the fusion was transparent, since the final **t* of the two negatives clearly comes from the initial of *zhī* (OC **tjəg*); but the final **n* of *yān* and *rán* cannot be explained so conveniently, since in Classical Chinese there is no common third-person pronoun or demonstrative beginning with **n*. This suggests that these two fusion words must originally have arisen in a dialect which did have such a form. Such a possibility is corroborated by the appearance in later Chinese of such forms as *ěr* (MC *ńźje:*, OC **njidx*) and *nà* (MC *nâ-*), both meaning 'that'. Even in the Classical period *ruò* (MC *ńźjak*, OC **njak*) was occasionally employed as a demonstrative adjective meaning 'this'.[2]

Compounds were relatively few in number in Old Chinese. Moreover, the degree of cohesion between the elements of a compound in the early period was considerably smaller than it became in later times. A compound term like *shīlǚ* 'troops' consists of two independent free morphemes, *shī* 'a military contingent of 3,500 troops' and *lǚ* 'a military contingent of 500 men'. Taken together they form a word meaning 'troops (in general)'. This is quite different from the modern equivalent of this term, *jūnduì*, where neither *jūn* 'military, army' nor *duì* 'ranks, group, crew' is syntactically free; both occur only as members of compounds, and cannot function alone as independent nouns or adjectives. As a result, one has the feeling that the modern compound is a much more cohesive and fixed unit than its corresponding Classical counterpart. In the course of its historical development, Chinese developed an ever greater number of compounds; this was chiefly due to phonological attrition, which greatly decreased the number of phonologically distinct syllables in the language, but the increasing complexity of Chinese culture probably also played a role in this process. As more and more terms were required to meet the needs of an expanding civilization, compounding was virtually the only way to create needed new words in a language like

Chinese which was so poor in derivational processes. In this regard, it is well to remember that a language rarely increases the overall number of its morphemes except by borrowing, and, as we have seen, Chinese generally has been resistant to borrowing throughout most of its history.

Old Chinese was very rich in reduplicates and semi-reduplicates. For the most part the forms were expressive or vividly descriptive adjectives and adverbs. Reduplicates simply repeat the same syllable twice: *wēiwēi* 'tall and grand', *yúyú* 'happy and at ease', *kǎnkǎn* 'with fervor and assurance.' Semi-reduplicates were of two kinds, rhyming and alliterative. In rhyming semi-reduplicates, only the final part of the syllable was reduplicated: *xiāoyáo* 'free and unfettered', *páihuái* 'hesitate, pace up and down'. In alliterative semi-reduplicates, only the initial of the syllable was repeated: *cēncī* 'uneven, irregular', *chóuchú* 'shilly-shally'. Although the majority of semi-reduplicates are descriptive in some sense, a few are nouns and verbs, as the following examples illustrate: *mínglíng* 'insect found on mulberry trees', *púfú* 'crawl', *xīshuài* (MC *sjet ṣjuet*) 'cricket'.

4.3 Word classes

Classical Chinese, because of its lack of morphology, is extremely resistant to any formal word class analysis. The problem is further complicated by the extraordinary freedom that almost any word enjoys to enter into what one might call atypical syntactic functions; nouns can function like verbs; verbs and adjectives, likewise, may be used like nouns or adverbs, depending on the syntactic and semantic context. One is sometimes tempted to think that Old Chinese lacked word classes altogether, and that words simply took their function from their position in the sentence, but this would be an extreme position to hold. A more measured approach would be to posit the existence of word classes, but to recognize that most words may function as other parts of speech depending on their place in the sentence; according to this view, certain words, for example, are essentially nouns but may, under certain conditions, be used as verbs, adjectives or adverbs. This does not exclude the possibility that there are cases of class overlap, that is, that some words may belong to more than one class simultaneously.[3] The word *shí* 'stone', for example, is a noun; if one encountered it used as a verb, it would certainly be felt to be a very untypical use. Another word, *shì* 'matter, affair, work' is also frequently found used as a verb in the sense of 'to serve, to work'. According to George Kennedy (1964, 323), in the text of the *Mencius*, *shì* is about evenly divided between its nominal and verbal uses. Based on this and other similar cases, Kennedy concluded that "in the final analysis word-classes cannot be defined, hence ... Chinese grammar must start from different premises." Unfortunately, Kennedy never produced a grammar based on these "different premises," so it remains unclear how such a grammar could be written.

Chinese words can be generally classified from two points of view. A very ancient native division is that of *xūzì* 'empty words' and *shízì* 'full words'. The former are what one might call "function words," words lacking a concrete meaning, used to show various kinds of grammatical relationships; to this category belong pronouns, demonstratives, particles of various sorts, and prepositions. *Xūzì* are limited in number, and form a closed class. Full words, on the other hand, have concrete meaning; they form an open class which includes mainly nouns, verbs and adjectives. Another general division of words is into substantives and predicatives. Substantives include nouns and other words which behave syntactically like nouns – pronouns, demonstratives, localizers and time words. Predicatives are those words which typically function as predicates or adjuncts to the predicate – verbs, adjectives, prepositions, adverbs and a few other small lexical classes.

A tentative scheme of word classes for Classical Chinese is outlined below. It should be kept in mind that there is no generally accepted set of word classes for any stage of early Chinese; what is given here is to some degree a composite of several different attempts to establish a set of word classes for the Classical language.[4]

Nouns typically function as subjects or objects. Notionally they are names of objects, substances, people and places. Nouns, under certain conditions, may function as verbs. For example, nouns referring to people (names of professions, titles, kinship terms) are frequently used in the verbal sense of 'to fulfil the duties of ..., to behave as ... should'.[5]

(1) Cài   hóu   yín   ér   bú   fù
PNAME MARQUIS PROFLIGATE CONJ NEG FATHER
'The marquis of Cai was profligate and would not fulfil his duties as a father'

Names of tools may be used with an object with the meaning 'perform an action using ... as a tool' as in (2):

(2) biān   zhī   jiàn   xuè
WHIP HIM SEE BLOOD
'lashed him and saw blood'

Before the locative preposition *yú*, a noun may be interpreted as an intransitive verb:

Table 4.3. Personal pronouns in Classical Chinese

First person (A)	yú (MC jiwo, OC *rag)
(B)	wú (MC nguo, OC *ngag)
	wǒ (MC ngâ:, OC *ngarx)
Second person	rǔ (MC ńźjwo:, OC *njagx)
	ěr (MC ńźje:, OC *njidx)
Third person	qí (MC gï, OC *gjəg)
	zhī (MC tśï, OC *tjəg)
	yān (MC jän, OC *gwjan)

(3) Jìn   shī   jūn   yú   Lúliǔ
PNAME TROOPS ARMY PREP PNAME
'The Jìn troops encamped [armied] at Lúliǔ'

Pronouns are of various types – personal, demonstrative, interrogative and distributive. They all function as substitutes for nouns, but differ from nouns in that they cannot take preposed modifiers. Personal pronouns are characterized by a proliferation of different forms; even when one limits oneself to the Classical period, the number of forms is surprisingly great, and a number of scholars have suspected that this is due to dialectal variation. Here only the most common forms will be examined; these are shown in Table 4.3.

Classical Chinese knew no distinction between singular and plural forms for either nouns or pronouns. When context required a distinction, various devices could be resorted to, one of which was to add a word meaning 'group' or 'associates': wú chái 'we (collectively)', ěr bèi 'you (as a group)'. There are two sets of first person pronouns; type A in Old Chinese had an initial *r, while type B had an initial *ng. In the Classical period it is difficult to find any clear-cut distinction between the two types.[6] There was, on the other hand, an apparent division of labor between wú and wǒ. Wú is generally used as a subject or as a possessive attribute; wǒ is mostly restricted to the object position. When wǒ is used as a subject, it seems to have a contrastive sense: 'I (but no one else)', 'we (but not you or others)'.[7]

For the second-person pronouns it is more difficult to draw any consistent distinction. Even individual texts rarely reveal any significant pattern. In addition to the forms given in Table 4.3, two other second-person pronouns appear in various Classical texts: ér (MC ńźï, OC *njəg) and ruò (MC ńźjak, OC *njak). These forms likewise show no consistent syntactic distinctions.

The third-person pronominal forms, unlike those of the first and second person, exhibit a very sharply defined division of labor. Qí is used only attributively in the sense of 'his, her, its, their'; *zhī* is restricted to use as an object pronoun. *Yān*, as we have seen, is a fusion of the preposition *yú* and a demonstrative or pronominal form beginning with **n*; it functions as a kind of dative-locative form, replacing the juxtaposition of *yú* 'in, at, to, etc.' and *zhī*, the third-person objective pronoun. Strictly speaking there is no third-person subject pronoun; when required for emphasis or contrast, the demonstrative *bǐ* (MC *pje:*, OC **pjarx*) is employed.

There was a tendency in Classical Chinese (as well as in later periods) to avoid the use of personal pronouns in certain circumstances. The second-person forms were generally viewed as intimate, and were chiefly used among equals or to inferiors. When speaking to a person of higher station it was necessary to have recourse to various honorific substitutes. Among the common substitutes employed in this way were *zǐ* 'master' and *jūn* 'lord'. Similarly, when addressing superiors it was common to use deferential forms for the first-person pronouns; in Classical texts, for example, lower-level functionaries often use *chén* 'servant, vassal' when talking to people of higher rank.

The two most common demonstratives are *cǐ* (MC *tshje:*, OC **tshjarx*) 'this', and *bǐ* 'that'. A third demonstrative is *shì* (MC *źje:*, OC **djigx*) 'this'; there is a tendency to use *shì* more when reference is made to something in the general linguistic context, while *cǐ* is more likely to occur when reference is made to something actually present (Lǚ 1944; Yakhontov 1965, 70).

Classical Chinese does not have indefinite pronouns corresponding to English 'something' and 'nothing'. These notions are generally expressed with the nominalizing particle *suǒ* used together with the existential verb *yǒu* or its negative counterpart *wú*. Compare example sentences (4) and (5).

(4) wú yǒu suǒ jiàn
   I   HAVE NOM SEE
   'I saw something'

(5) wú wú   suǒ yán yě
   I   NOT-HAVE NOM SAY PCL
   'I didn't say anything'

The most common interrogative pronouns are *hé* (MC *γâ*, OC **gar*) 'what' and *shúi* (MC *źwi*, OC **djəd*) 'who'. *Hé* is generally restricted to the predicate; *shúi* also occurs more commonly as a part of the predicate than as a subject. In addition to its use as a pronoun, *hé* may also function as an interrogative adjective and adverb: *hé rén* 'which person?', 'what sort of person?'; as an adverb it means 'why, how' or 'where': *hé wèi* 'why be afraid', *niú hé zhī* OX

WHERE GO 'where is the ox going?' In addition to these two very common interrogatives, the following also occur in many texts: *xī* (MC *yiei*, OC **gig*) 'what,
where', *hú* (MC *yuo*, OC **gag*) 'what, how', *ān* (MC *ʔân*, OC **ʔan*) 'what,
where'. The forms *hé bù* and *hú bù* are often fused into a single syllable *hé* (MC
yâp, OC **gap*).

The Classical Chinese distributive pronouns are the following: *shú* (MC *źjuk*,
OC **djəkw*) 'which one?', *mò* (MC *mâk*, OC **mak*) 'no-one', *gè* (MC *kâk*, OC
*kak) 'each one', and *huò* (MC *ɣwək*, OC **gwək*) 'someone'. *Shú* and *gè* may
refer to both people and things; *mò* and *huò* more generally refer to human
beings. All the distributives occur immediately before the verb.

Localizers are words showing spatial orientation; these include the names of
the four directions *dōng* 'east', *nán* 'south', *xī* 'west', *běi* 'north' and the more
general terms of orientation *shàng* 'above', *xià* 'below', *nèi* 'inside', *wài* 'outside',
qián 'front', *hòu* 'back' and *zhōng* 'middle'. Used after a noun, a localizer shows
location with regard to the noun itself: *shān shàng* 'on (top of) the mountain',
mén nèi 'inside the gate', *shù xià* 'under a tree'. Used before a verb, the localizers
can indicate the direction of an action: *xī yóu* 'travel westward'.

Time words refer to various divisions of time or to points in time relative to the
present: *rì* 'day, daily', *yuè* 'month', *jīn* 'now', *xī* 'formerly'. More will be said
about the use of time words below.

The word classes discussed up to this point have all been substantives of various types. Below those classes that either function as predicates or adjuncts to
the predicate will be discussed.

Verbs are predicatives per excellence. In most languages it is fairly easy to
make a distinction between transitive and intransitive verbs. In Classical Chinese,
however, it is frustratingly difficult to establish this distinction with any con-
sistency. One feels intuitively that verbs like *shā* 'kill' and *shí* 'eat' are transitive
and that verbs like *lái* 'come' and *kū* 'weep' are intransitive; but when one looks
for some sort of formal criterion on which to base this distinction, it turns out to
be very elusive. Both types of verbs can take objects, including the formally
marked objective pronoun *zhī*. To make matters more difficult, even nouns can
be used as "transitive" verbs under certain circumstances. But while much work
remains to be done on the problem of transitivity in Classical Chinese, certain
preliminary observations can be made. Transitive verbs normally occur with
objects; intransitive verbs typically occur without objects; when intransitive verbs
have an object, the verb must be understood in a causative or putative sense
(consider X as Y). When transitive verbs occur without an object, either a pronominal object must be understood or they must be taken in a passive sense.
Example sentences (6)–(10) illustrate these situations.

(6) lǎo   zhě   shí   ròu
OLD NOM EAT MEAT
'The old will eat meat'

(7) yī   lái
DOCTOR COME
'A doctor came'

(8) jì   lái   zhī   zé   ān   zhī
PRF COME THEM THEN CONTENT THEM
'Having caused them to come, then make them content'

(9) zì   qiǎo   ér   zhuō   rén
SELF CLEVER CONJ STUPID PEOPLE
'considers himself clever and considers other people stupid'

(10) zhí   mù   xiān   fá
STRAIGHT TREE FIRST CHOP-DOWN
'Straight trees are chopped down first'

Sentence (6) shows an example of a transitive verb with its object following it. In sentences (7) and (8) *lái* 'come' is shown first in its basic intransitive function and then in a derived causative usage. Sentence (9) illustrates the putative use of two adjectives (which in Chinese are a species of intransitive verb). Sentence (10) is a good example of the passive use of the transitive verb *fá* when it occurs without a following object.

Adjectives are intransitive verbs of quality; they admit modification by attributes of degree, and may occur in comparative constructions: *zhì shàn* MOST GOOD 'best', *gāo yú Tài Shān* TALL PREP TAI MOUNTAIN 'taller than Mt Tai'. As indicated above, adjectives can take objects in a causative or putative sense.

Auxiliary verbs are verbs that take other verbs as their object and for the most part express various modal notions. Examples of these will be given in section 4.4 below.

Classical Chinese prepositions, like their counterparts in Modern Chinese (cf. section 7.4) are all verbal in origin; most of them in fact can occur as main verbs as well as prepositions. Prepositions form a small class of words which function for the most part to show various relationships between the main verb and its attendant nouns; the chief prepositions and their functions are shown in Table 4.4. The three forms in group 1 are probably variants of a single morpheme in the Classical language. There is a tendency to use the second *yú* (**gwjag*) more before place words and the first one (**Pjag*) more before personal names and

Table 4.4. Classical Chinese prepositions

Preposition	Middle Chinese	Old Chinese	Function
1. yú	ʔjwo	*ʔjag	locative
yú	ju	*gwjag	locative
hū	ɣuo	*gwag	locative
2. zì	dzi-	*dzidh	ablative
yóu	jiəu	*rəgw	ablative
3. wèi	jwe-	*gwjarh	benefactive
4. yǔ	jiwo:	*ragx	comitative
5. yǐ	jiï:	*rəgx	instrumental

pronouns; *hū* occurs only in postverbal position.[8] Clauses headed by *yú* can occur either preverbally or postverbally, with the postverbal position being much more common. The range of meaning of *yú* (and its variants) is very wide; depending on context, it can have such different meanings as 'to', 'toward', 'than', 'by' and 'from'. Both *zì* and *yóu* occur as ablative prepositions; *zì* frequently occurs after the main verb. *Wèi* means 'for (the sake of)'; in addition to its benefactive sense, it also often serves as a marker of causality or purpose. Preposition number 4, *yǔ*, expresses the idea of 'together with', 'accompanying'. *Yǐ* is one of the most important grammatical elements in Classical Chinese; in addition to its primary instrumental meaning, it is also used to express purpose, conjunction and several other important grammatical functions. The following sentences exemplify some of the more frequently encountered uses of these prepositions.

(11) wéi   xiǎo   mén   yú   dà   mén   zhī   cè
MAKE SMALL GATE PREP BIG GATE SUB SIDE
'[They] made a small gate at the side of the large gate'

(12) yǒu   péng   zì   yuǎn   fāng   lái
HAVE FRIENDS PREP FAR REGION COME
'to have friends come from far regions'

(13) wèi   zhǎng   zhě   zhé   zhī
PREP ELDER NOM BREAK-OFF BRANCH
'break off a branch for an older person'

(14) wú   yǔ   Húi   yán   zhōng   rì
I   PREP PNAME SPEAK WHOLE DAY
'I spoke with [Yan] Hui for a whole day'

(15) jī   zhī yǐ gē

ATTACK HIM PREP DAGGER-AX

'attacked him with a dagger-ax'

Clauses formed with *yǐ* may either precede or follow the verb; the position after the verb generally focuses attention on the means or instrument, while the position before the verb emphasizes the verb somewhat more.

Pro-verbs are words that can substitute for specific verbs; in Classical Chinese the most important pro-verb is *rán* 'act in this (or that) way': *zǐ wú rán* YOU DON'T ACT-IN-THAT-WAY 'don't act like that'. The corresponding interrogative form is *hé rú*: *zǐ jiāng hé rú* YOU FUTURE HOW ACT 'how do you plan to act?'

Adverbs precede and modify the predicate of a sentence. They fall into several subcategories. The following are examples of some adverbs of scope: *jiē* 'all, in all cases', *yì* 'also', *guǒ* 'truly, indeed', *gù* 'originally'. Adverbs of degree modify adjectives: *zùi* 'most, in the highest degree', *yóu* 'especially', *mí* 'even more'. (Adverbs of degree, as a class, developed rather late in the history of the Classical language; in the earlier period, degree was most often expressed by independent predicate adjectives or by particles.) Time adverbs indicate various temporal and aspectual relationships; examples are *fāng* 'just in the process of ...', *jiāng* 'in the future', *lǚ* 'frequently'. Note that words like *jīn* 'now' and *xī* 'formerly' are not adverbs but time words (a kind of substantive), since they usually precede the subject of the sentence. Syntactically the various negatives occupy the same position in the sentence as adverbs and may be considered a species of adverb; they will be discussed below in a special section.

Particles are bound forms occurring at the beginning or end of the sentence, or between the subject and the predicate; the subordinative particle *zhī* is unique in that it occurs between a modifier and a following noun. Particles bear a variety of modal and emotional nuances, as well as serving to mark such important grammatical functions as nominalization and subordination. They will be discussed below in their relevant sections.

Conjunctions are connectives which occur between nouns; the two most commonly used are *yǔ* 'and' (written with the same character as the preposition *yǔ* 'with') and *jí* 'and'.

Classical Chinese has a set of interjections used to express surprise, disappointment, joy and other emotional states; some common examples are *xī* 'expression of surprise or shock', *jiēhū* 'expression of regret or sorrow' and *chìjiē* 'expression of anger'.

4.4 The Classical Chinese sentence

There are basically two types of sentence in Classical Chinese, the nominal (or copular) sentence and the verbal sentence. In a nominal sentence, both the subject and the predicate are nouns, pronouns or noun phrases; in a verbal sentence, the subject is a noun, pronoun or noun phrase, and the predicate consists of a verb with its adjuncts. Adverbs and certain particles may occur between the subject and predicate; before the subject, time words and certain particles (*gài*, *fú*) are permitted. A number of particles can follow the predicate. Occasionally an adjectival or nominal predicate, followed by one of the emphatic particles *zāi* or *yĭ*, precedes the subject, as in example (16).

(16) jūnzĭ   zāi ruò   rén
GENTLEMAN PCL THAT MAN
'This man is truly a gentleman'

The nominal sentence has a classificatory, equative or explanatory function. Its most common form is SP *yĕ*, where *yĕ* is a particle denoting factuality; its negation is S *fēi* P (*yĕ*).

(17) Wén   wáng wŏ shī   yĕ
PNAME KING MY TEACHER PCL
'King Wén is my teacher'

(18) zĭ   fēi   wŏ
YOU NEG I
'You are not I'

The interrogative form of a nominal sentence has the final particle *yú* (MC *jiwo*, OC **rag*) which is thought to be a fusion of *yĕ* (MC *jia:*, OC **riagx*) and the interrogative particle *hū* (MC *γuo*, OC **gwag*).

(19) shì   Kŏng Qiū zhī tú   yú
THIS PNAME SUB DISCIPLE QUES
'Is this a disciple of Kŏng Qiū?'

Other types of sentence are sometimes included under the heading of copular sentences. Of particular importance are sentences containing the verb *wéi*; the basic meaning of *wéi* is 'to make', but by extension it also means 'to be considered as' ('be made as') or 'to function as'. In this sense it frequently occurs in sentences referring to professions or functions.

(20) kěyǐ wéi shī   yǐ
CAN BE TEACHER PCL
'[He] can [then] be a teacher'

In some cases, however, *wéi* seems to have lost its verbal sense entirely and to function purely as a copula:

(21) zǐ   wéi shéi ... wéi Zhòng Yóu
YOU BE WHO   BE PNAME
'Who are you? ... [I] am Zhòng Yóu'

The predicate of a verbal sentence can be quite complex. At its simplest it consists of a single verb: *zǐ chū* MASTER GO-OUT 'the master went out'. In the case of a transitive verb and an object, the usual order is verb–object. When there is an indirect object, several orders are possible: the indirect object may precede the direct object without any overt marking, as in example (22).

(22) gōng cì   zhī shí
DUKE BESTOW HIM FOOD
'The duke gave him food'

The object may be preposed by means of the preposition *yǐ*, as in the following example:

(23) Yáo   yǐ   tiān-xià yǔ   Shùn
PNAME PREP WORLD GIVE PNAME
'Yao gave the world to Shùn'

Still another possibility is to place the indirect object after the direct object with the aid of the preposition *yú*.

(24) tuō   qí qī zǐ   yú qí yǒu
ENTRUST HIS WIFE CHILDREN PREP HIS FRIEND
'entrusted his wife and children to his friend'

Sometimes to bring the direct object into sharper focus it can be placed before the verb; in this case either the pronoun *zhī* or *shì* is placed between the object and the verb:

(25) wǒ qiě   xián   zhī yòng
I FUTURE WORTHY THEM EMPLOY
'I will employ the worthy'

Existential sentences form a special category; they are not nominal sentences because they contain a verb, either *yǒu* or its negative counterpart *wú*. Although syntactically both *yǒu* and *wú* take objects (including the overtly marked objective pronoun *zhī*), the object is, semantically speaking, a pseudo-object, since there is no real transitive relationship with the verb; the object is clearly the thing or person of which existence is predicated.[9] There are several types of existential sentence. The simplest type has no subject: *yǒu rén yú cǐ* THERE-IS MAN PREP HERE 'there is a man here'. A more common type begins with a place word: *shān yǒu qiǎo sōng* MOUNTAIN THERE-IS TALL PINE 'there is a tall pine on the mountain'. When *yǒu* or *wú* have a pronominal or human subject, the sentence has a possessive sense: *zǐ yǒu chē mǎ* YOU THERE-IS CARRIAGE HORSE 'you have carriages and horses'. Although such possessive sentences are a special subclass of existential sentence, they do not differ structurally from existential sentences beginning with place words; in fact they are in complementary distribution. Both types could be used in parallel constructions without any apparent incongruence.[10]

4.5 Some grammatical operations

In this section, such topics as negation, interrogation, mood, tense aspect, voice, time and place and modality will be briefly examined.

Classical Chinese is characterized by an unusually large number of negatives; in the Classical period, some of these were already felt to be archaic and some others may have been of dialectal origin. The negatives fall into two groups, one of which had initial $*p$ and the other initial $*m$. The most important negatives and their functions are given below.

1. *bù* (MC *pjəu*, OC $*pjəg$). This is the ordinary negator of verbs and adjectives: *bú xiào* 'doesn't laugh', *bù gāo* 'not tall'. With action verbs it is sometimes said that *bù* negates the present and future while *wèi* (see below) negates the past. This is not quite exact. *Bù* can also refer to the past, in which case it carries an overtone of deliberateness:

(26) Bó Yí bù yǔ è rén yán
　　　PNAME NEG WITH EVIL PERSON SPEAK
　　　'Bó Yí would not speak with evil persons'

Wèi, by way of contrast, is simply a factual assertion that something did not happen.

2. *fú* (MC *pjuət*, OC $*pjət$). As pointed out above, *fú* is thought to be a fusion of *bù* plus the objective third person pronoun *zhī*: *fú dé* 'will not obtain it'.

3. *fēi* (MC *pjuəi*, OC **pjəd*). This form serves as a negative copula: *fēi mǎ* 'it is not a horse'.

4. *wú* (MC *mju*, OC **mjag*). *Wú* is the negation of the existential verb *yǒu*: *wú mǎ* 'there is no horse, doesn't have a horse'.

5. *wú* (MC *mju*, OC **mjag*). Homophonous with and often written with the same character as number 4, *wú* is used to form negative imperatives: *wú lái* 'don't come'. It is also used to express negative wishes and commands as well as negative potentiality in dependent clauses: *yù wú yǔ* WANT NEG GIVE 'didn't want to give it', *kěyǐ sǐ, kěyǐ wú sǐ* MAY DIE MAY NEG DIE 'is able to die and is able not to die'.

6. *wù* (MC *mjuət*, OC **mjət*). Parallel to *fú*, *wù* is thought to be a fusion of *wú* (in its imperative sense) and *zhī*: *wù qǔ* 'don't take it'. In the case of both *fú* and *wù* (both of which are thought to incorporate third-person object pronouns), it should be remembered that such an analysis does not hold either in the Preclassical or in the Postclassical period.

7. *wèi* (MC *mjuəi-*, OC *mjədh*). *Wèi* is generally defined as 'not yet, hasn't ... yet'. Such a translation undoubtedly works in a great number of cases, but it does not bring out with sufficient clarity its basic function. *Wèi* contrasts with *bù*, which carries the idea of deliberately not carrying out an action; this is especially clear when *bù* refers to actions that took place in the past. *Wèi*, on the other hand, simply focuses on whether an action occurred or not, without reference to the subject's intention (Lǚ 1944, §14.22).

The simplest form of the imperative consists of a verb used alone: *lái* 'come!' Various particles may be used to make a command sound less blunt; the most common of these are *yǐ*, *zāi* and *hū*. The negative imperative, as we have seen, is formed with *wú* or *wù*: *wú lái* 'don't come'.

Interrogative sentences are of two types: yes/no questions, and questions eliciting specific information. The first type is formed with question particles placed at the end of the sentence; of the three commonly used particles, *hū* is the most neutral and straightforward; *yú* is felt to be less blunt in tone than *hū*, while *yé* carries to some extent a tone of surprise (Liú 1958, 237).

(27) ruò fēi wú dí   rén   hū
    YOU NEG MY ENEMY PERSON QUES
    'Aren't you my enemy?'

(28) fēi   fūzǐ   zhī yǒu   yé
NEG MASTER PCL FRIEND QUES
'Aren't [you] the master's friend?'

Questions containing a request for specific information, as opposed to a simple yes/no answer, contain a question word. In questions of this type, final question particles are not used. Examples of several of these were given above. The following additional question words are commonly found in Classical texts: *yān* (MC *ʔjän*, OC **ʔjan*) 'how, where, what', *wū* (MC *ʔuo*, OC **ʔag*) 'how', *jǐ* (MC *kjei:*, OC **kjədx*) 'how many, how much'. A grammatical peculiarity of question words is that, when they occur as objects to verbs, they precede the verb, as the following two examples illustrate:

(29) niú hé   zhī
OX WHERE GO
'Where is the ox going?'

(30) bù   suǒ   hé   huò
NEG SEARCH WHAT OBTAIN
'If one doesn't search, what will he obtain?'

Sentence-final particles, in addition to being used to express interrogation, also serve to convey overtones of certainty, finality, supposition, surprise and limitation. The two most important sentence particles are *yě* and *yǐ* (MC *jï:*, OC **gwjəgx*), which convey very different meanings and in most respects can be considered as antonyms. *Yě* conveys a sense of factuality, of 'this is the way things are'; it implies that the situation or state described in the sentence is not subject to change. *Yǐ*, on the other hand, conveys a sense of change, either that something has now come about that formerly was not so, or that some change will inevitably or imminently come about; it imparts a dynamic quality to a sentence where *yě* imparts a more static sense. Examine the following sentence from the *Analects* of Confucius (16.11):

(31) wú wén   qí   yǔ   yǐ, wèi jiàn qí   rén   yě
I   HEAR THAT TALK PCL NEG SEE THAT PERSON PCL
'I have heard that sort of talk, but have not seen that sort of person'

The *yǐ* of the first clause shows that this is something that has already come about, whereas the *yě* of the second clause reinforces the non-dynamic and factual nature of the assertion; note that there is a kind of natural semantic affinity between the factual negative *wèi* and the particle *yě*. The particle *zāi* (MC *tsɒi*, OC **tsɔg*) is frequently used to express approval or praise: *měi zāi* 'it is beautiful indeed'. *Ěr* (MC *ńźï*, OC **njəgx*) is thought to be a fusion of *ér yǐ* 'and it's finished'; *ěr* lends a sense of finality or limitation to a sentence, as example (32) shows:

(32) Yáo   Shùn   yǔ   rén   tóng   ěr
PNAME PNAME WITH PERSON SAME PCL
'Yáo and Shùn were just the same as other people'

The *ěr* in this sentence shows that the speaker considers what he has said to be final, and that any further argument or discussion will be of no use.

There are two sentence-initial particles, *gài* and *fú*. The first of these is used to express supposition or uncertainty; it may often be translated 'probably' or 'presumably'. *Fú*, on the other hand, shows that the speaker is expressing a proposition which he considers well-established or obvious.

Classical Chinese, like the modern language, has a set of modal auxiliaries which are used to express potentiality, volition, obligation and other related notions. Most of these words (with the exception of *yù* 'to want') are adjectives when used independently: *néng* 'be able' when used alone means 'capable'; *kě* 'can' used alone means 'permissible'. The most frequently used auxiliaries are given below.

1. *kě* (MC *khâ:*, OC **kharx*). *Kě* expresses potentiality; when used directly before a transitive verb, it most often has a passive sense: *kě shā* 'can be killed'. *Kěyǐ* imparts an active meaning to a following verb: *kěyǐ shā* 'can kill (him)'.

2. *néng* (MC *nəng*, OC **nəng*). Potentiality is also expressed with *néng*: *bù néng sǐ* 'cannot die'.

3. *yù* (MC *jiwok*, OC **grjuk*). This auxiliary expresses volition: *yù shí* 'want to eat'.

4. *bì* (MC *pjiet*, OC **pjit*). *Bì* is the most common way used to express obligation or necessity: *bì suǒ liáng yī* AUX SEARCH GOOD DOCTOR 'must search for a good doctor'. *Bì* is also used to express inevitability or certainty: *qí yán bì xìn* HIS WORDS AUX RELIABLE 'his words are certainly reliable'.

5. *yí* (MC *ngje*, OC **ngjar*). A milder degree of obligation is expressed by *yí*: *yí qǔ* 'ought to take it'.

Some other common auxiliaries are *zú* 'worth ... -ing', *kěn* 'be willing', *rěn* 'bear to', *gǎn* 'dare to', *qǐng* 'may (I) be permitted to'.

The modal auxiliary *qí* (MC *gï*, OC **gjag*), unlike the auxiliaries just discussed, never occurs as an independent predicate. Because it is syntactically bound, some grammarians prefer to consider it a particle rather than an auxiliary, but the fact that semantically it expresses a number of modal notions supports its being treated together with the modal auxiliaries. One of the important functions of *qí* is to express conjecture or inference:

(33) Qí   shī   qí   dùn
PNAME ARMY AUX FLEE
'The army of the state of Qí has probably fled'

In another common use, it functions to give a sentence an advisory or mild imperative tone:

(34) Jūn qí   dài   zhī
YOU AUX WAIT THEM
'You should wait for them'

In conjunction with a final question particle, *qí* is used to form rhetorical questions:

(35) qí   néng jiǔ   hū
AUX CAN LONG-TIME QUES
'Is it possible that it can last long?'

Various relationships of the agent to the action expressed by a verb are subsumed under the heading of "grammatical voice". In Classical Chinese the verb itself is totally unmarked for voice (as well as tense and aspect), but these relationships can be expressed syntactically by means of preverbal auxiliaries, prepositions and changes in word order.

A transitive verb used predicatively without an object may be interpreted in a passive sense even though there is no overt marking for a passive construction:

(36) xīzhě   Lóng Féng zhǎn
FORMERLY PNAME   BEHEAD
'Formerly Lóng Féng was beheaded'

In some cases, when a verb is used in a passive sense, it is given a different pronunciation in the Classical reading tradition; some examples of this were given in section 4.2 (Table 4.2). Normally when a verb is to be taken as a passive, it is preceded by *jiàn* 'to perceive, to see' or (less commonly) by *shòu* 'to receive, to suffer'. If the agent is mentioned, it is marked by the preposition *yú* following the verb.[11]

(37) Pénchéng Guā jiàn   shā
 PNAME   PASS KILL
 'Pénchéng Guā was killed'

(38) Cài Zé jiàn zhú   yú Zhào
 PNAME PASS EXPEL BY PNAME
 'Cai Ze was expelled by the state of Zhao'

In late Classical Chinese, *bèi* also came to be used as a passive marker; at approximately the same time (third to fourth centuries BC), another passive sentence construction began to appear formed with the quasi-copula *wéi* plus a nominalized verb preceded by *suǒ*; sentence (39) is a typical example of this new construction:

(39) wéi shé   suǒ shí
 BE SNAKE NOM EAT
 '[You] were eaten by a snake'

Intransitive verbs (including adjectives) may be interpreted in a causative sense when they occur with a following object: *lái* 'come', *lái zhī* 'caused him (her, them) to come'. Sentences (40) and (41) are further examples of this construction:

(40) wǒ néng qǐ   sǐ   rén
 I   CAN RISE DEAD PERSON
 'I can make dead people arise!'

(41) jǔ   shǒu chū   láng
 RAISE HAND COME-OUT WOLF
 'Raise your hand and cause the wolf to come out'

Even some normally transitive verbs may be used with causative meaning; these verbs normally do not take human objects, so the danger of ambiguity is not great. *Shí zhī*, which in some contexts means 'ate it', in certain other contexts must be interpreted as 'make him eat (it), feed him'. Some verbs of this type are given a special departing-tone pronunciation in the Classical reading tradition: *yǐn* (MC *ʔjəm:*) 'drinks', *yìn* (MC *ʔjəm-*) 'gives to drink, waters'. Obviously verbs which typically take human objects could not normally be used in this manner. A more analytic form of the causative is formed by means of causative verbs *shǐ* and *lìng*: *shǐ wǒ sù sǐ* CAUSE ME QICKLY DIE 'make me to die quickly'.

A reflexive construction is formed by placing the reflexive pronoun *zì* (MC *dzi-*, OC **dzjidh*) before the verb: *zì zhī* 'know oneself'. Reciprocal action is shown by a preposed *xiāng* (MC *sjang*, OC **sjang*): *bù xiāng jiàn* 'do not see one another'.

4.6 Place and time adjuncts

Place adjuncts in Classical Chinese are most frequently placed after the verb phrase (note that this is just the opposite of the situation in the modern language, in which place adjuncts occur more often in front of the verb). If the verb has an object, the place adjunct follows the object. The preposition *yú* is normally used to mark place expressions, but it may be omitted; such unmarked place adjuncts are especially frequent in late Classical Chinese, and in the Post-classical literary language. Examples (42)–(44) illustrate various types of place adjuncts:

(42) Páng Juān sǐ   yú   cǐ   shù zhī xià
     PNAME   DIE PREP THIS TREE SUB UNDER
     'Páng Juān died under this tree'

(43) Bāo   yú   dào   bìng sǐ
     PNAME PREP ROAD ILL DIE
     '[Wáng] Bāo died of illness on the road'

(44) cǐ   shí   Pèi   gōng yì   qǐ   Pèi
     THIS TIME PNAME DUKE ALSO RISE PNAME
     'At this time the duke of Pèi also rose [in revolt] in the region of Pèi'

Example (42) illustrates the most usual construction; in sentence (43) the place adjunct occurs before the verb. In (44) the place adjunct is unmarked, and occurs immediately following the verb.

Time adjuncts are of several types. Basically they can be divided into those that tell when an event occurred and those that refer to the duration of an event. The first type occurs before the verb and, depending on its scope, may precede the subject or follow it; at the beginning of the sentence it has the entire sentence as its scope; after the subject and before the verb, it modifies the verbal phrase only. Time adjuncts are usually unmarked, but they may occasionally be introduced by the preposition *yú*. Some examples of 'time when' adjuncts are shown in the following sentences.

(45) míng rì   sùi   xíng
     NEXT DAY THEN GO
     '[He] then departed on the following day'

(46) zǐ   yú   shì rì   kū
     MASTER PREP THIS DAY WEEP
     'The master wept on this day'

(47) jīn   rì   wǒ jí   zuò
PRESENT DAY MY ILLNESS FLARE-UP
'Today my illness flared up'

Duration adjuncts come after the verb:

(48) zǐ   lái   jǐ   rì   yǐ
YOU COME HOW-MANY DAY PCL
'How many days have you been here?'

Time expressions indicating how long it has been since an action has taken place precede the verb:

(49) sān   rì   bù   shí
THREE DAY NEG EAT
'He wouldn't eat for three days'

It is interesting that the rules for the placement of time adjuncts are the same for both Classical and Modern Chinese. Place adjuncts, on the other hand, have for the most part different placement rules in the two stages of the language.

4.7 Nominal and verbal modification

As a general rule in Classical Chinese, modifiers precede the elements which they modify. The marker of nominal subordination is *zhī* (MC *tśï*, OC **tjəg*), but in the case of short modifiers (especially if they are monosyllables) it is normally omitted: *shēn shuǐ* 'deep water', *liú shuǐ* 'flowing water'. Nouns can be freely modified by adjectives, verbs and other nouns: *gāo shān* 'high mountain', *fēi niǎo* 'flying bird', *shí tián* 'stony field' (where *shí* is a noun meaning 'stone').[12] Examples (50) and (51) illustrate the use of *zhī* in nominal modification.

(50) dà   xiǎo   zhī yù
GREAT SMALL SUB LAWSUIT
'greater and lesser lawsuits'

(51) zhì   néng   zhī shì
WISDOM ABILITY SUB SCHOLAR
'scholars of wisdom and ability'

Relative clauses are a type of noun modification in Classical Chinese. Like other modifiers, relative clauses may take *zhī* as a marker of subordination, but this is not obligatory. (Note, however, that in Modern Chinese the corresponding marker of nominal subordination *de* cannot be omitted after a relative clause; see section 7.5.) Two different types of relative clause can be derived from a simple transitive sentence like *niú gēng tián* OX PLOW FIELD 'the ox plows the field': if the subject becomes the head noun, example (52) will result:

(52) gēng tián (zhī) niú
PLOW FIELD (SUB) OX
'the ox that plows the field'

If, on the other hand, the object noun is made the head of the phrase, then the particle *suǒ* must occur before the verb, as in (53):

(53) niú suǒ gēng (zhī) tián
OX NOM PLOW (SUB) FIELD
'the field that was plowed by the ox'

Adverbial modifiers also obey the general rule which requires that modifying elements always precede the words which they modify. Examples (54)–(57) illustrate the use of adjectives, nouns, localizers and verbs used as adverbial adjuncts. In the case of verbal modifiers, the verbal conjunctive particle *ér* (MC *ńźï*, OC **njəg*) is required between the modifier and its head.

(54) wǒ míng gào zǐ
I CLEAR INFORM YOU
'I clearly inform you'

(55) shǐ rén lì ér tí
PIG MAN STAND CONJ WEEP
'The pig, standing up in human fashion, wept'

(56) dōng fá Wèi
EAST ATTACK PNAME
'[He] attacked the state of Wèi in the east'

(57) kū ér sòng zhī
WEEP SUB SEE-OFF HIM
'[He] saw him off weeping'

4.8 Nominalization

There are basically four ways in which verbs or verbal expressions can be nominalized in Classical Chinese. In the simplest case, a verb may be interpreted in a nominal sense if it occupies a position in the sentence typically reserved for nouns; for example, if it occurs in the subject or object position, it will normally be translated as an infinitive or verbal noun in English: *hào xué* BE-FOND-OF STUDY 'fond of studying', *qiú jiù* REQUEST SAVE 'requests to be saved'; (58) is an example of a verb being used as a subject:

(58) xué   yì   yǒu   yì   hū
LEARN ALSO HAVE BENEFIT QUES
'Is learning also beneficial?'

A subject–predicate construction can be nominalized by inserting the subordinative particle *zhī* between the two constituents; for example, *Mèngzǐ qù Qí* MENCIUS DEPART PNAME 'Mencius departed from the state of Qí' can be converted into the noun phrase *Mèngzǐ zhī qù Qí* 'Mencius' departing from the state of Qi' in this way. Noun phrases of this type have many syntactic functions; phrases that occur as objects to verbs of perception, for example, are always nominalized in this fashion:

(59) wú zhī   niǎo zhī néng fēi
I   KNOW BIRD SUB CAN FLY
'I know that birds can fly'

Even when a noun clause of this type would lack an overt third-person subject pronoun when used independently, it must take the third person genitive pronoun *qí* when subordinated in this way:

(60) wú zhī   qí   néng fēi
I   KNOW ITS CAN FLY
'I know that it can fly'

The two remaining types of nominalization may be called agential and objective nominalization. In the first case, the particle *zhě* is placed after a verb or verb phrase, and the resulting form is a noun phrase of agent: *shā zhě* 'one who kills', *shā rén zhě* 'one who kills people'. *Zhě* may also occur with adjectives, in which case the resulting phrase simply refers to the person or thing of which the quality designated by the adjective is predicated: *dà zhě* 'big ones, big things', *rén zhě* 'those who are benevolent'.

Noun phrases referring to the object of a transitive verb are formed by placing the particle *suǒ* before the verb: *suǒ shā* 'that which was killed'; when *suǒ* is used in this way with adjectives, the latter must be interpreted in a causative or putative sense: *qí suǒ shàn* HIS NOM GOOD 'that which he considers to be good'.

4.9 Conjoining constructions

In the case of nouns, conjunction is frequently expressed by simple juxtaposition: *rén mǎ* 'people and horses'. Alternatively the conjunctions *yǔ* and *jí* may be used: *rén yǔ mǎ* 'people and horses'. Clauses may be joined without any overt marking of conjunction, as in example (30) above. It is more usual, however, to find clauses joined by the two connectives *ér* and *zé* (MC *tsək*, OC **tsək*). Of these two connectives, *ér* forms the closer and smoother transition; it may express conjunction pure and simple (like the English word 'and') or it may have an adversative sense (English 'but'). It is often used to set the scene for or express the attendant circumstances of another action:

(61) míng   gǔ   ér   gōng   zhī
     SOUND DRUM CONJ ATTACK HIM
     'attack him beating drums'

Another common usage of *ér* is to show temporal sequence as in the following sentence:

(62) tīng   qí   yán   ér   guān   qí   xíng
     LISTEN HIS WORD CONJ OBSERVE HIS ACTION
     'listen to his words and (then) observe his actions'

In contrast to *ér*, *zé* forms a sharper transition between two clauses; the sense of a complex sentence containing *zé* is most often 'if ... then ...' or 'when ... then ...'. The clause introduced by *zé* is normally to be construed as the logical outcome of the first clause. Examples (63) and (64) illustrate the force of *zé* used as a connective:

(63) xué   ér   bù   sī   zé   wǎng
     STUDY CONJ NEG THINK CONJ VAIN
     'If one studies but does not think, then it is in vain'

(64) zhì   zé   xíng   yǐ
     ARRIVE CONJ LEAVE PCL
     'When he arrived, he had already left'

In Classical Chinese (as well as in the modern language) conditional and temporal sentences are frequently unmarked; this is not to say that they cannot be explicitly marked, however. Conditional clauses may contain one of several words meaning 'if': *rú* (MC *ńźjwo*, OC **njag*), *ruò* (MC *ńźjak*, OC **njak*), and *gǒu* (MC *kəu:*, OC **kugx*). Temporal clauses may be preceded by *jí* or *bǐ*, both of which basically mean 'to reach', or they may be followed by the noun *shí* meaning 'time'.

(65) zǐ   ruò yù   zhàn   zé   wú tùi   shè
     YOU IF WANT BATTLE CONJ I RETREAT ONE-DAY'S-MARCH
     'If you wish to do battle, then I will withdraw one day's march'

(66) jí   fǎn   shì   bà
WHEN RETURN MARKET FINISH
'When he returned, the market had disbanded'

4.10 The classical literary language in later ages

As indicated at the beginning of this chapter, in the centuries following the Classical period the written language changed much more slowly than did the vernacular; this is of course a phenomenon well known in several other parts of the world. It would be a mistake, however, to think that the literary language of the Postclassical period remained absolutely static. Although most writers made a conscious attempt to imitate classical models, there were inevitably features of this language which were not fully understood and which consequently were not correctly emulated; moreover, changes in society necessitated the constant creation of new words to accommodate new concepts and changes in the environment and material culture. Thus the later literary language was by no means identical with the Classical language of the Eastern Zhou dynasty; nonetheless, it remained much closer to its Classical model than it did to the progressively evolving vernacular dialects.

As Lǚ Shūxiāng (1944) has pointed out, it is useful to divide the later literary language into two rather different currents. In one, a conscious attempt was made to reproduce as faithfully as possible the model prose of the Classical era. Although, here and there, even this "canonical" literary language reveals its age by vernacular intrusions and lapses from genuine Classical usage, by and large it is very close to its model. But from the very beginning of the Postclassical period there was another current, in which a more relaxed attitude was taken toward the Classical standards; this variety of literary Chinese, while in general remaining within the confines of proper literary usage, permitted the intrusion of vernacular elements more freely. This more vulgar variety of the written language is often encountered in informal writing – personal jottings, letters, routine official documents, contracts, popular religious writings and certain kinds of literature destined for common consumption.

In neither variety of literary Chinese does one find a complete or even partially complete record of the contemporary vernacular. The vernacular rather simply peeks through here and there in the form of a non-Classical pronominal form or the use of a vernacular grammatical construction. The vernacular features are of course extremely valuable to the linguist studying the history of Chinese grammar, but they rarely allow the reconstruction of anything approaching a complete picture of the vernacular of the period in question.

While vernacular forms of Chinese were leaving their mark on the literary language of different periods, the reverse process was also at work, as elements of the literary language were constantly being absorbed in the vernacular. This came about in several ways. The speech of members of the literate educated classes was naturally influenced by literary norms, especially in the area of vocabulary. Their language, being the most prestigious variety of spoken Chinese, was then imitated by people of lower social classes, many of whom were illiterate or at best only semiliterate. Another avenue of influence was probably genres of oral literature, especially drama and story-telling. These oral art forms, although basically in the vernacular, tend to be filled with literary phrases and constructions. It would seem that, in a literate society like that of China, it is very difficult to draw a rigidly strict line between the literary language and the vernacular, even when the written language differs greatly in structure and lexicon from the spoken language.

Literary Chinese survived as the predominant form of writing in China well into the first half of the twentieth century. Beginning in the 1920s the written vernacular (*báihuà*) gradually came to replace the literary language (*wényán*); at the present time, the old literary language is to all intents and purposes defunct; it is now studied by students of Chinese literature and history in much the same way that Latin and Greek are studied in Western countries. But in another sense it has not died out completely, for the modern written language, while essentially based on the spoken language of the capital, Peking, still employs a rather high proportion of literary vocabulary and grammatical constructions. Moreover, most neologisms are based on the morphemes of the Classical period rather than on those of any modern vernacular. For example, the Classical word for 'foot', *zú*, is totally obsolete in the spoken language, but is still widely used in calques and other new lexical formations: *zújī* 'footprint', *zúqiú* 'football, soccer', *lìzú* 'get a foothold'. Such common words as *hūrán* 'suddenly', *suīrán* 'although', *jìshǐ* 'even if', *suǒwèi* 'so-called', and *rán'ér* 'however', which are purely literary in origin, are frequently to be encountered not only in formal writing but even in everyday speech. A common modern phrase like *yǐ cǐ wéi zhǔn* 'using this as a criterion' is literary both in its grammatical structure and in its choice of morphemes. The Classical literary element in the modern written language is so important that it is hard to imagine anyone mastering the modern language without some acquaintance with the Classical language. This is undoubtedly the most important reason for continuing the teaching of Classical Chinese and the later literary language in present-day Chinese secondary schools.

Nowadays very few people write in a purely literary style, and the number of people able to do so is rapidly diminishing. Nonetheless the influence of literary Chinese is all pervasive, and a good knowledge of China's three-millennia-long

Classical literary tradition remains a virtual necessity for any educated person in Chinese society. The role played by the Classical and later literary languages is in many ways similar to that played by Latin in modern European languages; Latin itself is hardly written any more, but its spirit lives on in the way Europeans (and others who use European languages) think, speak and write. Latin (along with Greek) is also the source of most new scientific and technical terminology. Like the Western classical languages, Classical Chinese is deeply rooted in Chinese culture, and will inevitably continue to play an important role in future Chinese linguistic development.

Further reading

Chou Fa-kao 1959, 1961, 1962. *A historical grammar of Ancient Chinese*, part 1, *Syntax*; part 2, *Morphology*; part 3, *Substitution*. Taibei: Academia Sinica, Special Publications 39. [A comprehensive treatment of Classical Chinese grammar written in Chinese. Chou's work gives copious bibliographic references to works of other scholars, both Chinese and Western.]

Kennedy, George A. 1964. Word-classes in Classical Chinese. In *Selected works of George A. Kennedy*, ed. Tien-yi Li. New Haven: Far Eastern Publications. [This article represents an attempt to write a grammar of *Mencius* based on formal structural principles.]

Lǚ Shūxiāng 1944. *Zhōngguó wénfǎ yàolüè*. Shanghai: Commercial Press. Reprinted, Peking, 1982. [Although this grammar treats both the modern and earlier literary languages together, it contains many valuable insights concerning the grammar of the Classical language.]

Yakhontov, S. E. 1965. *Drevnekitajskij Jazyk*. Moscow: Nauka. [An excellent sketch of Classical Chinese grammar, written in Russian.]

5

The rise and development of the written vernacular

5.1 Sources for the study of the early vernacular

As indicated in the last chapter, literary Chinese, although it was modeled on the Classical prose of the late Zhou and Han dynasties, was not an absolutely timeless and uniform language. One thing that undoubtedly influenced the literary language in later ages were various forms of spoken or vernacular Chinese. Vernacular elements were particularly evident in two types of writing: religious (especially Buddhist) texts and various genres of popular literature. It is generally these sources that the student of the historical grammar of Chinese finds the richest.

It is no accident that religious writings play such a prominent role in the study of vernacular language. Missionaries, by the very nature of their work, try to present their teachings in a simple and easily accessible language. Thus, already in the Eastern Han dynasty (AD 25–200) Buddhist works (consisting almost entirely of translations and paraphrases of Indian originals) have a strong vernacular flavor, and this continues to be the case through succeeding centuries down to the Song dynasty. Collections of popular verse and stories are also good sources for the study of early vernacular forms. A third important source for the study of the early spoken language are works containing passages in direct speech; examples of this can be found in the official dynastic histories, anecdotal collections, drama and certain types of popular narrative.

In the period before the Tang dynasty, one rarely finds full-fledged vernacular texts; what one finds instead are texts, basically written in the literary language, but with various degrees of vernacular overlay; the quantity of such vernacular elements varies from source to source, but in no case can one point to a particular text and say unequivocally that it is written in a purely vernacular style. All the texts represent to one degree or another a mixture of the literary and spoken languages. This naturally complicates the work of anyone who is engaged in the study of the history of the syntax and lexicon of Chinese. The mere fact that a strongly vernacular-colored text of the sixth or seventh century contains literary words like *qí* 'his', *zhī* 'genitive marker' or *fēi* 'is not' does not allow one to conclude automatically that these words were still current in the popular speech of that period. If in the same text, however, one encounters a vernacular form like *bú-shì* used to mean 'is not', one has relatively strong grounds for suspecting that the use of *fēi* in the same text is a literary form which had already been replaced by *bú-shì* in the spoken language of that time. By examining texts in this way, a general chronology of vernacular elements can be established, but one must keep in mind that the corpus of written Chinese is immense, and there is always the possibility that the date of the appearance of any given vernacular element will have to be revised backward as still earlier attestations are discovered.

By Tang times many (if not most) of the features that are associated with the fully developed vernacular of Song and Yuan times are already found. By and large the nascent vernacular of Tang can be identified as a variety of Northern Chinese (see Chapter 8). It is possible that there exist some heterodialectal features here and there, but clearly the basis of the language is a variety of Old Mandarin. It seems quite likely that the written vernacular at all stages was closely connected to the development of a spoken koine based on the language of the national capital which, with only a few short-lived exceptions, was located in Mandarin-speaking areas from the beginning of the Tang dynasty.

In the following sections of this chapter, some of the chief features of early vernacular Chinese will be inspected. It should be borne in mind that the study of historical grammar in Chinese is in many ways still in its infancy, and that there are many uncertainties concerning the details of dating even the most important vernacular innovations. Nevertheless, the broad outline of what happened is relatively clear.

5.2 Nouns, measures and localizers

In Classical Chinese most words, whether verbs or nouns, were monosyllabic. As the phonological system of Chinese underwent simplification, the total number of phonologically distinct syllables decreased. For example, in the widely used *Xīnhuá zìdiǎn*, there are twenty-five characters pronounced *jiàn*; in the *Qièyùn* system, these twenty-five characters represented eighteen distinct syllables; at a still earlier period it is possible that there were even more distinctions. Given this progressively radical reduction in the overall number of contrasting syllables, and the consequent falling together of many words once phonologically distinct, it is not surprising that the old one-word/one-syllable pattern began to weaken, and that the number of disyllabic words began to increase. Disyllabic words were basically formed in two ways – by compounding and by affixation. Compounds undoubtedly already existed in the Old Chinese period, but, as we have seen, they were limited in number and were structurally less cohesive units than modern compounds. The history of nominal compounding has unfortunately not been studied in a detailed way, so it is difficult to give a clear picture of developments in this area. The situation concerning affixes is much clearer.

The earliest vernacular prefix for which we have ample textual documentation is *ā*. Although this prefix is no longer used in the Peking dialect, it is still widely employed in a great many southern dialects as a prefix to kinship terms and personal names. As a familiar prefix for nicknames, it may go back to the Han dynasty and is well attested from the Three Kingdoms period (AD 220–65) on. The character with which this prefix is written originally meant 'the slope of a hill'; in its use to write the prefix *ā*, it is apparently used for its sound-value alone. Some early examples are the following: *ā-mŭ* 'mother' (Han), *ā-dŏu*, the familiar name of Liú Chán (Three Kingdoms period), *ā-nú* 'younger brother' (Jìn), *ā-wēng* 'grandfather' (Jìn). From an early date *ā* is also found as a prefix to personal pronouns: *ā-shúi* 'who', *ā-nĭ* 'you', *ā-nóng* 'I'; a vestige of this usage may survive in the first-person plural pronoun *a' la'* in the modern Níngbō dialect (Chao 1928, 95).

The appearance of *lăo* 'old' as a prefix denoting familiarity is somewhat later than that of *ā*. One must be careful to distinguish *lăo* in its primary meaning of 'old' from its grammatical function as a prefix of familiarity; the first cases of the prefix *lăo* are used with surnames as a form of familiar address. The earliest unambiguous examples of this usage occur in Tang texts; more than one example of this usage can be found in the works of the famous Tang poet Bái Jūyì (772–846). *Lăo* as a prefix to the names of certain familiar (but generally disliked or feared) animals and birds also shows up for the first time in Tang texts; there are Tang examples for both *lăo-shŭ* 'mouse' and *lăo-yā* 'crow'; *lăo-hŭ* 'tiger' does not seem to appear until the Song dynasty, however.

The two prefixes described above are relatively limited in their occurrence, generally being found only in certain semantic categories. The common noun suffixes *zĭ*, *ér* and *tóu*, however, are all-pervasive in many modern dialects. *Zĭ* and *ér* both mean 'son' or 'child', and they both clearly originated as diminutive suffixes. The use of the morpheme meaning 'child' as a marker of the diminutive is still commonly found in some southern dialects; in the Guăngzhōu dialect, for example, *tsai*³ 'son, child' is used in this way: *tɔ*¹ 'knife', *tɔ*¹ *tsai*³ 'small knife'; likewise, the Fuzhōu dialect employs *kiaŋ*³ 'child' in the same way: *to*¹ 'knife', *to*¹ *kiaŋ*³ 'small knife'. As in the case of *lăo*, caution is required in searching for early examples of *zĭ* and *ér* used as suffixes. In Modern Chinese the suffix *zĭ* can be distinguished from *zĭ* used as an element in a compound by the fact that the former form is always atonic. *Ér* in its suffixal form is not only atonic, it has even lost its syllabicity (cf. section 7.3). From the use of both of these suffixes in Tang verse it is clear that at that time they were scanned as full syllables which retained both their tones and syllabicity intact. From the earliest times one can find examples of compounds in which *zĭ* is the second element; in the Classical period, *zĭ* can almost always be interpreted either as 'child' or as some semantic extension of 'child': *nán-zĭ* 'male child', *hŭ-zĭ* 'baby tiger', *zhōu-zĭ* 'boat boy, boatman'. It is better to treat such cases as these as examples of compounding rather than suffixation, but the use of *zĭ* as a diminutive marker begins quite early. Its use in nouns denoting small round objects goes back to the Classical period; Mencius, for example, has *móu-zĭ* 'pupil of the eye'. The use of *zĭ* as a suffix to animal names is also ancient: such forms as *māo-zĭ* 'cat', *yĭ-zĭ* 'ant', *hé-zĭ* 'raccoon-dog' can be encountered in Nanbeichao sources. As a suffix to names of tools and vessels of various types, it is also common; the following examples are from the pre-Tang period: *dāo-zĭ* 'small knife', *lóng-zĭ* 'small cage', *wèng-zĭ* 'jar'.

In the pre-Tang era, *zĭ* as a nominal suffix seems by and large to retain its diminutive meaning and occasionally, by extension, a pejorative sense. By the Tang dynasty, however, *zĭ* is found as a suffix to virtually any class of noun, including some that refer to large objects: *chē-zĭ* 'carriage', *tíng-zĭ* 'pavilion', *zhái-zĭ* 'residence'. Other examples showing the wide range of nouns to which the suffix *zĭ* was attached in the Tang dynasty are *qié-zĭ* 'eggplant', *ăo-zĭ* 'jacket', *wō-zĭ* 'lapdog', *yàn-zĭ* 'swallow' (the bird), *fēi-zĭ* 'concubine', *lì-zĭ* 'rainhat'.

The use of *ér* as a grammatical suffix is later than the use of *zĭ*, although its semantic development was undoubtedly very similar. In general, however, *ér* carries a more familiar tone than does *zĭ*. As Wáng Lì (1957) has pointed out, the difficulty of determining whether a particular occurrence of *ér* carried its full tone or not means that it is sometimes hard to distinguish cases where *ér* is used in its etymological sense of 'child' and those cases where it is used as a sort of familiar diminutive suffix. Nonetheless, by the Tang dynasty *ér* as a suffix was already widespread; the following examples are all taken from Tang sources: *yàn-ér* 'wild goose', *fēng-ér* 'bee', *yú-ér* 'fish', *píng-ér* 'bottle, jug'. As a rule in Tang texts the use of *ér* as a suffix is mainly limited to animate nouns except for a few cases. By the Song dynasty it is found with nouns of all categories including designations for inanimate things: *xiăo chē-ér* 'small carriage', *hú-lú-ér* 'little gourd'. In later sources the use of *ér* is even more extensive.

The suffix *tóu* is more restricted in use than either *zĭ* or *ér*. Its appearance as a noun suffix is nonetheless quite early; examples of its use as a suffix to localizers (cf. section 7.5) can already be found in Nanbeichao and Tang texts: *lĭ-tóu* 'inside', *qián-tóu* 'front', *hòu-tóu* 'back'. By the Tang dynasty it is common as a general noun suffix: *shí-tóu* 'stone', *zhěn-tóu* 'pillow', *gǔ-tóu* 'bone'. All of these examples are still current in the standard language of today.

One of the most distinctive characteristics of Modern Chinese is the use of measures or classifiers. In Classical times, on the other hand, the use of measures was the exception rather than the rule. (Here the term "measure" is limited to what Y. R. Chao (1968) called "individual measure" words associated with particular nouns; quantity and container measures like 'catty' or 'bucket of' are probably in universal use.) In pre-Han times numerals and demonstratives normally occurred immediately in front of the noun they referred to: *sān rén* 'three people'. In the few rare cases when measures were employed, they were placed after the noun: *mǎ sān-pǐ* HORSE THREE-MEASURE 'three horses'. But although the beginnings of the use of measures with numerals are already evident in this early period, their widespread use does not begin until the Han dynasty; by the Nanbeichao period the use of measures with numerals is commonplace. According to Liú Shìrú (1956b), a good proportion of the individual measures used today can already be found in Nanbeichao sources. Several of the commonest measures which arose at that period are listed and commented on below.

1. *méi*. This measure is already attested in Han dynasty works like the *Shǐjì* (second century BC) and *Wú yuè chūnqiū* (Eastern Han). The original meaning of *méi* was 'tree-trunk', but its use as a measure seems to have arisen from a somewhat later meaning 'chip, counter' (Liú 1956b). In the Nanbeichao period it is used with concrete nouns of every category, and was clearly the most versatile measure in use. Today it is totally obsolete in the standard language, but as a loanword it survives as a commonly used measure in Japanese.

2. *gè*. This is the most widely used measure in the modern standard language, corresponding in its versatility to *méi* in Nanbeichao times. The original meaning of *gè* was 'bamboo-stalk', but by the late Classical period it already appears as a general measure used with nouns of many different semantic categories. By the Nanbeichao period its range of usage expanded, and it can even be found in conjunction with the noun *rén* 'man, person' and other nouns referring to human beings. In Tang its usage is extended to abstract nouns as well (Liú 1956b, 85).

3. *tóu*. This measure, literally meaning 'head', is mostly used to refer to things having heads, especially animals: *tóngshòu yì-tóu* BRONZE-ANIMAL ONE-HEAD 'one bronze animal'; *dú shí-tóu* CALF TEN-HEAD 'ten calves'. Nowadays *tóu* as a measure is limited to livestock, but in the Nanbeichao period it could refer to

wild animals, birds and even insects and fish: *hǔ sān-tóu* 'three tigers', *yú shièr-tóu* 'twelve fish'.

4. *běn.* This measure originally meant 'root, stem'. In its earliest use as a measure it usually refers to plants of various kinds: *wǔshí-běn cōng* FIFTY-MEASURE ONION 'fifty onion plants'. By Nanbeichao times, it commonly occurs as a measure for books; it is only this usage that has survived into Modern Chinese. It is not entirely clear how a word originally meaning 'root' could come to be used as a measure for books.[1]

5. *tiáo.* From its original meaning of 'branch' *tiáo* came to be used as a measure for long, slender, branchlike objects: *yì-tiáo shéng* 'one rope' (second century AD). The use of *tiáo* as a measure for abstract things ('matters', 'affairs', 'items of business', etc.) has an interesting semantic history. In the Han dynasty, documents were mostly written on slender wooden or bamboo strips. An item of business, when written down, became in effect a "strip"; quite naturally *tiáo* was used as a measure for these strips; from there it was easily transferred to the matters written on the strips. This usage survives in the modern language in such expressions as *yì-tiáo xīnwén* 'an item of news'.

6. *zhī.* This is one of the few words which seems to have been a measure from the very beginning; already in the *Shuōwén jiězì* it is defined as a measure word for single birds. In the post-Han era (third to seventh centuries AD), it often occurs as a measure for birds: *jī yì-zhī* 'one chicken'. From its meaning 'single' (as opposed to a pair), it is also used to refer to one of the things that naturally occur in pairs: *yángtuǐ yì-zhī* 'one leg of mutton'. By further extension *zhī* came to be used as a measure for any long hard object: *shí shǐ-zhī* 'ten arrows'. By Tang times *zhī* was generalized even more, and came to be used with such nouns as *chuán* 'boat' and *yǐ-zǐ* 'chair'. In the modern standard language, *zhī* is one of the most common measures; it is commonly found in many of the same uses as those described above for the Nanbeichao and Tang periods. In the Fúzhōu dialect it has become the most general measure, corresponding in most regards to *gè* in the standard language; in this dialect it even occurs with *nøiŋ*[2] 'person'.

From this brief examination of the early use of measures, several observations can be made. In the first place, it is obvious that measures as a grammatical class arose by and large out of words that were originally nouns. Secondly, in their early history, numeral measure combinations tended to occur more commonly after the nouns to which they were attached. As a result of the general Chinese tendency to place modifying elements before the elements they modify, the reverse order became more and more usual from the Nanbeichao period onwards.

In Modern Chinese, the use of measures with numerals modifying nouns is obligatory; but it is very difficult to say just when this situation was first established. According to Wáng Lì (1957), the extensive use of measures in Nanbeichao texts suggests that measures were already obligatory with numerals before nouns in the popular spoken language at that time, and that survivals of the older Classical order (where numerals normally preceded nouns directly) in texts of that period are simply cases of copying the Classical model.

In the Classical period, localizers (*shàng* 'above', *xià* 'below', *nèi* 'inside', etc.) were all monosyllabic. The development of disyllabic forms consisting of the localizer morpheme plus a suffix occurs already at the very end of the Classical period. Forms with a suffixed *tóu* already appear in Han dynasty sources and have continued in use down to the present time (see above). Another common suffix for localizers, *biān* (originally meaning 'side'), makes its appearance in the Tang dynasty (Ohta 1958). The basic morphemes of spatial orientation have changed very little (see section 4.3), the sole exception being *lǐ*, which has replaced *nèi* totally in the spoken language. Although *lǐ* in the sense of 'inside' occurs in Classical texts, it was much less common than *nèi* at that time. By the Jìn dynasty it appears commonly as a localizer. The disyllabic form *lǐ-tóu* is attested in Tang sources. This suggests that *lǐ* had probably by and large replaced *nèi* by this time in the spoken language.

5.3 Pronominal forms

As regards personal pronouns, three important developments took place between the Classical period and the Tang dynasty. The first of these was the breakdown of the so-called "case" system – that is, the gradual disappearance of the differences in syntactic function between such forms as *wú* and *wǒ*. Secondly, the old third-person forms *qí* and *zhī* came to be replaced by new forms which could function without change in all syntactic environments. The third important change was the development of true plural forms. Let us examine each of these in turn.

As seen in the last chapter, there was in general a division of labor between pronominal forms like *wú* and *wǒ* for the first person and *qí* and *zhī* for the third. Even in the Classical period, there are signs of a breakdown in the distinction of the first-person pronoun, a situation that becomes more pronounced in the Han and later periods. In Nanbeichao and Tang times, there is effectively no real grammatical difference between *wú* and *wǒ*. How is this development to be interpreted? In modern dialects it is doubtful that *wú* survives anywhere as a first-person pronoun. Gurevich (1974) has observed that, in some of the early Buddhist translations which she studied, *wú* had disappeared altogether; in others a clear predilection for the use of *wǒ* can be observed. Gurevich concludes on the basis of these facts that *wú* gradually fell from use as a colloquial form in the period between Han and Tang. Its continued appearance in texts is to be explained as a classicism. Such a hypothesis would accord wel! with the distribution of pronominal forms in Modern Chinese dialects.

In the case of second-person pronouns, both *ěr* and *rǔ* are found commonly in Nanbeichao texts in all syntactic positions. A third form, *nǐ*, is well attested from the Tang on. In actuality, *nǐ* (MC *nï:*) is nothing more than a phonological variant of *ěr* (MC *ńźje:*); according to the *Guǎngyùn*, *nǐ* was a northwestern dialect form; it may well have been diffused widely throughout the country from the Sui-Tang capital of Chángān which was located in the northwest. Modern dialectal forms of the second-person pronoun can almost all be derived from either *rǔ* or *nǐ*; forms from *rǔ* are limited, it would seem, to the coastal Mǐn dialects (see 9.4).

In Classical Chinese there was no third-person pronoun for use in the subject position; *qí* served as a sort of genitive form and *zhī* as an accusative. In the post-Han period, there was a tendency for *qí* to encroach upon uses earlier reserved for *zhī*; at the same time *qí* begins to appear in the subject position. This reflects a further breaking down of the distinct "case" functions characteristic of personal pronouns in the pre-Han era. *Qí* appears to have survived in a few Wú dialects as a general third-person pronoun (Chao 1928, 96). Another form *yī* (MC *ʔi*), in origin a demonstrative, begins to appear in about the fourth or fifth century and is quite common in Tang texts; *yī* survives today in a number of Wú dialects (including Shànghǎi) and in the coastal Mǐn dialects, and sporadically in a few other areas.[2] Another third-person pronoun that makes its appearance at approximately the same time is *qú* (MC *gjwo*). *Qú* survives as the usual third-person form in a great number of contemporary dialects in southern and central China, including dialects belonging to the Yuè, Kèjiā, Gàn, Xiāng, Mǐn and Wú groups.

In the case of both *yī* and *qú* there was no restriction on their syntactic use; they could occur freely in the subject, object or attributive positions. In this way they differed markedly from *zhī* and *qí*, both of which were employed in strictly defined, mutually exclusive environments. The appearance of these third-person forms effectively marks the end of the Classical pronominal system.

The development of the third person pronoun *tā*, now almost universal in Mandarin dialects, is somewhat more complicated than that of *yī* and *qú*. Originally *tā* meant 'other'; in the Classical language it could be used to modify any noun (including those referring to human beings), but when used alone it referred only to non-animate nouns. Only in Nanbeichao texts does it begin to be used in reference to humans in the sense of 'the other one', 'others' or 'someone else'. There has been much controversy over whether *tā* ever occurs in the purely pronominal sense of 'he' or 'she' in pre-Tang texts. The consensus now seems to be that there are no truly unambiguous textual occurrences of *tā* as a third person personal pronoun in any text predating the Tang dynasty.[3] The first unambiguous examples of *tā* in the sense of 'he' or 'she' are from the early Tang (seventh century AD); by the high Tang (eighth century) its occurrence is well attested.

Modern dialects possess a great variety of demonstratives. Here only the most common of these, *zhè* 'this' and *nà* 'that', will be examined. Both forms are first seen in Tang texts.[4] In the earliest examples of their use, neither form occurs with a measure (as in modern usage) but both precede the nouns they modify directly. There is a lack of agreement concerning the etymology of both *zhè* and *nà*. Lǚ Shūxiāng (1947) is of the opinion that *zhè* originated from *zhě*, the marker of agentive nominalization in Classical Chinese (see section 4.7). Although *zhě* would fit quite well phonologically, it is not so apt semantically or syntactically. As Wáng Lì (1957) points out, *zhě* in Classical Chinese occurs after the element it refers to, whereas the demonstrative *zhè* is always placed in front of the noun it modifies. But despite semantic and grammatical discrepancies, one cannot rule out altogether the possibility of this etymology. Wáng Lì (1957) is inclined to view the Classical demonstrative *zhī* 'this' as the origin of *zhè*; semantically and syntactically *zhī* would be perfect, but phonologically it presents problems: how does one explain the shift from *zhī* (MC *tśï*) to *zhè* (MC *tśja:*)? At the moment there would appear to be no entirely satisfactory answer to any of these problems.

There is greater agreement about the origin of the far demonstrative *nà*. Classical Chinese possessed a demonstrative *ruò* (MC *ńźjak ~ ńźja:*); in post-Han times a related demonstrative *ěr* (MC *ńźje:*) appears. Phonologically *nà* (MC *nâ-*) would seem to have definite phonological relation to these forms; semantically and syntactically there is almost perfect agreement.

Two Classical interrogatives have survived intact into Modern Chinese: *shúi* 'who' and *jǐ* 'how many' are used in much the same way in contemporary Mandarin dialects as they were in pre-Han Chinese.[5] Words for 'what', 'which' and 'how', on the other hand, are all innovations.

In an insightful article, Zhāng Hùiyīng (1982) has shown that *shénme*, the standard modern word for 'what', comes from *shí wù* (MC *źjəp mjuət*). This form (in a number of different phonological shapes) makes its first appearance in the

Tang dynasty. *Shí wù* originally meant 'vessels, household utensils, things (of various sorts)'. The development of an interrogative meaning 'what' from a meaning 'thing' finds a parallel in modern Italian, where *cosa* 'thing' is also used to mean 'what'. A similar development can be seen in some Mǐn dialects, where a morpheme meaning 'thing' in some dialects means 'what' in others; e.g. Xiamen *miʔ⁸ kiã⁶* 'thing', Jiàn'ōu *mi⁴ ti⁶* 'thing', Cháozhōu *miʔ⁸ kai²* 'what'; in the Xiàmén dialect itself *miʔ⁸* occurs as a constituent in the word for 'what', *sim³ miʔ⁸*.[6]

The interrogative *nǎ* 'which (one)' is attested earlier than the corresponding demonstrative *nà*.[7] In the Nanbeichao period it normally occurs in the combinations *nǎdé* and *nǎkě*, both meaning 'why', 'how could it be that ... ', 'how is it possible that ...': *nǎdé dú yǐn* WHY ALONE DRINK 'why are you drinking alone?' In Buddhist texts of the same period it sometimes has the meaning of 'where': *dāng nǎ qiú zhī* SHOULD WHERE SEEK IT 'where should one seek it?' Note that in both cases, *nǎ* is used adverbially; as an adjunct to nouns and measure words, it does not appear until the Tang dynasty (Ohta 1958).

In Tang dynasty texts the interrogative adverb *zhēng* 'how' appears for the first time. It has a corresponding demonstrative adverb *néng* 'in that way, thus'. The origin of both these forms is at present unclear. In the late Tang and Wudai periods, a different form begins to be found; it consists of the verb *zuò* (MC *tsuo-*) plus one of several variants of the morpheme meaning 'thing, what' discussed in relation to the origins of modern *shénme*: *zuò mò* (MC *muət*), *zuò wù* (MC *mjuət*), *zuò mó* (MC *muâ*). In the Wudai period, a fusion word *zěn* (from an earlier **zěm*) based on these forms appears for the first time. It is this fusion form that is directly ancestral to the modern *zěnme* 'how'. *Zhème* 'in this way' and *nàme* 'in that way' were probably analogically based on this form.

One of the distinctive characteristics of Classical Chinese pronouns was their lack of a number distinction. In Han and post-Han texts, one can begin to encounter personal pronouns followed by various markers of plurality of which *děng*, *cáo* and *bèi* are the most common. It is doubtful that number had become an obligatory category for personal pronouns before the late Tang dynasty; at an earlier transitional stage, various plural markers could optionally be added to personal pronouns when it was necessary to avoid ambiguity. The fact that Modern Chinese dialects (all of which have number as an obligatory category for personal pronouns) have created an almost bewildering number of different plural formations suggests that the development of an obligatory number distinction for pronouns occurred rather late.

Forms ancestral to the plural suffix *men* (used in almost all Mandarin dialects as well as in the standard language) do not appear in this form until the Song dynasty. There are several theories about the origin of this suffix; the most likely explanation, it seems to me, is that it is in origin a fusion of *měi* 'each, every' and *rén* 'person'. Although such a disyllabic form apparently does not occur textually, Yuan dynasty texts employ *měi* alone as a plural suffix to pronouns. The fact that it is restricted to pronominal forms and human nouns also supports this hypothesis.[8]

A distinction between inclusive and exclusive for first-person plural pronouns is not universal in Modern Chinese dialects, but the standard language has inherited such a distinction from the northern dialect of Song and Yuan times: *wǒmen* 'we (exclusive)', *zámen* 'we (inclusive)'. What is the origin of the inclusive form? There seems to be little doubt that *zá* derives from a fusion of *zì* (MC *dzi-*) 'self' and *jiā* (MC *ka*) 'family'. *Zìjiā* in the sense of 'self' is already found in Tang texts. By Song times it begins to appear in the sense of 'I' and 'we (inclusive)' (Ohta 1958). The fused form *zá* also dates from the Song dynasty.

Various fusions of pronominal forms plus the plural suffix *men* developed at approximately the same time. *Nín* (earlier **nǐm*) first appears as a simple plural form of *nǐ* 'you'; later it developed into a polite singular form, the usage still found in the standard language today. *Ǎn* (earlier **ǎm* or **ǒm*) is a fusion of *wǒ* plus *men*; in the Song dynasty it is already attested in its use as a singular form meaning 'I'; today it survives only in non-standard dialects. Likewise, *zán*, the fusion of *zá* and *men* in the sense of 'I' or 'we (inclusive)', attested since the Yuan dynasty, is no longer common in standard Chinese.

5.4 Predicatives

In the period between Classical Chinese and the present, great changes took place in the structure of the predicate. These changes include the following: (1) the development of verbal compounds of several types; (2) the appearance of a new aspectual system; (3) the emergence of a new set of verbal auxiliaries; (4) the appearance of a new copular verb; (5) changes in the negation system; (6) the appearance of many new adverbs; (7) a great increase in the number of prepositions; and (8) changes in the expression of the passive and causative. Each of these important changes will be considered in turn below.

In Classical Chinese there were no verbal compounds; when two closely linked verbs occurred in a single phrase, they had to be separated by the verbal connective *ér*. By the Western Han dynasty, however, linked verbs without an intervening *ér* begin to make an appearance (Zhǔ 1958). In the several centuries following the Han dynasty, the use of these verbal collocations greatly increased. Gurevich, who has studied these forms in Buddhist texts of the third to fifth centuries, divides such verbal compounds into several classes. In her 1974 work on the grammar of these early Buddhist sources, she sets up three basic categories: (1) synonym or near-synonym compounds, (2) verbs with resultative complements, and (3) verbs with directional complements. The first of these categories consists of compounds of two verbs that are either synonymous or nearly so; these forms allow of no insertions between their components, and form a class of bound verbal compounds. Some examples of such compounds of this type are *xǐhuān* 'to be happy', *xiǎngniàn* 'to think about' and *sǐwáng* 'to perish'; in all these cases the compounds are made up of two verbs very similar or identical in meaning. (It is interesting to note that all three of the verbs cited above are still in common use today.)

Gurevich's second category consists of compounds of a transitive verb plus a second verbal element (the complement) which indicates in some sense the result of the action of the first verb. The form *dǎ-shā*, for example, is comprised of *dǎ* 'to hit, to strike' and *shā* 'to kill', yielding a compound meaning 'to hit and kill', 'to beat to death'. Some resultative complements merely show that the action denoted by the first verb had a result in a very general sense: *zhuó-dé* CHOP-OBTAIN 'succeeded in chopping, chopped down'.

The third category studied by Gurevich are combinations of a verb plus a complement showing the direction of the action: *liú-chū* FLOW-GO OUT 'flows out', *fēi-lái* FLY-COME 'came flying'.

The first category of these compound verbs consists of forms which are fixed lexical units; if they occur with an object, it can only occur after the compound as a whole. In the case of the second and third categories, on the other hand, the cohesion between the two elements is not so tight; although objects may occur after these forms as in the case of the first type of verbal compound, they are often placed between the two elements. Thus alongside an example like *shāo-shā cháng-shòu wáng* BURN-KILL PNAME KING 'burned King Changshou [lit. "long life"] to death', one can encounter *dǎ gāng pò* HIT JAR BREAK 'hit and broke the jar'. This shows that the degree of cohesion between the elements of these kinds of compounds was still relatively weak at this time. In the later history of the language, the link between verbs and their resultative complements became stronger, and this sort of separation of a verb from its result was no longer allowed. In the case of complements showing direction, however, this sort of discontinuity is still found; parallel to a Nanbeichao example like *sòng shí lái* SEND FOOD COME 'send food here', one can find a modern form like *sòng dōngxi lái* 'send some things here'. In both the earlier and the modern languages it is also possible to find cases where the objects to compound verbs of this category follow the directional complement.

The most important development in the aspectual system between the period of Classical Chinese and the modern standard language was the appearance of the verbal suffixes *le* and *zhe*. In Classical Chinese perfected action was indicated by the use of the preverbal particle *jì*; this particle progressively came to be replaced by *yǐ* in the late Classical period and the Han dynasty. In the popular Buddhist texts examined by Gurevich, although both of these preverbal perfective markers continue to be used, there is a clear tendency for *yǐ* to move to the end of the clause. Where the Classical language would have had *wáng jì chū* KING PERF GO-OUT '(after) the king went out', the language of these early Buddhist sources may have *wáng chū yǐ* with the marker of completed action at the end. In the case of transitive verbs having objects, *yǐ* follows the object; *wáng jiàn zéi yǐ* KING SEE BANDIT PERF 'when the king saw the bandit'. This grammatical frame of V O PERF is found very commonly in Nanbeichao texts; in addition to *yǐ*, several other perfective markers, all derived from verbs meaning 'finish, come to an end', are found; the most important of these are *bì*, *jìng* and *qì*. The popular Buddhist texts of the Tang dynasty (*biànwén*) contain many examples of this construction; but in this period another perfective verb, *liǎo* (MC *lieu:*), progressively begins to oust the above-mentioned forms, so that the most common perfective construction in these texts eventually becomes V (O) *liǎo*.[9] By the tenth century, cases of V *liǎo* O have begun to make an appearance. T. L. Mei (1981b) has suggested that this new word order was influenced by the movement of resultative and potential complements to a postverbal position at the same period; the tendency to place *liǎo* after the verb was also undoubtedly influenced by the fact that resultative complements by their very nature carry with them the notion of completed action. By the Song dynasty the modern construction of V *liǎo* (= *le*) O is firmly established in the written vernacular.[10]

The history of the continuative suffix *zhe* is much less clear. According to Lǚ Shūxiāng (1940) and Zhào Jīnmíng (1979), the character *zhuó* (the stressed reading pronunciation of *zhe*) is already commonly found after verbs in the Tang dynasty, both in poetry and in popular Buddhist literature. There is no doubt that *zhe* derives from a Middle Chinese word *djak*, which meant 'to be attached, to come in contact with'. In Nanbeichao texts this morpheme is found as a verbal suffix whose function is to show location: *zuò zhuó xī qián* SIT ATTACH KNEE FRONT 'sits in front of his knees'.[11] Several Chinese scholars (Lǚ 1940; Wáng Lì 1957; Zhào 1979) believe that the continuative suffix *zhe* derives from this early usage; this is certainly possible, but one would like to see a little more supporting evidence in favor of this hypothesis. The same Middle Chinese morpheme *djak* is also attested quite early as a resultative complement which functions to show that the action of the preceding verb was carried out successfully; this usage has survived into the modern language in the stressed form *zháo*.

To express the notion of an indefinite past for which the Classical language employed *cháng*, a new preverbal particle *céng* (MC *dzəng*) appears in the Han dynasty.[12] In Nanbeichao and Tang texts it is quite common. In conjunction with the negatives *bù* and *wèi* it means 'never' or 'not yet': *wèi céng jiàn* 'never saw'. Although the use of *céng* alone has disappeared from modern spoken forms of Chinese, it survives in its negative form (frequently in the form of a fusion word) in numerous central and southern dialects: Sūzhōu *fən*[1] (from *fəʔ*[7] and *zən*[2] 'ever'), Guăngzhōu *mei*[6] *tshaŋ*[2]. In the standard language *céng* has been replaced by the suffix *guo*. This use of *guo* (derived from the verb *guò* 'to pass') appears to have been a Song dynasty development.

Verbal modality is commonly expressed by means of preposed auxiliary verbs at all stages of Chinese. The only exception to this general rule is the expression of potentiality by suffixing *dé*, in origin a verb meaning 'obtain'. In Han texts it can already be encountered as the second element in verbal compounds in which the first verb in some sense refers to acquisition: *căi-dé* 'obtain by gathering', *xué-dé* 'obtain through study', *măi-dé* 'obtain by buying'. In some cases this postposed *dé* merely served to show that the action of the first verb was carried through to a successful conclusion. (See the example *zhuó-dé* above.) These collocations of verb plus *dé* were negated by placing the negatives *bù* or *wèi* before the *dé*. It is easy to see how a form like *măi wèi dé* 'didn't succeed in buying' could be interpreted as 'couldn't buy'. It is no doubt in this way that a suffixed *dé* came to perform its potential function. By the Tang dynasty the use of a suffixed *dé* to express potentiality is common. The usage has survived in all forms of the modern language.

With the exception of the aforementioned construction, modality continued to be expressed by means of auxiliary verbs. Such Classical auxiliary verbs as *kěyǐ* 'can, may', *néng* 'can' and *găn* 'dare' continued in common use after the Classical period and are still employed today. Others such as *yù* 'want' and *bì* 'must' dropped out of the colloquial language and were replaced with various innovations; the following are the chief of these:

1. *dāng* (MC *tâng*). *Dāng* appears in late Classical texts in the sense of 'ought to, should'. By Han times this usage is common. In the Nanbeichao sources studied by Gurevich, in addition to this meaning, *dāng* also often functions like the classical *jiāng* as a marker of future action. In the modern language *dāng* has disappeared as a free form, but it survives in the compound auxiliary *yīngdāng* 'ought, should'.

2. *yào* (MC *ʔjiäu-*). In modern standard Chinese, *yào* is used to express obligation ('must, have to'), volition, and as a marker of future action. According to Ohta (1958, 200) the use of *yào* as an auxiliary verb is of Tang vintage.

3. *xiè* (MC *γai:*). In Tang texts *xiè* (written with the same character as *jiě* 'to untie, to explain') occurs as an auxiliary verb expressing potentiality: *bú xiè shuō* 'cannot speak'. In the later written vernacular, *xiè* was for the most part replaced by *huì* (MC *γuâi-*), which in Tang times was found only in the meaning of 'to understand'. *Xiè* is preserved as an auxiliary verb with potential meaning in the modern Mǐn dialects: Fúzhōu *a*[6], Xiàmén *ue*[6], Jiànyáng *hai*[5].

4. *xū* (MC *sju*). As an auxiliary expressing obligation, *xū* was rare in Classical texts, but becomes common in the post-Han period. The use of *děi* (MC *tək*) to express obligation does not appear until the Tang and Wudai periods (Ohta 1958, 197).

Surely one of the most important developments in Postclassical Chinese was the appearance of a copular verb. In the last chapter we saw that the Classical language had no such verb; a copular sentence took the form X Y *yě*, X representing the subject and Y the predicate. The corresponding negative form was X *fēi* Y (*yě*), *fēi* being the negator of nominal predicates. By the Han dynasty, the Classical demonstrative *shì* begins to be used as a marker of nominal predication. One of the clearest early examples is the following sentence taken from Sīmǎ Qiān's *Shǐjì*:

qí shì wú dì yú
HE *shì* MY BROTHER QUES
'Is he my (younger) brother?'

The most widely accepted view concerning how a demonstrative meaning 'this' could come to develop into a copular verb is that it originated as a reiteration of the subject, much as in Russian one can use *èto* 'this' as a sort of emphatic marker of nominal predication.[13] This explanation is quite plausible, but another factor may have reinforced this development. Already in Classical Chinese one often finds the collocation *shì fēi* meaning 'right and wrong'; this shows that in some sense *shì* was considered to be the opposite of *fēi* in the Classical period. Since *fēi* was the regular negation used with nominal predicates, it would only have been natural to regard *shì* as its affirmative counterpart, thus allowing *shì* to fill what came to be perceived as an empty slot in affirmative nominal sentences.[14] In Nanbeichao texts the use of *shì* as a copular verb is common, indicating that in the spoken language of that time the new construction with *shì* had probably already replaced the older Classical construction. Initially *fēi* was used as the negative counterpart of the new copular *shì*; as *shì* came more and more to be felt as a verb, the compound form *fēishì* developed; this form can be found in numerous Nanbeichao texts. By the Tang dynasty *fēi* was analogically replaced by the more general negative *bù*, and *fēi* dropped from the spoken language altogether.

The great plethora of negative forms found in Classical Chinese was greatly reduced in the later vernacular. Classical *fú* (MC *pjuət*) survived in the guise of *bù* and became the most common negative (cf. section 3.6).

The question of the origin of the modern negative *méi* is more difficult. It is written with a character which in Middle Chinese meant 'sink, submerge'; the Tang pronunciation of this character was *m(u)ət*. Ohta (1958, 301) is of the opinion that the later negative *méi* derives from this word. While this is possible both semantically and phonologically, I think it rather more likely that the origin of *méi* is to be found in the classical negative *wèi* (MC *mjuei-*). Just as modern *bù* comes from a form ending in *t*, *méi* also originates from an older form having a final *t*, in origin probably a fusion of *wèi* plus *zhī* (OC **tjəg*), the third person objective pronoun. The resultant form (MC **mjuət*) like *bù* lost its palatal medial, yielding a Middle Chinese *m(u)ət*. In Tang texts this negative form is sometimes written with *wù* (the same character as the negative imperative *wù*) but more commonly with the graph meaning 'sink' or 'submerge' mentioned above (Lü 1955). After *m(u)ət* lost its final stop, it became **mə*; the final glide in the modern form *méi* has been added due to contamination with the initial of *yǒu* 'there is, have' with which it is regularly associated.[15]

The expression of negative imperatives underwent many changes in the medieval period. As the ordinary prohibitive forms came to be viewed as too blunt and impolite, they were replaced by various circumlocutions which in their turn often came to be felt as too blunt and were then replaced by newer, less offensive forms. One of the first of these circumlocutions to become popular was the use of *mò* which, in the Classical language, meant 'no-one'. Rather than saying 'don't do' something, it was felt to be less blunt to say 'no-one' does such and such a thing. Examples of *mò* used in this way are already found in Han dynasty sources. In Nanbeichao and Tang texts its use is very common, but today it survives only in a few southern dialects. In the Tang dynasty several other forms of attenuated prohibition were commonly used. One of these was the use of *xiū* 'to rest, take a rest from', as in *xiū chàng* 'don't sing'. Another was the use of such forms as *bù yào* 'there is no need', *bù xū* 'it is unnecessary' and *bú yòng* 'there is no need'. Of these three expressions, *bú yào* and *bú yòng* have survived in the modern standard language.

The most common prohibitives in the modern Peking dialect are *bié* and *béng* (also pronounced *bing* by some speakers). The latter form is a fusion based on *bú yòng*. *Bié* is often said to be a fusion of *bú* and *yào*, but this is not entirely convincing from a phonological point of view; if it were truly a fusion form, one would expect something like **biáo* rather than *bié*.[16] Another objection to the fusion theory of the origin of *bié* is that *bié yào* also occurs. Ohta Tatsuo (1958, 303) thinks that *bié* (which is written with a graph meaning 'other, different'), in the light of the history of the development of other Postclassical prohibitives, was more likely in origin a circumlocution meaning 'otherly, differently'; thus, a form like *bié shuō* originally meant 'do something other than speaking – don't speak'. I personally find Ohta's explanation more attractive than the fusion theory.[17]

An immense number of new adverbs begin to appear in the Postclassical period. A few of these will be examined here to give a general idea of this development.

The adverb *dōu*, which in modern Chinese means 'completely, all', first appears in late Han and Nanbeichao sources. The character used for writing *dōu* originally meant a 'large town or city'. It is possible that this meaning comes from a more basic verbal of 'assemble together (in a place)' and hence developed the meaning 'general, altogether' (Lǐ Xíngjiàn 1958). Be that as it may, by the Nanbeichao period, *dōu* is used adverbially in the sense of 'completely, altogether, in totality': *dōu jìn* 'completely exhausted'. According to Gurevich, the meaning 'all' referring back to the subject is already found in the Nanbeichao Buddhist translations studied by her: *hóu zhòng dōu bìng* MONKEY GROUP ALL ILL 'the group of monkeys all fell ill'. This latter usage became progressively common in the Tang and Song dynasties and has survived into most Modern Chinese dialects.

Classical Chinese, strictly speaking, had no adverbs of degree, degree being expressed most commonly by means of predicate adjectives. By the Han dynasty, however, degree adverbs like *jí* 'extremely', *zùi* 'most' and *tài* 'too' become relatively common. The most common adverb of degree in modern Chinese, *hěn* 'very', originates from the adjective *hěn* 'fierce, ruthless'; the use of *hěn* as an adverb seems to have originated in the Yuan dynasty. The use of *dǐng* to form the superlative degree of adjectives is much later than the use of *zùi*, but it is found already in Song texts.

The adverb *biàn* 'right away, immediately' is no longer used in the spoken language, but is a prominent feature of the earlier written vernacular. It is first seen in this sense in the Eastern Han. It is common in Nanbeichao and later texts. In modern colloquial Chinese *biàn* has for the most part been replaced by *jiù*; the use of *jiù* in this meaning (it was originally a verb meaning 'to approach') is thought to be Yuan dynasty phenomenon.

For the notion 'only', the Classical language most commonly employed *wéi* or *dú*. By late Han a new adverb, *dàn*, appears used in this sense. *Dàn* is very common throughout the Nanbeichao period and later. In Modern Chinese it chiefly survives in the compounds *dànshi* 'however' and *búdàn* 'not only'. The most common modern adverb used in the sense of only is *zhǐ*; the use of *zhǐ* in this meaning (written with several different but homophonous characters) dates back to Classical times. It is not clear when *jiù* (written with the same character as *jiù* meaning 'at once') began to be used in the sense of 'only'.

Along with the proliferation of new adverbs, the Postclassical language saw both the development of a number of new prepositions and the tendency for certain late and rarely employed prepositions to be used progressively more at the expense of the older, more Classical forms. To this latter category of increasingly high-frequency prepositions belong such forms as *zài* '(located) in or at', *cóng* 'from' and *xiàng* 'towards'. All three of these words are found functioning as prepositions in early texts, but their use becomes much more frequent in the late Classical and Postclassical period. *Zài* gradually encroached on the territory once occupied by the Classical preposition *yú*, eventually replacing it in the spoken language.[18] The three prepositions *zài*, *cóng* and *xiàng* are all still commonly used in the modern standard vernacular.

The preposition *wèi* was used in a benefactive sense in the Classical language and is still frequently used in this way, but its use in the modern language almost certainly represents a literary borrowing. The corresponding colloquial form is *gěi* which is derived from the verb meaning 'to give'. *Gěi* in both its verbal and prepositional uses described here appears to be a rather late development. In pre-Qing dynasty texts, the notion of 'to give' is generally still expressed by means of the Classical verb *yǔ* (MC *jiwo:*). It is interesting to note that *yǔ* quite early began to be used as a preposition with a benefactive sense 'for the sake of'. This undoubtedly reflects a very early association of the verb 'to give' with a derived propositional use meaning 'for the benefit of'.

In Classical Chinese the notion of instrumentality was shown with the preposition *yǐ*. The verb *yòng* 'to use' is already found used as an instrumental preposition in late Classical texts, a usage still found in the modern standard language. The use of verbs meaning 'to hold' to express the instrumental function begins very early. In the early Buddhist translations, for example, *chí* (MC *ḍï*) 'to hold' is found used in this fashion: *chí dāo gē ròu* HOLD KNIFE CUT MEAT 'cut meat with a knife'. In later texts the verbs *bǎ* 'to grasp with the hand' and *jiāng* 'to take in the hand, help, accompany' are also used to indicate an instrument: *bǎ qián mǎi yào* GRASP MONEY BUY MEDICINE 'buy medicine with money'.

One of the major differences between Classical Chinese and later vernacular forms is the expression of the passive. The use of *bèi* to show that the subject of a clause in some sense suffers or undergoes the action of the verb is a late Classical innovation; in this usage it merely replaced the earlier use of *jiàn* (Wáng Lì 1957). In the Nanbeichao period, *bèi* begins to appear followed by the agent of the passive verb; this construction is already similar in most respects to the modern passive construction in the standard language. The use of *bèi* in the modern vernacular is most likely a literary borrowing; the more popular and colloquial construction employs *jiào* or *ràng* as markers of the passive. A curious thing about this modern construction is the use of what are basically causative verbs to express a passive meaning.[19] Ohta (1958, 247) cites two early examples of the use of *jiào* to mark an apparent passive, one from the late Tang poet Bái Jūyì, another from the Song poet Sū Shì. If these examples are indeed authentic passive constructions, they would appear to be quite isolated at this early period.[20] It is interesting to note here that in Manchu, the language of the ruling house in the last imperial dynasty, the passive and causative are formed with one and the same suffix. Even if this particular usage arose in Chinese before the Qing dynasty, this fact may help to explain why *jiào* and *ràng* have tended to oust their competitors in most northern dialects.

The use of intransitive verbs and adjectives in a causative sense was a prominent feature of the Classical language. An intransitive verb like *pò* 'be broken, be crushed' could take an object and then be interpreted in a transitive sense: *pò zhī* 'crushed it'. In the Han dynasty, a new construction consisting of a transitive verb plus an intransitive complement (either a verb or an adjective) began to put in an appearance; the grammatical function of these compounds was that of a causative verb. In place of *pò zhī*, one begins to see forms like *gōng-pò zhī* ATTACK-CRUSH IT 'attacked and demolished it'. This is undoubtedly an indication that in the spoken language of that time, these compound verbs were beginning to replace the older construction, whereby an intransitive verb or adjective could be employed directly in a causative sense. As Chinese developed in later periods, this new way of expressing causatives became progressively more popular, eventually replacing the older construction altogether.

Classical Chinese had a second way of expressing the causative: this was through the use of causative verbs such as *shǐ* and *lìng*: *shǐ zhī lái* CAUSE HIM COME 'make him come'. This construction has remained very stable throughout the history of Chinese; *shǐ* can still be used in this way in the modern language. The only real change that has taken place is that a number of new causative verbs have come into use; among the more common are *ràng* and *jiào*, or, when a less blunt tone is required, *qǐng*: *jiào tā lái* 'tell him to come', *qǐng tā lái* 'ask (request) him to come'.

5.5 Changes in word order

The order of elements in a Chinese sentence has remained remarkably stable over the last two millennia. The chief differences may be subsumed under two headings: (1) the position of pronominal and interrogative objects with respect to the verb, and (2) the shift of place and instrumental phrases to a position in front of the verb.

In Chapter 4, we saw that pronominal objects came between the negative and the verb in Classical Chinese: *wèi zhī shí* NEG IT EAT 'didn't eat it'. By the Han dynasty, one encounters numerous cases of pronominal objects placed after negated verbs: *mò zhī wǒ fú* NO-ONE KNOW ME PCL 'no-one knows me'. Such examples are even more numerous in Nanbeichao texts. This has led Wáng Lì (1957) to conclude that by this period this word order change was essentially completed in the spoken language.

One can observe a very similar development in the case of interrogative pronouns used as objects to verbs: in the Classical language, these elements appeared regularly in front of the verb. By Han times, a shift to the postverbal position can already be observed. Judging from the very frequent appearance of these elements after the verb in the several centuries following the Han dynasty, it seems probable that in the colloquial language of that time interrogative pronouns used as objects had already been regularly shifted to the position after the verb.

In the Classical language, the normal place for instrumental and place phrases introduced by a preposition was after the main verb. At about the same time that *zài* begins to replace *yú* as the most common preposition used to introduce place phrases, a tendency to move such phrases before the verb can also be observed. In the pre-Han literary language, the instrumental preposition *yǐ* could either precede or follow the verb phrase. When it functioned to indicate a reason for the action, it could only precede the verb. With the demise of the preposition *yǐ* in the spoken language and its replacement with later equivalents such as *yòng*, *chí* and *bǎ*, instrumental phrases were also moved to a preverbal position. Again, as in the case of place phrases, it is very difficult to date this change exactly, but to judge from the widespread use of new prepositions to express instrumentality already in Nanbeichao texts, it must have taken place at about this time (Gurevich 1974).

Of utmost importance in the history of Chinese syntax is the development of what Y. R. Chao (1967, 342ff) called the pretransitive construction. This construction entails the placement of the direct object in front of the verb by means of a so-called "pretransitive preposition". The two most common prepositions used for this purpose were in origin both markers of instrumentality; moreover, they both derive from full independent verbs meaning 'to hold in the hand'. Of these two verbs, *jiāng* is apparently the older and *bǎ* somewhat more recent. According to both Wáng Lì (1957) and Liú Jiān (1982), both verbs, when used prepositionally, were initially used to indicate an instrument: examples of this usage are found already in early Tang sources. By mid-Tang, cases where the two prepositions clearly mark the direct object of the main verb begin to make an appearance. The instrumental use of both these prepositions continued alongside their newer, pretransitive function right down until the Qing dynasty, when the two functions became clearly separated. (Wáng Lì 1957, 414). In the modern spoken language, only *bǎ* is used as a pretransitive preposition; *jiāng*, however, is still commonly used in the written language.

In the current standard language not all prepositional phrases precede the verb. Phrases headed by *zài*, *dào* and *gěi* may occur postverbally; the general rule is that phrases formed with these prepositions occur immediately after the verb when the focus of the sentence in which they occur is on the preposition and its object rather than on the verb itself. Moreover, the set of verbs to which each of the above-mentioned prepositions can be postposed is quite restricted.

The word order changes described here have been one of the reasons that has led a number of linguists to propose that Chinese is changing from a basically subject–verb–object language into a subject–object–verb language. Their arguments are supported by a number of alleged word order universals proposed by Joseph Greenberg in 1963; but, as Chauncy Chu (1984) has pointed out, the proponents of this theory of word order change have taken Greenberg's proposed universals as established facts when in reality they are only preliminary observations still in need of further study and verification. This being the case, it would seem to be premature to use these "universals" as arguments for historical syntactic change. Another problem with the theory that Chinese is in the process of becoming an SOV language is that it is not at all clear that the proposed changes are as dramatic as their proponents have painted them to be. In Classical Chinese prepositional phrases were already permitted before the verb; the movement of place and instrumental phrases to a preverbal position can be viewed as the generalization of a pattern already present in the language. When one also considers that, in the modern language, prepositional phrases may still follow the verb under certain conditions, it is doubtful that any major typological change has taken place at all: in both the Classical and modern language, prepositional phrases occurred both in front of and after the verb phrase proper, even though the rules determining the placement of the phrases are somewhat different. As for the preposing of direct objects, it is clear that this has been possible at all stages of the language.[21] The real question, to my mind, is not so much whether Chinese has developed a new word order, but the relative frequency and importance of preverbal objects at various stages of its history, a question that still remains to be studied in depth.

Further reading

Gurevich, I. S. 1974. *Očerk grammatiki kitajskogo jazyka III–IV vv.* Moscow: Nauka. [A description of the language of the earliest Buddhist translations – a treasure trove for the study of early vernacular elements.]

Gurevich, I. S. and Zograf, I. T. 1982. *Xrestomatija po istorii kitajskogo jazyka III–XV vv.* Moscow: Nauka. [A collection of semi-vernacular and vernacular texts from the end of the Han down to the Ming dynasty. Brief descriptions of the vernacular of each period are included.]

Ohta, Tatsuo 1958. *Chūgokugo rekishi bunpō.* Tokyo: Kōnan Shoten. [The standard Japanese source for early vernacular Chinese.]

Wáng Lì 1957. *Hànyǔ shǐgǎo.* Peking: Kēxué Chūbǎnshè. [A valuable history of the Chinese language; the second section deals with the history of morphology and syntax.]

6

The modern standard language I

6.1 The formation of the modern standard language

At the present time China (both the mainland and Táiwān) has an officially recognized standard language which is taught in the schools and employed in all governmental and official transactions. This situation is a relatively recent development. During the Qing dynasty, the last of the imperial dynasties, the official language (if indeed one can speak of such a concept at that time) was the Tungusic language of the ruling house, Manchu; this can be seen from the fact that during most of the Qing dynasty the term *guóyǔ* 'national language' referred to Manchu and not to Chinese.[1] Historically, the term *guóyǔ* seems mainly to have been employed by dynasties whose rulers were not Chinese, but some northern group like the Tabgach, the Jurchens, or the Mongols.[2] But it is clear that during dynasties of this sort, the vast bulk of governmental business was transacted in Chinese and not in the languages of the ruling elite. In the Qing dynasty, the ordinary written administrative language was a late form of literary Chinese; officials communicated orally in a variety of Peking dialect, often strongly influenced by the local native dialect of the speaker, which was referred to as *guānhuà* 'the officials' (or mandarins') language'. Neither of these forms of bureaucratic Chinese was codified in any fashion; they simply developed as a natural response to the need for a practical medium to carry on the day-to-day business of the empire.

At the beginning of this century, during the declining years of the Qing dynasty, various individuals concerned with China's entry into the modern world began to realize the importance of a uniform and officially sanctioned national standard language, both as a tool of education and administration and as a symbol of national unity. At this time, not only was literacy not widespread, but the vast masses of China knew only their local dialects, which in many cases could only be understood and employed in a very restricted geographic region.

The problem of establishing a uniform national language possessed two aspects: the formation of a new literary standard, and the promotion of a single form of spoken Chinese which could serve as the means of communication among people coming from different parts of the country. Among reform-minded intellectuals it was generally recognized that the traditional literary language, even in an updated and modernized version, could not serve as a vehicle of expanded literacy; moreover, a new normalized form of spoken Chinese would have to replace the uncodified lingua franca known as *guānhuà*.

As early as 1909 the Ministry of Education promulgated a program for promoting the teaching and study of *guānhuà* in Chinese schools. In the following year a proposal was made to the Minister of Education that the term *guānhuà* be replaced by the more appropriate designation *guóyŭ* 'national language' (Liú Fù 1925, 14).[3] At this early period, *guóyŭ* was principally seen as a sort of a language of school and administration, but not of literature – for this purpose, the traditional literary language (*wényán*) was to be preserved.

Hú Shì (1891–1962) and Chén Dúxiù (1880–1942) led the battle to do away with the old literary langage in favor of a new vernacular literary standard based on the language of such traditional *báihuà* literary classics as *Shŭi hŭ zhuàn* and the *Hóng lóu mèng*. The written vernacular, as we have seen in Chapter 5, had already gone through a long period of development, beginning as far back as the Tang and Song dynasties. After the 1919 May Fourth Movement, a movement which began as a student protest against Japanese imperialism but soon expanded to demands for literary and cultural reform as well, *báihuà* quickly became accepted as the normal written medium in China.

While there was general agreement about what were to be the bases of both a new spoken and written national language – the spoken standard was to be a continuation of *guānhuà*, and the new literary language was to be based on the old *báihuà* classics – it soon became apparent that, in the case of spoken language at least, a definite norm of pronunciation would have to be adopted. *Guānhuà* had its roots in the language of the former imperial capital of Peking. In its use as a general interregional administrative lingua franca, it had shed a number of Peking localisms in favor of more widespread and generally understood equivalents. Unfortunately, at the conference convened in 1913 by the new Republican Ministry of Education for the purpose of establishing a unified pronunciation of characters, the standard agreed upon was a cross-dialectal compromise which in fact corresponded to no single living dialect at that time (Liú Fù 1925, 19ff). This artificial standard was used in the 1919 compilation *Guóyīn zìdiăn* [*Dictionary of national pronunciation*], which was intended as a guide to correct pronunciation, but within two years of its publication it was severely criticized for its impracticality. In 1924 the Preparatory Committee for the

Unification of the National Language came out in favor of making Peking pronunciation standard; the publication in 1932 of the Peking-based *Guóyīn chángyòng zìhùi* [*A glossary of frequently used characters in National Pronunciation*] by the Nationalist government settled, temporarily at least, the controversy over the norm of pronunciation (Sofronov 1979, 103).

Almost simultaneously with the controversy just described, another approach to the problem of creating a national language was being developed. Under the influence of Soviet plans to latinize the scripts of the Turkic peoples of the USSR, Qú Qiūbái (1899–1935) and others took a strong stand in favor of abolishing Chinese characters altogether and replacing them with a Latin-type script.[4] To do this, Qú proposed a standard language based on the speech of the newly emerging proletariat, a kind of superdialectal form of the old *guānhuà*. Qú referred to this language as *pǔtōnghuà* 'the common language' to distinguish it from the Peking-based *guóyǔ*, which he considered an upper-class, bureaucratic form of Chinese not easily accessible to the masses. For similar reasons he also repudiated the *báihuà* literary language that emerged from the May Fourth Movement; the literary language, in his view, had to be purged of its *wényán* elements and brought into a much closer relationship with the spoken language, *pǔtōnghuà*.[5]

After the victory of the Chinese communists in 1949, the views espoused by Qú and his followers came into conflict with those of the proponents of *guóyǔ*. A series of meetings and a spirited press debate on language policy ensued. By 1955, a compromise was reached: the national language of China would officially be known as *pǔtōnghuà*, but *pǔtōnghuà* was defined as "the common language of China, based on the northern dialects, with the Peking phonological system as its norm of pronunciation". It would appear from this definition that proponents of *pǔtōnghuà* were conceded only the name of the new standard while the supporters of the older *guóyǔ* movement won on most matters of substance. Looked at today, it is indeed difficult to see any substantial differences between the goals of the promoters of *guóyǔ* in the 1930s and the goals of the present movement to promote *pǔtōnghuà*.

6.2 The problem of nomenclature

From the preceding section it is evident that the process of forming a standard language in China has been quite complex. One result of the process has been a proliferation of names for the Chinese language; since each of these names has particular historical nuances and sociolinguistic overtones, they will be examined in more detail in this section.

1. *guānhuà*. This term, now virtually obsolete, refers primarily to the common superdialectal lingua franca employed in imperial China. This "officials'" or "mandarins'" language was loosely based on the Peking dialect, but was spoken in numerous regional varieties, often no more than very slightly altered forms of regional dialects. No attempt was made to establish a norm for the pronunciation of *guānhuà*; it was a purely spontaneous development in response to the need to administer a large multilingual and multidialectal empire.

The English term "Mandarin" as a designation of the standard language, and as a term for the large dialect group to which the standard language belongs, is obviously merely a translation of *guānhuà*. In view of the fact that the Chinese now avoid this term in referring to the standard language, it is clearly inappropriate to retain the term "Mandarin" in English in this sense: one should rather use "Chinese" as the ordinary correct designation of the modern standard language; in contexts where this might be ambiguous, "Standard Chinese" should be employed. However, for lack of a better term, "Mandarin" may be retained as the name of the large dialect group to which such regional forms of Chinese as those of Peking, Xīān, Chéngdū and Nánjīng belong.

2. *báihuà*. The vernacular literary language as opposed to the Classical literary language, *wényán*. Such a vernacular-based form of written Chinese has been employed since Tang and Song times. Its use was originally limited to certain genres of popular literature; after the May Fourth Movement, it became the ordinary form of written Chinese. For all practical purposes it has now completely replaced literary Chinese.

Modern *báihuà* still contains a relatively strong *wényán* element; attempts to purge the modern written language of its literary components have not been entirely successful; although at the present time *wényán* influence on *báihuà* seems to be gradually diminishing, current *báihuà* is still by no means identical to the spoken standard.

3. *guóyǔ*. This term, as we have seen, replaced *guānhuà* as the name of the common national language in the early part of this century. *Guóyǔ* is the national language as opposed to foreign languages, non-Chinese languages within China, and non-standard dialects. In its codified form it is in effect a form of the Peking dialect, stripped of its more restricted localisms and enriched with a certain number of words and phrases from other dialects. The term has been abandoned in mainland China for reasons already alluded to, but it continues to be used as the name of the standard language in Táiwān.

4. *pǔtōnghuà*. This is the official name of the standard language in the People's Republic of China. Although originally *pǔtōnghuà* 'the common language' referred to a rather loosely defined and uncodified koine rather as the older term *guānhuà* did, it has since the mid-1950s been defined in such a way that it is difficult to see how it actually differs from *guóyǔ*, the designation which it replaced. Like *guóyǔ* before it, it is a standard language based on the dialect of Peking and serves as the official medium of schools and all other governmental organs.

5. *hànyǔ*. Literally 'the language of the Hans', that is, the ethnic Chinese. In practice, this term seems to be gaining currency at the expense of *pǔtōnghuà*. It is the usual term in all academic writing; Chinese linguists, for example, rarely use *pǔtōnghuà* when referring to the standard language. The standard monolingual dictionary currently in use is called the *Xiàndài hànyǔ cídiǎn* [*A modern Chinese (hànyǔ) dictionary*]; to use *pǔtōnghuà* in this context would sound awkward. From such academic usage, *hànyǔ* has now entered the spoken language, and it is not at all unusual to be asked, *nǐ huì shuō hànyǔ ma?* ('Do you speak Chinese?').

Strictly speaking, *hànyǔ* may refer to any variety of spoken or written Chinese, as in such terms as *gǔdài hànyǔ* 'Old Chinese', *hànyǔ fāngyán* 'Chinese dialect', etc., but it is more and more coming to be accepted as a way of referring to the standard national language. *Pǔtōnghuà* as a name for Standard Chinese is curiously inexplicit; in its literal sense it merely means 'common language', and lacks any specific reference to the Chinese either as an ethnic or as a cultural entity. If used as a term for distinguishing the standard form of the language from regional, nonstandard dialects, it has a certain utility; but as a general designation of Standard Chinese as opposed to other national languages it is too nebulous. For this reason, it is not surprising that an explicitly ethnic name like *hànyǔ* should gain currency at the expense of a purely functional designation like *pǔtōnghuà*.

6. *zhōngguohuà*. *Zhōngguohuà* (literally 'the language of China') is an old term which refers only to spoken forms of Chinese. It may be used of dialects as well as of the standard language. It is strongly colloquial in flavor, and is probably losing ground to more modern terms.

7. *zhōngwén*. This term, unlike the last, refers both to written and spoken forms of Chinese. The second element, *wén*, strictly means 'written language', but this term in everyday usage can refer to spoken language as well. Although *zhōngwén*

enjoys no official status as a name for the Chinese language, it has wide currency; indeed there are some contexts in which it is obligatory: as a modifier for
nouns referring to various forms of printed matter – books, newspapers, maga-
zines, pictorials, etc. – it is the only admissible form meaning 'Chinese'. For
example, to say anything other than *zhōngwén bào* for 'Chinese language newspaper' would be unacceptable to many speakers of Chinese.

6.3 Phonology of the standard language – preliminaries

The only aspect of the modern language that is strictly codified is its phonology.
According to the official definition of *pǔtōnghuà*, Peking pronunciation is standard. This means that, to describe the phonology of the standard language, all
one has to do is to describe the speech of an average native speaker of the Peking
dialect. This is not to say that Peking speech is absolutely uniform, but the
differences between speakers are so few and so minor as to be negligible. As a
general rule, speakers of *pǔtōnghuà* from other regions of China speak varieties
strongly colored by local speech habits, but this does not change the fact that the
only officially sanctioned pronunciation is that of Peking.

We have already indicated in Chapter 1 that Chinese is monosyllabic from a
morphemic point of view: almost every syllable corresponds to a morpheme.
There is a sense in which Chinese is also phonologically monosyllabic. In almost
all descriptions of Chinese, the syllable is taken as a kind of self-contained entity
which forms the basis of phonological description. It may be that this approach
is to some extent influenced by the writing system in which each unit represents a
single syllable, but other factors enter in as well. It would seem, for example, in
historical comparison that the syllable is the largest relevant unit; another important feature of Chinese dialects (and perhaps of other monosyllabic languages as
well) is that any one dialect contains a fixed number of possible syllables. Even
when new terms are borrowed from foreign languages, they are interpreted
in terms of the existing set of syllables: former president Nixon's name, for
example, was interpreted variously as *ní-kè-sōng*, *ní-kè-xùn*, and *ní-kè-sūn*. A
further consideration is that most phonological processes affect the syllable
without reference to its lower level constituents.

The basic insights of medieval phonologists into syllabic structure have continued to maintain their validity, despite recurrent attempts to reinterpret Chinese phonology in ways more in conformity with Western linguistic theories. In
the traditional scheme, it will be remembered, the syllable (which is the maximum relevant unit of phonological description) is divided into an initial, final
and tone. The initial is the consonantal onset to the syllable; in both medieval
and modern Chinese this always consists of a single consonant. The final is the

Table 6.1. Peking initials

	Unaspirated stops	Aspirated stops	Nasals	Fricatives	Voiced continuants
Labials	b [b̥]	p [p']	m [m]	f [f]	w [w]
Alveolars	d [d̥]	t [t']	n [n]		l [l]
Dental sibilants	z [ts]	c [ts']		s [s]	
Retroflexes	zh [tʂ]	ch [tʂ']		sh [ʂ]	r [ɻ]
Palatals	j [tɕ]	q [tɕ']		x [ɕ]	y [j]
Gutturals	g [g̊]	k [k']		h [χ]	ŋ [ʁ]

remainder of the syllable minus the tone; it may be further broken down into a medial, a main vowel and an ending; of these elements only the main vowel is obligatory. Tone, which pertains to the entire syllable, is primarily characterized by voice pitch, although other features like length, intensity and glottality may also play a role in its perception.

In the following sections we will examine the sound system of Standard Chinese, using as our point of departure the official *pīnyīn* spelling system now widely used for pedagogical purposes in the People's Republic of China and overseas.

6.4 The initials

Table 6.1 charts the twenty-four initials of the Peking dialect.[6]

1. *Manner of articulation.* Standard Chinese has a primary distinction of obstruents (stops, affricates and fricatives) and sonorants (nasals, laterals and semivowels). The obstruents are all voiceless, the sonorants all voiced; this pattern is found in a majority of Chinese dialects, only the dialects of the Wú group and a few Xiāng dialects being exceptions. The stops and affricates fall into two contrasting series, one unaspirated, the other aspirated. The unaspirated series (*b, d, z*, etc.) is lenis, and often gives the impression of being voiced to the untrained ear. The second series (*p, t, c*, etc.) is strongly aspirated.

2. *Place of articulation.* Of the labials, *b, p* and *m* are bilabials; *f* is a labiodental. The alveolar consonants (*d, t, n, l*) are articulated with the tip of the tongue against the front part of the alveolar ridge, in a slightly more advanced position than the corresponding English sounds. The dental sibilants (*z, c, s*) have a point of articulation somewhat forward of that for the alveolars: during their production the tip of the tongue is placed against the back of the upper teeth.

The retroflex sounds are pronounced with the front of the tongue retracted to a position just behind the alveolar ridge. Before unrounded vowels, Chinese retroflexes are pronounced with spread lips; this is contrary to the English speaker's habit of pronouncing *j*, *ch*, *sh* and *r* with slightly rounded lips even before unrounded vowels. Chinese *r* is sometimes described as the voiced counterpart of *sh* [ʂ]: [ʐ]. Such a description is, however, misleading; the Chinese *r* is pronounced with less friction than the comparable English fricative, and acoustically sounds much closer to the usual American pronunciation of *r*. Moreover, to consider *r* the voiced counterpart of *sh* would be tantamount to recognizing voicing as a distinctive feature in the phonological system of Chinese, a distinction which is otherwise unneeded.

Chinese palatals are articulated with the blade of the tongue placed against the front part of the palate; simultaneously the free front part of the tongue is raised toward the alveolar ridge. The English sounds *j* [ʤ], *ch* [tʃ] and *sh* [ʃ] fall somewhere between the Chinese retroflexes and the palatals, and the typical English-speaking student of Chinese has a difficult time learning to distinguish Chinese pairs like *shao* [ʂǎo], and *xiao* [ɕiǎo].

Following Chao (1968, 21), I use the term guttural to include the velars (*g* and *k*) and uvulars (*h* and ɢ); *g* and *k* are both produced by placing the back of the tongue against the soft palate; *h* is articulated farther back, in the region of the uvula. The zero initial has a number of possible articulations; a majority of Peking speakers employ a very weak voiced uvular fricative [ʁ]; this is particularly obvious when a syllable with this initial occurs after another syllable ending in a final nasal: in the expression *fān-àn* 'to reverse a verdict', there is no linkage or liaison between the final *n* of the first syllable and the beginning of the second, showing that *àn* does not have a purely vocalic onset.[7]

Many Chinese dialects have no distinction between the dental sibilants and the retroflex series of stops and fricatives. When speakers of such dialects learn the standard language, they almost always fail to distinguish the two series properly; average *pǔtōnghuà* speakers from such widely separated places as Shànghǎi, Fú-zhōu, Táiběi and Chéngdū will typically pronounce *shān* 'mountain' the same as *sān* 'three', *chí* 'slow' the same as *cí* 'word', *zhēng* 'to steam' the same as *Zēng* 'a surname', and so forth. The ability to distinguish the two series correctly has become one of the chief hallmarks of elegant standard pronunciation.

3. *Phonemic status of the palatals.* Most of the consonants described above contrast phonemically with one another. The palatals, however, are in complementary distribution with three different series: the dental sibilants, the retroflexes

Table 6.2. Peking finals

					pīnyīn						
(i)	e	a	ei	ai	ou	ao	en	an	eng	ang	er
i	ie	ia			iu	iao	in	ian	ing	iang	
u	(u)o	ua	ui	uai			un	uan	ong	uang	
ü	üe						ün	üan	iong		
					IPA						
ʐ/ɻ	ɣʌ	ʌ	ei	ae	oʊ	ɑo	ən	an	ʌŋ	ɑŋ	əɻ
i	iɛ<	iʌ			ioʊ	iɑo	in	iɛn	iɴ	iɑŋ	
u	uo	uʌ	ueɪ	uae			uən	uan	ɔɴ	uɑŋ	
y	yɛ<						yɪn	yan	yɔɴ		

and the velars. The latter three series never occur before high front vowels (*i* and *ü*), whereas the palatals are found only in this position. This has posed one of the classic problems of phonemic analysis. Hartman (1944) and Hockett (1947) interpreted the palatals as allophones of the dental sibilants before palatal semivowels; Martin (1957) considered the palatals to be allophones of the velar series of initials, an interpretation which Chao considers closest to the "feeling of the native" (1968, 21).

Most romanizations of Chinese which have been devised for English-speaking students have placed the palatals together with the retroflexes, presumably because the two series sound very close to the average speaker of English. The official *pīnyīn* system (as well as the older *zhùyīn fúhào* alphabet) retains the palatals as a separate series.

6.5 The finals

The elements making up the final are the medial, the main vowel and the syllabic ending; this analysis of the final has already been discussed in Chapter 2. The finals in *pīnyīn*, along with their values in IPA, are shown in Table 6.2.

Finals in the first row display a primary two-way contrast between a low *a*-like vowel and a closer mid vowel with a very wide range of allophonic variation. Generally speaking, main vowels have fronter values before final -*i* and -*n* and backer values before -*u* (or -*o* in *pīnyīn*) and -*ng*. In addition, the mid vowel becomes rounded in the immediate vicinity of labial elements. The high vowels *i*, *ü* and *u* occur both independently as finals (*di, jü, gu*, etc.) and as medials (*die, jüe, guo*).

Below we will comment on the pronunciation of each of the finals, attempting to give a rather detailed phonetic description of their various constituent elements.[8]

1. *i, ü, u.* In *pīnyīn, i* is used to represent three very different sounds. After the dental sibilants and retroflexes it represents a voiced syllabic prolongation of the initial; it represents a weak syllabic [ʐ] in the case of the sibilants, and it represents a weak syllabic retroflex continuant [ɻ] in the case of the retroflexes. From the point of view of acoustic phonetics, the retroflex variety of *i* shows up as a lower and somewhat more front vowel than the sibilant variety does (Howie 1976, 64). After all other initials, *i* represents a high front unrounded [i]. In Standard Chinese *i* never occurs after the guttural initials. The two rounded high vowels *ü* and *u* contrast only after *n* and *l*; otherwise *ü* occurs only with the palatals and *u* only with the remaining non-palatal initials. Because of this complementarity, the umlaut over *u* is generally omitted except after *n* and *l* as a matter of practical orthography: *xüe* is written *xue, yüan* as *yuan, jü* as *ju*, etc. The vowel *u* has a very high and very back articulation, giving it a very different auditory impression from the usual English pronunciation of *u* which is lower and more centralized; *ü* is a high front, strongly rounded vowel.

As can be seen from Table 6.2, *i, ü* and *u* all function as medials as well as main vowels; *i* and *u* (*o*) also appear as syllabic finals. As a medial, *i* has a very narrow value after labials and palatals, but a somewhat laxer and more open variant after the alveolar initials; compare *pian* [pʼiɛn] and *tian* [tʼɪɛn]. Medial *ü* and *u* are anticipated, and are to some degree articulated simultaneously with the initial.

2. *e, ie, uo, üe.* These four finals illustrate the three medials; in traditional terminology, finals lacking a medial are called *kāikǒu* 'open-mouth' finals; those having a medial *i* are called *qíchǐ* 'even-teeth' finals; those having medial *u* are designated *hékǒu* 'closed-mouth' finals; and those with *ü cuōkǒu* 'puckered-mouth' finals. As an independent final, *e* is a back unrounded vowel; it begins relatively high and then descends to a more open value: [ɣʌ]. After *i* and *ü, e* has a fronted articulation, but in comparison with the nuclear vowel of *ian* [iɛn], the vowel of these two finals is somewhat retracted, hence the transcriptions [iɛ<], and [y<]. The final *uo* is an example of the mid vowel becoming rounded in the vicinity of another labial element; toward the end of its articulation the [o] of this final becomes somewhat unrounded. In *pīnyīn* orthography, this final is written without the medial *u* after labial initials; thus, *bo* is written instead of *buo, fo* instead of *fuo*, etc. Nonetheless, it is still possible to hear a weak medial *u* between the initial and main vowel in these cases.

3. *a, ia, ua.* In all three of these finals, the value of the *a* is central, neither particularly fronted nor backed. Following Y. R. Chao we symbolize this quality with a small capital *a*: [ᴀ].

4. *ei, ui.* In the final *ei* the main vowel has a very close front allophone, [e]. The final written *ui* in *pīnyīn* is phonetically [ueɪ]; the *e* is more prominent in tones 3 and 4 than in tones 1 and 2; according to some linguists the [e] is also more prominent after guttural initials.

5. *ai, uai.* In these two finals *a* has a very fronted articulation, [a], or even [æ]. Formerly a final *iai* was recognized, but it is now considered obsolete.

6. *ou, iu.* The mid vowel phoneme is also realized as [o] in the final *ou* due to the influence of the labial ending; *iu* is phonetically [ioʊ]. It is similar to the final *ui* in that the vowel [o] is more prominent in tones 3 and 4 than in tones 1 and 2.

7. *ao, iao.* The *a* of these two finals is very back: [ɑ].

8. *en, in, un, ün.* The *e* in *en* is a mid, central unrounded vowel, the so-called neutral vowel *schwa.* The final *un* is phonetically [uən]; the [ə] is more prominent in the third and fourth tones than in the other two tones; it is reportedly also more prominent after the guttural initials. The vowel of the final *ün* often tends to become unrounded just before the final *n*: [yɪn]. After the close vowels *i, ü, u* and *e*, final nasals as a general rule are longer and articulated more forcefully than after low vowels (Lǐ Róng 1963, 33).

9. *an, ian, uan, üan.* In all these finals the *a* has a front articulation. In *ian* it falls between [æ] and [ɛ]; as pointed out above, the main vowel of *ian* is a genuine front vowel, and is not retracted toward the central region as in the case of the finals *ie* and *üe.*

10. *eng, ing, ong, iong.* The *e* of the final *eng* is pronounced farther back than the *e* in *en*: [ʌŋ]. In the speech of many Peking speakers the final *ng* in *ing* has a uvular articulation. The *o* in *ong* is not as low as that in the finals *uo* and *ou*: the medial of *iong* is actually rounded: [yoN]. On phonological grounds it would be better to identify the main vowel of these two finals with *u* rather than with the vowels of the finals *uo* and *ou* since, as we have seen, the vowels of these two finals belong to the mid vowel phoneme together with *e*.

11. *ang, iang, uang.* The *a* of *ang* and *uang* is very back: [ɑ]; in *iang* it is somewhat more central: [iʌŋ].

12. *er.* This final represents a retroflexed central vowel very similar to the *er* in the American English pronunciation of *berth.* The vowel quality is somewhat

higher in tones 1 and 2 ([əɹ]), than in tones 3 and 4 ([ɐɹ]), but in both cases the final is produced by a single tongue gesture with coarticulated retroflexion, which, for the sake of convenience, is symbolized by retroflex *r* following the vowel.

A few linguists recognize syllables ending in *m*; but the forms they cite occur only in fast speech and always have corresponding disyllabic variants: *tām ~ tāmen* 'they', *nèm ~ nèmma* 'in that way', *shém ~ shénma* 'what'.

From a phonemic point of view, Standard Chinese exhibits five vocalic contrasts: three high vowels (*i, ü, u*) and two non-high vowels (*e* and *a*). That these five vowels indeed contrast with one another can be shown by the following five minimally contrasting words: *lì* 'profit, benefit', *lǜ* 'green', *lù* 'road', *lè* 'happy', *là* 'pungent, hot'. (The *pīnyīn* finals (*u*)*o*, *ui*, *ou*, and *iu* are better interpreted phonologically as *ue*, *uei*, *eu* and *ieu* respectively; the finals *ong* and *iong*, as we have indicated, can be reinterpreted as *ung* and *iung*, thus eliminating the apparent contrast between *o* and *e* in certain finals.) Numerous attempts to deny vocalic status to the high vowels have been made (Hartman 1944; Hockett 1947; Martin 1957); in these analyses the high vowels are viewed as semivowels which join with the simple initials to form complex syllabic onsets. The actual vowels one hears, then, are interpreted as syllabic prolongations of these complex initials: for example, a syllable like *pi* is analyzed as a complex initial sequence /*pj*/ followed by a non-distinctive vocalization; similarly, the sibilant and retroflex vowels are interpreted as syllabic prolongations of the sibilant and retroflex initials respectively. In analyses of this kind, tone is considered to be the basic determinant of syllabicity, and vowels are not an essential component of syllables. It is not entirely clear what the advantages of this 'two-vowel' approach are, especially in view of the fact that how one interprets medials phonologically appears to have no effect on further phonological processes in the language. It must also be admitted that this sort of manipulation of syllabic elements does a certain violence to the phonetic facts.

In addition to the primary set of finals discussed above, Standard Chinese also possesses a series of so-called "rhotacized" (*ér-huà*) finals; morphemically these finals consist of one of the primary finals followed by the subsyllabic suffix -*r* (see section 7.3). The effects of this process are several: (1) the syllabic endings *i* and *n* are dropped, (2) front vowels become centralized, and (3) final *ng* fuses with *r* to form a nasalized retroflexed vowel. All the finals affected by these changes are listed below, along with the resulting rhotacized forms of *pīnyīn*.

Finals in *pīnyīn*	Finals in IPA
air anr	ʌɹ
ianr	iʌɹ
uair uanr	uʌɹ
üanr	yʌɹ
eir enr ir (after dentals and retroflexes)	əɹ
inr ir (after other initials)	iəɹ
uir unr	uəɹ
ür ünr	yəɹ
angr	ɑ̃ɹ
iangr	iɑ̃ɹ
uangr	uɑ̃ɹ
engr	ə̃ɹ
ingr	iə̃ɹ
ongr	uə̃ɹ
iongr	yə̃ɹ

One of the hotly debated questions of language policy is to what extent rhotacization should be adopted as a feature of the standard language. Many nonnortherners are unable to pronounce such forms correctly and avoid the -*r* suffix as much as possible, even in those cases where it serves to distinguish different grammatical categories: for *huà huàr* 'to paint a picture' many southerners will say *huà huà*. It would appear that for a long time to come the use or non-use of this suffix will serve to distinguish Peking speakers from others, or at least to distinguish northerners from southerners.

6.6 Tones

In addition to an initial and a final, every Chinese word (at least when it is pronounced in isolation) has a tone. The tones of Chinese words are every bit as important as the initials and finals; to mispronounce a tone is analogous to mispronouncing a consonant or vowel in English.

Tones are perceived principally as differences in pitch, although intensity and duration also provide important secondary auditory cues for the identification of discrete tones. In describing tones, pitch is used in a purely relative sense; actual pitch is determined by many variables such as sex, age, individual voice differences and even emotional state.

In 1930 Y. R. Chao introduced a very convenient and accurate method of describing the pitch of tones in Chinese. In his system, pitch is plotted on a vertical scale which represents the normal voice range of a speaker; the scale is divided into five points, on which 1 is the lowest point and 5 the highest; 3 is mid pitch, 4 half-high, and 2 half-low. A tone can be described by indicating its beginning and ending point; in a few cases where tones have concave (falling–rising) or convex (rising–falling) contour it is necessary to give one intermediate point as well. The following examples will illustrate how the system works.

[44] a level tone beginning at the half-high level and continuing at the same pitch throughout

[35] a rising tone beginning at the mid point of person's normal speaking range and rising to its upper limit

[52] a falling tone beginning at the upper limit of one's normal range and falling to a point just short of its lower limit

[242] a convex tone, first rising from the half-low point to the half-high point and then falling back to its original starting point

[313] a concave tone, falling first from mid to low pitch and then rising back to its original starting point

Chao's system of tonal notation can be used to draw "tone letters" or simple graphs of tonal contours: [55] for example can be represented by the graph ⌐, [51] would be ⌐, etc. For reasons of convenience we will only use the numerical notation in the remainder of this book.

Tones are usually described in their isolation forms. In many cases these isolation forms are for all practical purposes identical to the values that tones have when preceded and followed by other syllables, but in other cases the contextual variants of tones can be very different. When speaking about such contextual variants, two different situations should be distinguished. The changes that take place may be no more than phonetic variants or allophones of the tone in question; in other cases, the new shape that a tone assumes in a given context may actually coincide with the value of another distinct tone in the same context. The first case can be referred to as phonetic sandhi and the second as phonemic sandhi. In the description of the four tones of Standard Chinese given below both types will be encountered.

The four tones of Standard Chinese are not the same as the four Classical tones (*píng*, *shǎng*, *qù* and *rù*) described in Chapter 2. Because of numerous splits and mergers of the Classical categories, the tonal systems of very few modern dialects show a straightforward one-to-one relationship to the categories found in the *Qièyùn*. This problem will be discussed more fully in Chapters 8 and 9.

The phonetic make-up of the four tones of the standard language can be described as follows:[9]

1. The first tone is high level. It is relatively constant in its intensity (loudness) and somewhat longer than tones 2 and 4, but shorter than tone 3. In Chao's notation it is [55]. Examples: *gē* 'song', *tīng* 'listen', *dōng* 'east'.

2. The second tone is high rising. It begins in about the middle of the speaker's normal speaking range and rises abruptly to the top of his range. It tends to rise in intensity toward the end and is short in duration. It can be represented as [35] on the tonal scale. Examples: *ná* 'hold in the hand', *jiáo* 'chew', *líng* 'zero'.

3. The third tone has two basic variants. When it is pronounced in isolation, it begins low, falls to the very bottom limit of the voice and then rises to a half-high level. It loses intensity after its inception but shows a small rise toward the very end; it is the longest of the tones in duration. It is generally described as [214] on the tonal scale. Examples of the third tone: *mǎi* 'buy', *mǎ* 'horse', *dǒng* 'understand'.

When the third tone occurs before any tone except another third tone, it becomes what is commonly known as a "half third"; that is, it loses its final rise and remains low throughout: [21]. It should be pointed out here that the half third is in fact the more common variant of the third tone, since the isolation form occurs only when a word is uttered alone or when it occurs at the end of a phrase, clause or sentence. The examination of virtually any text written in the modern language will confirm this.

When the third tone occurs before another third tone syllable, it changes to a second tone. Charles Hockett (1947) considered this so-called "raised third" tone a separate tonal phoneme, but subsequent perceptual tests done by Dreher and Lee (1966) and Wang and Li (1967) established that native speakers are unable to make a consistent distinction between second tones and raised third tones. Since pairs like *mái mǎ* 'bury a horse' and *mǎi mǎ* 'buy a horse' cannot be distinguished by native Peking speakers when they hear them, the raised third tone before another third tone must be considered a case of morphophonemic tone sandhi, and not just a phonetic variant or allophone.

4. The fourth tone is high falling. It begins at the top of the speaker's pitch range and falls abruptly to the bottom limit of his voice. The fourth tone diminishes in intensity toward the end, and is the shortest of the four tones in duration. Its value on the tonal scale is [51]. Examples: *liù* 'six', *nèn* 'tender', *qù* 'go'.

In addition to the cases of tone sandhi mentioned in conjunction with the third tone above, one other minor case should be mentioned. In a three-syllable combination, if the second syllable is a second tone (either an original second tone or a raised third) and the first syllable is either a first or second tone, the middle syllable changes to a first tone in rapid speech. In slow speech, or if the final syllable is atonic, this rule does not apply: *liánhéguó* 'United Nations' is pronounced *liánhēguó*, and *tā mǎi mǎ* 'he buys a horse' becomes *tā māi mǎ*.

6.7   Stress and intonation

Some people assume that because Chinese is a tone language it cannot have the sort of intonational patterns found, for example, in English. They apparently think that pitch cannot function at the lexical level (tone) and at the syntactic level (intonation) at the same time. But this is not so. In fact, in addition to tone, Standard Chinese possesses both stress and intonation.

In the most widely accepted analysis of stress, three degrees are recognized (Chao 1968, 35): normal, weak and contrastive. Normal stress is characterized by the presence of a perceptible tonal contour, but it lacks the exaggerated duration and intensity of syllables carrying contrastive stress. In a sequence of syllables all having normal stress, the strongest phonetic stress falls on the last syllable, the second strongest on the first syllable and the weakest on the intervening syllables. These varying degrees of normal stress are completely predictable, and can hence be considered allophones of a single stress phoneme.

Contrastive stress has a wider pitch range and greater intensity than normal stress and can occur anywhere in a sequence of syllables. For example, in the phrase *yǔyán yánjiūsuǒ* 'linguistics institute' the normal pattern would require the strongest stress to fall on *suǒ*, the last syllable, the second strongest stress on *yǔ*, the first syllable, and so on. If contrastive stress is placed on *yǔ*, however, the normal pattern is displaced and the strongest stress is shifted to *yǔ*.

Weakly stressed syllables (*qīngshēngzì*) are variously known as neutral tones, atonic syllables or weak syllables. The term "neutral tone" implies that weakly stressed syllables are a kind of "fifth tone". From both a synchronic and a diachronic perspective, this is misleading. Unlike the four basic tones, weakly stressed syllables cannot be pronounced in isolation; when an element which normally has weak stress is cited in isolation, as for example when a teacher of grammar discusses a certain particle like *le* or *ba*, it must be supplied with a tone (usually a first tone). Moreover, the phonetic value of a weakly stressed syllable is determined almost entirely by the tone of the preceding syllable. Historically, such syllables may come from any of the Middle Chinese tones, and even synchronically they can usually be connected with tonic morphemes which occur in other combinations.

Weak syllables are very short in duration and have a very reduced tone range;

the pitch of such syllables is determined by the preceding tone: it is half-low after the first tone, mid pitch after a second tone, half-high after a third tone, low after a fourth tone. In two-syllable combinations followed by a pause the contour is slightly falling, but other contours may occur in more complex tonal environments. Weakly stressed syllables are also characterized by a number of other phonetic features. The unaspirated consonants, which are voiceless when they occur in syllables with normal or contrastive stress, become fully voiced in weakened position. In rapid speech the following reductions may take place: the retroflex affricates and fricatives may become *r* and the corresponding palatals may become *y*; vowels tend to become centralized even to the point of losing the primary phonological distinction between *e* and *a*; vowels after *f*, *c*, *s*, *ch* and *sh* tend to become voiceless after a fourth tone.

Weak stress is an essential feature of the standard language, and of most northern dialects, but because its occurrence is lexically determined it is difficult for non-Peking speakers to master. Speakers of *pǔtōnghuà* from many regions in South China, however, employ only a very small number of weakly stressed syllables, and these are chiefly limited to grammatical suffixes and particles. Speakers of the Peking dialect are frequently able to detect non-native speakers of their dialect by their improper use of weak stress, even when other aspects of the outsider's pronunciation are correct.

Chinese intonation can be thought of as a band which represents the scale on which the tones are plotted, but which can itself rise and fall. When the intonational band rises, for example, then the pitch of a given tone will rise in absolute terms, but its relative relation to other syllables in the phrase or clause will remain constant. The intonation of ordinary statements, for example, falls slightly toward the end (this is especially noticeable in long sentences). As a result of this, a first tone at the beginning of a statement will be pronounced somewhat higher than one near the end. Unmarked questions and questions ending in the interrogative particle *ma* have an overall higher pitch than simple statements. Chao (1968, 40–4) has described a number of other intonational patterns for Standard Chinese, but we still lack a detailed and comprehensive study of this subject.

6.8 Morphophonemics

We have already described several morphophonemic alternations in connection with the process of -*r* suffixation and tone sandhi. These cases are all strictly phonological processes; that is, the changes described take place whenever those particular phonological categories are present in the relevant environments. There are other cases of morphophonemic alternation which affect only certain morphemes, and hence cannot be viewed as general phonological rules. We will examine a few of these cases below.

In section 6.6 the sandhi behavior of the third tone was described. The change to a second tone which occurs before another third tone is automatic irrespective of what morpheme is involved; it ordinarily takes place even when the second syllable has weak stress: *xiáojie* (*xiǎo + jiě*) 'young lady, miss', *zóuzou* (*zǒu + zǒu*) 'take a walk'.[10] In a few such combinations (mostly kinship terms or terms of endearment), the expected shift does not occur: *bǎobao* (*bǎo + bǎo*) 'little precious' – term of endearment for babies, *jiějie* (*jiě + jiě*) 'elder sister', *shěnshen* (*shěn + shěn*) 'aunt – wife of father's younger brother', etc. Since such forms depart from the regular pattern of tonal change, they must be learned individually by the student of Chinese or listed as exceptions by the grammarian.

There are also a few isolated cases in which particular morphemes exhibit tone sandhi alternations which cannot be subsumed under regular phonological rules. The two morphemes *yī* 'one' and *bù* 'not' both undergo the same set of tonal changes: before tones 1, 2 and 3 they are pronounced in the fourth tone; before a following fourth tone they are pronounced in the second tone. Examples: *yìzhāng* 'one sheet', *bùnán* 'not difficult', *bùhǎo* 'not good', *yícùn* 'one inch', *búqù* 'not go'. The numerals *qī* and *bā* can optionally change to a second tone before a following fourth-tone syllable: *qīwàn* (or *qíwàn*) '70,000', *báhào* (or *bāhào*) 'the eighth day of the month'.

Somewhat different are cases where a particular morpheme shows tonal changes only in certain words. The bound morpheme for 'bone' when pronounced in isolation is *gǔ*, as it is in many compounds such as *jizhūigǔ* 'spine', but in the ordinary word for 'bone' which is formed with the noun suffix -*tou* it has a second tone: *gútou*. Even more complicated is the morpheme for 'finger': in the ordinary word for 'finger' (also formed with the suffix -*tou*) it has a second tone, *zhítou*, but in *zhījia* 'fingernail' it has a first tone. Its etymological third tone appears in a number of words such as *dàmuzhǐ* 'thumb' and *shízhǐ* 'index finger'. Tonal behavior of this sort is sporadic and, fortunately for the foreign learner of Chinese, rather rare.

Chao (1968, 45) has pointed out that several particles, *a*, *e* and *ou*, unlike other words which begin with vowels in the better-known transcription systems, lack the weak voiced uvular fricative onset usually associated with such words. An important result of this is that with these particles the syllabic ending of a preceding syllable can be elided; this gives rise to a number of different allomorphs for each of these particles; in the case of *a*, these allomorphs (*a*, *ya*, *wa*, *na*) are provided with different characters; these alternations can be observed in the following example:

kuài dianr lái ya   'Come quickly'
nín hǎo wa?   'How are you?'
nàr yǒu rén na?   'Is there someone there?'

In comparison with a majority of the world's languages, morphophonemic alternation plays a minor role in most Chinese dialects. Where it does occur, it is most common in the form of tone sandhi. This is perhaps a result of the generally autonomous nature of the syllable in all historical stages of Chinese.[11]

Further reading

Chao, Yuen Ren 1948. *Mandarin primer*. Cambridge: Harvard University Press. [This book contains a splendid introduction containing useful information on most of the matters touched upon in this chapter and in the next.]

De Francis, John 1953. *Nationalism and language reform in China*. Princeton: Princeton University Press. [A useful introduction to the early history of language reform and language policy in China.]

Kratochvil, Paul 1968. *The Chinese language today: features of an emerging standard.* London: Hutchinson. [An informative general introduction to the modern standard language.]

Sofronov, M. V. 1979. *Kitajskij jazyk i kitajskoe obščestvo*. Moscow: Nauka. [A detailed and up-to-date treatment of language policy and sociolinguistic problems in modern China.]

7

The modern standard language II

7.1 The study of grammar in China

As we have seen, China has a very rich tradition of phonological study; the study of grammar, on the other hand, is a rather recent development. Although one can find observations concerning grammar in traditional philological works, the systematic study of this subject did not begin until the late nineteenth century. Mǎ Jiànzhōng (1845–1900) was the first person to write a systematic grammar of Chinese, the *Mǎ shì wéntōng*; his book, modeled on Western classical grammar, was concerned with the Classical written language which in the late nineteenth century was still the most common form of written Chinese. Mǎ's work was very important in the further development of Chinese grammar, and its influence can be seen in much of the grammatical work up until the 1940s.

In the late 1930s a reaction set in against the sort of imitative grammar that the *Mǎ shì wéntōng* represented. Led by Chén Wàngdào (1890–1977), a group of Chinese linguists and scholars began to advocate the establishment of a new grammatical framework that would better reflect the basic nature of the Chinese language. These men were all influenced to one degree or another by Western linguists such as de Saussure, Jespersen and Bloomfield. A lively debate was carried on in a number of journals concerning such problems as form classes (parts of speech), the peculiarities of Chinese grammar, the differences between *báihuà* and *wényán*, word order, and the establishment of formal categories in grammar. The result of this debate was to free Chinese grammar from the classical Western model and set it on a course of its own (Lǚ Bìsōng 1980).

The 1940s saw the publication of two important grammars, both influenced by the debate described above. Lǚ Shūxiāng's *Zhōngguó wénfǎ yàolüè* [*Sketch of Chinese grammar*] and Wáng Lì's *Zhōngguó xiàndài yǔfǎ* [*Modern Chinese grammar*] both drew on the ideas of Western linguists like Jespersen and Bloomfield and attempted to describe Chinese grammatical structure in such a way as to bring out its individuality. Lǚ's book treated both the vernacular and literary languages, since at that time both forms of the language were still routinely taught in schools. Wáng's grammar was a grammar of the vernacular language, his examples mostly being taken from early vernacular novels, especially the *Hónglóu mèng*. Both works played an important role in putting Chinese grammatical studies on a new course.

Yuen Ren Chao's *Mandarin primer* was published in 1948 as a textbook for American students learning Chinese. Chao's grammatical approach was that of the American structuralist school founded by Leonard Bloomfield. The introductory grammatical sketch of this book was translated into Chinese under the title *Běijīng kǒuyǔ yǔfǎ* [*Grammar of the Peking colloquial language*] by Lǐ Róng in 1952. This short translation had a tremendous impact in China; it effectively introduced the methodology of structuralism to a wide Chinese audience, and its interpretations were eagerly adopted by the more innovative linguists of that time. Its influence is especially evident in *Xiàndài hànyǔ yǔfǎ jiǎnghuà* [*Introduction to modern Chinese grammar*] edited by Dīng Shēngshù and a group of associated linguists. This book, which originated as a series of articles in the journal *Zhōngguó yǔwén*, is widely regarded as one of the outstanding works on grammar produced in China; it helped give the ideas of structuralism even wider currency.

Twenty years after the publication of the *Mandarin primer*, Yuen Ren Chao's *A grammar of spoken Chinese* came out. This monumental work was the first really comprehensive reference grammar of Chinese written in English. It sums up the results of more than twenty years of both Chinese and Western writing on Chinese grammar, much of which was either directly or indirectly inspired by Chao's own earlier work (Xú and Yè 1979, 170). A Chinese translation of Chao's grammar by Lǚ Shūxiāng was published in Peking in 1980 (Lǚ Shūxiāng 1980a).

By the late 1960s American structuralism had largely yielded its place to a new movement, transformational generative grammar. On the eve of the Cultural Revolution in China (1966–76), the first samplings of the ideas of this new school appeared in articles by Zhū Déxī and Lǚ Shūxiāng in *Zhōngguó yǔwén*, but subsequent events effectively choked off any further developments in this area (Xú and Yè 1979, 172). A rich literature on Chinese grammar written from the point of view of transformational and post-structuralist grammar has appeared in the last twenty years in the United States (much of it published in the *Journal of Chinese Linguistics*).[1] These studies have yet to influence grammarians in China to any great degree, although there are signs of a burgeoning interest in the new linguistics; only the future will tell whether these ideas will take root or not.

In the following sections we will attempt to give a basic outline of Chinese grammar, hoping in the process to give some idea of how Chinese "works." The point of view is by and large that of the structuralist school which prevailed in the 1950s and 1960s; these are views which still hold sway in China, and they are available in several definitive syntheses, especially Chao's 1968 grammar. The intent is not to reject or deprecate more recent writing; it is merely that most post-structuralist analyses are still at a preliminary or even experimental stage and it would be well-nigh impossible to present these ideas in an organized and coherent manner in the space allotted.

7.2 The morpheme

The morpheme is at once the smallest meaningful unit in a language and the smallest relevant unit in grammatical analysis. In both Classical and Modern Chinese, the great majority of morphemes coincide phonologically with a monosyllable; stated conversely, almost every syllable can be analyzed as an independent morpheme. Since the basic graphic unit, the character (*zì*), is also monosyllabic, it is clear that the overwhelming majority of characters represent single morphemes. Classical and Modern Chinese differ, in that polysyllabic words were much rarer in the Classical language than they are in the modern language.

Modern Chinese, as can be seen from any good dictionary, contains thousands of disyllabic and trisyllabic words; in almost all cases, however, such words can be analyzed as strings of monosyllabic morphemes. Although a considerable number of polysyllabic morphemes can be found, they are probably not significantly more numerous than those found in Classical Chinese. Examples of such polysyllabic morphemes in Modern Chinese are the following: *bòhe* 'mint', *zhānglàng* 'cockroach', *dīle* 'to carry hanging at one's side', *hàshimǎ* 'a kind of Manchurian frog used in Chinese medicine'. The only subsyllabic morpheme is the nominal suffix -*r*, which will be discussed below.

Looked at from the point of view of their propensity to combine with other morphemes, morphemes can be divided into several types; those that can be uttered independently are *free*; morphemes which always occur in conjunction with another morpheme are *bound*. This is not an absolute dichotomy, since morphemes may be bound in one context and free in another; a morpheme is considered free if it is free in any context and bound only if it is bound in all contexts; thus, *gǒu* 'dog' is free, although it is bound in certain compounds like *mǔgǒu* 'bitch' and *gǒuxióng* 'dog-bear, i.e. small bear'; *hóu* 'monkey', on the other hand, is always bound – *hóuzi* 'monkey', *hóuxì* 'a monkey act', etc.

Morphemes can also be characterized by the degree of versatility with which they occur with other morphemes; they are considered *versatile* if they enter into combination with relative ease and *restricted* if they occur only in a very small number of contexts. Bound morphemes are mostly, but not always, restricted;

likewise free morphemes are typically versatile. Chao (1968) cites the verb *mián* 'to sleep, used only of silkworms only at a certain point in their development' as an example of a free but highly restricted morpheme. There are quite a number of bound versatile morphemes, including the demonstratives *zhè* 'this' and *nà* 'that', the ordinal prefix *dì*, the nominal suffix *zi* and the localizing suffix *li*.

7.3 The word

In the Chinese writing system, morphemes (characters) are strung together one after another without any indication of word boundaries; the reader supplies the necessary boundaries as he reads along. Although it is fairly easy to identify words intuitively in Chinese, it is much more difficult to define the concept rigorously. Perhaps the difficulty is particularly evident in Chinese because the word is not a unit in the writing system, and it is not so easy to take it for granted as it is in most writing systems. In their *Xiàndài hànyǔ yǔfǎ jiǎnghuà*, Dīng Shēngshù and his coauthors define a word (*cí*) as a unit "which has a specific meaning and can be used freely." While this definition may not please everyone, especially traditional structuralists who try to avoid using meaning as a criterion in linguistic definitions, it can stand as an expression of the intuitive criteria that most native speakers use when asked to make word divisions. For a detailed discussion of the manifold difficulties encountered in defining the concept of word in Chinese, the reader is referred to Chao's extended discussion of the question (1968, 136–93).

At its simplest, a word consists of a single morpheme: *rén* 'human being', *chī* 'eat', *wǒ* 'I, me', *hěn* 'very', *zhòng* 'heavy', *gēn* 'and', *yōu!* interjection of surprise, *hāla* 'rancid', *jiēba* 'to stutter'. This class of words is very large and contains many of the most basic elements of the lexicon. Another large class of words consists of a simple morpheme plus a word-formative suffix. Two common noun suffixes of this type are -*zi* and -*r*. The first of these has no function but to form nouns, generally from a bound morpheme; it is highly versatile: *bízi* 'nose', *zhuōzi* 'table', *lúzi* 'stove', *mánzi* 'barbarian', *lǐngzi* 'collar', etc. The suffix -*r* is also a noun formative, but unlike -*zi* it frequently conveys a sense that the object it is attached to is something everyday and familiar; in some cases it may carry either a diminutive or a slightly pejorative overtone: *xìngr* 'apricot', *lǐr* 'lining', *huàr* 'picture', *zǐr* 'seed', *qiúr* 'globule, small ball' (cf. *qiú* 'ball'), *guānr* '(petty) official'. The -*r* suffix is found with only a very few verbs, mostly of a very colloquial nature, the only one in common use being *wánr* 'to play'. A much more restricted noun-formant suffix is -*tou*: *mùtou* 'wood', *shítou* 'stone', *gútou* 'bone'.

A few words seem to be formed by a process of tonal change: *mǎi* 'to buy' and *mài* 'to sell'; *dīngzi* 'nail' and *dìng* 'to nail'; *liáng* 'to measure' and *liàng* 'quantity'. This process is limited to just a few pairs of this sort, and is now totally unproductive.

A few quasi-prefixes exist: the *lǎo-* in *lǎohǔ* 'tiger', *lǎoshǔ* 'mouse, rat', *lǎoyīng* 'hawk', and *lǎogua* 'crow' denotes a sort of respectful familiarity towards harmful creatures. Ordinal numbers are formed with the prefix *dì-*: *dìsān* 'third', *dìliù* 'sixth'.

Reduplication is used to form words of several types. Kinship terms account for a large number of reduplicates: *bàba* 'father', *lǎolao* 'maternal grandmother', *gēge* 'older brother'. Reduplicated forms are found among other classes of nouns and parts of speech as well: *xīngxing* 'ape', *rénrén* 'everybody', *yǎngyang* 'itches', *chángcháng* 'often'. Reduplication also has a number of grammatical functions; a reduplicated measure has the sense of 'every': *běnběn* 'every volume'. Reduplicated verbs form what Chao calls a 'tentative' aspect, which has several different nuances depending on the particular verb: *zuòzuo* 'sit for a while', *kànkan* 'take a look' from *zuò* 'to sit' and *kàn* 'to look'.

By far the greatest number of words in the dictionary are compounds. A compound consists of at least two morphemes neither of which is an affix; *zhuōzi* 'table' is not a compound because it is composed of a root morpheme plus a suffix, but *zhuōbù* 'tablecloth' is a compound because it is made up of two root morphemes. Compounding is the most productive process of word formation in the modern language; new terminology, especially that of a technical or scientific nature, is almost all formed in this way. Some of the elements in modern compounds recur so frequently that they have virtually attained the status of affixes; an example of this is *xué* (literally 'learning') which is used to translate *-logy* in such words as *xīnlǐxué* 'psychology', *dìzhìxué* 'geology' and *shēngwùxué* 'biology'.

The analysis and classification of compounds is a very complex study. Lù Zhìwěi (1964) and Yuen Ren Chao (1968) have made very detailed studies of the different types of compounds. Lù and Chao found that all the syntactic relationships found in phrases and sentences – subject–predicate, coordination, attribute–head (subordination), verb–object, and verb–complement – are all found in compounds as well. In the absence of any well-defined phonological criteria for distinguishing words from phrases, this has made it difficult to draw a hard and fast boundary between morphology and syntax in Chinese. This question has undoubtedly been one of the most vexed problems in modern Chinese grammar, but it is also one of its most urgent tasks because of its practical implications, particularly the alphabeticization of Chinese, which has a direct bearing on such pragmatic issues as language reform, the teaching of Chinese in elementary and middle schools, and lexicography.

7.4 Word classes

Traditional Chinese philologists divided words into 'full words' (*shící*) and 'empty words' (*xūcí*). Full words are those that have a concrete meaning and empty words are words which have more abstract meanings and are for the most part employed to show grammatical relationships; the distinction is similar to that drawn by some modern linguists between content and function words. Mǎ Jiànzhōng was the first Chinese scholar to apply the Western notion of word classes (parts of speech) to Chinese in a systematic way. Since that time, the problem of word classes has been a central concern of Chinese linguists. Mǎ simply borrowed the categories of Western classical grammar and adapted them to his Chinese material. Later linguists attempted to define Chinese word classes on the basis of their syntactic behavior, leaving aside semantic considerations as much as possible. Although the results of this procedure have differed with the analytic criteria employed, there is a fairly high degree of agreement, at least as regards the major classes. The scheme outlined below is close to that found in several widely used grammars.

Full words fall into six classes: nouns, verbs, adjectives, numerals, measures and pronouns. A noun (*míngcí*) is a word that can be modified by a demonstrative-measure compound: *shū* 'book' can follow *zhè-běn* 'this (volume)', hence it is a noun. A verb (*dòngcí*) is a word that can immediately be negated by *bù* 'not' and can be followed by a set of typically verbal suffixes like *-le* 'suffix for perfect aspect', and *-zhe* 'suffix for durative aspect'. Adjectives (*xíngróngcí*) are generally considered to be a species of verb (Chao calls them intransitive verbs of state) since they can be negated by *bù* and can function independently as predicates; the difference between adjectives and verbs proper is that adjectives can be modified by *hěn* 'very' and verbs proper cannot.

Numerals (*shùcí*) are bound morphemes which express quantity; they are ordinarily followed by a measure (*liàngcí*); measures are bound morphemes that follow either numerals or demonstratives (*zhǐshì dàicí*). Numerals and demonstratives must be followed by an appropriate measure before they modify a noun: *yí-ge rén* 'one MEASURE man', *nà-liàng chē* 'that MEASURE car', etc.

Pronouns are deictic words, that is, words which point to persons or things in the speaking situation; syntactically they generally behave like nouns, but unlike nouns they normally do not admit of modification. The personal pronouns are shown in Table 7.1.

The third-person pronoun distinguishes gender in the written language where separate graphs have artificially been devised for 'he', 'she' and 'it'; in the spoken language all three forms have the same pronunciation. The inclusive–exclusive distinction is found in many northern dialects, in most Mǐn dialects and in a

Table 7.1. Personal pronouns

wǒ	'I, me'	wǒmen	'we' (exclusive), 'us'
		zánmen	'we' (inclusive), 'us'
nǐ	'you' (plain)	nǐmen	'you' (plural)
nín	'you' (polite)		
tā	'he, she, it'	tāmen	'they, them'
	'him, her'		

number of Wú dialects, but is uncommon elsewhere. Even in the standard language *wǒmen* not infrequently replaces *zánmen*, and functions as both an exclusive and inclusive pronoun. The demonstrative pronouns are *zhè* (*zhèi*) 'this' and *nà* (*nèi*) 'that'; they are usually found joined to a measure in both their pronominal and their adjectival uses. Other words commonly included among the pronouns are *shénme* 'what?', *nǎ* (*něi*) 'which one?', *zìjǐ* 'oneself' and *měi* 'each'.

The empty word classes are adverbs, prepositions, conjunctions, particles, interjections and onomatopoeia. Adverbs (*fùcí*) modify verbs and adjectives and are usually bound: *zhǐ* 'only', *jiànjiàn* 'gradually', *hěn* 'very', *zùi* 'most'. Chinese grammarians generally include the negatives *bù*, *méi* and *bié* among the adverbs on the basis of their syntactic behavior. Adverbial modifiers derived from full words are distinguished from adverbs proper as 'adverbial adjuncts' (*zhuàngcí*); such forms are frequently followed by the adverbial suffix *-de*: *mànmānrde* 'slowly', derived from *màn* 'slow'.

Chinese prepositions (*jiècí*) originate from verbs, and are used to show various grammatical relationships which will be touched upon below. Conjunctions (*liáncí*) comprise various connectives: *hé* 'and', *érqiě* 'moreover', *suóyi* 'therefore'.

Particles (*zhùcí*) are a group of generally monosyllabic, atonal forms used to show a number of different grammatical relationships or subjective and modal overtones; Chinese grammarians include verbal and noun suffixes in this class. Examples of particles are *de* 'subordinative particle', *ma* 'sentential interrogative particle', *a* 'vocative particle' and *ba* 'advisative particle'.

Interjections (*tàncí*) are asyntactic forms used to express warnings, call others' attention, or give verbal expression to some emotional state. Phonologically they reveal certain irregularities in having elements which are not a part of the normal phonemic inventory, like a voiced [ɦ] and a front central vowel *ê* [ɛ]. Examples: *ɦa* 'huh?', *ê* [ɛ] 'hey you!'. Onomatopoeic words (*xiàngshēngcí*) are words that imitate sounds of the natural world; syntactically they may be nominal or adverbial adjuncts: *huālā* 'the sound of rain falling', *gūlōng* 'the sound of thunder or a large vehicle moving along'.

As in English, there is considerable class overlap in Chinese: *li* can be either a noun 'plow' or a verb 'to plow'. A high proportion of modern disyllabic verbs can also do service as nouns: *pīpíng* 'criticize, criticism', *zŭzhī* 'organize, organization'. This sort of class overlap was much more common in the Classical language than it is now. Modern Chinese, in fact, probably has no more such cases than does English.

7.5 Expression of grammatical categories

Chinese possesses very little of what was traditionally known as inflectional morphology; affixes therefore play only a minor role in the expression of grammatical relationships. Word order, particles and prepositions carry most of the burden of showing how the elements of a sentence relate to one another. In this section, rather than examining the function of each of these devices, I will examine a number of universally recognized grammatical categories and see how they are expressed in Chinese.

1. *Number.* Number is obligatorily expressed only for the pronouns. The same plural suffix found in the pronouns, *-men*, can also be employed with nouns referring to human beings; however, the resulting forms differ from English plural nouns in several ways. They are not used with numerals; they are not obligatory in any context; and they tend to refer to groups of people taken collectively. Examples: *háizimen'* '(a certain group of) children', *lǎoshīmen* 'the teachers'. Although number is only rarely indicated morphologically, it is shown in other ways when necessary; for example, demonstratives are shown to be plural by use of the plural measure *-xiē*: *nàxiē rén* 'those people'. A plural subject or object can be indicated by the use of the adverb *dōu*, usually translated 'all', but often no more than a device for showing plurality:

(1) *shū   dōu zài   zhuōzishang*
    BOOK ALL LOCATED-ON TABLE-TOP[2]
    'The books are (all) on the table'

Number can of course also be expressed through the use of various quantifiers such as *yŏude*, 'some', *yíge* 'one, a', *jǐge* 'several', or *hěn duō* 'many'. Foreign students of Chinese often have difficulty in getting used to the fact that number is for the most part an optional category in Chinese, unlike in most European languages, where it is obligatory.

2. *Definite and indefinite reference.* Similar to number is the category of definite and indefinite reference. Chinese lacks articles, but there is surprisingly little ambiguity as a result. Definite elements may be overtly marked by modifiers that themselves are inherently definite, such as the demonstratives and possessive pronouns; nouns which lack such definite modifiers can still be shown to be definite by putting them at the beginning of the sentence, or at least before the verb. Compare the following two sentences:

(2) *wǒ méi gěi   ta   shū*
     I   NEG GIVE HER BOOK
    'I didn't give her a (*or* any) book'

(3) *shū   wǒ méi gěi   ta*
     BOOK I   NEG GIVE HER
    'I didn't give her the book(s)'

3. *Subordination and modification.* In Chinese all modifiers precede the elements which they modify. A single suffix, *-de*, serves to indicate all cases of nominal subordination, including that of possession.

(4) *wǒde diànshìjī*
     I *de* TELEVISION-SET
    'my television set'

(5) *jīntiān   shàngwǔ   de hùi*
     TODAY MORNING *de* MEETING
    'this morning's meeting'

(6) *qīnggōngyè   de fāzhǎn*
     LIGHT-INDUSTRY *de* DEVELOPMENT
    'the development of light industry'

This usage of *de* is similar to the genitive case of many languages; but, unlike the genitive in most languages, *de* is also used to mark modifying clauses:

(7) *nǐ   gěi   tāmen de qián*
     YOU GIVE THEM *de* MONEY
    'the money that you gave them'

(8) *xǐhuan chōuyān de rén*
     LIKE   SMOKE *de* PEOPLE
    'people who like to smoke'

Monosyllabic adjectives and certain nouns referring to geographical entities can normally modify nouns directly without an intervening *de*: *hǎo shū* 'good book', *Zhōngguo shū* 'Chinese book'. Chao (1968, 285) considers such combinations without *de* as quasi-compounds, that is, more like words than phrases. Polysyllabic adjectives or adjectives modified by an adverb of degree generally require a *de*: *hěn hǎo de shū* 'a very good book', *yǒuyìsi de shū* 'an interesting book'.[3]

4. *Case relationships.* If we take case in an abstract sense to refer to those grammatical devices used to show the relationship between nouns and verbs in a sentence, then case relationships in Chinese (as in English) are mostly expressed by means of prepositions. From an historical perspective it is clear that Chinese prepositions all derive from earlier verbs; some grammarians still consider them a type of verb – in the *Mandarin primer* Chao defined verb prepositions as "verbs which are usually in the first position in verbal expressions in series," but in his *Grammar of spoken Chinese* he considers them a transitional category which he defines by enumeration. Even from a purely synchronic perspective, the verbal nature of prepositions is evident, since in many cases the same words that function as prepositions still function as full verbs as well. Prepositions along with their object always occur together with another verbal phrase which they precede.

Both the agent of a transitive verb and the subject of an intransitive verb are unmarked, and both precede the verb; an indefinite direct object follows the verb, and is likewise unmarked. Definite objects may also follow the verb, especially if they are of certain inherently definite types. Providing certain rather complex conditions are met, they may also occur with what Chao (1968, 342) calls the "pretransitive" preposition *bǎ*.

(9) *wǒ dǎle   ta*
  I   HIT-PERF HIM
  'I hit him'

(10) *nǐ   shénme shíhou lái*
  YOU WHAT TIME COME
  'When are you coming?'

(11) *háizi   bǎ   fàn   chī-wán   le*
  CHILD ACC-PREP RICE EAT-FINISH PCL
  'The child has eaten the rice'

The *bǎ* construction (illustrated in example (11)) has been the subject of much debate among Chinese and foreign grammarians; the studies of Henri Frei (1956; 1957), Wáng Huán (1959), and Chao (1968) are considered classic.

With certain verbs denoting existence, appearance and disappearance, the logical subject of a verb may come after it: *xià-yǔ* 'FALL RAIN – rains', *zǒule yíge rén* 'LEAVE-PERF A PERSON – a person left', *chū tàiyang le* 'APPEAR SUN PCL – the sun has come up'.

The dative (indirect object or beneficiary of an action) can be shown either by its position after the verb or by the preposition *gěi* 'to, for':

(12) *wǒ gěile   ta   yìběn shū*
     I   GIVE-PERF HIM A   BOOK
     'I gave him a book'

(13) *gěi ta   dǎ   ge diànhuà*
     TO HER MAKE A   PHONE(CALL)
     'Telephone her'

(14) *tā   àirén gěi   ta   lǐfà*
     HIS WIFE FOR HIM CUT-HAIR
     'His wife cuts his hair for him'

In the standard language the indirect object always precedes the direct object; however, in some dialects (Shànghǎi, Guǎngzhōu) the reverse order is employed.

The preposition for the instrumental is either *yòng* or (more colloquially) *ná*: *yòng dāo qiē ròu* 'WITH KNIFE CUT MEAT – cut meat with a knife', *ná chǐ liáng* 'WITH RULER MEASURE – measure with a rule'. The comitative relationship is expressed with *gēn*: *gēn mèimei qù* 'WITH YOUNGER-SISTER GO – go with one's younger sister'.

The above prepositions ('cases') all express what are generally known as grammatical functions (Lyons 1968, 295). Another set of prepositions are associated with what are known as local functions. *Zài* is the locative preposition *par excellence*; it is used to indicate where an action takes place: *zài kètīng shuìjiào* 'LOCATED LIVING-ROOM SLEEP – sleep in the living room'. This and the other local prepositions are frequently associated with nouns followed by a simple or complex localizer. Simple localizers are bound morphemes suffixed to nouns to indicate certain spatial relationships; in the spoken language only *-li* 'in(side)' and *-shang* 'above, on top' occur with any degree of versatility: *wūli* 'in the room, indoors', *zhuōzishang* 'on (top of) the table'. Complex localizers are formed by suffixing one of several elements to a bound localizer; the suffixes in order of their colloquial frequency are *-tou*, *-bian(r)*, and *-mian(r)*. Examples: *shū zài zhuōzi shàngbian* 'BOOK LOCATED TABLE ABOVE – the book is on the table'; *tā zài mén wàibianr* 'HE LOCATED GATE OUTSIDE – he is outside the gate'. Other common complex localizers are *lǐbian* 'inside', *xiàbian* 'underneath', *hòubian* 'behind', *qiánbian* 'in front', *yòubian* 'right side', *zuǒbian* 'left side'.

Table 7.2. Chinese prepositions

Preposition	Meaning as full verb	Case function
bǎ	'grasp'	accusative
gěi	'give'	dative, benefactive
yòng	'use'	instrumental
ná	'take'	instrumental
gēn	'follow'	comitative
zài	'be present'	locative
cóng	'follow' [4]	ablative
dào	'arrive'	terminal

The ablative relationship is shown by the preposition *cóng*.

(15) *Zhāng tóngzhì cóng Shànghǎi lái*
ZHANG COMRADE FROM SHANGHAI COME
'Comrade Zhang is coming from Shanghai'

Destination is expressed with the preposition *dào*: *dào Běijīng qù* 'TO PEKING GO – go to Peking'. Both *cóng* and *dào* often occur with phrases containing localizers.

Table 7.2 shows the most important Chinese prepositions, their meanings as full verbs and their 'case' functions.

5. *Aspect and voice.* Chinese, like a number of other East Asian languages, is an aspect and not a tense language; this means that Chinese is concerned with telling whether actions are completed or not, or whether they are actually in progress or not. The plotting of action along some sort of time axis, so important in tense languages, is not a feature of Chinese.

Completed action or perfective aspect is shown by the verbal suffix *-le*:

(16) *wǒ kànle nèibĕnr shū*
I READ-PERF THAT BOOK
'I read that book'

(17) *nǐ chīle fàn zài qù ba*
YOU EAT-PERF FOOD THEN GO PCL
'Go after you have eaten'

Example (17) shows that the verbal suffix *-le* may refer to the future as well as to the past (as in example (16)); this demonstrates neatly that we are dealing with aspect and not with tense. Uncompleted action or imperfect aspect is unmarked

– that is, there is no suffix or other overt marking associated with it:

(18) *zuótian   wǎnshang wǒ kàn   shū*
YESTERDAY EVENING I   READ BOOK
'I read yesterday evening'

In (18) the verb is imperfective; note, however, that this does not necessarily mean that the action was not completed; rather, it indicates that completion is not at issue in this particular sentence. The speaker is merely describing what he did last evening, without reference to whether he completed it or not. The perfective can be described as the marked member of the aspect opposition, in that it specifically indicates whether the action was carried through to completion or not; the imperfect simply leaves the question open.

Actions can be shown to be durative in several ways; perhaps the most common nowadays is to place *zài* (written with the same character as the locative *zài* described above) before the verb: *tāmen zài chīfàn* 'THEY DUR EAT-FOOD – they are (*or* were) eating'. Another, somewhat less common, durative form has the suffix *-zhe* after the verb:

(19) *tāmen zhèng kāizhe   hùi   ne*
THEY JUST HOLD-DUR MEETING PCL
'They are just now holding a meeting'

More commonly the verbal suffix *-zhe* is used to form stative verbs from action verbs: *chuān yīfu* 'puts on clothing', *chuānzhe yīfu* 'is wearing clothing'. Another frequent use of *-zhe* is to form dependent adverbial clauses:

(20) *màozhe   dà xuě   shàng   shān*
BRAVE-DUR BIG SNOW ASCEND MOUNTAIN
'ascend a mountain braving the heavy snow'

Chinese verbs in themselves lack any distinction of active and passive; *chī* can mean either 'eat' or 'be eaten', as is evident from Chao's (1968, 75) well-known example: *yú chīle* meaning either 'the fish has eaten (it)' or 'the fish has been eaten'. The passive sense of a verb can be made explicit by supplying an agent, expressed by means of one of several prepositions; the most common colloquial agentive prepositions are *ràng* and *jiào*; somewhat more formal is *bèi*. The two following examples can be considered typical passive sentences:

(21) *Xiǎoling   ràng bàba   dǎle*
XIAOLING BY   FATHER BEAT-PERF
'Xiaoling was beaten by father'

(22) *tā bèi dàjiā   pīpíngle*
HE BY EVERYONE CRITICIZE-PERF
'He was criticized by everyone'

In the colloquial language, passives are for the most part restricted either to verbs of an unfavorable meaning or to verbs denoting disposal or separation. In the modern written language, however, the passive is found in a much wider range of semantic contexts; this is mostly due to the influence of Western languages like English and Russian.

6. *Negation.* From a syntactic point of view, negatives behave like adverbs in that they precede and modify verbs. *Bù* can be used with any verb except the existential verb *yǒu*, which is invariably negated with *méi*: *búqù* 'doesn't go, won't go, wouldn't go', *bùhǎo* 'not good'. *Méi* is the existential negative: *méi(yǒu) shū* 'there is no book, doesn't have a book'; it also is the negation of the perfective and durative aspects: *méi lái* 'didn't come, hasn't come yet', *méi(yǒu) zuòzhe* 'not (actually) sitting'. Negative commands are formed with *búyaò* (literally 'not-want') or *bié*: *nǐ bié qù* 'don't go'.

7. *Modality.* The expression of modality is a vast topic that we can only touch upon briefly here. The various modalities which in English are expressed by modal auxiliaries are also as a rule expressed by modal auxiliary verbs in Chinese. In this section we will examine several of these. Most of the Chinese modal auxiliary verbs have more than one function, and there is a certain amount of semantic overlap among them, especially in the case of those verbs expressing possibility, permission and potentiality. Note that auxiliary verbs are always negated with *bù* and not with *méi*.

Volition is most commonly expressed by the verb *yào*: *yào qù* 'wants to go'; negative volition may be *búyào* but more usually it is *bùxiǎng* or *búyuànyi*; both *xiǎng* and *yuànyi* are also volitional auxiliaries: *xiǎng lái* 'wants to come', *yuànyi kànshū* 'wants to read, feels like reading'.

Obligation may be expressed in several ways: *děi* 'must, have to' expresses strong obligation; its negation is either *búyòng* or *búbì* and never **bùděi*. A weaker degree of obligation may be shown with *yīnggāi* or *yīngdāng* 'ought, should'; both of these auxiliaries can be negated in the ordinary way with *bù*.

The auxiliary *huì* (negation: *búhuì*) is used for the expression of possibility.

(23) *tā   jīntian huì   lái*
SHE TODAY MAY COME
'She may come today'

Hùi as an auxiliary also has the common meaning of 'to know how to, to possess the requisite knowledge to': *hùi kāichē* 'knows how to drive a car'. In the Peking dialect, *néng* is more common than *hùi* as an expression of probability: *tā jīntian néng lái* 'she may come today' (Lü *et al.* 1980, 369).

Kéyi is the most common verb denoting permission:

(24) *zhèr   bùkéyi   yóuyŏng*
     HERE NEG-PERMITTED SWIM
     'One may not swim here'

In interrogative and negative sentences *néng* often carries the same meaning: *bùnéng chōuyān* 'one may not smoke', *néng cānjiā ma?* 'may one attend?'.

The expression of potentiality is rather complicated; the most general auxiliary used for this notion is *néng*: *néng zŏulù* 'can walk', *bùnéng shíxiàn* 'cannot be carried out'. With two large classes of complex verbs another device for indicating potentiality is more common. The two classes of verbs are verb–directional complement and verb–resultative complement compounds; the first of these constructions consists of a verb plus a complement indicating the direction of the action: *ná-shanglai* 'HOLD-COME UP – bring up (here)', *zŏu-jìnqu* 'WALK-GO-IN – walk in (there)'. Verb–resultative complement constructions are composed of a verb plus a complement expressing the result of the action: *dă-sĭ* 'BEAT-DIE – beat to death', *chī-băo* 'EAT-SATISFIED – eat one's fill'. In both types of constructions potentiality is generally expressed by placing an infixed *de* between the two parts of the construction: *ná-de-shanglai* 'can bring up here', *chī-de-băo* 'can eat one's fill'; in the corresponding negative form, *de* is replaced by *bu*: *ná-bu-shanglai* 'cannot bring up (here)', *chī-bu-băo* 'cannot eat one's fill'.

7.6 The Chinese sentence

At the most general level Chinese sentences can be divided into major and minor types; major sentences contain both a subject and a predicate: *wŏ qù* 'I will go'; a minor sentence contains only a predicate: *qù* '[I'll] go'. The frequent omission of pronominal subjects means that minor sentences are more common in Chinese than in English. Major sentences can be subdivided into simple subject–predicate sentences and composite sentences; a composite sentence is formed of two or more simple sentences (either major or minor) in close combination; if the components are in a coordinate relationship, it is a compound sentence: *wŏ qù, Zhāng Sān yě qù* 'I'm going and Zhang San's going too'. A complex sentence results when the component parts are in any of several noncoordinate relationships: *yàoshi nĭ qù, wŏ jiù búqù* 'If you go, then I won't go'.

Many Chinese grammarians have remarked on the considerable semantic looseness that characterizes the relationship of subject and predicate in Chinese. Chao (1968, 69ff) defines the grammatical meaning of subject and predicate as that of 'topic' and 'comment': the subject is that about which something is said. Looked at in this way, the subject of a sentence may stand in a number of different logical relationships to the predicate. It may, for example, be the agent (shīshì) of a transitive verb: wǒ dǎle ta 'I HIT-PERF HIM – I hit him'; it may also be the patient or recipient of the action (shòushì): gōngzuò zuò-wán le 'WORK DO-FINISH PCL – the work is already finished'. In other cases it may be merely an object about which some quality is predicated: tāde shūfǎ hǎo 'HER CALLIGRAPHY GOOD – her calligraphy is good'. It may also be an instrument: dàwǎn hē tāng, xiǎowǎn chī fàn 'BIG-BOWL DRINK SOUP SMALL-BOWL EAT RICE – the big bowls are for eating soup and the small bowls are for eating rice'.

Among Chinese grammarians, it is common to consider place and time words at the beginning of a sentence as subjects: míngtian huì xiàxuě ma? 'TOMORROW MAY SNOW QUES – will it snow tomorrow?'; wūli hěn lěng 'IN-ROOM VERY COLD – it's quite cold in the room'. Many linguists would probably tend to reject this analysis in favor of considering such elements time and place adjuncts. It must be admitted, however, that such a distinction is more difficult to draw in Chinese than in English. A sentence like Běijīng méiyou zōngshù 'PEKING NEG-BE PALM-TREE' can be translated either as 'Peking has no palm trees', in which case 'Peking' would appear to be the subject, or as 'In Peking there are no palm trees', in which case 'Peking' would seem to serve as an adjunct of place; but in fact such a distinction can be posited only on the basis of the differing English translations. It seems quite doubtful that the Chinese sentence per se is ambiguous and represents more than one semantic structure. Even if it is possible to distinguish time and place adjuncts from subjects in such sentences, certainly the line separating the two analyses is much less distinct in Chinese than in English.

Looked at from the point of view of the predicate, Chinese sentences may be divided into many types, some of which closely parallel analogous English sentences in their basic structure; above we have already briefly discussed the relative positions of verbs, objects and subjects in sentences containing action verbs. Here we will limit our remarks to a few points where Chinese and English show a significant difference.

Copular (or nominal) sentences may contain no verb at all: jīntian wǔhào 'TODAY FIFTH (OF THE MONTH) – today is the fifth', wǒ àirén guǎngdōngrén 'MY WIFE CANTONESE – my wife is Cantonese'. The more usual form of this type of sentence contains the copular verb shì 'is, are'; this verb, unlike its English counterpart, has only a copular function. Although it can be negated directly by *bù* like other verbs, it takes none of the aspect markers. As in the case of subject and predicate, the relationship between *shì* and its complement is varied; the most common relationship is that of equality or class membership, as in (25) and (26) respectively:

(25) *Zhāng   Sān   shì   tā   fùqin*
ZHANG SAN IS HIS FATHER
'Zhang San is his father'

(26) *zhèxiē   xuésheng   dōu   shì   Zhōngguórén*
THESE STUDENTS ALL ARE CHINESE
'All these students are Chinese'

Sometimes a copular predicate merely explains or comments on the topic of the sentence in a loose manner; for example, if a person is asked, 'Why are you at home during the daytime?', he might reply *wǒ shi wǎnshang de kè* 'I AM EVENING *de* CLASS – my classes are in the evening'. Sentences of this type are very common, especially in the colloquial language.

Existential sentences contain *yǒu* which, as we have seen, is always negated with *méi*; unlike *shì*, it may take all the aspectual suffixes. An existential sentence may occur with or without a place adjunct: *yǒu fàn ma?* 'BE RICE QUES? – is there any rice?'; *zhèr méiyou rén* 'HERE NEG-BE PEOPLE – there is no-one here'.

In Chinese, as in a number of other East Asian languages, possession is expressed by means of an existential predicate: *wǒ yǒu shū* 'I have a book' is exactly parallel to Manchu *minde bithe bi*, literally 'to-me book be'. John Lyons (1968, 393) has pointed out that sentences (27) and (28) bear the same transformational relationship to one another as do (29) and (30):

(27) *shū   zài   zhuōzishang*
BOOK LOCATED TABLE-TOP
'The book is on the table'

(28) *zhuōzishang   yǒu   shū*
TABLE-TOP HAVE BOOK
'There is a book on the table'

(29) *shū   shì wǒde*
BOOK IS MINE
'The book is mine'

(30) *wǒ yǒu   shū*
I HAVE BOOK
'I have a book'

In (27) and (29) 'book' is definite, in (28) and (30) it is indefinite. Structurally, the only real difference between (28) and (30) is that the word *zhuōzi* is inanimate and *wǒ* is animate; and it is this, and not the difference between two different verbs *yǒu*, one meaning 'have' and another meaning 'be', that determines the choice of 'there is' or 'have' in the English translation. If we use an unnaturally literal translation like 'there is a book by me (*or* at me)', the parallelism of (28) and (30) is perfectly clear. It is interesting to note that the Russian translation of (30), *u menja jest' kniga* literally means 'by me there-is (a) book'. We must conclude that attempts to analyze *yǒu* as two different words, one meaning 'there is' and the other meaning 'have', distort the actual structure of Chinese.

Almost all Chinese grammars divide sentences into declarative, interrogative and imperative types. Chao (1968, 58–9) observes that declarative sentences have truth value, that is, they can be judged to be true or false. Questions, on the other hand, have information value; they are requests for information. Commands have what he calls compliance value; the request, order or plea contained in such a sentence can be complied with or rejected.

Declarative sentences can be said to be unmarked. Questions, on the other hand, are marked, and fall into several distinct categories. Questions asking for specific information contain one of a set of question words; in addition to those already mentioned above, the most common are *duōshao* 'how much, how many?' *zěnme* 'how?', *wèi shénme* 'why?', *nǎr* 'where?', and *shénme shíhou* 'when?'. Questions containing question words have the same word order as the corresponding answer: *nǐ yào shénme?* 'YOU WANT WHAT – what do you want?'; *wǒ yào nàběn shū* 'I want that book'.

Questions which require a "yes" or "no" answer are of two types; the simpler type is formed by the use of sentence particles, of which *ma* is the most common: *nǐ qù ma?* 'YOU GO QUES – are you going?'. The other type is formed by juxtaposing two choices or alternatives for the listener to choose between: *nǐ hē shuǐ hē chá?* 'YOU DRINK WATER DRINK TEA – are you going to drink water or tea?'. An especially common subtype of the choice question is formed by offering a choice between a verb and its negative: *nǐ qù búqù?* 'YOU GO NEG-GO – are you going?'. An important restriction on this question form is that it cannot be employed if the verb is modified by an adverb; one can only say *nǐ yě qù ma?* 'YOU ALSO GO QUES – are you going also?'; **nǐ yě qù búqù?* is ungrammatical.

Imperatives are generally expressed by the verb alone: *qù* 'go!'. The presence of a second-person pronoun is somewhat more usual in Chinese than in English: *nǐ qù* '(you) go'. Imperatives may be made less blunt by the use of the advisative particle *ba*: *nǐmen lái ba* 'you (pl.) come, why don't you come?'. Imperatives are negated with *búyào* or *bié*; the latter form is generally considered to be a contraction of *búyào* (see, however, sec. 5.4). In Chinese it is difficult to separate the imperative proper (which refers to the second person) from wishes or commands concerning the first and third persons; all of them employ the particle *ba* and are negated with *búyào* or *bié*.

(31) *zánmen   zǒu   ba*   *zánmen   bié zǒu*
    WE (incl) LEAVE PCL   WE NEG LEAVE
    'Let's go'   'Let's not go'

(32) *Zhāng   Sān   qù ba*   *Zhāng   Sān bié   qù*
    ZHANG SAN GO PCL   ZHANG SAN NEG GO
    'Let Zhang San go'   'Don't let Zhang San go'

While the use of *ba* is usual in sentences like (31) and (32) which refer to the first and the third persons, it may be absent if the injunction is considered urgent: *zánmen kuài zǒu!* 'let's go quickly!'.

7.7 Traditional Chinese lexicography

Although China never really developed a native grammatical tradition, lexicography has been a central concern of philologists since the Han dynasty. The first Chinese dictionary is generally considered to be the *Ěryǎ*. The material that went into the *Ěryǎ* consisted of collections of glosses on old Classical texts, and was in some cases very old. According to the most generally held modern opinion, such older materials were assembled and augmented by Han classicists, the final result of this process being the *Ěryǎ* as we know it (Liú 1963, 81). This first Chinese "dictionary" is arranged by semantic categories; under each category the entries consist of lists of synonyms (or near synonyms) glossed by a word from the standard Han literary language. No attempt is made at indicating pronunciation.[5]

The Han dynasty saw the birth of another type of dictionary, the *Shuōwén jiězì* of Xǔ Shèn. This dictionary of Chinese graphs was completed in AD 100 and presented to the Emperor in AD 121 (Liú 1963, 6). We saw in Chapter 3 what an important source this dictionary is for the study of the evolution of the Chinese script. Looked at from a purely lexicographical point of view, it has a number of serious defects. Its definitions are frequently tainted by cosmological speculation, based either on phonetic similarity of one word to another or on the graphic make-up of the entry. From this we can see that the author was basically more interested in getting at some kind of metaphysical significance of words than in defining them according to their actual use in texts. The *Shuōwén* arranges characters according to a system of radicals, a device which in principle is still used commonly in present-day dictionary making. Unfortunately, Xǔ Shèn's system was overly elaborate and employed in an inconsistent way, making his dictionary difficult to use without the aid of a modern index. Since in the first century AD the Chinese had still not worked out an adequate way to indicate pronunciation, the attempts made to record pronunciation are only approximate. Despite such shortcomings, however, Xǔ's work remains one of the most important sources for the study of Old Chinese, in both its phonological and its semantic aspects.

The Nanbeichao period saw the development of a third kind of dictionary, the rhyme book. These were the first dictionaries to be arranged according to sound; the structure of the most important of these, the *Qièyùn*, has already been described in Chapter 2. Lexicographically these dictionaries were a great advance over the previous two types in that, employing the device of *fǎnqiè*, they gave a clear and accurate indication of pronunciation. In the course of their development, however, they became more and more conservative, imitating their predecessors in an ever more slavish fashion, with the result that their *fǎnqiè* spellings ceased to represent in any way the current literary practice of their time. The definitions of words in the rhyme books are generally terse, and only here and there are they based explicitly on textual occurrences.

By the sixth century AD the three basic principles of Chinese lexicographic arrangement were already in use: the *Ěryǎ* and related works were arranged according to semantic categories. For all its obvious drawbacks – arbitrariness of classification, lack of any strict principle of ordering within categories, and the great difficulty experienced by users in finding entries – this system of arrangement continued to be used down to very recently.

In the *Shuōwén jiězì*, entries were ordered according to their graphic structure; graphs were decomposed into *radicals* (*bùshǒu*) and a remainder. Xǔ Shèn's system was clumsy and applied without rigor, but in later dictionaries the principle was refined; in the process Xǔ Shèn's 540 radicals were reduced to 214 by the time of the Ming dynasty dictionary *Zìhùi*; this and later dictionaries arranged graphs belonging to a single radical according to the number of residual strokes, making the finding of entries a relatively simple matter. This "radical-stroke" system remains one of the most common forms of lexicographic arrangement today.

The phonetic system of arrangement established by the early rhyme books has also persisted down to the present. After alphabetic writing was introduced by Westerners in the nineteenth century, arrangement by alphabetic order came to predominate, even in monolingual native dictionaries.

With perhaps the exception of the *Zhōngyuán yīnyùn*, there were few (if any) advances in Chinese lexicography between the sixth and seventeenth centuries. New dictionaries were generally no more than minor revisions and enlargements of older works, and the old models were almost always followed. Méi Yīngzuò's *Zìhuì* (completed around 1615) represents the first important lexicographic advance after this long period. In his dictionary he greatly simplified and rationalized the traditional set of radicals, and introduced the principle of ordering graphs according to the number of residual strokes. He also employed the current *kǎishū* (standard) form of characters then current as the basis of his dictionary. (Earlier dictionaries arranged according to radicals employed the obsolete seal script.) In this way he made his work easily accessible to the general literate public. In addition to using the traditional *fǎnqiè* spellings, Méi indicated pronunciation by commonly used homophonous characters, no doubt in recognition of the fact that it was almost impossible for the average reader to derive correct current readings from Tang dynasty *fǎnqiè*. Variant pronunciations of a single graph were meticulously recorded. *Zìhuì* definitions are for the most part brief but clear; and reference to a text is almost always given by way of example.

The importance of Méi's innovations is confirmed by the fact that they were promptly imitated by others. The most important of the works based on Méi's model was undoubtedly the *Kāngxī zìdiǎn*, produced under imperial order by a committee of lexicographers headed by Zhāng Yùshū and Chén Tíngjìng; it was completed in 1716 after five years of work. More comprehensive than the *Zìhuì* and its successive redactions, the *Kāngxī zìdiǎn* soon became the standard dictionary of Chinese characters, and continues to be used widely today.[6] This dictionary in turn exercised a strong influence on subsequent Chinese lexicography.

Traditional lexica of the sort described above had a common characteristic: they were all concerned with the explication of ancient texts. Only very rarely did they record elements of the spoken language, or even characters associated with vulgar vernacular literature. It was only with the advent of European missionaries and government functionaries that dictionaries began to take notice of various forms of vernacular Chinese.

7.8   The rise of bilingual dictionaries

The foreigners who began to arrive in China in the late Ming dynasty found it necessary to learn both spoken and written Chinese. This need gave rise to the first grammars and bilingual dictionaries.[7] In this section I will limit myself to a few remarks concerning early Chinese–English dictionaries.

The main thing that distinguishes early Western lexicography of the Chinese language from traditional native work (aside, of course, from the fact that the definitions are in a second language) is the use of the Latin alphabet to indicate pronunciation. Since Westerners in China were faced with learning to speak

Chinese as well as learning how to read and write it, early lexicographers mixed both vernacular and literary material together in the same dictionary, generally without any indication of which words or definitions belonged to which style. This was a serious defect in all Chinese–English dictionaries up until very recently. The dictionaries of Robert Morrison (1815–23) and Walter Medhurst (1842–3) were characterized by serious defects in indicating pronunciation: Morrison, for example, failed to distinguish aspirated and unaspirated stops, and Medhurst, although he recognized the distinction, often inserted aspiration marks in the wrong words (Giles 1912, viii). Samuel Williams' *Syllabic dictionary of the Chinese language* (1874) was apparently the first dictionary to get this distinction sorted out properly. These early dictionaries were much concerned with the entering tone, which had already ceased to exist in the Peking dialect of the nineteenth century; this was no doubt the legacy of the *Wǔfāng yuányīn*, a simple rhyme book compiled by Fán Téngfèng at the beginning of the Qing dynasty and subsequently widely used in North China.

Herbert A. Giles' *Chinese–English dictionary* was the first truly adequate Chinese–English dictionary. The 1912 revised version in two volumes contained 13,848 characters plus a vast number of compounds and phrases. Pronunciation was based on current Peking usage, and was by and large free of the artificiality found in earlier works. Giles modified the transcription of Thomas Wade, creating what has come to be known as the Wade–Giles system of romanization; for many years this system served as the standard transcription in scholarly sinological works in English, but it is now slowly but surely yielding its place to the newer *pīnyīn* system. Like his predecessors, Giles mixed literary and colloquial definitions together without distinction. While Giles' dictionary remains a rich depository of nineteenth-century Peking colloquial words and phrases, in other respects it has been superseded by later dictionaries.

English-speaking students up until the 1970s relied chiefly on R. H. Mathews' *Chinese–English dictionary*, first published in 1931 by the China Inland Mission in Shanghai. From a lexicographic point of view, Mathews' dictionary was no advance over Giles'; its only real advantage was that it was more compact and up-to-date with regard to modern terminology. Otherwise, it scrambled together without differentiation words from the earliest texts of Chinese literature with contemporary neologisms. The most serious problem with the dictionary, however, was its treatment of pronunciation. As Yuen Ren Chao points out in his introduction to the 1943 reprint, it contains three disparate systems of pronunciations: current Peking pronunciation, the ephemeral standard promulgated in the 1919 *Guóyīn zìdiǎn* which became obsolete only one year after its publication, and a third system employed by the China Inland Mission. The result of this is that, although the entries are in alphabetic order, it is often frustratingly difficult to find a particular entry unless one is familiar with these various systems of transcription.

The influence of American structural linguistics is very much in evidence in two small dictionaries produced during the Second World War. Y. R. Chao's and L. S. Yang's *Concise dictionary of spoken Chinese* (1947) made a number of highly important lexicographic innovations. The dictionary is of single characters arranged in the traditional radical-stroke order. Characters of a purely literary nature are excluded unless they occur in some well-known colloquial phrase or are commonly employed in the modern written style; such entries are clearly marked *L* 'literary'. Other entries are distinguished according to whether they are 'free' *F* or 'bound' *B* (see above). Measure words, called "auxiliary nouns" in the dictionary, are marked *AN* and the types of nouns they occur with are listed. In compounds which are given as examples, atonal (neutral tone) syllables are clearly marked by placing a period before the syllable which is pronounced without tone.

Chao and Yang as a rule did not indicate word classes (with the exception of *AN*); they contended that in most cases class membership was made clear by the English gloss, and marking it would be redundant: if *chy* is defined by the English verb 'to eat', then it is itself also a verb. Only in cases of ambiguity are word classes specified; *jyfang* 'fat' is marked *n.* 'noun' since English 'fat' can also be an adjective.

Pronunciation of main entries is given in National Romanization, a system officially adopted by the Chinese government in 1928. The most distinctive feature of National Romanization was that it used spelling to distinguish the four tones: *tou* (first tone), *tour* (tone 2), *toou* (third tone), *tow* (tone 4). Although this system had its ardent devotees for many years, it is little used now. Wade–Giles readings are also given in parentheses following those in National Romanization. Chao and Yang also gave certain historical information concerning pronunciation, indicating for example which words originally ended in -*p*, -*t* and -*k* and which words had older voiced initials. The synchronic justification for including such information was that all these distinctions survive in other important modern dialects, and that such knowledge would aid in the learning of a second dialect.

The anonymous *Dictionary of spoken Chinese* issued by the War Department in 1945 represents a more ambitious lexicographic experiment. To begin with, it contains both Chinese–English and English–Chinese sections. In the Chinese–English part the entries are not single characters, as in almost all earlier dictionaries, but monosyllabic and polysyllabic words; these are entered in strict alphabetic order, without regard to the way they are written in the Chinese script. It is a dictionary of the spoken language; Chinese characters, although given in the Chinese–English section for the main entries, are treated as secondary. This represents a radical departure from all earlier Chinese–English dictionaries, which were primarily dictionaries of Chinese characters *(hànzì)* and not of the spoken language as such. A newly devised romanization system, the ancestor of the well-known Yale system, was employed throughout. Meticulous attention was paid to recording authentic colloquial pronunciation, especially stress.

The War Department dictionary was very much concerned with recording how words are actually used; its chief function was to show the user of the dictionary how to employ the entries in actual speech. This contrasts sharply with other bilingual Chinese dictionaries, whose chief function was to allow the user to decode written texts. The function of words was described chiefly through classifying them into one of twelve major grammatical categories: adjective (A), demonstrative (Dem), adverb (H), intransitive verb (I), conjunction (J), co-verb (K), measure (M), noun (N), numeral (Num), pronoun (Pron), resultative compound (RC) and transitive verb (V). Most of these categories were further divided into subcategories, e.g., "time nouns" (Ntime) and "transitive verbs followed by two nominal forms" (V2). One or more examples of actual usage were provided for most entries; for nouns the proper measure words were indicated.

The English–Chinese section is chiefly concerned with providing Chinese equivalents for a relatively small basic stock of English vocabulary. The entries are quite elaborate, providing Chinese equivalents and examples for a large number of different semantic nuances of the English entry.

Both Chao and Yang and the War Department dictionary reflected the shift of concern from the written to the spoken language which was so characteristic of the structuralist school in the United States. In both dictionaries we can observe the authors attempting not just to provide their Chinese entries with English equivalents but to demonstrate through grammatical categorization and examples how they are actually used. In retrospect, it would seem that Chao and Yang took a more practical approach to the problem of categorization. The sort of detailed syntactic analysis upon which the War Department dictionary depends is likely to be based on a theory of linguistic analysis which, although it may remain popular for a few years, is almost certain to be replaced by a more fashionable theory sooner or later; since a dictionary is a tool that must serve the needs of its users for many years if it is to be successful, its grammatical apparatus must be simple and as free as possible from passing linguistic fashions.

Another factor that favors the simpler Chao and Yang approach is that the more complex a grammatical apparatus becomes the more difficult it is to place the entries in their correct categories; Chinese has been especially intractable when it comes to establishing clear-cut word classes, a fact that should give potential lexicographers pause.

The War Department dictionary was never widely distributed and used, but it gave rise to two well-known dictionaries which to a great extent were modeled on it: the Institute of Far Eastern Languages at Yale University published the *Dictionary of spoken Chinese* in 1966. Fred Fangyu Wang later published a two-volume *Mandarin Chinese dictionary* closely modeled on the Yale and older War Department works. With these dictionaries, American efforts in Chinese lexicography effectively ceased.

7.9   Modern lexicography in China

In the 1910s and 1920s, China faced the problem of establishing a new written and spoken standard language. As we have seen, the basis for such a language already existed in the traditional written vernacular, *báihuà*, and in the administrative lingua franca, *guānhuà*, which had already slowly begun to take on the role of a national language at the end of the Qing dynasty. The compilation of a dictionary which could serve as an authority for correct pronunciation was one of the pressing needs felt by those active in the national language movement. The first standard for pronunciation decided on in 1913 by the Society for Unification of the National Language was a highly artificial compromise, containing features of both Northern and Southern Chinese (see section 6.1). This short-lived standard was the basis of the 1919 *Guóyīn zìdiǎn* [*Dictionary of national pronunciation*] (already mentioned above in connection with Mathews' dictionary). Since there were no native speakers of this standard "dialect", its impracticality was eventually realized and in 1932 the Peking dialect was officially recognized as the standard of pronunciation for the national language.

In 1936 the *Guóyǔ cídiǎn* was published in four volumes. This large dictionary was compiled by the Zhōngguó dàcídiǎn biānzuǎnchù [Compilation Section for a Comprehensive Chinese Dictionary] of the Ministry of Education. This was the first large-scale dictionary of the modern standard language; its twofold purpose was to fix the correct pronunciation of a large proportion of the Chinese lexicon, both modern and ancient, and for the first time to list the *words* (and not merely the characters) of the standard language. The main entries were Chinese characters arranged phonetically according to the National Phonetic Letters (*zhùyīn zìmǔ*), a partly alphabetic, partly syllabic script devised specifically for indicating the pronunciation of Chinese characters; this script, inspired partially by the

Japanese *kana* syllabaries, was given official status in 1919 and continues to be used in Táiwān today. Pronunciations were also given in National Romanization, the system later used in Chao and Yang's *Concise dictionary*. After the definitions of the main entry, compounds beginning with the character being defined were listed in the order of the National Phonetic Letters. Great care was taken to indicate neutral tone syllables in compounds, and to designate where the *-r* suffix occurred.

Although the emphasis was on the modern language, a large amount of purely Classical and literary material was also included, with no attempt being made to differentiate literary from vernacular entries. Definitions, which were mostly written in simple literary Chinese, were generally brief, since the main purpose of the dictionary was the standardization of pronunciation and not the detailed definition of words. The dictionary had no grammatical apparatus, so the reader was left to infer word classes either from the definitions or from the short examples given for some of the entries. Examples were mostly drawn from Classical and older vernacular literary works; sources unfortunately were limited to giving only the name of the book in which the quotation occurred. A great wealth of proper names were included; this was particularly useful since the dictionary came to be viewed as authoritative in cases of ambiguous readings in personal and place names.

The *Guóyǔ cídiǎn* in many ways set excellent standards for Chinese lexicography, particularly in the area of pronunciation, but due to the war with Japan and the ensuing civil war, little progress was made in this area until the 1950s. A one-volume abridged version of the *Guóyǔ cídiǎn* appeared in 1947; this handy condensation has gone through several reprintings, both in mainland China and in Táiwān.

In 1953 the first edition of the important *Xīnhuá zìdiǎn* appeared in Peking. This small, pocket-size dictionary, the first to be published by a national publishing house after the 1949 revolution, replaced the older *Guóyǔ cídiǎn* as the standard guide to pronunciation. It had gone through five editions by 1980, and yet another revision is expected.

The *Xīnhuá zìdiǎn* [*New China dictionary*] is primarily a dictionary of Chinese characters, as its name indicates.[8] Compounds or phrases are given primarily as aids to explaining different nuances of the entries. The most common arrangement of entries for the dictionary has been by phonetic order; the dictionary now employs the official *pīnyīn* system of romanization but gives the older *zhùyīn zìmǔ* spellings as well, no doubt as an aid to older users who were educated before the advent of *pīnyīn*. The 1980 revised edition contains 11,100 characters and 3,500 illustrative compounds and phrases.

Entries include both vernacular and literary words; although no overt attempt is made to differentiate the two types of vocabulary, the definitions and examples almost always make it clear to which category a particular word belongs. The definitions of vernacular words are as a general rule more detailed, and at least one example of usage is given. The definitions of literary words are terse and lack examples, unless they occur as common bound components of words current in the present standard language, in which case illustrative compounds and phrases are given. Words with a strongly local or dialectal flavor are marked as such. Care is taken in the case of nouns to indicate if the *-zi* or *-r* suffixes are employed. From the examples given for vernacular entries it is usually possible to judge whether they are free or bound; thus, to an experienced user the *Xīnhuá zìdiǎn* provides nearly as much grammatical information as the Chao and Yang dictionary does.

Several important lexicographic projects were nearing completion when the Great Cultural Revolution broke out in 1966. The *Xīnhuá zìdiǎn*, for all its good qualities, was too concise to meet all the needs of Chinese students and the general educated public; in 1958 the lexicography section of the Institute of Linguistics of the Academy of Sciences began the compilation of a medium-sized dictionary of Chinese, which was to contain not only single characters but a large percentage of the compound words in use in the modern standard language. A limited number of volumes of a preliminary version (*shiyòngběn*) were printed in 1960 and 1965, in order to allow a select group of scholars and other concerned individuals to put forth their criticisms and suggestions. The dictionary was originally to have been published in 1966, but publication was put off because of the Cultural Revolution. Another preliminary edition was prepared in 1973; in 1974 this version was subjected to scathing political criticism by the then powerful radical clique which later came to be known as the "Gang of Four", and publication was again delayed. After all these vicissitudes, the *Xiàndài hànyǔ cídiǎn* [*Dictionary of modern Chinese*] was finally published for general distribution in 1978 after the downfall of its detractors.

The *Xiàndài hànyǔ cídiǎn* is an official dictionary whose chief aim is the establishment of a standard lexicon and pronunciation for modern Chinese. It contains approximately 56,000 entries, arranged phonetically according to *pīnyīn* romanization. Main entries are characters; compounds, phrases and idioms are listed alphabetically under each main entry. Like the earlier *Guóyǔ cídiǎn*, this dictionary is concerned with determining word boundaries, and great care is taken in this regard. The elements of words are joined: *Zhōngguó* 'China', *yǔfǎ* 'grammar', *xuéxí* 'study'. Where there is felt to be a somewhat weaker degree of cohesion, a dash is placed between the elements: *děngyāo-sānjiǎoxíng* 'isosceles triangle'. When the parts of a word are separable, as in the case of many verb–object compounds, a slanting equal sign is inserted: *guò⧸jié* 'celebrate a holiday', *chī⧸fàn* 'eat (food)'.

Pronunciation is given in the *pīnyīn* system. Obligatory neutral tones are shown by a period in front of the syllable in question (a device borrowed from Chao's *Mandarin primer*) and the absence of a tone mark on the second syllable: *wǒ.men* 'we', *lǎ.ba* 'horn'; optional neutral tone syllables are indicated by a period also, but with all the tone marks retained: *yīn.wèi.* 'because'. Facultative uses of the *-r* suffix are given in parentheses. Variant pronunciations of characters are cross-listed.

While the *Xiàndài hànyǔ cídiǎn* has followed the lead of the already excellent *Guóyǔ cídiǎn* and *Xīnhuá zìdiǎn* in matters of pronunciation, it surpasses both of these dictionaries in the quality of its definitions; this can be seen in two features, the specification of word classes and an attempt to characterize entries stylistically.

The *Xiàndài hànyǔ cídiǎn* implicitly divides words into two categories: full words (nouns, verbs, adjectives) and empty words (all other parts of speech). In the case of the first category, no attempt is made to classify entries into their individual word classes; the editors apparently feel that the definitions and examples make these distinctions sufficiently clear. Empty words are classified into eleven different subclasses: pronouns, demonstratives, interrogative pronouns (*yíwèn dàicí*), numerals, measures, adverbs, conjunctions, prepositions, particles, exclamations and onomatopoeics. This set of word classes is very close to that employed in current Chinese pedagogical grammars.

In addition to parts of speech, the dictionary also discriminates several stylistic categories. The great majority of entries are unmarked and assumed to be stylistically neutral. Entries marked *shū* are limited to the written language (*shū-miànyǔ*); those marked *kǒu* are used mainly in the spoken language (*kǒuyǔ*). (In neither case is the distinction an absolute one: words usually restricted to the written language may occur in certain types of very formal speech, and very colloquial words appear not infrequently in informal writing, especially in the recording of dialogue.) Dialectal words are identified by the designation *fāng* (for *fāngyán* 'dialect'); this may refer to the Peking dialect or to other local dialects. Archaicisms are identified by the designation *gǔ* (for *gǔcíyǔ*). Some single characters are followed by a small square with an *x* inside it; this indicates that the entry is rarely used in the modern language. A small diamond-shaped symbol preceding an example of usage means that the definition is to be taken in a metaphorical sense.

The *Xiàndài hànyǔ cídiǎn* is an outstanding example of lexicography, comparable to the best efforts produced in other countries. It sets a high standard for future dictionary compilers, and is bound to have a lasting effect in this field. Lexicography is enjoying a renaissance in present-day China; projects of all types are reported to be under way; it is unlikely that all this work will be of the same high quality as the *Xiàndài hànyǔ cídiǎn*, but the days when the student of Chinese had to depend on defective and poorly constructed dictionaries would seem to be drawing to a close.

Further reading

Chao, Yuen Ren 1968. *A grammar of spoken Chinese.* Berkeley and Los Angeles: University of California Press. [The most comprehensive study of modern Chinese grammar in English.]

Dīng, Shēngshù *et al.* 1961. *Xiàndài hànyǔ yǔfǎ jiǎnghuà.* Peking: Shāngwù Yìnshūguǎn. [A succinct synthesis of some of the best work on Chinese grammar in China in the 1950s.]

Hashimoto, Anne Yue 1971. Mandarin syntactic structures. *Unicorn (Chi-Lin)* 8. Princeton: Chinese Linguistics Project. [A brief outline of modern Chinese grammar from the point of view of the transformational school.]

8

Dialectal variation in North and Central China

8.1 Classification of Chinese dialects

The first scientific classification of the Chinese dialects was proposed by Li Fang-kuei in 1937. In Li's original classification there were nine groups, but three of them were clearly Mandarin subgroups (distinguished only by geographic tags) and the last group is simply an amalgam of dialects that cannot be fitted conveniently into other groups. Li's scheme has been widely accepted, and has become one of the main foundations on which Chinese dialectological research has been based; it is essentially the classification employed by Yuán Jiāhuá in his 1961 standard handbook *Hànyǔ fāngyán gàiyào* [*An outline of the Chinese dialects*]. Yuán's groups are the following:

1. Mandarin (Běifānghuà)   3. Xiāng   5. Kèjiā (Hakka)   7. Mǐn
2. Wú   4. Gàn   6. Yuè (Cantonese)

I will examine each of these groups in detail below; but before proceeding to the consideration of the particular dialect groups, it will be useful to consider the question of dialect classification more generally. One question that naturally arises concerning the scheme given here is how these groups are interrelated. There has been a tendency to view the seven groups as more or less independent, each group related to each other group in approximately the same degree. The single exception has been the proposal that the Gàn and Kèjiā groups are especially closely related (Luó 1950).

The traditional classification is mainly based on a single criterion – the development of the Middle Chinese voiced stops into the modern dialects. In general, this criterion works fairly well; some minor difficulties with it will be examined in the discussions of the separate dialect groups. Since the voiced initials probably persisted in the North down to the tenth or eleventh centuries at least, this dialectal classification is clearly valid only for a relatively recent historical period.

Without rejecting the traditional scheme, I would like to propose a new set of criteria or diagnostic features which will provide a framework that both has

Table 8.1. Classificatory criteria for Chinese dialects

	Bj	Xa	Km	Sz	Wz	Cs	Sf	Nc	Mx	Gz	Fz	Jo
1.	+	+	+	−	−	+	+	−	−	−	−	−
2.	+	+	+	−	−	−	−	−	−	−	−	−
3.	+	+	+	+	+	+	+	+	−	−	−	−
4.	+	+	+	+	+	−	−	−	−	−	−	−
5.	+	+	+	−	−	−	−	−	−	−	−	−
6.	+	+	+	+	+	+	+	+	−	−	−	−
7.	+	+	+	−	−	+	?	+	−	−	−	−
8.	+	+	+	+	+	+	−	+	−	−	−	−
9.	+	+	+	+	+	−	−	−	−	−	−	−
10.	+	+	+	±	−	±	?	−	−	−	−	−

greater historical depth and shows more clearly the internal relationships which obtain among the various subgroups. This framework is based on a number of criteria – phonological, grammatical and lexical. Below these criteria are described and then applied to a representative sample of dialects, and a discussion of some of their implications follows.

I have chosen ten features which I think can be applied in a straightforward manner, and which will produce a relatively clear-cut result; the criteria will be given in the form of statements for which a positive (+) or negative (−) reply can be made for any given dialect. In some cases both a positive and negative response is possible. The features are as follow:

1. The third-person pronoun is *tā* or cognate to it.
2. The subordinative particle is *de* (*di*) or cognate to it.
3. The ordinary negative is *bù* or cognate to it.
4. The gender marker for animals is prefixed, as in the word for 'hen' *mǔjī*.
5. There is a register distinction only in the *píng* tonal category.
6. Velars are palatalized before *i*.
7. *Zhàn* or words cognate to it are used for 'to stand'.
8. *Zǒu* or words cognate to it are used for 'to walk'.
9. *Érzi* or words cognate to it are used for 'son'.
10. *Fángzi* or words cognate to it are used for 'house'.

In Table 8.1 the ten criteria given here are applied to twelve dialects, given roughly in a north-to-south order: Běijīng (Bj), Xīān (Xa), Kūnmíng (Km), Sūzhōu (Sz), Wēnzhōu (Wz), Chángshā (Cs), Shuāngfēng (Sf), Nánchāng (Nc), Méixiàn (Mx), Guǎngzhōu (Gz), Fúzhōu (Fz), Jiànōu (Jo).[1] The features plotted on the table allow us to divide the dialects into three large groups. The three dialects on the left of the table have plus values for all the diagnostic features; we will designate this group of dialects the *Northern group*. The Northern group coincides exactly with the Mandarin (Běifāng) group of the traditional classification.

The four dialects at the right of the table have minus values for all the diagnostic features. We will refer to this group as the *Southern group*. It includes the Kèjiā, Yuè and Mǐn groups.

The remaining dialects show mixed values for the features plotted on the table; these dialects are clearly transitional, possessing northern features in some cases, southern features in others. We will call these dialects the *Central group*. With the exception of certain dialects in Zhèjiāng province, they are almost all spoken along the southern bank of the Yangtze or along its southern tributaries. This group includes the Wú, Gàn and Xiāng groups of the traditional scheme.

Of the three groups proposed here, the Northern group is by far the most homogeneous, despite the fact that it occupies the most extensive territory and comprises the great majority of Chinese speakers. Of the essential historical and geographic unity of this group there can be no doubt; the Central and Southern groups on the other hand, exhibit an extraordinary diversity, especially in phonology and lexicon. We will examine all these groups in detail in the remainder of this chapter and in the next.

8.2 Historical factors in dialect development

In the second millennium BC, the language which is ancestral to the modern Chinese dialects was spoken on the North China Plain along the banks of the Yellow River. How far it had spread at that time beyond this nuclear area, we have no way of knowing, nor do we know anything about dialectal diversity in that ancient period. It is clear, however, that in the succeeding millennium Chinese began to spread into new areas both to the north and south, a process that has continued throughout Chinese history right down to the present. In the Chūnqiū period (770–476 BC), we get the first signs of dialectal differences, both in explicit references to dialects in texts and in clear dialectal differences among the texts themselves. At the same time, it is evident that a kind of refined standard had arisen which was considered especially appropriate for the recitation of literary texts such as the *Shūjīng* [*The book of history*] and *Shījīng* [*The book of odes*] and in performing rites. This so-called *yǎyán*, which was based on the dialect of the Zhōu royal domain, may also have served as a common language for communication across dialect boundaries (Yuán 1960, 17). This common language continued to exist and function throughout the Zhànguó period (475–221 BC) and formed the basis of the Qin-Han standard language (Zhōu and Wú 1956, x). Thus we see that from a very early period there were two opposed

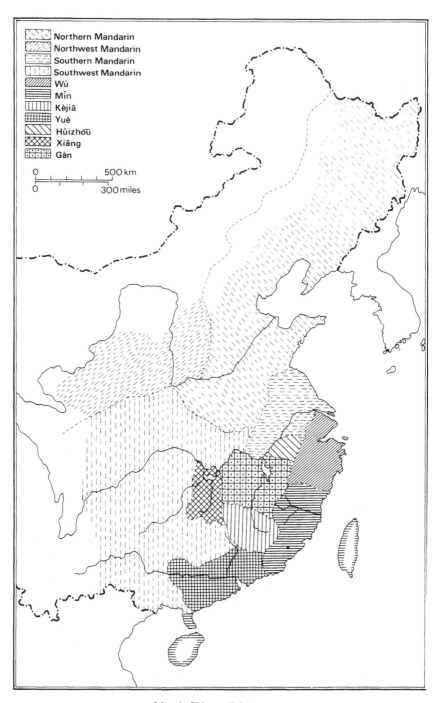

Map 1. Chinese dialect areas

forces operating on Chinese linguistic territory: the spread of the language to ever more distant regions gave rise to a centrifugal force to create increasingly greater differences in the local varieties of the language; but at the same time the standard or common language created a centripetal counterbalance, the effect of which was to bring the regional varieties into greater uniformity. The interplay of these two forces can be observed in most periods of Chinese history.

In periods of political consolidation the influence of a central standard language used in administration has been especially strong. During the first great imperial unification of the Qin and Han dynasties, a strict policy of standardization touching all spheres of life, including language, was put into effect. But at the very time when pressures toward linguistic uniformity were strongest, vast new territories were brought under Chinese rule and into the Chinese cultural sphere, laying the seeds of the great dialectal diversity found in present-day China. The colonization that these new conquests brought in their wake carried the Chinese language for the first time to the areas of Lǐngnán (modern Guǎngdōng and Guǎngxī provinces), Fújiàn and southern Jiāngxī. It was this colonization that ultimately led to the formation of the Southern dialect group mentioned above.

In the Han dynasty appeared the first work devoted to dialect vocabulary, the *Fāngyán* of Yáng Xióng (58 BC–AD 18). It is from the title of this book that the modern word for 'dialect' (*fāngyán* – lit. 'regional speech') is taken. Yáng Xióng's work is a rather random sample of dialect words, some taken from earlier texts, some of which he personally elicited from contemporary dialect speakers; the words are defined in terms of the current Han standard language and recorded in Chinese characters. From the book one can get a general idea concerning Han dialect areas, but because of the nature of the Chinese script, it is difficult (perhaps impossible) to deduce anything about the phonological systems of these dialects. It also seems that only a few of the regional terms recorded by Yáng Xióng can be connected with modern dialect words.

From the end of the Han until the beginning of the Sui dynasty (581–618), China was, with the exception of the short-lived Western Jìn dynasty (265–316), politically divided. The South saw a succession of short, weak dynasties, while the North was fragmented into a series of ephemeral states ruled over by several different, non-Chinese peoples. This period of almost four centuries of political and cultural division had a profound effect on Chinese linguistic history. In the south, the dialects of the recently colonized territories were in many cases left to develop relatively independently of the influence of a strong standard language. In the north there was even less possibility of any unifying linguistic force; and in addition there existed the strong superstratum influence of the non-Chinese languages of the ruling peoples. The period of disunity between the Han and the Sui-Tang dynasties must be viewed as the period in which the various dialect groups and subgroups had their beginnings.

Social factors can also be seen at work during this period. When the Western Jìn dynasty fell in 316, the aristocracy and bureaucrats migrated *en masse* to the region south of the Yangtze, and together with the older local aristocracy formed the ruling class of the Southern dynasties. The fleeing Jìn gentry brought with them their own prestigious northern dialect, which then became the basis of a new southern literary standard; it seems to have differed considerably from the language which the older inhabitants of the region south of the Yangtze spoke (Chén 1936). These older inhabitants used dialects which descended from the language of earlier Han settlers and which perhaps, in some cases, went back even to the dialects of the Zhànguó period. It is not unreasonable to assume that the aristocratic dialect of these recent northern immigrants deeply influenced the local patois, even replacing them in some cases. The northern influence would have been especially strong in the region along the Yangtze and around the southern capital of Jīnlíng, the present-day Nánjīng. We may even speculate that the older dialects of this region were originally much closer to those of the Southern group, nowadays represented in their purest form by the Mǐn dialects, and that the present transitional nature of the Central group is due in large measure to the influence of the imported northern standard described here.

The Sui dynasty reunified China in 581; itself short-lived, it ushered in what culturally speaking was China's golden age, the Tang dynasty (618–907). During the course of this dynasty, a common vernacular and literary standard developed which was based on the dialect of the capital city Chángān. We may assume that dialectal diversity was already fairly great at this period, and that consequently this common vernacular or koine was used extensively in government and commerce, and in the Buddhist and Taoist churches. In its literary form, that is, in its role as the standard way in which texts were read, it profoundly influenced all the local dialects of China; this influence was so great that the reading pronunciations of characters go back to this Tang standard in all Chinese dialects, with only a few scattered and vestigial survivals of an earlier standard. In its role as a common vernacular, the Tang koine no doubt replaced many older local dialects altogether; in other cases it had a profound influence on the grammar and lexicon of local forms of speech without actually taking their places. In general the influence of the Tang koine and its related literary standard was so strong that the dialectal map of China was altered in a very fundamental way.

As we have already seen in Chapter 2, a new koine developed during the foreign dynasties of Liao, Jin and Yuan. This language became the vehicle of a

flourishing vernacular literature, and an indispensable tool of imperial administration. This new standard, which had as its base the region around Peking, has
influenced local dialects chiefly at the level of the spoken language; in a vast
majority of cases the local reading pronunciations are still continuations of the
older Tang standard.[2]

These successive standard languages or koines have given rise to a rather complex situation of stratification in virtually every modern Chinese dialect, a situation that must be taken into account if we are to understand Chinese linguistic
history.

8.3   Degree of diversity among the Chinese dialects

One often hears it said that the Chinese dialects are really different languages.
In practical terms they must often be treated as such; in some universities, for
example, Cantonese is offered alongside the standard language in Asian language departments, just as German and Dutch are both taught in departments of
Germanic languages. But the question of what constitutes a language and what
constitutes a dialect cannot be answered in an absolute way; nonetheless, it is
important to keep in mind that the differences among the Chinese dialects are
very considerable. To the historical linguist Chinese is rather more like a language family than a single language made up of a number of regional forms. The
Chinese dialectal complex is in many ways analogous to the Romance language
family in Europe: both have their roots in a large-scale imperial expansion that
took place in the centuries just preceding and just following the birth of Christ,
the Qin-Han empire in the case of China and the Roman empire in the case of
Europe; in both instances the imperial language was carried by armies and settlers
to areas previously occupied by speakers of different languages; in the course of
their development both were affected by these "substratum languages"; in both
cases, the newly developing vernaculars existed alongside an antiquated written
language and were profoundly influenced by it. In view of these parallels, it
would not be surprising if we found about the same degree of diversity among
the Chinese dialects as we do among the Romance languages, and in fact I
believe this to be the case. To take an extreme example, there is probably as
much difference between the dialects of Peking and Cháozhōu as there is between
Italian and French; the Hǎinán Mǐn dialects are as different from the Xīān dialect as Spanish is from Rumanian.[3]

There are literally scores of mutually non-intelligible varieties of Chinese. The
greatest diversity is to be found in the Central and Southern zones, while the
Northern Group is on the whole quite homogeneous; a person from Harbin in
northern Manchuria has little difficulty understanding a native of Kūnmíng some

3,200 kilometers away (Yuán 1960, 23). In the Central zone there are some relatively large areas, comprising many counties in some cases, which share a mutually intelligible form of speech, such as the region around Shànghǎi; in other cases the dialects of adjacent counties would appear to be totally unintelligible, as in Southern Húnán. Dialectal diversity reaches its highest degree in the Southern zone, especially in Fújiàn province, where most of the Mǐn dialects are spoken; in this region every county generally has its own distinctive dialect which often differs quite radically from those in neighboring counties, and in some cases even neighboring villages use forms of speech that are totally mutually unintelligible. Within the confines of Zhōngshān county near Macao, for example, varieties of Mǐn, Kèjiā and Yuè are found side by side.

8.4 Dialect geography

No comprehensive dialect survey for the whole of China has ever been carried to completion. Surveys of separate provinces were undertaken in the 1930s and 1940s under the direction of Y. R. Chao. These surveys were by design very simple, the general intention being to get a general idea of the dialectal situation of vast areas in a rather short period of time. The first of such surveys to be published was the *Húběi fāngyán diàochá bàogào* [*A report on a survey of the dialects of Hupei*], which came out in 1948. After the nationalist government moved to Táiwān in 1950, the remaining materials of these surveys have been edited and published by S. F. Yang, a member of the Institute of History and Philology of the Academia Sinica. To date the surveys of Yúnnán (Yang 1969a), Húnán (Yang 1974) and Sìchuān (Yang 1984) have appeared.

Less comprehensive surveys have been carried out for other regions; Y. R. Chao's *Studies in the modern Wu dialects* (1928) was a ground-breaking work for this type of study. Bái Dízhōu and Yù Shìcháng published a similar study of northwestern Mandarin dialects in 1954. A more recent example of this sort of survey is the *Jiāngsūshěng hé Shànghǎishì fāngyán gàikuàng* [*A survey of the dialects of Jiāngsū province and the city of Shanghai*] published in 1960 in Nánjīng. An abridged but very important survey report on the dialects of Fújiàn was published in the journal *Zhōngguó yǔwén* by Pān Màodǐng and his associates in 1963. Pān's work is significant because he and his co-workers departed from the usual pattern of basing their survey solely on lists of character readings and concentrated instead on collecting the popular vocabulary of the dialects which they surveyed.

Between 1956 and 1958, a limited dialect survey of most of the counties of China was carried out pursuant to a directive issued by the Ministry of Education (Lǐ Róng 1963). The chief aim of this project was to obtain an overall picture of dialect variation in different regions of China with a view to facilitating the teaching and the promotion of the official national language, *pǔtōnghuà*; the main emphasis, as in the earlier surveys, was on phonological variation, but with the special aim of comparing local phonological systems with that of the standard language. Unfortunately only a few of the results of this survey have been published; descriptions that have appeared mostly have a very practical pedagogical orientation, and generally are of limited utility to the dialectologist.

At the present time our knowledge of Chinese dialect geography is sketchy and incomplete. It has also been criticized for its excessive emphasis on character readings as opposed to the real, everyday, living vocabulary of the dialects (Grottaers 1943). Such an approach, which in the last analysis is the legacy of Karlgren's *Études*, was justified earlier in this century, when vast areas of China were totally unknown to the dialectologist and an efficient and quick method of mapping gross dialectal features was called for, but at present it seems to us that a new technique, similar to the one employed by Pān Màodìng and his colleagues in Fújiàn, is called for. Ultimately it is only on the basis of an analysis of the popular dialect vocabulary that a true picture of Chinese dialectal relationships can be drawn.

8.5 Dialect boundaries

We know very little about the nature of dialect boundaries in China, and until we have more extensive and detailed dialect atlases, this situation is unlikely to change. In a few cases, however, we can make some preliminary observations; it is possible, for example, to speak of strong and weak dialect boundaries. As an example of a strong boundary, we can cite the demarcation which separates Wú and Mǐn, one of the strongest dialect boundaries to be found in China. The Mǐn dialects, as we shall see, are a very well-defined grouping, exhibiting unmistakable characteristics in phonology, grammar and lexicon. When one compares a Mǐn dialect like that of Zhèróng, which is spoken very near the Mǐn–Wú border, with the Wú dialect of Wēnzhōu in southern Zhèjiāng, one immediately senses that one is dealing with two utterly different varieties of Chinese. Table 8.2 compares some of the important features of the Zhèróng and Wēnzhōu dialects.[4]

From the table it can be seen that the basic vocabulary of these two dialects is quite different, and the list could be extended almost indefinitely. The last four items illustrate the typical development of the Middle Chinese voiced stops in the two groups: they are retained in Wēnzhōu, as they are consistently in Wú, but correspond to voiceless stops in the Mǐn dialects, where they are sometimes aspirated and sometimes not, according to a fixed, lexically determined pattern.

Table 8.2. Comparison of Wēnzhōu and Zhèróng features

	Wēnzhōu	Zhèróng
'I, me'	η^4	ηua^3
'you'	ni^4	ny^3
'he/she'	gi^2	i^1
'what?'	$ga^2\ ni^2$	$ni^1\ no\unicode{0294}^7$
'not'	fu^3	n^6
'walk'	$tsau^3$	$kia\eta^2$
'pot'	$\hbar o^8\ \eta$	$tia\eta^3$
'dog'	kau^3	$khen^3$
'head'	diu^2	$thau^2$
'copper'	$do\eta^2$	$t\alpha\eta^2$
'nose'	bi^8	phi^5
'thin'	bo^8	$po\unicode{0294}^8$

The boundary between Mǐn and Kèjiā, unlike that between Mǐn and Wú, cannot be drawn so sharply. In the far western and southwestern parts of Fújiàn province, there are dialects which are clearly transitional between the two groups; we will look at some of these dialects in Chapter 9.

An example of a very weak dialectal boundary is that dividing the Xiāng dialects from Mandarin. The dialects found along this boundary possess many similarities, due to centuries of slow infiltration of northern features into the area. It may well be that many dialects which we now consider southwestern Mandarin were originally of the Xiāng type, and have been slowly assimilated to the northern type in the course of recent centuries. From our admittedly limited data, we can tentatively say that both abrupt and gradual dialect boundaries may be found in China, but, for the most part, we are presently unable to delimit the dialect groups with any great precision. The study of the borders between the various dialect groups is one of the most challenging tasks of current Chinese dialectology.

8.6 The Mandarin dialects

The Mandarin dialects, which are spoken by about 70 per cent of China's Hàn population, are found everywhere north of the Yangtze River, except for those border regions where non-Hàn languages predominate. In addition, they are found throughout most of the southwest; in this latter region they are often spoken in proximity to minority languages such as Tibetan, Zhuàng and Miao. In the south-eastern area, where non-Mandarin dialects are the rule, one can find Mandarin-speaking "islands" here and there, such as the city of Nánpíng in northwestern Fújiàn (Pān 1963). Until fairly recently, few Mandarin speakers emigrated overseas; since the end of the Second World War, however, this situation has changed and significant colonies of Mandarin-speaking Chinese can be found in many cities of Europe and North America.

Chinese linguists classify Mandarin into four subgroups: (1) northern Mandarin, spoken in the provinces of Héběi (including the city of Peking), Hénán, Shāndōng, northern Ānhūi, Manchuria and parts of Inner Mongolia; (2) northwestern Mandarin, spoken in Shānxī, Shǎnxī, Gānsù, Qīnghǎi, Níngxià and parts of western Inner Mongolia; (3) southwestern Mandarin, spoken in Húběi, Sìchuān, Yúnnán, Guìzhōu, northwestern Guǎngxī, and the northwestern corner of Húnán; (4) eastern Mandarin (also referred to as the Jiāng-Huái dialects), spoken in central Ānhūi, and Jiāngsū north of the Yangtze, as well as in the region of Nánjīng. Of these subgroups, southwestern Mandarin is the most homogeneous, while the northwestern group, especially in Shānxī province, displays the highest degree of diversity.

The Mandarin dialects are important not only because of their vast numbers of speakers and the extensive territory they occupy, but because the standard language is based on a northern Mandarin dialect, that of Peking. In its standard form it is learned not only by members of the Hàn nationally throughout China, but also by the speakers of minority languages; due to its prestige and wide use, it exerts a strong influence on all the Chinese dialects and on the non-Hàn languages of China.

Mandarin dialects are clearly distinctive with respect to their phonology, grammar and lexicon. No other dialect group, with perhaps the exception of Mǐn, can be characterized so neatly. Let us first examine some of the phonological features of these dialects.

The Middle Chinese voiced obstruents (stops, affricates and fricatives) have all become devoiced in Mandarin, in effect eliminating voicing as a distinctive feature in the phonological systems of these dialects. In the case of the stops and affricates, the typical Mandarin development is to voiceless aspirates in the *píng* tone, voiceless non-aspirates in the non-*píng* (or *zè*) tones. This is often given as the defining characteristic of Mandarin as a group, and it is true that the great majority of dialects obey this rule; but there are a few Mandarin dialects in which the Middle Chinese voiced stops become aspirates in the non-*píng* tones as well as in the *píng* tone. Examples of this type of development can be found in Tóngguān in Shǎnxī (Lí 1944), and Língbǎo in Hénán (Yang and Ching 1971). Another minor difficulty with this criterion is that it is quite similar to the pattern found in standard Cantonese (see Chapter 9). So, while the development of the voiced stops will not serve to identify a Mandarin dialect infallibly, taken

Table 8.3. Development of Middle Chinese voiced stops in Mandarin dialects

	Middle Chinese	Peking	Yángzhōu	Xīān	Chéngdū	Língbǎo
'head'	dəu	thou²	thʏ²	thou²	thəu²	thou²
'long'	ḍjang	tʂhaŋ²	tshaŋ²	tʂhaŋ²	tshaŋ²	tʂhaŋ²
'tea'	ḍa	tʂha²	tsha²	tsha²	tsha²	tsha²
'nose'	bji-	pi²	piəʔ⁷	phi²	pi²	phi²
'bean'	dəu-	tou⁵	tʏ⁵	tou⁵	təu⁵	thou⁵
'white'	bɐk	pai²	pɔʔ⁷	pei²	pe²	phiɛ²

Table 8.4. Maximal inventory of Mandarin consonants

	Labials	Plain apicals	Apical sibilants	Retroflexes	Palatals	Velars
Voiceless unaspirated	p	t	ts	tʂ	tɕ	k
Voiceless aspirated	ph	th	tsh	tʂh	tɕh	kh
Nasals	m	n				(ŋ)
Fricatives	f		s	ʂ	ɕ	x
Sonorants	(w)	l		ɻ	(j)	

together with other criteria it is of great importance. Table 8.3 is a sampling of dialectal words illustrating this development; the first three words are *píng* tone words and the remaining words are all *zè* tone words.[5]

The general uniformity of the Mandarin dialects allows us to set up a set of initials which represents a kind of maximal overall pattern which will account for most of the dialects of the group.[6] The following general observations can be made concerning Mandarin initial consonants:

(1) In many dialects there is a confusion of *f* and *x* before rounded vowels; where Peking has *fu* and *xu* as distinct syllables, Chéngdū has only *fu* for both.

(2) Both *w* and *j* may or may not be distinct from *u* and *i* phonemically, depending upon one's syllable analysis; some dialects have a *v* corresponding to Peking *w*.

(3) Many Mandarin dialects (and dialects of other groups as well) confuse *n* and *l* in various ways; in some they are in free variation, as in Lánzhōu; others have only *l* (Nánjīng) or only *n* (Chóngqìng).

(4) Palatalization of Middle Chinese velars before high front vowels is virtually a universal feature of Mandarin dialects: $ki > t\varphi i$, $khy > t\varphi hy$, $xia > \varphi ia$, etc. In some dialects such palatalized forms, traditionally referred to as *tuányīn* 'round sounds', are kept separate from *tsi, tshy, sia*, which are called *jiān-yīn* 'sharp sounds'. Many other dialects, like the standard language, have merged these two series.

(5) The standard language, as we have seen, distinguishes a series of retroflex sibilants from a plain dental (or alveolar) series. Such a distinction is found in almost all the northern and northwestern Mandarin dialects, although the incidence of one or the other series in any given word is by no means uniform. The southwestern and eastern groups as a rule do not make the distinction. In some northwestern dialects, including that of Xīān, the retroflex consonants have become labiodentals before back rounded vowels: $t\varsigma u > pfu$, $t\varsigma huan > pfhan$, $\varsigma uei > fei$, etc.

(6) The retroflex semivowel *r* has a variety of correspondences; in a few dialects it has dropped entirely; in others it is *z* (Chéngdū), *l* (Yángzhōu), or *n* (Hànkǒu).

(7) In those dialects which have initial η, it is not the reflex of Middle Chinese *ng* but rather corresponds to the zero initial of the Peking dialect, being merely a sort of automatic onset in words which earlier began with vowels.

The Mandarin finals, when compared with those of Middle Chinese, have been simplified considerably. Perhaps the most striking difference between the two systems is the attrition of final consonants. Middle Chinese, it will be recalled, had six final consonants: *m, n, ng, p, t, k*. Of the nasals, Mandarin dialects have retained only *n* and η; in Chapter 2 we saw that the Yuan dynasty rhyme book, *Zhōngyuán yīnyùn*, still retained final *m*, so we know that this final must have persisted in certain Mandarin dialects until a relatively late date. The evolution of the final stops has been more complex. In the southwestern dialects they are totally lost in most areas; in the Jiāng-Huái region (eastern Mandarin) they have mostly merged as glottal stop. In northwestern and northern Mandarin both types of development can be found. Table 8.5 illustrates the development of the Middle Chinese final consonants in a number of representative dialects.[7]

With the exception of certain areas in the southwest, eastern Shānxī and the region around Nánjīng, Mandarin regularly has the three medials *i, y* and *u*, as in *\varphi ian, \varphi yan, suan*; in Chinese these three types of syllables are called *qíchǐ, cuōkǒu* and *hékǒu* respectively. The incidence of the rounded medials is markedly varied in different regions; the loss of medial *u* after apical initials is a particularly common development.

Table 8.5. Development of the Middle Chinese final consonants in Mandarin dialects

	Middle Chinese	Peking	Yángzhōu	Xīān	Chéngdū	Língbǎo
'three'	sâm	san¹	sæ̃¹	sã¹	san¹	sã¹
'umbrella'	sân:	san³	sæ̃³	sã³	san³	sã³
'mulberry'	sâng	saŋ¹	saŋ¹	saŋ¹	saŋ¹	saŋ¹
'twelfth month'	lâp	la⁵	næʔ⁷	la¹	na²	la¹
'pungent'	lât	la⁵	næʔ⁷	la¹	na²	la¹
'drop'	lâk	luo⁵	naʔ⁷	luo¹	no²	luo¹

Leaving aside the medials and those finals which contain a single high vowel, most Mandarin dialects show a basic vocalic contrast between two degrees of openness, usually represented as *a* and *ǝ*; while other non-high vowels sometimes occur, they do not ordinarily contrast with *a* and *ǝ* phonemically. We will see soon that a three-way contrast of non-high vowels is one of the features of the Central dialects.

Apical and retroflex vowels are a feature found in many Chinese dialects, but are especially prevalent in the Northern and Central groups. In addition to the unrounded apical [ɿ] and the retroflex [ʅ] vowels described for the standard language, a few dialects also possess rounded counterparts, a rounded apical vowel [ɥ] and a rounded retroflex vowel [ʮ] respectively.

Dialects of the Northern zone are generally rich in diphthongs and triphthongs, in conspicuous contrast to the Wú dialects, for example, where such combinations are much rarer. This may be viewed as a conservative feature when compared with Middle Chinese, in which vocalic clusters abounded.

From a comparative point of view, Mandarin dialects have a small number of tones. A few dialects have only three tones, such as Línchéng in Héběi. More typically four tones are found, as in the Peking dialect. In the Jiāng-Huái region five tones are not uncommon. A few Mandarin dialects with six tones have been reported along the boundary that separates the Northern and the Central dialects. Many Mandarin dialects (perhaps a majority) show a tonal pattern similar to that described for Peking: the *píng* tone occurs in two registers, the *yīnpíng* in words which in Middle Chinese had voiceless initials, and the *yángpíng* in words which in Middle Chinese had voiced initials: here and there one can encounter dialects in which these two categories have merged, for example, Zhāngjiākǒu in Héběi and Tàiyuán in Shānxī. No Mandarin dialect (as far as is known) shows a register distinction for the *shǎng* tone; words with voiced obstruent initials of this

Table 8.6. Tonal development in Mandarin dialects

Middle Chinese categories	Píng		Shǎng		Qù		Rù	
	Yīn	Yáng	Yīn	Yáng	Yīn	Yáng	Yīn	Yáng
Peking	1	2	3		5		1, 2 3, 5	2, 5
Yángzhōu	1	2	3		5		7	
Xīān	1	2	3		5		1	2
Chéngdū	1	2	3		5		2	
Tàiyuán	1		3		5		7	8

tone in Middle Chinese have become *qù* tone, while those with sonorant initials have merged with words in the upper *shǎng* tone to form a single *shǎng* category. A register distinction for the *qù* tone is exceedingly rare, found apparently only in a few dialects spoken in the border region between the Northern and Central dialects; examples of such dialects are Huángméi and Máchéng in eastern Húběi and Nántōng in Jiāngsū. The Middle Chinese *rù* tone has evolved in many different ways; in some conservative dialects it is retained as a distinct category: such is the case in Nánjīng and Yángzhōu in the Jiāng-Huái region, Tàiyuán in Shānxī, and Zhāngjiākǒu in Héběi. More typically it has merged with other tonal categories; in some cases the merger has been quite regular as in Chéngdū where all *rù* tone words have become *yángpíng*, but in other cases the distribution is only partly predictable, as in the standard language. The occurrence of atonal or unstressed syllables is universal in Mandarin dialects, but by no means limited to this group. Table 8.6 illustrates the development of tonal categories in five Mandarin dialects.[8]

It was remarked earlier that tonal values vary immensely from dialect to dialect. Table 8.7 provides a sampling of Mandarin tonal values.[9]

In the areas of lexicon and grammar, the Northern dialects can be clearly distinguished from other groups.[10] One of the most typical of Mandarin features is the pronominal system. Virtually all these dialects possess the same set of pronouns as the standard language. Of these, the third person form *tha*[1] is distinctively Northern; when it is found in a Central dialect, its occurrence there can usually be attributed to Northern influence. The Mandarin dialects are further characterized by their use of a common plural suffix, *-mən* in the standard language, but with many local variants depending upon the phonology of the par-

Table 8.7. Mandarin tonal values

Tonal category	1	2	3	5	7	8
Peking	55	35	214	51	–	–
Yángzhōu	21	35	31	55	4?	–
Xīān	31	24	42	55	–	–
Chéngdū	44	31	53	13	–	–
Língbǎo	31	35	55	22	–	–
Tàiyuán	11	—	53	55	21?	54?

Table 8.8. Mandarin pronouns

	'I'	'you'	'he/she'	'my'	'we'
Peking	uo^3	ni^3	tha^1	uo^3 tə	uo^3 mən
Yángzhōu	o^3	$liɪ^3$	tha^1	o^3 tiɪ	o^3 məŋ
Xīān	$ŋə^3$	ni^3	tha^1	$ŋə^3$ ti	$ŋə^3$ mẽ
Chéngdū	$ŋo^3$	ni^3	tha^1	$ŋo^3$ ni²	$ŋo^3$ mən
Língbǎo	$ŋɣ^3$	ni^3	tha^1	$ŋɣ^3$ ti	$ŋɣ^3$ mẽ

ticular dialect. The isogloss which separates the Northern type of pronominal system from the Southern type runs approximately along the Yangtze River.

Another related feature of the Northern dialects is the general subordinative particle, which is *tə* or *ti* in most dialects. This form, as Demiéville (1950) has shown, descends from the Classical word of similar function *zhī* (MC *tsï*, <OC **tjəg*). In contrast to Northern forms with initial dentals, Southern dialects employ forms with a velar (or zero) initial. As a general rule, dialects in which *tha¹* is the third-person pronoun have *tə* or *ti* as the subordinative suffix, while those which employ a Southern pronominal form for the third person have a subordinate suffix beginning with a velar or zero initial. The isogloss for this feature also coincides roughly with the Yangtze River; taken together, these two isoglosses are among the most ancient and important found in China. Examples of Mandarin pronominal forms are given in Table 8.8.

Like the pronouns, the Mandarin demonstratives are quite uniform. The near demonstrative is everywhere cognate to the *tʂə⁵* of the standard language; most dialects also employ forms related to the standard *na⁵* for the far demonstrative; Xīān and a few other Northwestern dialects have *uo³* or related forms.

Negative morphemes differ widely in the various dialect groups. Mandarin dialects have a general verbal negative *pu⁵*, and an existential negative ('there is not', 'has not') *mei²*; the second of these also does service as a verbal negator meaning 'not yet'; in non-Mandarin dialects a different form is often found for this last function.

It is not easy to find basic lexical items which are restricted entirely to the Mandarin group. On the one hand this is because the Mandarin dialects and the other groups have a common origin and consequently share a large proportion of their basic vocabularies; another and more important reason for this is that Northern features have been steadily borrowed by the Central and Southern dialects for many centuries. Here we will mention a few items which we believe are typically Mandarin, and which can be used as diagnostic features for identifying Mandarin dialects.

Among the basic verbs of motion, forms for 'come' and 'go' are of common origin throughout China; 'walk' and 'run', on the other hand, show a good deal of variation. Mandarin uses a verb *tsou*³ which in earlier Chinese meant 'run' (MC *tsəu:*); Southern dialects employ the older word *ɕiŋ*² (MC *yɐng*) and retain *tsou*³ in its original sense of 'run'. Since the older word for 'run' has been appropriated in the new sense of 'walk', another word has appeared in its place, namely *phau*³. Early Chinese used the verb *li*⁵ (MC *ljəp*) to mean 'stand', but only a few modern dialects have retained this word. Northern dialects employ *tʂan*⁵ (MC *ʈǎm-*), where Southern dialects use a verb that in Middle Chinese was read *gje:*. A typical Mandarin dialect will have the set *tsou*³ 'walk', *phau*³ 'run' and *tʂan*⁵ 'stand', whereas in the South one finds reflexes of Middle Chinese *yɐng* 'walk', *tsəu:* 'run' and *gje:* 'stand' for these same notions.

Kinship terms in general do not have much diagnostic value in dialect classification. Two exceptions are the words for 'son' and 'daughter-in-law'; Northern Chinese has *ər*² *tsï* and *ɕi*² *fu(r)* (MC *sjək bju:*) respectively. For 'son' the Central and Southern dialects use a variety of different locutions, some of which we will examine in due course; for 'daughter-in-law', Southern Chinese employs a term which literally means 'new woman (or wife)' (MC *sjen bju:*). In modern dialects the difference between the Northern and Southern terms for 'daughter-in-law' is chiefly reflected by the presence of a nasal final in the first syllable of the word in the South but an open or glottal stop final in the North. Table 8.9 illustrates the distribution of the lexical items discussed here in a number of representative dialects; 1–3 are Mandarin; 4 is Wú; 5 is Xiāng; 6 is Gàn; 7 is Kèjiā; 8 is Yuè; 9 is Mǐn.[11]

8.7 The Central dialects

We saw at the beginning of this chapter that the Chinese dialects can be divided into two clear-cut types: a Northern type, to which all the Mandarin dialects belong, and a Southern type, to which the Kèjiā, Yuè and Mǐn groups belong.

Table 8.9. Diagnostic lexical items

	'walk'	'run'	'stand'	'son'	'daughter-in-law'
1. Peking	tsou³	phau³	tṣan⁵	ər² tsï	ɕi² fər
2. Yángzhōu	tsɤɯ³	phɔ³	tsɛ̃⁵	a² tsɛ	ɕiə?⁷ fu
3. Chéngdū	tsəu³	phau³	tsan⁵	ər²	ɕi² fər
4. Wēnzhōu	tsau³	zei⁸	ge⁴	ŋ²	səŋ¹ vøy⁶
5. Chángshā	tsəu³	phau³	tsan⁵	tsai³	ɕi² fu
6. Nánchāng	tsɛu³	phau³	tɕhi⁶	tsai³	ɕin¹ fu⁶
7. Méixiàn	haŋ²	tsɛu³	khi¹	lai⁵ ɛ	sim¹ khiu¹
8. Guǎngzhōu	ha:ŋ²	tsau³	khei⁴	tsai³	sam¹ phou⁴
9. Xiàmén	kiã²	tsau³	khia⁶	kiã³	sin¹ pu⁶

Between these two types a large transitional zone intervenes in which the dialects exhibit both Northern and Southern features. I view the Northern and Southern groups as subgroups of Chinese in the conventional sense of the term, but it is doubtful whether the Central dialects can be viewed as a subgroup in the same sense. It is my view that this zone is the result of centuries of Northern linguistic intrusions into a region that originally was home to dialects of a more purely Southern type; in the course of many centuries, the original Southern features of these dialects have been progressively eroded, leaving dialects of mixe·' type such as those we find today. When examined in their present-day form, it is difficult to determine if the dialects of this zone themselves possessed some sort of original unity or if their only common feature is simply their transitionality. Their single common phonological trait at present would seem to be that they all treat the Middle Chinese voiced stops in a uniform way: in Wú they are retained; in Gàn they all become voiceless aspirates; in Xiāng they all become non-aspirates with voicing preserved to varying degrees in different dialects. However, it must be noted that other groups also share this feature so that it cannot serve as a sufficient condition for identifying a Central dialect. One can also observe a tendency to maintain a phonemic contrast between *a* and *o* in syllables ending in *n* (and *m*): this contrast does not however extend to the Xiāng dialects.[12]

The Central dialects are tonally more complex than those of the North; specifically, they retain a register distinction for the *qù* tone, a feature extremely rare in Mandarin as we have seen. In most areas the *rù* tone is retained as a separate category. The number of tones ranges from five in some Xiāng dialects to eight in certain conservative Wú dialects.

The Central dialects employ pronouns of the Southern type, except where Mandarin influence is strong and *tha*[1] has been imported; likewise, forms with velar initials are the rule for the subordinative particle. The common negative is cognate to Northern *pu⁵*. (I consider the Wú negatives – Sūzhōu *fəʔ⁷*, Wēnzhōu *fu³*, etc. – as well as forms beginning with *p* all to be reflexes of Middle Chinese *pjuət*.) It is significant that there is no Central dialect with a negative cognate to those of the Southern group (Guǎngzhōu *m²*, Kèjiā *m²*, Xiàmén *m⁶*, etc.).

With the exception of a few sites, there are only very sketchy data on the Central dialects. Until we have more extensive descriptions, it will remain difficult to interpret these dialects in a proper historico-linguistic context. In view of the presently limited nature of our information on this group, the remarks offered above should be considered tentative.

8.8 The Wú dialects

The Wú dialects are spoken in Jiāngsū south of the Yangtze, with the exception of the region around Nánjīng, which is Mandarin-speaking. In addition, Wú is spoken on Chóngmíng island in the Yangtze estuary and in a few localities north of the river. The province of Zhèjiāng is mostly within the Wú area; some localities in the southwestern part of the province, such as Qìngyuán and Lóngquán, are apparently not Wú, however.[13] A few counties in northeastern Jiāngxī (Yùshān, Guǎngfēng) are also reported to be within the boundaries of the Wú group. Like Mandarin, Wú has been carried overseas only in relatively recent times.

Wú is usually divided into a northern (Jiāngsū) type and a southern (Zhèjiāng) type (Chao 1967, 100), but the details on which such a division is based are not entirely clear. According to Yuán Jiāhuá (1960), the dialects of the southern part of Zhèjiāng such as Wēnzhōu, Jīnhuá, Yǒngkāng and Qúzhōu are very different from the typical northern Wú dialects in vocabulary; Yuán thinks that this may be due to influence from other dialect groups. Y. R. Chao (1967) has observed that in the Wú dialects of Zhèjiāng there is less divergence between reading and spoken pronunciations of characters, showing that southern Wú is more purely Wú than the northern dialects of this group, which are strongly influenced by Mandarin. A fully satisfactory solution to the problem of Wú subgrouping will have to await more complete descriptions and glossaries of a wider variety of Wú dialects.

The most prominent phonological trait of Wú is the uniform preservation of a three-way distinction of initial stops. In addition to voiceless aspirated and unaspirated stops, all the Wú dialects possess a third series, whose precise phonetic nature differs somewhat from region to region. In most of the northern Wú dialects, the third series has a lenis voiceless onset followed by breathy voice or murmur when they occur initially in a phrase [b̥ɦ, d̥ɦ], etc.; when they occur after another syllable in a phrase, however, they are fully voiced. In the southern part

Table 8.10. Shànghǎi initials

	Labials	Dentals	Alveolar sibilants	Palatals	Velars	Glottals
Unaspirated stops	p	t	ts	tɕ	k	
Aspirated stops	ph	th	tsh	tɕh	kh	
Voiced stops	b	d		dʑ	g	
Voiceless fricatives	f		s	ɕ		h
Voiced fricatives	v		z	ʑ		ɦ
Nasals	m	n		ɲ	ŋ	
Liquids	w	l		j		

of Zhèjiāng this series is voiced throughout, and is without any perceptible breathy voice or murmur: [b, d, g], etc. The voiceless unaspirated stops of Wú, in comparison with the voiceless non-aspirates of Peking and most Mandarin dialects, are very fortis, giving a rather "hard" or "crisp" impression. To give an idea of the consonantal system of a typical Wú dialect, the initials of the Shànghǎi dialect are shown in Table 8.10.[14] From the table we can see that the most striking difference between Wú and Mandarin is the presence of a feature of voicing which serves to distinguish almost all the obstruents into two types, one voiced, one voiceless. Here and there, other Wú dialects make a few more distinctions than are made in Shànghǎi: a few dialects have *dz* in addition to *z*; there are also a few dialects which have a separate alveopalatal (or retroflex) series of affricates and fricatives which contrast with the plain alveolar and palatal sibilants. Palatalization of velars before high front vowels is usual for Wú.

Viewed historically, the Wú initials are more conservative than those of Mandarin. In addition to the preservation of the voiceless/voiced contrast which we have already noted, the following points are also to be found. Middle Chinese *ng* is retained in Wú as a separate and distinctive initial; although in general a part of the Middle Chinese bilabials have dentilabialized (as they have in a majority of Chinese dialects), in a few popular words initial *m* is preserved where Mandarin has *w* (from an earlier *v*): Shànghǎi has *məŋ²* 'ask' (with a reading pronunciation *vəŋ²*) and *m²* 'have not' (with a reading pronunciation *vu²*); cf. Mandarin *wèn* and *wú* respectively (Chao 1967, 95).

Wú dialects, as a rule, have a very rich inventory of vocalic contrasts. Table 8.11 gives the vowels found in the Shànghǎi dialect. The vowels *i, e, ɛ, ï, ə,* and *a* are all unrounded; the others are rounded to some degree. Shànghǎi and a number of other Wú dialects lack diphthongs of the descending type, *ai, ou,* etc., as a consequence of monophthongization: where the standard language has *lai* and

Table 8.11. Shànghǎi vowels

	Front	Central	Back
High	i y	ï	u
Upper mid	e ø		o
Lower mid	ε	ə ɵ	ɔ
Low		a	

lou, Shànghǎi has *lɛ* and *lə*. There are two medials, *i* and *u*; some Wú dialects may have an additional medial *y*. In the Shànghǎi dialect there are basically three types of finals: open, that is, ending in one of the vowels in Table 8.11; nasal, ending in *ŋ*; and abrupt, ending in glottal stop. The occurrence of vowels before final *ŋ* and *ʔ* is restricted to *i, ə, a, u, o,* and *ɔ*. Apical (and more rarely retroflex) vowels are as prevalent in Wú as they are in Mandarin, if not more so. On the whole, however, Wú dialects tend to have a much richer inventory of vocalic contrasts than do Mandarin dialects; on the other hand, as we have already pointed out, Mandarin dialects are richer in diphthongs and triphthongs.

Middle Chinese final *m* and *n* tend to be lost in most Wú dialects after low vowels: *sâm > sɛ, nậm > nə*, etc. Final *ng* either nasalizes a preceding vowel or is retained as a velar nasal: *tâng > tɔ̃* or *taŋ*. From a synchronic point of view, most Wú dialects have a simple contrast of nasal and non-nasal finals: in nasal finals, the actual phonetic realization of nasality is conditioned by the preceding vowel. In Sūzhōu, for example, *ŋ* is found after the low and back vowels, *n* after front and central vowels. Wēnzhōu has only final *ŋ*.

The Shànghǎi tonal system is not typical for the Wú dialects, most of which have seven or eight tones (Chao 1967). To give some idea of the tones of Wú dialects, I have charted the tonal systems of several different dialects in Table 8.12. It is clear from the table that the Wú dialects as a whole maintain a very strict distinction between the upper (*yīn*) and lower (*yáng*) registers in all tonal categories. This is not surprising in view of the fact that the feature which gave rise to different registers, namely a contrast of voiced and voiceless initials, is still retained in Wú; in many Wú dialects the lower register is characterized by a breathy aspiration or murmur, even with sonorant initials. In some northern Wú dialects the *shǎng* tone behaves as in Mandarin: words with sonorant initials merge with the upper shǎng, while those with obstruent initials go over to the lower *qù* category. In Zhèjiāng (with the exception of Hángzhōu) the lower *shǎng* is commonly preserved as a distinct category, and sonorant and obstruent initials are treated alike. Where the *rù* tone is preserved as a separate category, it is

Table 8.12. Wú tonal systems

Middle Chinese categories	Píng		Shăng		Qù		Rù	
	Yīn	Yáng	Yīn	Yáng	Yīn	Yáng	Yīn	Yáng
Shànghăi	1	2	3	2	3	2	7	8
Sūzhōu	1	2	3	6	5	6	7	8
Hángzhōu	1	2	3	6	5	6	7	8
Shàoxīng	1	2	3	4	5	6	7	8
Yǒngkāng	1	2	3	4	5	6	3	4
Wēnzhōu	1	2	3	4	5	6	7	8

Table 8.13. Wú tonal values

Tonal category	1	2	3	4	5	6	7	8
Shànghăi	42	24	35	—	—	—	55	23
Sūzhōu	44	24	41	—	513	(3)31	44	23
Hángzhōu	44	213	41	—	445	11	54	12
Shàoxīng	51	231	335	113	33	11	45	12
Yǒngkāng	44	22	35	13	52	24(1)	—	—
Wēnzhōu	44	31	45	24	42	11	23	12

Note: Underlining of a tonal value indicates that the tone in question is shorter or more abrupt than those which are not underlined.

generally characterized by the presence of a final glottal stop. Table 8.13 gives the phonetic values of the tonal categories in Table 8.12. It illustrates that lower-register tones in Wú are regularly lower in pitch than their corresponding upper-register counterparts.

Tone sandhi is a consistent feature of all Wú dialects. This means that in many cases (or in most cases, in some dialects) tones undergo changes when they occur in phrases consisting of two or more syllables. Actually Wú is part of a "sandhi zone" in southeastern China that stretches from the Yangtze River in the north to the Cháozhōu region of Guǎngdōng, and includes many Mǐn dialects as well as Wú dialects. All the dialects in this zone possess rather intricate rules of tone sandhi, but the mechanics operate differently from dialect to dialect.[15]

In sharp contrast to Mandarin, Wú displays a great deal of variety in its basic

Table 8.14. Wú pronominal forms

	'I'	'you'	'he/she'	'my'	'we'
Dānyáng	ηou³	η³	tha¹	ηou³ kəη⁷	ηou³ dzi²
Sūzhōu	ηəu⁶	ne⁶	li¹	ηəu⁶ kəη	ɲi²
Shànghǎi	ηu²	noη²	ji²	ηu² gəη⁷	ɲi²
Hángzhōu	ηɔ³	ni³	tha¹	ηɔ³ tiη⁷	ηɔ³ men
Shàoxīng	ηo⁴	noη⁸	ji²	ηo⁴ gəη⁸	ηa⁴ laη⁸
Yǒngkāng	ηoi⁴	n⁴	gou²	ηoi⁴ ke¹	ηoi⁴ lø⁶ noη²
Wēnzhōu	η⁴	ɲi⁴	gi²	η⁴ gai⁶	η⁴ le²

vocabulary, particularly in pronouns and demonstratives. A sample of Wú pronominal forms is shown in Table 8.14.[16] All the first-person pronouns can be viewed as reflexes of Middle Chinese *ngâ:*, which is also ancestral to the Mandarin forms and those in most other dialects as well. The second-person pronouns do not appear to have a common origin, and their etymological roots are not absolutely clear at present. The greatest variety is to be observed in the third-person pronouns: Dānyáng and Hángzhōu both have *tha¹*, clearly of Mandarin origin; the Shànghǎi and Shàoxīng forms are both cognate to Middle Chinese *ʔi*, a pronoun otherwise attested mainly in the Mǐn dialects. The southern Zhèjiāng dialects of Yǒngkāng and Wēnzhōu have forms which are probably to be associated with Middle Chinese *gjwo*, which is probably the source of most Southern third-person pronouns. This obvious disparity among third-person pronominal forms suggests that the unity of Wú as a subgroup perhaps rests more on its typological similarities than on deep historical roots.

This disparity of basic vocabulary is confirmed by the Wú demonstratives. For 'this' a number of dialects have *kəʔ⁷* or *keʔ⁷* (Dānyáng, Hángzhōu, Shàoxīng); Sūzhōu has *ke¹*, and Wēnzhōu has *ki⁷*. There is even greater variation for 'that': Dānyáng and Yǒngkāng both have *kou⁵*, Sūzhōu has *kue¹*, Shànghǎi has *i¹* (related to its third person pronoun *ji²*?), Hángzhōu has *la³*, Shàoxīng has *haŋ⁵* and Wēnzhōu *hi³*.

Wú negatives are fairly homogeneous. Corresponding to Mandarin *bù*, Wú has forms with a labiodental initial; a distinction between an existential negative and a preverbal form meaning 'not yet' is consistently maintained; this latter form generally consists of the general negative plus a following *zəŋ* or *dzəŋ*; the corresponding form in Mandarin, *bùcéng*, is found only in premodern prose, and if it was ever current in Mandarin vernaculars, it is now totally obsolete. A representative set of Wú negatives is given in Table 8.15. The Wēnzhōu negative for 'not yet' is not a typical Wú formation but is related rather to corresponding

Table 8.15. Wú negatives

	General negative	Existential negative	'not yet'
Dānyáng	fəʔ⁷	n² tsəʔ⁷	fəʔ⁷ dzəŋ²
Sūzhōu	fəʔ⁷	m² pəʔ⁷	fən¹
Shànghǎi	vəʔ⁷	m² məʔ⁸	vəʔ⁷ zəŋ²
Shàoxīng	veʔ⁸	ɲ¹ iou¹	veʔ⁸ ziŋ²
Wēnzhōu	fu³	n⁵ nau⁴	mei⁶

Southern forms: Guǎngzhōu *mei⁶*, Xiamen *be⁶*, Fuzhou *mui⁶*, all of which are derived from the Classical Chinese *wèi* (MC *mjuei-*).

The Hángzhōu dialect occupies a special place among the Wú dialects. In phonology it possesses all the typical Wú features discussed above: a three-way division of initial stop contrasts, seven tones, a *rù* tone ending in glottal stop. Lexically and grammatically, however, Hángzhōu is very like Mandarin: the third-person pronoun is *tha¹*, the subordinative particle is *tiʔ* and the plural suffix is *men*; it does not make a distinction between the existential negative and the form meaning 'not yet' – *məʔ⁸ iou³* being used for both; this form is an exact correspondence to Mandarin *méiyou*. Chao's (1967) description of the Hángzhōu dialect as having a Wú phonology and a Mandarin vocabulary is quite apt. The historical explanation for this state of affairs is that Hángzhōu became the capital of the Southern Song dynasty (1127–1279) when North China fell to the Jurchens in the twelfth century. The northern court and bureaucracy brought along their northern dialect much as the fugitive Jìn aristocrats had brought a northern dialect to Jīnlíng some 800 years earlier. We can hypothesize that the local population adopted the prestigious northern dialect of the new immigrants, not integrally, but by replacing the lexicon of their original dialect item by item, using the corresponding local Wú morphemes in most cases rather than trying to copy the new dialect in all its details. In essence what happened was a relexification of the old local Wú dialect by a process similar to that observed in certain Creole languages by recent linguists (Whinnom 1965; 1971).

8.9 The Gàn dialects

The Gàn dialects as a group are known only in a sketchy fashion, so what we say here is of an especially tentative nature. The Gàn dialects are spoken chiefly in Jiāngxī province and in the eastern part of Húnán. The dialects of the southeastern corner of Húběi would also seem to be of this type. All of these dialects have voiceless aspirated stops in all tones for the Middle Chinese voiced stop and affricate initials. The Kèjiā dialects, as well as a few Mandarin and Mǐn dialects,

Table 8.16. Gàn and Jīxī pronominal forms

	'I'	'you'	'he/she'	'my'	'we'
Nánchāng	ŋɔ³	li³, n³	tɕhiɛ²	ŋɔ³ kɔ	ŋɔ³ tuŋ
Línchuān	ŋo³	li³	ke³	ŋo³ ko	ŋo³ koi¹ to¹ ɲin²
Fèngxīn	ŋo⁶	ɲi⁶	tɕi⁶	ŋo⁶ ko	ŋon³ li
Jīxī	a³	n³	ke²	a³ ne	a³ mæ̃²

also possess this feature. The convergence between Gàn and Kèjiā with regard to this development led Luó Chángpéi (1950) to propose that Gàn and Kèjiā formed a single group. Yuán Jiāhuá (1960, 128) rejected this view because, in its lexicon, Gàn resembles Wú and Xiāng more than it does Kèjiā. In our scheme, the Gàn dialects belong to the Central zone, and are clearly of a transitional type; so we follow Yuán Jiāhuá in keeping Gàn and Kèjiā separate. We will have more to say on this subject in the next chapter.

Gàn dialects as a rule have six or seven tones; a few have only five tones (Yang 1971). Those with six and seven tones have a register distinction for either the *qù* or the *rù* tone. Conservative dialects like that of Línchuān (Luó 1958) retain all the final consonants of Middle Chinese; Nánchāng, the representative dialect of the group, has merged final *m* and *p* with *n* and *t* respectively (Yang 1969b). Other Gàn dialects have reduced the inventory of final consonants even further.

Palatalization of velars before high front vowels is found in all Gàn dialects, as it is in the other Central dialects. The velar nasal *ng* survives as a separate initial. Viewed as a whole, there is very little that distinguishes the initials of Gàn from those of the other dialects which have lost voiced initials.

The vowels of Gàn dialects are rather like those of Mandarin, except that *a* and *o* contrast in finals like *an/on, am/om* and *ai/oi*. Contrasts of this type are common in many Central dialects. Like Mandarin, Gàn has a rich inventory of diphthongs and triphthongs. Luó Chángpéi cited as one of the features connecting Gàn and Kèjiā the pronunciation of Middle Chinese *əu* as *eu* (or *ɛu*), but this pronunciation is also found in western Mǐn dialects and would not appear to be a sufficient criterion for uniting Gàn and Kèjiā into a single subgroup.

The Gàn pronominal system is clearly of the Southern type. The third-person pronoun is related to the Middle Chinese *gjwo*; cognate forms are widely used throughout the adjoining regions where Kèjiā, Mǐn, Yuè and Xiāng dialects are spoken. The subordinative suffix generally has a velar initial, as do other dialects of the Central and Southern zones. The plural suffix varies from place to place. Gàn pronominal forms are shown in Table 8.16; for comparison, forms for the Jīxī dialect in southern Ānhūi are also given.[17]

The demonstratives of the Gàn dialects differ from the northern type: Nán-chāng has $k\rho^3$ for 'this' and $h\varepsilon^3$ for 'that'; Línchuān has koi^1 and e^1 respectively. Fèngxīn has hi^3 for 'this', he^3 for 'that'. The general negative is $p\rho t^7$ (Nánchāng, Fèngxīn) or put^7 (Línchuān), cognate to both Mandarin $bù$ and Wú $f\rho^2{}^7$. The existential negative is mau^6 in Nánchāng and Fèngxīn, mau^2 in Línchuān. These latter forms are typically Southern and cognates are found in Yuè, Kèjiā and Mǐn. As far as can be determined, Gàn does not distinguish an existential nega-tive from a form meaning 'not yet'; in this regard it resembles Mandarin more than Wú or the Southern dialects.

For 'to walk' $tseu^3$ is general. In Nánchāng, where $tsan^5$ and $t\rho hi^6$ coexist as verbs meaning 'to stand', $tsan^5$ is obviously a loan from a Northern dialect; Línchuān has only the usual Southern form $t\rho hi^6$ in this sense.

The Gàn dialects are located in a part of China which lies along one of the most convenient routes between north and south. The Gàn River, which flows through the province, has historically been one of the main routes between the Yangtze basin and the far south. The region has been more open to north-ern influence than most of the Wú-speaking area, and this is reflected in the rather strongly northern flavor of some of these dialects. Yuán Jiāhuá's (1960) observation that the Gàn dialects are not sharply differentiated from other dialects in their vicinity seems valid; this is at least partly due to the constant encroachment of northern elements into this easily accessible part of the Central zone.

With the data presently available to us, it is extremely difficult to draw the boundaries of the Gàn group. If the evolution of the Middle Chinese voiced stops to aspirates in all four tones is taken as the sole criterion for identify-ing a dialect of this group, then its territory would be very large indeed, but I have already remarked that it is doubtful whether such a simple criterion is acceptable. A typical example of the sort of problem we encounter in this region is the affiliation of the Huīzhōu dialects spoken south of the Yangtze in Ānhuī province. Chao and Yang (1965), in their description of the Jīxī dialect, observe that these dialects are difficult to classify, noting that they show fea-tures of several different groups. Jīxī has voiceless aspirates for all the Middle Chinese voiced stops; in this regard it is very like Gàn, which is spoken imme-diately to the south of the Huīzhōu area. Moreover, Jīxī has ke^2 as its third-person pronoun, almost identical to that of Línchuān, ke^3 (cf. Table 8.16). It would not be doing too much violence to the facts to consider Jīxī a variety of Gàn, differing from it mainly in having been even more strongly influenced by Northern Chinese, owing to its greater proximity to the Mandarin-speaking area.

Table 8.17. Preservation of voicing in Xiāng

	Middle Chinese	Chéngbù	Shuāngfēng	Shàoyáng	Chángshā
'snake'	dźje	dzie²	ɣio²	ze²	sɣ²
'peach'	dâu	dao²	də²	daɣ²	taɣ²
'sit'	dzuâ:	dzo⁶	dzu⁶	tso⁶	tso⁶
'together'	gjong-	goŋ⁶	gaŋ⁶	koŋ⁶	koŋ⁵
'cave'	dung-	doŋ⁶	daŋ⁶	toŋ⁶	toŋ⁵
'ten'	źjəp	zi⁷	ʂï⁷	sï⁷	sï⁷
'white'	bɐk	ba⁷	piɛ²	pe⁶	pɣ⁷

8.10 The Xiāng dialects

The Xiāng dialects have unaspirated reflexes for the Middle Chinese voiced stops in all four tones; more conservative dialects have retained voicing to some degree, while in the more evolved types the original voiced stops have become voiceless non-aspirated in all tonal categories. Yuán Jiāhuá (1960) refers to the latter type as "New Xiāng" and the more conservative types as "Old Xiāng." Both varieties of Xiāng are spoken in the central and southwestern parts of Húnán province.

From the *Húnán fāngyán diàochá bàogào* [*Report on a survey of the dialects of Húnán*] (Yang 1974), we can form a good general idea of this dialect group. From it we can see, for example, that only a small number of the dialects surveyed preserve voiced stops in all tones. We can also observe that the great majority of Xiāng dialects have undergone strong Northern influence; in some cases this influence has been so all-pervasive that only a very small number of Xiāng features have been preserved, and it is difficult to determine how such dialects should actually be classified. To get a clear idea of what a "pure" Xiāng dialect is, we will examine that of Chéngbù in the extreme southwestern corner of the province.

Chéngbù has voiced stops in all tonal categories; unlike the voiced stops of Wú, they are described as being fully voiced and lacking the aspiration or murmur associated with the voiced stops of many Wú dialects. Chéngbù has six tones: both the *píng* and *qù* tones are divided into an upper and lower register; the *shǎng* and *rù* tones lack a register distinction. (Six is the maximum number of tones recorded for any Xiāng dialect; varieties with four and five tones are also found.) The finals of Chéngbù generally resemble those of a southwestern Mandarin dialect; of the original Middle Chinese final stops only *n* and *ŋ* are preserved. Chángshā, one of the New Xiāng dialects, is like Chéngbù except that it has lost the voiced stops, having converted them uniformly into the corresponding voiceless non-aspirates. Table 8.17 illustrates the degree to which voicing has

Table 8.18. Xiāng pronominal forms

	'I'	'you'	'he/she'	'my'	'we'
Chéngbù	ŋo³	ɲi³	tɕi³	ŋo³ kə	ŋo³ ni
Qíyáng	ŋo³	ɲi³	ki¹	ŋo³ ti	ŋo³ næ
Shuāngfēng	aŋ	n³	tho¹	aŋ³ kə	ŋu³ nin²
Chángshā	ŋo³	n³ ~ ɲi³	tha¹	ŋo³ ti	ŋo³ mən

been preserved in several representative Xiāng dialects.[18] We can see that Xiāng presents a picture very different from that which we have seen in the Wú dialects: where Wú consistently preserves voiced (or murmured) stops in all tonal categories, the process of devoicing is already well advanced in the Xiāng group. Xiāng has lost all trace of the final stops originally found in the *rù* tone; again, this is a feature which distinguishes most Wú dialects from Xiāng.

When the group is viewed as a whole, the Xiāng lexicon is seen to be strongly mandarinized. Some of these dialects have been so strongly influenced by Northern dialects that they remind one of Hángzhōu in the Wú region, and it is quite probable that some of them have also undergone a similar process of relexification. A conservative dialect like Chéngbù still retains a strongly non-Mandarin (or Southern) element in its basic lexicon, counter to the general tendency just described. The Mandarin pronominal system has been widely adopted; fortunately the original Xiāng system still survives here and there, proving that the Mandarin type systems are an innovation. Table 8.18 gives a sample of Xiāng pronouns.[19] We can observe several degrees of mandarinization in the dialects in Table 8.18; Chéngbù represents a system still free of Mandarin influence; the other three dialects all exhibit such influences at varying stages.

In other lexical areas Xiāng also shows a mixture of northern and southern terms. Demonstratives tend to be non-northern even in the New Xiāng dialects; for example, Chángshā has *kei*[7] for 'this' and *lai*[5] for 'that'; Chéngbù has *ko*[5] and *ni*[5] respectively. For 'to stand', the more conservative dialects have words cognate to Middle Chinese *gje:*; mandarinized dialects use words cognate to *zhàn*. Xiāng shares its existential negative with Gàn: Chángshā *maɤ*[6], Shuāngfēng *mə*[6], Chengbu *mao*[6]. From available data it is not entirely clear whether any of the Xiāng dialects distinguishes the existential negative from a preverbal form meaning 'not yet'. Like the other Central dialects, Xiāng generally employs cognates of *bù* as the general negative.

From the Húnán *Survey* it is evident that the Xiāng dialects are undergoing erosion of their original non-northern features; in some dialects this process is virtually complete while in others it is still not advanced; a majority of the dialects seem to occupy an intermediate state in this respect. When examining this state of affairs, one wonders if the dialects of this group will not eventually lose their separate character altogether and merge into southwestern Mandarin.

Further reading

Chao, Yuen Ren 1967. Contrastive aspects of the Wu dialects. *Language* 43, 92–101. [The best concise overview of the Wú dialect group.]

Egerod, Søren 1967. Dialectology. In *Current trends in linguistics*, vol. 2, ed. Thomas A. Sebeok. The Hague: Mouton. [A good introductory description of the Chinese dialects.]

Li, Fang-kuei 1937. Languages and dialects. *The Chinese yearbook*. Reprinted with revisions in the *Journal of Chinese Linguistics* 1973, 1.1–13. [This article contains the classic formulation of the Chinese dialect groups.]

Yuán, Jiāhuá 1960. *Hànyǔ fāngyán gàiyào*. Peking: Wénzi Gǎigé Chūbǎnshè. [The standard handbook on Chinese dialects.]

9

The dialects of the Southeast

9.1 Common features found in the Southern dialects

In the scheme presented in Chapter 8, I placed the Mǐn, Kèjiā and Yuè dialects in a single category which I called the Southern group. It is my contention that these dialects were once much more similar to one another than they are at the present time, and that they can be viewed as sharing a common historical source. This source I shall call Old Southern Chinese; there is evidence that dialects of this type were once much more widely spread than they are today. It is very likely, for example, that the Wú dialects spoken in the trans-Yangtze region in the late Han, Sanguo and Western Jìn dynasties were a type of Old Southern Chinese; this view can be corroborated by material from Yáng Xióng's *Fāngyán* and the dialectal glosses of the Jìn dynasty scholar Guō Pú (276–324) as well as by Buddhist transcriptional evidence (Pulleyblank 1979). This ancient Wú dialect should not be confused with the modern Wú dialects discussed in Chapter 8, which are not of the Southern type.

When Fújiàn and Guǎngdōng (the present homeland of the Southern dialects) were first settled, the new immigrants brought with them varieties of Old Chinese. Isolated in the mountains and valleys of the far south, they no doubt quickly began to develop local peculiarities, influenced in many cases by the aboriginal languages found in various regions. In areas which for geographic or topographic reasons were more exposed to Northern influence, these archaic Southern Chinese dialects freely incorporated elements from each new wave of Northern immigration, while in other more remote and mountainous regions (like Fújiàn), they guarded their archaic aspect more faithfully. As a result of such external influences, over the course of two millennia, the original unity of these dialects became more and more obscured. Today, to the superficial observer, Mǐn, Kèjiā and Yuè appear very different from one another, but if one examines them closely with an eye to identifying their most ancient and autochthonous elements, one begins to see that they share some important features. These convergences, I

210

Table 9.1. Retention of bilabials in the Southern dialects

	MC	Peking	Yuè	Kèjiā	Mǐn (Xiàmén)
'float'	bjəu	fú	phou^2	feu^2	phu^2
'ax'	pju:	fŭ	(pou^3)	pu^3	pɔ^3
'woman'	bjəu:	fù	phou^4	fu^5	pu^6
'hatch'	bjəu-	fù	pou^6	phu^5	pu^6
'capsize'	phjuk	fù	phuk^7	phuk^7	phak^7
'fat'	bjuei	féi	fei^2	phui^2	pui^2
'bee'	phjwong	fēng	fuŋ^1	phuŋ^1	phaŋ^1

believe, point to a common origin for these dialects. Below we will examine some of the chief features which point in this direction.

The *Qièyùn* dictionary represents a stage of Chinese in which there were no labiodentals, but only bilabials. By the time of the rhyme tables, however, a goodly proportion of the *Qièyùn* bilabials had already become labiodentals. This process affected all the Northern and Central dialects without exception. Mǐn preserves bilabials in a large number of words which have become labiodentals in the Northern and Central dialects; Kèjiā also retains a significant number of such unchanged forms, as many in fact as do some Mǐn dialects. In the case of Yuè, the number of unshifted forms, while quite small, is still sufficient to establish that the oldest stratum of Yuè vocabulary goes back to a language in which labiodentalization did not take place. In Table 9.1 a selection of forms in Mǐn, Kèjiā and Yuè are given to illustrate this situation. (Yuè examples are Guǎngzhōu dialect except for 'ax' which is from the Yángjiāng dialect. Kèjiā forms are all from the Méixiàn dialect.)[1]

A feature which is perhaps related to the retention of bilabials in the Southern dialects is the strong resistance to the palatalization of velars. Actually Chinese has undergone two stages of palatalization. That which in post-*Qièyùn* times has affected virtually all of the Northern and Central dialects is comparatively recent; the Southern dialects have been virtually unaffected by this stage. The earlier one took place between the periods of Old and Middle Chinese; Middle Chinese forms like *tśje* 'branch', *tśhï:* 'tooth' and *tśi:* 'point' can be shown to derive from earlier velars; although the conditions under which this process took place are still controversial, the fact of its occurrence cannot be contested. The Mǐn dialects still preserve a few forms which did not undergo this earlier palatalization: Xiàmén *ki^1* 'branch', *khi^3* 'tooth', *ki^3* 'point'. Kèjiā apparently retains only a single velar form from this early period: *ki^1* 'branch'; no unshifted forms have been found in Yuè so far.[2] Taken together, these facts demonstrate an exceptionally strong resistance to any kind of affrication on the part of the Southern dialects throughout the entire course of their history.

Another development which reveals a deep-seated relationship among the three dialect groups is the development of the Old Chinese rhyme group *gē*. Li Fang-kuei (1971) reconstructs this rhyme group as *(u)ar*. In Middle Chinese this final had become *â* in plain syllables and *uâ* in *hékŏu* (rounded) syllables. The Northern and Central dialects all derive from a stage identical to that of Middle Chinese. In the South, however, we have evidence of a different development: in the ancestor of these dialects, *ar* became *âi* and *uar* became *oi*. Evidence for such a development is found not only in the Southern dialects which we are discussing here, but also in the earliest stratum of Chinese loanwords in Vietnamese and Yao. Both Yuè and Kèjiā preserve only vestiges of this development: Standard Cantonese has only *thaai*[4] (OC *dar* > MC *dâ:*) 'rudder of a boat' and *løy*[2] (OC *luar* > MC *luâ*) 'snail'; the Yuè dialect of Táishān has *ŋoi*[1] (OC *ngar* > MC *ngâ:*) 'I, me' and *koi*[1] (OC *kar* > MC *kâ-*) 'individual measure word' (Wong 1970). These two forms are also found in Kèjiā: *ŋai*[2] 'I, me', and *kai*[5] 'individual measure word'. The greatest number of such forms is found in Mǐn; the following examples (by no means a complete listing) are from the Fúzhōu dialect: *tuai*[6] 'rudder', *løi*[2] 'snail', *ŋuai*[3] 'I, me', *phuai*[5] (OC *phar* > MC *phua-*) 'broken', *soi*[6] (OC *dzuar* > MC *dzuâ:*) 'sit', *muai*[2] (OC *mar* > MC *muâ*) 'whet, sharpen'. To illustrate parallel forms from old loans into Vietnamese, we can cite *ngài* (OC *ngar* > MC *ngâ*) 'silkworm moth' and *mài* 'whet, sharpen'. Yuè and Kejiā must once have had many more words showing this Old Southern Chinese development, but at the present time, most words of this category have been replaced by forms which reflect the development found in the Northern and Central dialects. In general, the Old Southern basis of Yuè and Kèjiā survives only in vestiges like this, but fortunately enough still remains to make it possible to identify the ultimate roots of these dialects.

When looked at as a whole, the Southern dialects can be seen to possess a similar syllable structure. They typically have a simple set of initials in which voicing has been totally lost as a distinctive feature, not very different in this respect from the initials found in Mandarin and Gàn. A few dialects distinguish two sets of sibilants (alveolar or dental vs. alveopalatal), but most do not. As we have already noted, velars are regularly retained before high front vowels. Perhaps their most distinctive characteristic is the retention of all six of the final consonants found in Middle Chinese. In all three subgroups, dialects are found which have merged two or more of these final consonants, but such dialects cannot be taken as representative of their respective groups. Among non-Southern

Table 9.2. Forms for 'poison' in Southern Chinese

	'poison' n.	'to poison'
Middle Chinese	duok	—
Mĭn (Fúzhōu)	tøik[8]	thau[5]
Yuè	tuk[8]	tou[6]
Kèjiā	thuk[8]	theu[5]

dialects, only in the more conservative Gàn dialects is a similar retention of final consonants found.

In the realm of lexicon and grammar, one form serves to distinguish the Southern dialects from those of the Northern and Central zones: these latter dialects all employ reflexes of Middle Chinese *pjuət* as the ordinary unmarked negator. Corresponding to this function, the Southern dialects use forms which can be reconstructed as a syllabic nasal *m*; in Yuè and Kèjiā this syllabic nasal negative belongs to the *píng* tonal category, but in Mĭn it belongs to the *shăng* (or *qù*) category. It has often been observed that Old Chinese possessed a rich array of negatives which could be divided into two groups: one group began with *p* and the other with *m*. The Northern and Central dialects retain forms from both sets; the Southern dialects, on the other hand, only have negatives beginning with *m*. For the existential negative, the Southern dialects have forms which might be reconstructed as *mău* (in MC terms); in Yuè it is lower *shăng* tone: *mou*[4]; in Kèjiā (Méixiàn) it is lower *píng* tone: *mo*[2]; in Mĭn it is either lower *píng* (in the coastal dialects) or lower *qù* (in some interior dialects). Forms closely related to this negative are also found widely in Gàn and Xiāng, where they agree tonally with the inland Mĭn dialects.

Another important lexico-grammatical feature linking Mĭn, Yuè and Kèjiā is the pair of forms, one nominal, one verbal, meaning 'poison'. In all these dialects the noun meaning 'poison' is *rù* tone and can be immediately associated with the attested Middle Chinese reading *duok*; the verb 'to poison', on the other hand, is *qù* tone, a pronunciation which cannot be found in any of the standard historical lexical sources (see Table 9.2).[3] Since it is hardly possible that such a pair of morphemes could represent innovations in each of the separate subgroups, and since such pairs are lacking in the Northern and Central dialects, these two words represent a powerful corroboration of the theory that Mĭn, Yuè and Kèjiā possess a common base.

In Chapter 1 a Mĭn word was cited for which I proposed an Austroasiatic etymology, namely the word for 'shaman' or 'spirit healer'. This term is also shared by Yuè and Kèjiā. In the Zhōngshān dialect of the Yuè group, it is *thuŋ*[2] *kuŋ¹ tsai³*; Kèjiā has *thuŋ² sin¹*.[4] These forms are important not only because they support the existence of a common Old Southern Chinese, but also because they provide evidence that this ancient variety of Chinese had an Austroasiatic substratum.

A number of common insect names also point to a common ancestor for the dialects under consideration here. The first of these is the word for 'cockroach': Mǐn (Xiàmén) *ka¹ tsuaʔ⁸*, Yuè *kaat⁸ tsaat⁸*, Kejia *tshat⁸*. These forms can all be derived from a common **dzât* (with or without a prefixed **kâ(t)*), a form not attested in the standard historical lexica, and limited to the Southern dialects. Terms for 'leech' also share a common element: Mǐn (Xiàmén) *gɔ² khi²*, Yuè *khei² na³*, Kèjiā *fu² khi²*.[5] A third insect name that suggests a common origin for these dialects is the word for 'louse' which, although it contains the common Chinese etymon for this creature, exhibits a distinctive morphological formation: in all these dialects the word consists of the common term for 'louse' (MC *sjet*) plus the suffix for female animals appropriate to each dialect: Mǐn (Xiàmén) *sat⁷ bu³*, Yuè *sat⁷ na³*, Kèjiā *set⁷ ma²*.

With very few exceptions, the Southern dialects have either reflexes of Middle Chinese *ʔi* or *gjwo* as the third person pronoun. Related forms are also widely distributed in the Central dialects, as we have seen, and consequently are not peculiar to the Southern zone. In the Central dialects such pronouns are perhaps among the few vestiges of the period when dialects of the Southern type were also spoken in that region. This also suggests that at the deepest historical level the Central and Southern dialects share a number of features in common; but by and large the Central dialects are the product of the post-Hàn migration of Northerners into the trans-Yangtze region.

To sum up, it is my view that the present-day dialects spoken south of the Yangtze are the result of successive accretions of Northern elements over an Old Southern Chinese base. In the case of those dialects spoken along the southern banks of the Yangtze and its tributaries, these accretions have been so great as to virtually inundate the dialects with elements of later Northern origin. Farther south, in the mountainous areas of Fújiàn and Guǎngdōng, the Old Southern Chinese element has survived to a greater degree, to the maximum extent in Mǐn, somewhat less so in Kèjiā, and only vestigially in Yuè.

9.2 The Yuè dialects

The Yuè dialects form a relatively homogeneous group of dialects spoken over wide areas of Guǎngdōng and Guǎngxī provinces. The term Cantonese, which is sometimes used interchangeably with Yuè, should be reserved for the dialect of the city of Guǎngzhōu (Canton) and not used as a general name for the group as a whole. According to Yuán Jiāhuá (1960, 179), Yuè dialects are to be found in approximately 100 counties in the two provinces mentioned above. O. Y. Hashimoto (1972), basing herself on published descriptions and her own field experience, mentions only half that number. Actually the Yuè-speaking area is poorly surveyed, and at the present time it is very difficult to say with certainty just what its limits might be. Another problem is the heterogeneous situation that prevails in almost all the Yuè region: it is common for Yuè dialects to coexist with Kèjiā and Mǐn dialects in the same county, and it is not always clear from published reports which variety actually predominates in a given locality. Despite the sketchy nature of our knowledge of Yuè dialect geography, it is fairly clear that Yuè dialects predominate in the deltas of the Pearl River (where Guǎngzhōu, the capital of Guǎngdōng province, is located) and the West River (Xī Jiāng). Yuè dialects are also spoken along most of the upper reaches of the West River and its tributaries. From this region they seem to have spread westward into much of southern Guǎngdōng and Guǎngxī.

Yuè dialects are also spoken by a large population overseas. Hashimoto (1972, 12) estimates that there are more than two million Yuè speakers in Southeast Asia with the main areas of concentration in Thailand, Malaysia, Singapore and Indonesia. Several hundred thousand Yuè dialect speakers are to be found in North America, and the number continues to increase because of accelerated immigration in recent years.

The language of Guǎngzhōu city enjoys the status of a prestige or standard language, not only among other Yuè speakers but even among Mǐn and Kèjiā speakers who inhabit Guǎngdōng province. This standard dialect is also the predominant dialect in the colonies of Hong Kong and Macao. Cantonese (in the narrow sense defined above) has a rich written folk literature; for the purpose of writing down this literature, a large number of special Cantonese characters have been developed; but this written form of Cantonese is rarely (if ever) used for formal writing of any kind.

As in the case of Mandarin, there are problems in applying the standard defining criterion to the Yuè dialects. According to this criterion the Middle Chinese voiced obstruents appear in Yuè dialects as voiceless aspirates in the *píng* tone, and in a small number of words in the *shǎng* tone, but as voiceless non-aspirates in the remaining tones. This in fact describes what is found in the Guǎngzhōu dialect, but does not apply to all the dialects of the group. Some Yùe dialects like Bóbái in Guǎngxī show voiceless aspirated reflexes for all the Middle Chinese voiced obstruents, irrespective of tonal category; others, like Téngxiàn and Cāngwú (both spoken in Guǎngxī) have voiceless unaspirated reflexes for the Middle Chinese voiced obstruents in all tones (Hashimoto 1972, 32). Two

Table 9.3. Yuè (Guǎngzhōu) initials

	Labials	Apicals	Sibilants	Velars	Labiovelars	Laryngeals
Voiceless unaspirated stops	p	t	ts	k	kw	(ʔ)
Voiceless aspirated stops	ph	th	tsh	kh	khw	
Nasals	m	n		ŋ	ŋw	
Fricatives	f		s			h
Liquids		l	j		w	

other characteristics, the retention of all the Middle Chinese final consonants
and a distinction of eight or more tones, are not sufficient criteria to distinguish
Yuè from the other Southern dialects. A fourth criterion, the split of the rù tone
into three (or even four) categories conditioned by vowel length, would however
seem to be peculiar to Yuè.

Compared to Wú and Xiāng, Yuè and the other Southern dialects have relatively simple initial systems. That of Guǎngzhōu (shown in Table 9.3) can be
considered fairly typical for a Yuè dialect.

Speakers of Standard Cantonese vary considerably in their pronunciation of
the sibilant initials; some use a dental articulation, while others employ a palatal
or alveopalatal pronunciation; most speakers palatalize the sibilants to some
degree before high front vowels (Yuán 1960, 183). The labiovelars are treated as
sequences of velars plus a back rounded medial by some linguists; considerations
of simplicity in describing syllable structure would seem to favor retention of a
separate set of labiovelars however (Hashimoto 1972, 138). Glottal stop may or
may not appear before syllables beginning with a vowel. Some speakers confuse
n and l, while others prefix a non-etymological ŋ to all words beginning with a
vowel. A majority of speakers, however, maintain a distinction among all these
initials (Yuán 1960, 183).

Although the Guǎngzhōu dialect possesses a single set of sibilant initials, some
outlying dialects of the group provide evidence that proto-Yuè must have had
two sets, corresponding in a general way to the distinction between dental and
retroflex sibilants in Northern Mandarin. This situation is illustrated in Table
9.4.[6] The forms there show that the distinction between the two varieties of
sibilants, where retained, is not necessarily reflected as two different points of
articulation; the shift of the dental sibilants to dental stops and s to a voiceless
lateral fricative and the retention of the alveopalatal series as sibilants is one of
the ways in which the distinction is kept.

Table 9.4. Yuè sibilants

	Peking	Guǎngzhōu	Yángjiāng	Zhōngshān	Táishān	Téngxiàn
'early'	tsau³	tsou³	tsou³	tsou³	tou³	tou³
'vegetable'	tshai⁵	tshoi⁵	tshoi⁵	tshoi⁵	thoi⁵	thɔi⁵
'die'	si³	sei³	ɬei³	si³	ɬei³	ɬi³
'needle'	tṣən¹	tsam¹	tsɐm¹	tsam¹	tsim¹	tsəm¹
'blow'	tṣhuei¹	tshøy¹	tshui¹	tshøy¹	tshui¹	tshøy¹
'stone'	ṣï²·	sek⁸	sɪk⁸	sia:k⁸	siak⁸	sek⁸

Yuè dialects vary greatly in the number of vocalic contrasts they possess, from a high of nine or ten vowel phonemes in Téngxiàn (Yue 1979) to a low of only five in Táishān (Chao 1951). With the exception of Téngxiàn, Yuè dialects lack rounded medials altogether; combinations like *uâ* have either monophthongized (**puân > pun*) or the medial has been reinterpreted as a part of the initial (**kuan >* kwan). A high front medial exists in most dialects, but has been lost in Guǎngzhōu by a process of monophthongization: **io > œ*, **ie > i*, etc. As a result Guǎngzhōu is one of the few Chinese dialects which lacks medials altogether. Seven of the eight vowels of Guǎngzhōu may stand alone as main vowels: *i, y, e, œ, u, o, aa* [a:]; one of them, *a* [ɐ] must be followed by a glide (*i* or *u*) or one of the final consonants. A phonetic distinction between long and short vowels is one of the characteristics of Guǎngzhōu finals (Hashimoto 1972, 152ff). In syllables with short vowels, the ending (glide or final nasal) is comparatively long, and syllables with long vowels have comparatively shorter endings. In syllables with final stops the long/short distinction is carried almost entirely by the vowel. This length distinction is closely related to the development of the *rù* tone in all Yuè dialects, even those which have lost vocalic length such as Yángjiāng, Táishān and Téngxiàn, showing clearly that a long/short contrast must have been a feature of proto-Yuè.

The Yuè dialects are the most conservative group when it comes to the preservation of the Middle Chinese final consonants. Although a number of Mǐn dialects and most Kèjiā dialects retain all six of the old ending consonants, they do not always retain the consonants in the same words: in both Mǐn and Kèjiā there is a strong tendency to assimilate final velars to dentals after front vowels: *iŋ > in*, *ek > et*, etc. In Yuè, on the other hand, the old final consonants are preserved quite faithfully, with only the merest handful of exceptions.

Yuè dialects tend to have large numbers of tones. The typical Northern and Central merger of the lower *shǎng* and *qù* in words with obstruent initials is rare in words of popular origin. A distinctive Yuè development found in all the dialects is the split of the upper *rù* tone into two subtypes conditioned by phonetic

Table 9.5. Yuè tonal development

Middle Chinese categories	Píng		Shǎng		Qù		Rù		
	Yīn	Yáng	Yīn	Yáng	Yīn	Yáng	I	II	III
Guǎngzhōu	1	2	3	4	5	6	7a	7b	8
Yángjiāng	1	2	3		5	6	7a	7b	8
Zhōngshān	1	2	3		5		7		8
Táishān	1	2	3	1, 3	1	6	7a	7b	8
Téngxiàn	1	2	3	4	5	6	7a	7b	8

Table 9.6. Yuè tonal values

Tonal category	Guǎngzhōu	Yángjiāng	Zhōngshān	Táishān	Téngxiàn
1	53	33	55	33	42/44
2	21	443	51	11	231/11
3	35	21	13	45	55/35
4	24	—	—	—	24/35
5	44	24	22	—	33
6	33	454	—	42	22
7a	55	24	55	55	55
7b	44	21	—	33	33
8	33	454	22	32	22

vowel length; to my knowledge, such a development is found nowhere outside Yuè. This tripartite division of the *rù* tone is designated by roman numerals, I, II and III in Table 9.5; categories I and II are both from voiceless initials historically, with category I from short vowels and category II from long vowels.

In words of literary origin most dialects have numerous examples of original lower *shǎng* words which have become lower *qù*. Table 9.5 represents only the popular developments. Tonal values for the categories of the above table are shown in Table 9.6.

One noteworthy feature of the Guǎngzhōu tones is that the lower or *yáng* tones (designated by even numbers in our scheme) consistently have a lower pitch value than the upper or *yīn* tones. As Table 9.6 shows, however, this is not always the case in the other Yuè dialects. The Téngxiàn dialect has two variants for the *píng* and *shǎng* categories; this is probably due to influence from Standard Cantonese (Yue 1979, 10).

Some Yuè dialects have so-called "changed" tones. In both Guǎngzhōu and Táishān, for example, the tones of certain words, chiefly nouns, have a tonal contour different from that of their etymological category when used in everyday familiar speech. In Guǎngzhōu the word for 'thief' has the reading [tshaak³³] in formal contexts but as an independent word in ordinary speech it is pronounced [tshaak³⁵]. This change is considered a kind of morphological process, the meaning of which is 'everyday familiarity with the object in question'. In function it is very similar to the *ér-huà* phenomenon described for the standard language and many Mandarin dialects.

Each of the three subgroups of the Southern dialects has certain characteristic lexical items by which it can be identified. O. Y. Hashimoto (1972, 15–19) gives a long list of such words for the Yuè dialects; here are a few of them:

(1) 'give' Guǎngzhōu *pei³*, Zhōngshān *pi³*, Táishān *i³* (< *pi³*), Téngxiàn *ʔbi³*

(2) 'thing' Guǎngzhōu *ie³*, Zhōngshān *ia³*, Yángjiāng *ie³*, Táishān *ie³*, Téngxiàn *ie⁵*

The following three suffixes (among others) are limited to Yuè dialects:

(3) 'suffix for human males (slightly pejorative)' Guǎngzhōu *lou³*, Zhōngshān *lou³*, Yángjiāng *lou³*, Táishān *lo³*, Téngxiàn *lou³*

(4) 'suffix for female animals' Guǎngzhōu *na³*, Zhōngshān *na³*, Yángjiāng *na³*, Táishān *na³*, Téngxiàn *na³*

(5) 'verbal suffix for progressive aspect' Guǎngzhōu *kan³*, Zhōngshān *kan³*, Táishān *kin³*, Téngxiàn *kan³*

It is probably possible on the basis of even this short list to identify a Yuè dialect.

The Yuè pronominal system is of the usual Southern type. The first- and second-person pronouns are cognate to Peking *wǒ* and *nǐ* respectively; the third-person pronouns are mostly related to Middle Chinese *gjwo*, and to similar forms found throughout the Central and Southern dialects. Table 9.7 gives a sampling of pronouns from several Yuè dialects.[7]

The most common way of forming plural pronouns in Yuè dialects is by means of the suffix *tei⁶* or its dialectal cognate, as in Guǎngzhōu, Zhōngshān and Téngxiàn. Some dialects, like Táishān and Yángjiāng, however, make plural forms by a process of tonal change. Pronominal possession in Yuè is usually shown by placing the specific noun measure word between the pronoun

Table 9.7. Yuè pronouns

	'I, me'	'you'	'he/she'	'we'
Guǎngzhōu	ŋo⁴	nei⁴	khøy⁴	ŋo⁴ tei⁶
Zhōngshān	ŋo³	ni³	khy²	ŋo³ ti⁵
Yángjiāng	ŋo³	nei³	kei²	ŋok⁷ᵃ
Táishān[7]	ŋoi¹	ni¹	khui¹	ŋoi*
Téngxiàn	ŋɔ⁴	ni⁴	ky⁴	ŋɔ⁴ ti⁶

Table 9.8. Yuè demonstratives

	'this'	'that'	Demonstrative plural
Guǎngzhōu	ni¹	ko³	ti¹
Zhōngshān	ko¹	nu¹	nai¹
Yángjiāng	ko³	na³	nai⁵
Táishān	khoi*	niŋ*	nai³
Téngxiàn	ko⁵	a⁵	ʔdi¹

and the thing possessed: Guǎngzhōu khøy⁴ pun³ sy¹ 'he – measure – book = his book'. This usage appears to be peculiar to Yuè. Demonstratives show only partial agreement among the dialects as can be seen from Table 9.8. The suffix for forming plural demonstrative forms is also given.

At first sight it seems curious that ko (in various tones) should mean 'that' in Guǎngzhōu but 'this' in the other dialects. A possible explanation of this is that ko originally was a general demonstrative like French ce (cette) meaning either 'this' or 'that'. As the various Yuè dialects developed a contrast between near and far demonstratives, ko came to mean 'this' in some dialects and 'that' in others. The plural suffix for demonstratives clearly is of two types: forms with nasal initials are generally found south of the West River, and forms with a dental stop initial to the north of it.

Yuè negatives generally resemble those of Mǐn and Kèjiā; the relevant forms are listed in Table 9.9. The Yuè existential negative is distinguished from those of the other Southern and Central dialects by being in the shǎng tonal category; the corresponding Eastern Mǐn and Kèjiā forms are píng tone, while some Western Mǐn, Gàn and Xiāng dialects have corresponding forms in the qù tone. The tones of the Yuè forms are probably influenced by the tone of the existential verb jau⁴ 'there is, there are'. The Téngxiàn form for 'not yet ...' is similar to those found in the Wú dialects (see Table 8.15) and certain Western Mǐn dialects.

Table 9.9. Yuè negatives

	General negative	Existential negative	'not yet ...'
Guǎngzhōu	m²	mou⁴	mei⁶ (tshaŋ²)
Zhōngshān	m²	mou³	mi⁵
Yángjiāng	m²	mou³	mei⁶
Táishān⁷	m²	mo¹	mei⁶
Téngxiàn	m²	mau⁴	m² thəŋ²

Syntactically, Yuè dialects differ from those of the other groups in a number of interesting ways. The use of measures alone (without numerals or demonstratives) as definite determiners is found throughout the Yuè group and would seem to be limited to this group: Guǎngzhōu *tsek*[7b] *kai*[1] 'the chicken' as opposed to *jat*[7a] *tsek*[7b] *kai*[1] 'a chicken, one chicken'. Certain adverbs follow rather than precede the verbs they refer to, an order unknown in other Chinese dialect groups: Guǎngzhōu *høy*[5] *sin*[1] 'go first'; cf. Peking *xiān qù* 'first – go = go first'. Yuè shares with Wú dialects the order direct object–indirect object: Guǎngzhōu *pei*[3] *sy*[1] *ŋo*[4] 'give book me – give me the book'; Standard Chinese has the reverse order *gěi wǒ shū* 'give me book'. The pretransitive construction (*bǎ* sentences) seems to be foreign to Yuè dialects; sentences modeled on it, using *tsæŋ*[1] as the pretransitive marker, are much more limited in scope and probably represent a borrowing from some Northern dialect.

In general the Yuè dialects give the impression of being a well differentiated subvariety of Southern Chinese with a strong overlay of Northern Chinese elements. These elements, however, are clearly not of recent origin; rather, they point in many ways to the late Táng as their source. The strongest indication of this is that the phonological categories of Yuè can almost all be viewed as deriving from Late Middle Chinese which, as we have already indicated, was the variety of literary Chinese current in the middle to late Táng dynasty. It is perhaps not irrelevant in this regard that the Yuè-speaking peoples will commonly refer to themselves as *thoŋ*[2] *jan*[2] 'people of the Táng dynasty'.

9.3 The Kèjiā dialects

The name Kèjiā (in Cantonese *hak*[7d] *ka*[1], whence the common English form *Hakka*) means 'guest' or 'stranger'; the name was given to those Kèjiā who during recent times settled in areas already occupied by Yuè-speaking peoples. For a number of reasons, many non-Kèjiā people in Guǎngdōng developed a strong antipathy toward these "strangers", and the erroneous notion that the

Kèjiā were not ethnically Chinese but some sort of non-Han "barbarians" became widespread. This produced a strong reaction among Kèjiā intellectuals, beginning in the late nineteenth century; in articles and books they sought to prove that the Kèjiā were in origin immigrants from North China and just as "Chinese" as their Yuè and Mǐn detractors. According to the views of these defenders of Kèjiā integrity, the Kèjiā originally lived in North China – in southern Shānxī and the provinces of Hénán and Ānhūi; at the fall of the Western Jìn dynasty, these peoples moved southward into the present-day Hūizhōu region of southern Ānhūi and into northern Jiāngxī; later, as a result of disorder in the late Tang dynasty, a part of the Kèjiā moved into their present homeland in southwestern Fújiàn and northern Guǎngdōng (X. Luó 1933; C. Luó 1958). Of course what is meant by these formulations is that the *ancestors* of the present Kèjiās came from the places enumerated, since it would be grossly anachronistic to refer to "Kèjiās" at all before the modern period. While I would agree that the historical materials on which this analysis of Kèjiā origins rests (mostly local genealogical records) do point to a northern origin for a certain part of the Kèjiā population, I believe that it would be a mistake to confuse this with a theory of the Kèjiā dialect origins; this kind of material is relevant mainly to an analysis of the make-up of the Kèjiā population and perhaps their ethnic background. As we have already shown, however, the Kèjiā dialects belong to the Southern group; such a classification implies that at base these dialects have developed from a variety of Chinese that has been present in South China since Han and Sānguó times (first to third centuries AD), and that they thus predate the dialects brought south by the Western Jìn immigrants in the fourth century. In other words, as far as their origin is concerned, the Kèjiā dialects differ from Mǐn and Yuè mainly in the degree to which they have been influenced by later northern immigrations, and by several peculiarly Kèjiā innovations.

As we shall see below, Kèjiā has particularly close links to Mǐn, a fact that cannot be explained unless we assume that Mǐn and Kèjiā shared an early period of common development; the numerous pre-*Qièyùn* elements found in Mǐn prove that it must go back to dialects brought to the region in the second and third centuries BC. As to the alleged close ties between Kèjiā and Gàn, we believe that these are for the most part superficial. I have already pointed out that their most salient common feature, the uniform evolution of the Middle Chinese voiced obstruents to voiceless aspirates in all four tones, is also found in other groups, including Yuè and Mǐn. In Table 9.10 I have selected a number of words in Kèjiā and Gàn for comparison. Kèjiā forms are from the Méixiàn dialect spoken in Guǎngzhōu (often referred to as standard Hakka) and from the Huáyáng dialect spoken in Sìchuān province; Gàn material is from the Nánchāng and

Table 9.10. Comparison of Kèjiā and Gàn vocabulary

	Méixiàn	Huáyáng	Nánchāng	Línchuān
1. 'I, me'	ŋai²	ŋai²	ŋɔ³	ŋo³
2. General negative	m²	m²	pət⁷	put⁷
3. 'rooster'	kɛ¹ kuŋ¹	kai¹ kuŋ¹	tɕi¹ kuŋ ~ iɔŋ⁶ tɕi¹	hau² tɕi¹
4. 'son'	lai⁵	nai⁵	tsai³	tsai³
5. 'nose'	phi⁵	phi⁵	phit⁷	phit⁸
6. Copula 'is'	hɛ⁵	xie⁵	sï⁶	si⁶

Línchuān dialects, both spoken in Jiāngxī province.[8] This short list of words illustrates some very fundamental differences between Kèjiā and Gàn in the area of basic vocabulary. (1) The Kèjiā first person pronouns show the Old Southern Chinese development of the *gē* group: *ar* > *ai; the Gàn forms, on the other hand, show the typical Northern and Central development to *o* or *ɔ*. (2) The Kèjiā negatives are related to forms found in Yuè and Mǐn, while the Gàn forms are connected with those found in Northern and Central dialects. (3) The Southern dialects, as we have seen, suffix the gender markers for domestic animals while in the North they are prefixed. In Kèjiā, as one would expect in a Southern dialect, such forms are regularly suffixed. In the Gàn dialects both orders are found; of the relevant forms given in the *Hànyǔ fāngyán gàiyào* (Yuán 1960) for the Nánchāng dialect, five have prefixed gender markers and four employ suffixes; it is probable that the suffixed forms are older, and that those with prefixes represent the influence of Northern Chinese. Since the suffixed forms are almost certainly the older type, this shows that Nánchāng and Línchuān have undergone strong Northern influence even in their most basic lexicon. (4) The Gàn word for 'son' is also found in Xiāng and Yuè, whereas the Kèjiā word is peculiar to this group. (5) For 'nose', Gàn has a *rù* tone pronunciation, as do all the Northern and Central dialects; Kèjiā agrees with Yuè and Mǐn in having a *qù* tone pronunciation. (6) For its copular verb, Kèjiā, like most Yuè dialects, employ reflexes of Middle Chinese *ɣiei*- 'connect'; Gàn and the other dialect groups use forms cognate to Standard Chinese *shì* (MC *źjeː*).

Most of the similarities that have been pointed out in favor of the Gàn–Kèjiā subgrouping can be shown to be common to dialects of other groups as well. On the other hand, it is difficult to point to any feature of phonology or lexicon which is unique to these two groups. Unless more substantial evidence can be brought to bear on the problem, I believe Gàn and Kèjiā must be assigned to different groups.

Table 9.11. Kèjiā (Méixiàn) initials

	Labials	Apicals	Sibilants	Palatals	Velars	Laryngeals
Voiceless unaspirated stops	p	t	ts		k	(ʔ)
Voiceless aspirated stops	ph	th	tsh		kh	
Nasals	m	n		ɲ	ŋ	
Fricatives	f		s			h
Liquids	v	l		(j)		

Since most of the information concerning areas inhabited by Kèjiā speakers is not based on any sort of strict linguistic criterion, it is quite difficult to say what the geographic limits of this dialect group are, and the task is made all the more difficult by the rather limited amount of reliable data available to us. Most would agree that the Kèjiā heartland is to be found in the mountainous region east of the North River (Běi Jiāng) in northern Guǎngdōng; it is here that Méixiàn, whose dialect is often considered to be the "standard" form of Kèjiā, is located. Other regions that are generally recognized as being solidly Kèjiā-speaking are southwestern Fújiàn and the extreme southern part of Jiāngxī. Kèjiā-speakers are said to be found in over forty counties in Guǎngxī; in addition, much of Guǎngdōng province outside the areas mentioned above is said to have mixed Yuè–Kèjiā population. Isolated communities of Kèjiā-speakers are scattered in several parts of Sìchuān province; dialects of this group are also spoken on the islands of Hǎinán and Táiwān. Outside China, Kèjiā immigrants have founded communities in several Southeast Asian countries, chiefly in Malaysia, Indonesia, Thailand and Vietnam.

The initials of the Méixiàn dialect as shown in Table 9.11 can be viewed as representative for the group as a whole. Meixian *v* is described as lacking strong friction, so it seems best to classify it among the liquids; if it were considered a voiced fricative, one would have to recognize an anomalous voiced–voiceless contrast between two fricatives *f* and *v*. Some Kèjiā dialects contrast two series of sibilants, one dental or alveolar, the other alveopalatal. Syllables like *ian* might also be interpreted as having a semivowel initial: *jan*; some dialects have a strongly consonantal initial for words of this type: Hǎilù ʒan. Some linguists (Hashimoto 1973) consider palatal *ɲ* an allophone of *ŋ* which occurs before high front vowels.

Kèjiā finals, at least in the dialects known to us, consist of two facultative medials, *i* and *u* (Shātóujiǎo in the New Territories apparently lacks *u*), one of six nuclear vowels: *i, ï, u, e* (*ə*), *a, o* (Huáyáng has both *e* and *ə* but they do not contrast phonemically) and an ending. All the dialects have the vocalic endings *i* and *u*; most have the full complement of final consonants *m/p, n/t, ŋ/k*. Huáyáng, probably because of strong Mandarin influence, has glottal stop for *p, t* and *k*, and has merged *m* with *n*. It is worth noting that Kèjiā dialects lack front rounded vowels altogether, either as medials or as main vowels.

Unlike most of the tonal systems which we have considered up to this point, Kèjiā tones cannot be derived in a simple way from the phonological system of Middle Chinese (O'Connor 1976, 52). In general, Kèjiā tonal categories are the same as those of Middle Chinese, but it is necessary in some cases to assume extra initial distinctions in order to explain the development of register. In the dialects known to us, Kèjiā tonal development is quite uniform; below we will discuss the correspondences of the tonal categories in order.

The *píng* tone shows the usual split into an upper register type, which has developed from words which had voiceless initials at an earlier period, and a lower register type, from words with voiced initials. Kèjiā differs from other Chinese dialects (with the exception of certain Mǐn dialects) in that it has a significant number of words with sonorant initials which belong to the upper register category. Mandarin, Yuè and most other dialects also have a few words of this type, but they tend to be limited to words of an onomatopoeic or expressive nature, often etymologically obscure. Kèjiā, on the other hand, has among syllables with sonorant initials a number of popular words of concrete meaning belonging to the *yīnpíng* category. O'Connor (1976) has proposed that words of this type had voiceless nasal and lateral initials at an earlier stage of development. Common examples of this type are Méixiàn *mau*[1] 'body hair', *mun*[1] 'mosquito', *lam*[1] 'basket' and *luŋ*[1] 'deaf'.

Reflexes of the *shǎng* tone are rather complicated. Words which in Middle Chinese had voiceless initials regularly become *shǎng* tone in Kèjiā. Popular words which derive from earlier forms with voiced obstruent initials have merged with the upper *píng* tone; corresponding words of literary origin show the common shift to the lower *qù* tone: for example, in the Hǎilù dialect the popular pronunciation for the word 'younger brother' is *thai*[1], whereas the literary reading is *thi*[6]. There are also two developments with regard to words deriving from sonorant initials, but this split cannot be correlated neatly with the distinction between the popular and literary strata, since among both popular and literary words both types of development can be found. Moreover, there is a high degree of correlation as to the incidence of one or the other tone from dialect to dialect. M. Hashimoto (1973) considers the development of *shǎng* tone words with earlier sonorant (*cìzhuó*) initials to the *yīnpíng* category as a distinctively Kèjiā feature.

Table 9.12. Hǎilù tonal development

	Píng	Shǎng	Qù	Rù
All voiceless initials	1	3	5	7
Voiced obstruents	2	1 (6)	6	8
Voiced sonorants	2	1, 3	6	8

Table 9.13. Kèjiā tonal values

	1	2	3	5	6	7	8
Hǎilù	53	55	13	31	22	55	32
Méixiàn	44	12	31	42	—	21	44
Huáyáng	55	12	31	53	—	32	55
Shātóujiǎo	33	11	32	53	—	33	55

This is very important in view of the fact that the classic criterion of aspiration has been shown to be inadequate.

In more conservative dialects like Hǎilù, the *qù* tone is split into upper and lower registers strictly conditioned by the earlier presence of voicing in the initial. A few words with sonorant initials are found in the upper *qù* (Hǎilù *ma*[5] 'scold', *mian*[5] 'face'), no doubt due to the distinction of two series of sonorants already described for the *píng* tone. Several Kèjiā dialects have lost the lower *qù* tone: in Méixiàn it has merged with the upper *qù*; the same has happened in the dialect of Huáyáng spoken in the province of Sìchuān.

The development of the *rù* tone has been rather like that of the *píng* and *qù* tones. The upper and lower *rù* (found in all the dialects) for the most part are determined by the presence or absence of voicing at an earlier stage of the language. A small number of words with sonorant initials in the upper *rù* strengthens the hypothesis of a two-way contrast in the sonorants in the dialect ancestral to Kèjiā. I will discuss this topic in more detail when I come to a discussion of Mǐn–Kèjiā parallel development at the end of this chapter.

Table 9.12 shows the development in tones in the Hǎilù dialect. According to O'Connor (1976, 12) the tonal system of this dialect is identical to that reconstructed for proto-Kèjiā. The voiceless initials include nasals and laterals as well as obstruents; since the *Qièyùn* system knows no such bipartite division of sonorants, it cannot be considered directly ancestral to Kèjiā. Tonal values for several representative Kèjiā dialects are displayed in Table 9.13.

We have already looked at some aspects of Kèjiā vocabulary in examining

Table 9.14. Kèjiā pronouns

	'I, me'	'you'	'he/she'	'we'
Méixiàn	ŋai²	ɲi², n²	ki²	ŋai² teu¹ ɲin²
Hǎilù	ŋai²	ɲi²	ki²	ŋai² teu¹ ~ ŋai² lit⁷
Huáyáng	ŋai²	ɲi²	tɕi²	ŋai² nien¹

a possible Gàn–Kèjiā subgrouping. Lying as they do at a kind of crossroads, bordered on all sides by other dialect groups, Kèjiā dialects have very little vocabulary that is not also found elsewhere. The word for 'son' (Méixian *lài⁵*), already mentioned above, is one of the few exceptions. In its fundamental lexicon, Kèjiā has connections with both Mǐn and Yuè, and in a sense forms a link between the two groups. The influence of the Northern and Central dialects has also been relatively strong; one indication of this is the widespread use of a noun suffix (Méixiàn *e*, Hǎilù *l²*) cognate to Mandarin *er*. A few superficial similarities of this type, coupled with widely publicized attempts to prove the Northern origin of the Kèjiās, has led to the curious notion (widely believed in Táiwān, for example) that Kèjiā has a particularly close affinity to Mandarin. There is simply no basis for such a view; Kèjiā is a full-fledged Southern dialect and is no more closely related to Mandarin than Cantonese.

Kèjiā pronouns are quite homogeneous as illustrated in Table 9.14. The third-person pronoun is anomalous in having an unaspirated initial in a *yáng* tone, one of the very few such examples. Etymologically this word can be connected either with Middle Chinese *gjwo* or *gï*. The irregular tones of the first- and second-person forms (one would expect them to be tone 1 or 3) can be explained as assimilation to the tone of the third-person form. This sort of assimilation is quite common throughout China, and examples can be found in virtually all the dialect groups. Possessive pronouns are either formed by a suffix (Méixiàn *ke⁵*, Hǎilù *kai⁵*, Huáyáng *kieʔ⁷*) or are independent forms which may have originated as contractions of the pronoun plus the suffixes mentioned above: Méixiàn *ŋa¹* ~ *ŋai ke⁵*, Hǎilù *ŋai² kai⁵*, Huáyáng *ŋa¹* (*kieʔ⁷*), all 'my'.

The demonstratives are related among the various dialects. For 'this' Méixiàn has *li³* or *ke³*; Hǎilù has *li³* and Huáyáng *ti³*. Méixiàn has *ke⁵* for 'that'; Hǎilù has *kai²*; and Huáyáng has *kai⁵*. It is likely that the Kèjiā demonstratives are in some way related to those of the Yuè dialects.

Kèjiā negatives, as we have already pointed out, are of the Southern type. Only the form for 'not yet ...' departs from the pattern; here Kèjiā employs forms modeled on Medieval Mandarin *bùcéng*, but with the first element replaced by the usual Kèjiā negative *m²*. This negative exists both in a fused form – Méixiàn and Hǎilù *maŋ² < *m² tshaŋ²* – and an uncontracted form – Méixiàn *m² tshen²*, Huáyáng *m² ɲien²*. Similar formations are found in Western Mǐn, as we will see in the next section.

From most of the published material concerning the Kèjiā dialects, we get a picture of a group of very homogeneous dialects. It must be remembered, however, that we still have only scanty knowledge of the group as a whole. From the small amount of information given by Pān Màodǐng *et al.* (1963) concerning the Chángtīng dialect spoken in southwestern Fújiàn, it would appear that this dialect, commonly supposed to be Kèjiā, differs from the other well-described varieties in many important ways. It may be that what we generally refer to as Kèjiā is in actuality only one subgroup of a larger and more heterogeneous family.

9.4 The Mǐn dialects

Fújiàn province, together with the northeastern corner of Guǎngdōng province, is the homeland of the Mǐn-speaking peoples. This region is a peripheral area in the classic sense of the term: the absence of major rivers and a wildly mountainous terrain have always made access difficult, and it is not surprising that the dialects spoken here lie outside the mainstream of Chinese linguistic development. On the one hand, we find here numerous archaisms not preserved elsewhere, and, on the other hand, a whole series of local innovations which are peculiarly Mǐn. Long centuries of relative isolation and the lack of convenient lines of communication within the region itself have also led to strong internal differentiation; but despite the very considerable differences found among the Mǐn dialects themselves, this group is, next to Mandarin, the most distinctive and easily characterized group of Chinese dialects.

The Mǐn dialects can be most easily defined by examining the relationship between the Middle Chinese voiced (*quánzhuó*) stops and their correspondences in Mǐn. Table 9.15 compares a set of Middle Chinese words having initial *d* with their Mǐn cognates.[9] An examination of forms in the table shows that the Mǐn dialects have three different correspondences to Middle Chinese *d*. Since this three-way correspondence cannot be shown to be a conditioned split, it follows that Middle Chinese *d* represents the merger of three different phonemes present in an earlier stage of Chinese and that the earlier distinction is still preserved in Mǐn. The primary distinction in Mǐn is between an unaspirated *t* and an aspirated *th*. The unaspirated forms are further divided into those which appear as stops in Jiànyáng and those which show up as laterals. The primary two-way distinction is present in all Mǐn dialects, but the further division of the unaspi-

Table 9.15. Mǐn correspondences to Middle Chinese *d*

	MC	Fúzhōu	Xiàmén	Jiànyáng	Yǒngān
'hoof'	diei	te²	tue²	tai²	te²
'younger' brother'	diei:	tie⁶	ti⁶	tie⁵	te⁴
'bean'	dəu-	tau⁶	tau⁶	teu⁶	tø⁵
'break off'	duân:	touŋ³	tŋ⁶	tuŋ⁵	tŭm⁵
'weep'	diei	thie²	thi²	hie²	the²
'sugar'	dâng	thouŋ²	thŋ²	hɔŋ²	tham²
'stack up'	diep	thak⁸	thaʔ⁸	ha⁸	thɔ⁴
'head'	dəu	thau²	thau²	heu²	thø²
'bag'	dâi-	toi⁶	te⁶	lui⁶	tue⁵
'neck'	dəu-	tau⁶	tau⁶	lo⁶	—
'poison'	duok	tøik⁸	tak⁸	lo⁸	tau⁴
'copper'	dung	tøiŋ²	taŋ²	loŋ²	tãɯ²

Table 9.16. Voiced stop correspondence in Mǐn

	Xiàmén	Fúzhōu	Jiànyáng	Yǒngān
$*d^1$	t	t	t	t
$*d^2$	t	t	l	t
$*d^3$	th	th	h	th

rated initials into two types is preserved only in certain Northwestern Mǐn dialects of which Jiànyáng is only one example. It is finally important to note that there is a high degree of correlation among the various Mǐn dialects as to the incidence of an aspirated or unaspirated initial in any given word of this type. On the basis of this and similar evidence, I concluded (Norman 1973) that the Chinese dialects ancestral to Mǐn (proto-Mǐn) had three different phonemes corresponding to each of the Middle Chinese voiced stops; because of tonal correspondences, these are also assumed to have been voiced in proto-Mǐn. If we designate these three voiced dentals as $*d^1$, $*d^2$ and $*d^3$, we find the Mǐn reflexes shown in Table 9.16. We can use this pattern of correspondence to define a Mǐn dialect: simply stated, a Mǐn dialect is any Chinese dialect in which both aspirated and unaspirated stops occur in all the *yáng* (lower-register) tones, and in which the lexical incidence of the aspirated forms in any given word is in substantial agreement with that of the other dialects of the group. The list of words in Table 9.15 could be used as a diagnostic test: if a dialect has voiceless aspirated *th* in the words for 'weep', 'sugar', 'stack up' and 'head', but voiceless

Table 9.17. Relationship of Mǐn initials to tones in Shàowǔ and Jiānglè

	MC	Fúzhōng	Jiànyáng	Shàowǔ	Jiānglè
'long'	djang	toun^2	lɔŋ^9	thoŋ^2	thoŋ^2
'sugar'	dâng	thoun^2	hɔŋ^2	thoŋ^7	thoŋ^9
'shaman'	—	tøiŋ^2	loŋ^9	thuŋ^2	thuŋ^2
'insect'	djung	thøiŋ^2	hoŋ^2	thuŋ^7	thuŋ^9
'reside'	djo-	tiu^6	tiu^6	thy^6	thy^6
'tree'	źju-	tshiu^6	tshiu^6	tʃhy^5	tʃhy^5
'thin'	bâk	poʔ^8	vɔ^8	pho^6	pho^8
'hail'	båk	phøik^8	pho^8	phau^7	phio^5

Table 9.18. Tonal development of words with nasal initials in Mǐn

	MC	Fúzhōu	Jiànyáng	Shàowǔ	Jiānglè
'whet'	muâ	muai^2	moi^2	məi^2	mai^2
'hemp'	ma	muai^2	moi^2	məi^7	mai^9
'recognize'	ńźjen-	nein^6	noiŋ^6	nin^6	ŋiŋ^6
'allow (want)'	ńźjang-	nioŋ^6	nioŋ^6	nioŋ^5	ŋioŋ^5
'moon'	ngjwɐt	ŋuok^8	ŋye^8	ye^6	ŋø^8
'meat'	ńźjuk	nyk^8	ny^8	ny^7	ny^5

unaspirated *t* in the remainder of the words of the list, chances are very high that
it is a Mǐn dialect.

In the far western part of Fújiàn there is a small group of dialects in which
this Mǐn system is reflected, but in a different way. In these dialects (of which
Shàowǔ and Jiānglè are examples) tonal reflexes in the *píng*, *qù* and *rù* tones
differ depending on whether the initial of the word in question is aspirated or
not in Mǐn; this situation is illustrated in Table 9.17. Since tonal development
in Shàowǔ and Jiānglè cannot be explained except in terms of the Mǐn initial
system, it follows that they too should be considered Mǐn in some sense; this
affiliation is confirmed by other features as we shall see.

Shàowǔ and Jiānglè show a related type of behavior for words with nasal
initials: one set of words has the same series of tones found with words which
have unaspirated initials in Mǐn, and a second set has tones found with words
related to the Mǐn aspirated forms. This suggests that the dialect ancestral
to Mǐn had two series of contrasting nasals, which, judging from their tonal
behavior, may have been voiced and voiceless. Table 9.18 illustrates the phenomenon just described. The sources for Middle Chinese have only one series of
nasals, so we must again assume that Mǐn preserves features of an ancient dia-

Table 9.19. Mǐn reflexes of MC retroflex stops

	MC	Fúzhōu	Xiàmén	Jiànyáng	Yǒngān	Shàowǔ	Jiānglè
'bamboo'	ṭjuk	tøik⁷	tek⁷	ty⁷	ty⁷	ty⁷	ty⁹
'turn'	ṭjwän:	tioŋ³	tŋ³	lyeŋ³	tẽ³	thien³	thŏ⁹
'chopstick'	ḍjwo-	tøi⁶	ti⁶	ty⁶	ty⁶	thy⁶	thy⁶

lect related collaterally to Middle Chinese but differing from it in a number of important ways.

Another well-known and much discussed feature of the Mǐn dialects is the retention of dental stops where Middle Chinese has retroflex initials (shéshàngyīn), as Table 9.19 illustrates. In the other dialect groups these initials have all become affricates of one kind or another; Peking has zhú, zhuǎn and zhù for the three words respectively.

The retention of bilabials for the qīngchún initials of the rhyme tables is often considered a typical Mǐn trait; but, as I have already shown above, this is by no means an exclusively Min feature, and the mere presence of bilabials in words of this type is not sufficient reason for classifying a dialect as Mǐn.

Vocabulary is also a useful device for identifying a Mǐn dialect. The Mǐn dialects provide us with a great abundance of lexical forms which either are not found elsewhere or are very rare in non-Mǐn dialects. Below I list and comment on five words which, to my knowledge, are uniquely Mǐn.

1. 'Son, child'. Xiàmén kiã³, Fúzhōu kiaŋ³, Jiànyáng kyeŋ³, Yǒngān kyẽ³, Shàowǔ kin³, Jiānglè kieŋ³. This word is first attested in a poem by the Tang poet Gù Kuàng (725?–816?) who identifies the word as Mǐn. It is quite possible that it has an Austroasiatic origin; cf. Vietnamese con [kɔn], Mon kon, Bahnar kon, all meaning 'child' (Pinnow 1959, 111).

2. 'Cooking vessel, pot'. Xiàmén tiã³, Fúzhōu tiaŋ³, Jiànyáng tiaŋ³, Yǒngān tiɔ³, Shàowǔ tiaŋ³. These words are related to the word dǐng (MC tieng:) 'three-legged cooking vessel': by the Han dynasty in the standard written language this word had come to be associated almost exclusively with the ritual bronze tripod so familiar to Chinese art fanciers. The Mǐn dialects no doubt retain the more primitive meaning – simply 'cooking pot, caldron'.

3. '(Rice) field'. Xiàmén tshan², Fúzhōu tsheiŋ², Jiànyáng thaiŋ², Yǒngān tshī², Shàowǔ tshən⁷, Jiānglè tshãi⁹. On phonological grounds it seems quite unlikely

that this word is related to Peking *tián* (MC *dien*), since neither the initial nor the final correspond in a regular way.

4. 'Wear, put on (clothing)', Xiàmén *tsheŋ⁶*, Fúzhōu *søiŋ⁶*, Jiànyáng *tseŋ⁶*, Yǒngān *tsem⁵*, Shàowǔ *ʃuŋ⁶*, Jiānglè *ʃiuŋ⁶*. The etymology of these forms is obscure, and as far as is known cognates are not found outside the Mǐn group.

5. 'Tasteless, insipid, lacking salt'. Xiàmén *tsiã³*, Fúzhōu *tsiaŋ³*, Jiànyáng *liaŋ³*, Yǒngān *tsiɔ̃³*, Shàowǔ *tshien³*, Jiānglè *tshiaŋ⁹*. The Song dynasty rhyme dictionary *Jíyùn* contains a character with the reading *tsjäm:*, which corresponds both in form and meaning to these Mǐn words, but the word is apparently restricted to this dialect group.

There are a number of other words which are typically Mǐn, but which are also found in a few dialects on the periphery of the Mǐn area as well. We will cite only two of these as examples.

6. 'Slaughter, kill'. Xiàmén *thai²*, Fúzhōu *thai²*, Jiànyáng *hoi²*, Yǒngān *thi²*. Cognates are lacking in Shàowǔ and Jiānglè, but Kèjiā (Méixiàn) has *tshi²*, 'to slaughter' (Norman 1979).

7. 'House'. Xiàmén *tshu⁵*, Fúzhōu *tshio⁵*, Jiànyáng *tshio⁵*, Yǒngān *tʃhɯ⁵*, Shàowǔ *tʃho⁵*, Jiānglè *tʃho⁵*. These forms are related to *shù* (MC *śju-*) which, in addition to its verbal meaning of 'to guard the frontier', also had the nominal sense of 'a frontier outpost'. It is not improbable that the first houses built by Chinese settlers in the wilds of ancient Fújiàn were in fact 'outposts'. This word is found in all known Mǐn dialects. I have also recorded it for the southwestern Zhèjiāng dialect of Qìngyuán in the form *tshyi⁵* 'house'.

Geographically speaking, Mǐn dialects are spoken in all of Fújiàn province except for the southwestern corner, which is a part of the Kèjiā-speaking region. The northeastern part of Guǎngdōng, located immediately to the south of Fújiàn, is also Mǐn-speaking; the dialect of this area is often referred to by the former prefectural name of Cháozhōu. Mǐn-speaking islands are found at many points on the Guǎngdōng coast and even in some inland areas; the Léizhōu Peninsula and Hǎinán Island are also home to a number of dialects belonging to this group.

The majority of the inhabitants of Táiwān speak Mǐn dialects closely related

Table 9.20. Reflexes of the proto-Mǐn *l* and *lh* in the Mǐn dialects

	MC	Xiàmén	Fúzhōu	Jiànyáng	Yǒngān	Shàowǔ
'come'	lậi	lai²	li²	le²	la²	li²
'fall'	lâk	loʔ⁸	loʔ⁸	lɔ⁸	lau⁴	lo⁶
'flow'	ljəu	lau²	lau²	lau²	lø²	lou²
'green'	ljwok	lek⁸	lioʔ⁸	ly⁸	ly⁴	ly⁶
'snail'	luâ	le²	løi²	sui²	sue²	soi⁷
'basket'	lâm	nã²	laŋ²	saŋ²	sɔ̃²	san⁷
'egg'	luân:	nŋ⁶	lauŋ⁶	suŋ⁵	sǔm⁴	son³
'six'	ljuk	lak⁸	løik⁸	so⁸	(ly⁴)	su⁷

to that of Xiàmén in Southern Fújiàn. A large population of Mǐn-speakers is also found in southern Zhèjiāng along the coast. Mǐn-speaking communities have also been reported in Jiāngxī, Guǎngxī and Sìchuān (Yuán 1960, 241).

In addition to the Mǐn-speaking population in China itself, there are several million overseas Chinese who have a Mǐn dialect as their native language. This population is concentrated in Thailand, Malaysia, Singapore and Indonesia. Much of the Chinese population of Indochina was Mǐn-speaking before the mass pogroms and expulsions of recent years. In Southeast Asia, dialects of the Xiàmén type (so-called "Hokkien" dialects) predominate, except in Thailand, where Cháozhōu-speakers form the majority. Smaller communities of Fúzhōu, Pútián and Hǎinán dialect speakers are also to be found, especially in Malaysia.

Formerly scholars divided the Mǐn dialects into a Northern and a Southern group (Yuán 1960). Pān Màodǐng and his associates (1963), in the brief report on their Fújiàn dialect survey, however, proposed that the major division is between an Eastern and a Western group. Pān was basically correct in this reinterpretation, but he unfortunately considered dialects like Shàowǔ and Jiānglè to be Kèjiā; above I have given reasons for including them among the Mǐn dialects.

One very important isogloss separates the Eastern from the Western Mǐn dialects. Just as proto-Mǐn had two contrasting sets of nasals, it also had two varieties of *l*. On the basis of tonal behavior, it may be assumed that one of these *l*s was voiced (*l*) and that the other was voiceless (*lh*). In the Eastern dialects, the two varieties of *l* merged; in the Western dialects *l* remains *l*, but *lh* becomes either *s* or *ʃ*, depending on the dialect (Norman 1973). This development is shown in Table 9.20.

This same division is also reflected by differences of basic vocabulary; this is particularly evident in the case of the pronouns and demonstratives. For the first-person pronoun, all the dialects use forms related to *wǒ* (MC *ngâ:*). For the second person, the Eastern dialects employ cognates of *rǔ* (MC *ńźjwo:*), and for

Table 9.21: Mǐn pronouns and demonstratives

	'I'	'you'	'he/she'	'this'	'that'
Xiàmén	gua^3	li^3	i^1	tsit^7	hit^7
Jiēyáng	ua^3	lɯ^3	i^1	tsek^7	hek^7
Fúān[10]	ŋo^3	ni^3	i^1	tsa-	ha-
Fúzhōu	ŋuai^3	ny^3	i^1	tsi-	hi-
Jiànōu	ue^4	ni^4	ky^4	ioŋ^7	u^7
Jiànyáng	ŋue^9	noi^9	ky^2	i^7	u^7
Chóngān	ŋuai^1	nei^1	hou^1	i^7	u^7
Yǒngān	ŋuo^1	ŋi^1	ŋy^1	tʃo^3	uo^3
Shàowǔ	haŋ^3	hien^3	hu^3	tʃoŋ^7	oŋ^7
Jiānglè	ŋai^9	ne^9	ky^3	tʃia^3	va^9

Table 9.22. Mǐn negatives

	Ordinary negative	Existential negative	'not yet'
Xiàmén	m^6	bo^2	be^6
Jiēyáng	m^6	bo^2	bue^6
Fúān	m^6	mɔ^2	mui^6
Fúzhōu	ŋ^6	mo^2	mui^6
Jiànōu	eŋ^6	mau^3	naiŋ^3
Jiànyáng	oiŋ^5	mau^9	naiŋ^9
Chóngān	ŋ^5	mau^5	naiŋ^5
Yǒngān	ãɯ^5	maɯ^2	ãɯ^5 kɔ^7
Shàowǔ	ŋ^6	mau^6	mau^6
Jiānglè	ŋ^6	mo^6	ŋ^6 ŋaŋ^2

the third person forms related to *yī* (MC *ʔi*). In the Western dialects, the second-and third-person pronouns are cognate to *nǐ* (MC *ni:*) and *qú* (MC *gjwo*) respectively. The Shàowǔ dialect is quite peculiar in this regard, employing a set of forms whose etymology is totally obscure. The Western Mǐn pronouns on the whole are closely related to those found in Kèjiā, Yuè and a number of Central dialects; this is only one of several transitional features found in this subgroup. The pronouns and demonstratives of ten representative Mǐn dialects are given in Table 9.21.[10] The first four dialects belong to the Eastern subgroup, the last six to the Western subgroup.

We can observe a similar situation with regard to the negatives. The Eastern Mǐn dialects preserve forms cognate to Middle Chinese *mjwei-* 'not yet'; the Western dialects, on the other hand, have several different innovations. Table 9.22 gives a sampling of Mǐn negative forms.

From the two preceding tables it can be seen that the Eastern dialects are much more homogeneous than those of the west. There are two possible reasons for this. Communications within the Western area are quite difficult; until recently transportation was almost exclusively along the short swift rivers of the region; the result of this was that localities within the region were quite isolated from one another. In the East, however, travel up and down the seacoast by boat was not difficult, and as a result localities had more frequent contacts. Paradoxically, despite the internal isolation of the Western region, outside influences seem to have penetrated relatively more easily, and consequently one finds a greater proportion of non-Mǐn elements in these dialects.

Shàowǔ and Jiānglè obviously occupy a very special place within the Western Mǐn group. While retaining their Mǐn core, these dialects seem to have come under strong Gàn (or Kèjiā) influence at some point, and this has given them a strongly distinctive character within the Mǐn group. To distinguish these dialects from the more conventional Western Mǐn dialects like Jiànōu, Jiànyáng and Yǒngān, I propose that they be called Far Western Mǐn. Northwestern Mǐn consists of Jiànōu, Jiànyáng, Chóngān and the dialects of several adjacent counties; these dialects are characterized above all by a peculiar pattern of tonal development (Norman 1973). Yǒngān, while clearly a Western dialect with regard to its development of proto-Mǐn *lh to s or ʃ, is otherwise so peculiar that it merits being placed in a special Central Mǐn subgroup.

The Eastern Mǐn dialects can be divided into two large subgroups: Southern Mǐn, which includes Xiàmén (as well as almost all of southeastern Fújiàn), Cháozhōu in Guǎngdōng, and the Mǐn dialects of Táiwān and Hǎinán, is chiefly characterized by the development of a series of nasalized vowels from earlier combinations of a vowel plus a nasal consonant, and the denasalization of m, n and ŋ before oral vowels. Northeastern Mǐn is spoken in the northeastern part of Fújiàn, including the capital city of Fúzhōu. The Northeastern dialects are more heterogeneous than those of the Southern group; a few, like Fúān and Níngdé, are very conservative, preserving the full complement of old final consonants, while others like Fúzhōu have only final ŋ and ʔ.

From a phonetic point of view the Mǐn dialects do not differ greatly from other dialects found in southern China. The initials of seven Mǐn dialects are listed in Table 9.23. The initials here are contrasted only in a synchronic and phonetic sense, and no attempt is made to indicate diachronic correspondences.

A few comments on the Mǐn initials shown in Table 9.23 are in order.

1. In Southern Mǐn dialects (Xiàmén, Cháozhōu, Táiwān) nasals become denasalized before oral vowels: mi > bi, ni > li, ŋia > gia, etc. A nasal pronunciation is retained before nasalized vowels in all the Southern Mǐn dia-

Table 9.23. Mǐn initials

Xiàmén	Fúzhōu	Jiànōu	Jiànyáng	Yǒngān	Shàowǔ	Jiānglè
p	p	p	p	p	p	p
ph	ph	ph	ph	ph	ph	ph
m(b)	m	m	m	m	m	m
			v			
t	t	t	t	t	t	t
th	th	th	h	th	th	th
n(l)	n	n	n	n ~ l	n	n ~ l
	l	l	l		l	
ts	ts	ts	ts	ts	ts	ts
tsh	tsh	tsh	ts (th)	tsh	tsh	tsh
s	s	s	s	s	s	s
dz						
				tʃ	tʃ	tʃ
				tʃh	tʃh	tʃh
				ʃ	ʃ	ʃ
k	k	k	k	k	k	k
kh	kh	kh	kh	kh	kh	kh
ŋ(g)	ŋ	ŋ	ŋ	ŋ	ŋ	ŋ
h	h	x	x	h	h	h
(ʔ)	(ʔ)	(ʔ)	(ʔ)	(ʔ)	(ʔ)	(ʔ)

lects; in Cháozhōu, but not in Xiàmén, the nasal pronunciation is also kept before finals when they end in a nasal segment: Cháozhōu *naŋ* = Xiàmén *laŋ*. Jiànyáng *v* is a very lenis labiodental semivowel.

2. In Jiànyáng common Mǐn *th* become *h*; this shift is found sporadically elsewhere in Chinese (Táishān, Hǎinán Mǐn).

3. In Yǒngān and Jiānglè *n* and *l* are in free variation; the same word is sometimes pronounced with *n*, sometimes with *l*. In Xiàmén and closely related Southern Mǐn dialects, *n* and *l* are conditioned variants of the same phoneme.

4. Xiàmén *dz* and Cháozhōu *z* derive historically from **n* before high front vowels, but, viewed synchronically, they must be regarded as discrete phonemes because of interference of unshifted forms from the literary language. In Jiànyáng *tsh* occurs only before high front vowels; elsewhere it becomes *th*.

5. Only a few dialects on the periphery of the Mǐn-speaking area distinguish dental (or alveolar) sibilants from an alveopalatal set.

6. In virtually all Mǐn dialects, a non-phonemic glottal stop occurs before initial vowels, especially when such words are pronounced carefully or enunciated in isolation.

As might be expected in a dialect group of such heterogeneity, the Mĭn dialects vary greatly in the number of vocalic contrasts which they possess: Xiàmén has six oral vocalic contrasts and four nasalized vowels; Yŏngān has ten oral vowels and four nasalized vowels. The average number of oral vocalic contrasts in Mĭn dialects is about eight, generally higher than that found in other dialectal groups. A characteristic of all the Southern Mĭn dialects is the absence of front rounded vowels; one or two such vowels, however, is the rule for the Northeastern and Western dialects. Eastern Mĭn has only two contrasting medials, *i* and *u*, although *i* is allophonically rounded to [y] before rounded main vowels in several Northeastern dialects: Fúzhōu *kioŋ* is phonetically [kyoŋ]. In the West a three-way contrast of medials (*i, u, y*) is the common pattern. All the dialects have descending diphthongs ending in *i* and *u*; Yŏngān, in addition to diphthongs of this type, also has *aɯ*, ending in a back unrounded vowel. Apical vowels are not common, found only in Yŏngān and Jiānglè as far as is known.

The old final consonants are preserved to varying degrees. They are retained most faithfully in Níngdé and certain other Northeastern dialects. In Southern Mĭn, all six of the original final consonants remain in Xiàmén and adjacent regions, but as a general rule combinations of an open vowel plus a nasal have developed into nasalized vowels: **sâm > sã, *tân > tuã, *kioŋ > kiũ*, etc. In Cháozhōu final *n* has merged with *ŋ*, and the same process of nasalization just described for Xiàmén is found. In both Xiàmén and Cháozhōu the final stops behave in a parallel fashion, with *p, t* and *k* becoming glottal stop after open vowels: **sâp > saʔ*, **tât > tuaʔ, *kiok > kioʔ*, etc. Cháozhōu merges final *t* with *k*, but the distinction is retained in Xiàmén and in its allied dialects in southern Fújiàn. Fúzhōu has only final *ŋ* and glottal stop; some speakers, however, may make a distinction between final *k* and *ʔ*.

The Northwestern dialects of Jiàn'ōu and Jiànyáng retain only a single final nasal, *ŋ*. The final stops survive only as separate tonal categories. In Yŏngān the final stops are completely lost. In this dialect, the nasals seem to have first become nasalized vowels and then in some cases to have reemerged as final *m*: **oŋ > *ãu > am, *an > *ũ > ŭm*.

In Jiānglè the final stops are lost, surviving only as tonal distinctions; the nasals have merged into a single distinction, realized phonetically in different ways depending on the final: with *e* and *ai* the vowel is nasalized: *ẽ, ãi; ə, y* and *ø* have a following *n*; *ən, yn, øn*; the remaining vowels all have *ŋ*: *aŋ, iŋ, uŋ, oŋ*. Shàowǔ has merged *m* with *n*, but *ŋ* generally remains distinct. The Shàowǔ final stops have developed in a unique way: *p* becomes *n*, *t* becomes *i*, and *k* drops altogether. Table 9.24 gives examples of these various developments.

Tonal development in the Mĭn dialects as a whole cannot be described in

Table 9.24. Final consonants in Mǐn

	MC	Xiàmén	Fúzhōu	Níngdé	Jiànyáng	Jiānglè	Shàowǔ	Yǒngān
'three'	sâm	sã¹	saŋ¹	sam¹	saŋ¹	saŋ¹	san¹	sɔ̃¹
'deep'	śjəm	tshim¹	tshiŋ¹	tshim¹	tshiŋ¹	tʃhiuŋ¹	tʃhin¹	tʃhã¹
'duck'	ʔâp	aʔ⁷	aʔ⁷	ap⁷	a⁷	a³	an⁷	ɔ⁷
'ten'	źjəp	tsap⁸	seiʔ⁸	sep⁸	si⁸	ʃi⁸	ʃin⁶	sï⁴
'liver'	kân	kuã¹	kaŋ¹	kan¹	xueŋ¹	kuãi¹	hon¹	hŭm¹
'new'	sjen	sin¹	siŋ¹	sin¹	soiŋ¹	siŋ¹	sən¹	sã¹
'cockroach'	dzât	tsuaʔ⁸	saʔ⁸	sat⁸	lue⁸	tsha⁸	tshai⁶	tsuo⁴
'seven'	tshjet	tshit⁷	tsheiʔ⁷	tshe:t⁷	thoi⁷	tshi³	tshi⁷	tshi⁷
'long'	djang	tŋ²	touŋ²	tɔ:ŋ²	lɔŋ⁹	thoŋ²	thoŋ²	tam²
'winter'	tuong	taŋ¹	tøiŋ¹	tøŋ¹	toŋ¹	tuŋ¹	tuŋ¹	tãɯ¹
'drop'	lâk	loʔ⁸	loʔ⁸	lɔʔ⁸	lɔ⁸	lo⁸	lo⁶	naɯ⁴
'north'	pək	pak⁷	poik⁷	pɛ:k⁷	pe⁷	pa³	pə⁷	pa⁷

Table 9.25. Mǐn tonal development

Middle Chinese categories	Píng		Shǎng		Qù		Rù	
	Yīn	Yáng	Yīn	Yáng	Yīn	Yáng	Yīn	Yáng
Xiàmén	1	2	3	6	5	6	7	8
Jiēyáng	1	2	3	4	5	6	7	8
Fúzhōu	1	2	3	6	5	6(5)	7	8
Fúān	1	2	3	6	5	6(5)	7	8
Yǒngān	1	2	3	4	5		7	4

terms of the usual Middle Chinese categories which are adequate for most other dialect groups. Although the tones of Southern Mǐn and Yǒngān exhibit quite a straightforward development, the Northeastern, Northwestern and Far Western dialects present problems which can only be explained if we assume that proto-Mǐn had an initial system quite different from that of Middle Chinese. Tonal evolution in the Northwestern and Far Western dialects is especially complex; due to the complexity of the issues involved and limitations of space, I will not attempt to describe the tonal development of these very interesting dialects here.[11] In Table 9.25, tonal development in five Mǐn dialects is shown.

Words with nasal and lateral initials in the *shǎng* tone split into two types; one type merges with the *yīnshǎng* tone and the other follows words with obstruent

Table 9.26. Mǐn tonal values

	1	2	3	4	5	6	7	8
Xiàmén	55	24	51	—	11	33	32	55
Jiēyáng	33	55	53	35	213	11	22	55
Fúzhōu	55	41	22	—	13	342	24	55
Fúān	43	21	51	—	35	212	43	21
Yǒngān	53	32	21	43	35	—	13	—

initials into the *yángshǎng* or *yángqù* category. No conditioning factor has been discovered to explain this split. In Fúzhōu and Fúān those lower register *qù* tone words which have aspirated initials in the modern dialects have shifted to the *yīnqù* category. Table 9.26 lists the tonal values of the above dialects.

The Eastern Mǐn dialects, from the Zhèjiāng border south to the Cháozhōu region, all have relatively complex tone sandhi. The dialects of interior Fújiàn and the Mǐn dialects of Hǎinán island, on the other hand, either lack tone sandhi altogether or have only one or two instances of it. In addition to tone sandhi, the dialects of Northeastern Fújiàn have varying degrees of consonantal and vocalic sandhi; for example, in Fúān the word for 'heart' consists of two syllables pronounced [sem^{43}] and [kan^{43}] in isolation, but [sim^{33} man^{43}] when combined.

9.5 Mǐn and Kèjiā

I have already stated that I believe there is an especially close relationship between Mǐn and Kèjiā. In this section I will examine some of the evidence for this belief.

In addition to those phonological features already given as evidence for Old Southern Chinese, Kèjiā and Mǐn share at least three other common developments. Mǐn has dental stops corresponding to the Middle Chinese retroflexes (*shéshàngyīn*); Kèjiā retains vestiges of this same correspondence, as the following examples illustrate:

(1) Méixiàn *ti*^{1} (MC *ţje*) 'know': Xiàmén *ti*^{1}, Fúzhōu *ti*^{1}, Jiànōu *ti*^{1}

(2) Méixiàn *tui*^{1} (MC *ţjwi*) 'pursue': Xiàmén *tui*^{1}, Fúzhōu *tui*^{1}, Jiànōu *ty*^{1}

(3) Méixiàn *thi*^{1} (MC *ţhje*) 'sticky, birdlime': Xiàmén *thi*^{1}, Fúzhōu *thi*^{1}, Jiànōu *thi*^{1}

(4) Méixiàn *tuk*^{7} (MC *ţǎk*) 'peck': Xiàmén *tok*^{7}, Fúzhōu *tauk*^{7}, Jiànōu *tɔ*^{7}.

A more significant feature shared by these two dialect groups is a fairly large number of words with nasal and lateral initials which have upper-register tones in both dialect groups. Actually, in Mǐn only Shàowǔ and Jiānglè have upper-division tones in all cases; in Fúzhōu (and the other Northeastern dialects), the

Table 9.27. Upper-register nasals in Mǐn and Kèjiā

	MC	Hǎilù	Méixiàn	Shàowǔ	Fúzhōu	Jiēyáng
'scold'	ma-	ma⁵	ma⁵	ma⁵	ma⁵	mẽ⁶
'body hair'	mâu	mo¹	mau¹	mau⁷	mo²	mõ²
'face'	mjiän-	mian⁵	mien⁵	min⁵	meiŋ⁵	meŋ⁶
'eye'	mjuk	muk⁷	muk⁷	mu⁷	møik⁸	mãk⁸
'forehead'	ngɐk	ɲiak⁷	ɲiak⁷	nia⁷	ŋieʔ⁸	hiaʔ⁸
'meat'	ńźjuk	ɲiuk⁷	ɲiuk⁷	ny⁷	nyʔ⁸	nĕk⁸

Table 9.28. Upper-register laterals in Mǐn and Kèjiā

	MC	Hǎilù	Méixiàn	Shàowǔ	Jiànyáng	Fúzhōu
'basket'	lâm	lam¹	lam¹	san⁷	saŋ²	laŋ²
'fish scale'	ljəm	lin¹	lin²	sen⁷	saiŋ²	liŋ²
'six'	ljuk	liuk⁷	liuk⁷	su⁷	so⁸	løik⁸
'dew'	luo-	lu⁵	lu⁵	so⁵	so⁶	lou⁵
'deaf'	lung	luŋ¹	luŋ¹	suŋ⁷	soŋ²	løiŋ²

upper-register tone is present only in the *qù* tone. In the Southern Mǐn dialects, however, nasal initial words which have upper-register tones in Kèjiā and the Far Western Mǐn dialects of Shàowǔ and Jiānglè often retain the nasality of their initials before oral vowels, contrary to the general rule of denasalization described above. Table 9.27 illustrates this phenomenon. Both Hǎilù and Méixiàn forms are given because the upper and lower *qù* tones have merged in Méixiàn but are still kept separate in Hǎilù.

In the case of the laterals, where Kèjiā has upper-register tones, the Western Mǐn dialects have *s* (see Table 9.28).

These developments illustrated in Tables 9.27 and 9.28 cannot be explained in terms of the Middle Chinese phonological system. The conclusion that must be drawn from this is that a pre-*Qièyùn* dialect which had a contrast of voiced and voiceless nasals and laterals lies at the base of both Mǐn and Kèjiā. The high degree of agreement between these two dialect groups as regards this feature is strong testimony in favor of an early and fundamental link between them.

This close relationship can be confirmed by a considerable stock of common vocabulary unique to the two groups. To illustrate this, Table 9.29 gives ten items which (as far as I know) are restricted to the Mǐn–Kèjiā area. I believe that these lexical parallels are also evidence for an ancient connection between the two groups.

Table 9.29. Common Mǐn and Kèjiā vocabulary

	Hǎilù	Méixiàn	Jiānglè	Jiànyáng	Fúzhōu	Xiàmén
'saliva'	lan¹	lan¹	lãi⁹	lueŋ⁵	laŋ³	nuã³
'pullet'	lon⁶	lon⁵	ʃuãi⁵	—	—	nuã⁶
'bamboo tray'	—	liak⁸	lia⁸	—	lieʔ⁸	liaʔ⁸
'female'	ma²	ma²	ma²	ma²	—	—
'milk'	nen⁵	nen⁵	—	naiŋ¹	neiŋ²	leŋ²
'millet'	—	tai¹	—	—	tai¹	tai¹
'heel, elbow'	tʃaŋ¹	tsaŋ¹	tsaŋ¹	tiaŋ¹	taŋ¹	tĩ¹
'chicken louse'	—	tshi²	—	loi⁹	tai²	tai²
'slaughter'	tʃhï²	tshï²	—	hoi²	thai²	thai²
'vulva'	tʃï¹	tsï¹	—	—	tsi¹	tsi¹

The Far Western Mǐn dialects are especially close to Kèjiā, so much so that mainland Chinese linguists have classified them as such (Pān *et al.* 1963). While considering these dialects as Mǐn, I recognize that they occupy a kind of inter-mediate or transitional position between Mǐn and Kèjiā. In like manner the Northwestern Mǐn dialects can be viewed as transitional between Eastern Mǐn and the Far Western dialects, thus forming a link between the dialects of the Fújiàn coast and the Kèjiā hinterland.

9.6 Difficulties in classification

The vast majority of Chinese dialects known to us can be accommodated in one of the dialect groups described above, but it is well to remember that there are still extensive regions of China about which we know very little in a dialecto-logical sense. When we obtain reliable information on these areas, it may be necessary to posit new subgroups, or at least to alter our understanding of the presently accepted classification.

The Pǔchéng City dialect spoken in extreme north central Fújiàn is an excel-lent example of the sort of difficulty that can be encountered.[12] This dialect is quite different from the surrounding Northwestern Mǐn dialects, and indeed from any other dialect known to us at present. As a first step in trying to deter-mine its affiliation, it should be placed into one of the three major dialectal groupings described at the beginning of Chapter 8. Below these features are listed and a plus (+) or minus (−) value assigned for each.

1. The third person pronoun is ke^4, (−).
2. The subordinative particle is ke^5, (−).
3. The ordinary negative is η^1, (−).

Table 9.30. Development of Middle Chinese voiced initials in Mǐn and Pǔchéng

	MC	Fúzhōu	Jiànyáng	Pǔchéng
'long'	ḍjang	touŋ²	lɔŋ⁹	tsiaŋ²
'sugar'	dâng	thouŋ²	hɔŋ²	taŋ²
'copper'	dung	tøiŋ²	lɔŋ⁹	toŋ²
'insect'	ḍjung	thøiŋ²	hɔŋ²	toŋ²
'reside'	ḍju-	tiu⁶	tiu⁶	tsye⁶
'tree'	źju-	tshiu⁵	tshiu⁶	sye⁶
'thin'	bâk	poʔ⁸	vɔ⁸	pau⁷
'hail'	båk	phøik⁸	pho⁸	pau⁶

4. The gender marker for animals is suffixed: *kie¹ ku⁷* 'rooster', (−).
5. The *shǎng* and *qù* tones both have register distinctions, (−).
6. Velars are not palatalized before *i*, (−).
7. The word for 'to stand' is *kue⁴*, (−).
8. The word for 'to walk' is *tsiau³*, (+).
9. The word for 'son' is *kiãi³*, (−).
10. The word for 'house' is *tshye⁵*, (−).

On the basis of this list, Pǔchéng can be classified as a Southern dialect but with a single Northern (and Central) feature, namely the use of a cognate of Peking *zǒu* (MC *tsâu:*) for 'to walk'. This being the case, to which of the three Southern dialect groups should it be assigned? Kèjiā can be eliminated for the following reasons: (1) in Pǔchéng the Middle Chinese voiced obstruents have all become voiceless non-aspirates; (2) the *yángshǎng* is regularly preserved as a separate category and does not shift to the *yīnpíng* which, as we have seen, is the most typical of the Kèjiā phonological developments; (3) the Pǔchéng word for 'son' is unrelated to Kèjiā *lai⁵*. The list could be extended but the items already given are sufficient to show that Pǔchéng is not a Kèjiā dialect.

It is even clearer that Pǔchéng is not a Yuè dialect. It has only a single *rù* tone, undifferentiated for register. Moreover, it lacks all the unique Yuè lexical items listed in section 9.2.

From a phonological point of view, it is not very Mǐn-like. There is no trace to be found of the distinctive pattern of aspirated and unaspirated initials in words cognate to forms which in Middle Chinese had voiced obstruent initials. This is clear from the selection of forms in Table 9.30.

If we compare this table with Table 9.17 in section 9.4, it is obvious that

Table 9.31. Vocabulary common to Mǐn and Pǔchéng

	Fúzhōu	Jiànōu	Jiànyáng	Pǔchéng
'child'	kiaŋ³	kyeŋ³	kyeŋ³	kiãi³
'house'	tshio⁵	tshio⁵	tshio⁵	tshye⁵
'foot'	kha¹	khau¹	khau¹	khau¹
'leaf'	nioʔ⁸	nio⁸	nio⁸	ŋiau⁴
'stumble'	—	tueŋ³	tueŋ³	luãi³
'short'	tøi³	to³	tui³	lue³

Pǔchéng, unlike Shàowǔ and Jiānglè, shows not the slightest trace of the proto-Mǐn three-way distinction of voiced stops. The Pǔchéng stop system can, in fact, be derived quite easily from that of the *Qièyùn* language.

In my material there are only two words in which Pǔchéng preserves bilabials for the Late Middle Chinese labiodentals: *pu*⁷ 'belly' (MC *pjuk*, Peking *fù*) and *poŋ*² 'a surname' (MC *bjung*, Peking *féng*). In only one word was a Pǔchéng dental recorded for a Middle Chinese retroflex (*shéshàngyīn*): *toŋ*² 'insect' (MC *ḍjung*, Peking *chóng*). Thus we have only the merest vestiges of these typically conservative features found so extensively in Mǐn dialects. We must conclude that phonologically Pǔchéng has little in common with Mǐn.

When the Pǔchéng lexicon is examined, a surprisingly large number of forms otherwise recorded only for Mǐn dialects are encountered. Table 9.31 lists some of these words. In the last item of the table, we see that Pǔchéng lacks a final nasal in the word for 'short' (MC *tuân:*, Peking *duǎn*), a feature otherwise recorded only for Mǐn dialects. It also illustrates the peculiarly Pǔchéng development of *t* > *l*.

At the present time we have too little data on the dialects of the Mǐn periphery to interpret these cases of lexical convergence properly. Obviously they show that Pǔchéng has some sort of ties to Mǐn; but in other ways Pǔchéng is so little like Mǐn that one hesitates to call it a Mǐn dialect just on the basis of such lexical similarities. The Pǔchéng pronouns are quite different from those of any Mǐn dialect, and remind one rather of certain forms of Wú: *a*⁴ 'I, me'; *noŋ*⁴ 'you'; *ke*⁴ 'he/she'. The negatives are of the general Southern type, and do not help to place Pǔchéng into any particular group: *ŋ*¹ 'general negative' *mo*² 'existential negative, not yet'.

Since it is not possible to classify Pǔchéng, other than to place it among the Southern dialects, one has no alternative but to put it in a group all its own – the Pǔchéng group. Further field work may of course turn up some of its relatives.

Further reading

Bodman, Nicholas 1955, 1958. *Spoken Amoy Hokkien*, vols. 1, 2. Kuala Lumpur: Charles Grenier. [An excellent introduction to one of the most important Mǐn dialects.]

Hashimoto, Mantaro 1973. *The Hakka dialect: a linguistic study of its phonology, syntax and lexicon.* Cambridge: Cambridge University Press. [A comprehensive description of Kèjiā.]

Hashimoto, Oi-kan Yue 1972. *Phonology of Cantonese.* Cambridge: Cambridge University Press. [The most detailed and up-to-date treatment of Cantonese phonology.]

10

Language and society

10.1 Prestige of the different forms of Chinese

The sociolinguistic situation in China at the beginning of this century was quite different from what it is now. At that time *wényán*, the Classical literary language, was without question the most prestigious form of Chinese. It was the only truly national and supradialectal form of the language, and undoubtedly the single most important symbol of Chinese ethnicity and cultural unity. Its immense prestige was based on its role as the language of all higher culture, and the almost sacred character it possessed as the language of the Confucian Classics, which at that time still formed the foundation of the nation's political and quasi-religious ideology. In addition, the vast majority of Chinese literature, history, philosophy and technical writing was written in the Classical language. This language was also the language of administration both at the national and local levels.

Wényán was purely a written language; unlike comparable literary languages in the West, it could not be spoken. The chief reason for this was that no uniform pronunciation existed; each region had its own purely local method of reading Classical texts aloud; these local pronunciations were almost always based on (or at least closely related to) local dialectal pronunciation, forming as it were dialectal varieties of the literary language. Moreover, even if a uniform pronunciation of the Classical literary language had existed, it is doubtful that an oral version of Classical Chinese would have been fully intelligible because of the high degree of homonymy that would have been present.[1]

Since the Classical literary language differed from the spoken local forms of Chinese radically in almost all its aspects, it was a difficult and time-consuming task to learn it, and since education was available only to a small minority of people, knowledge of *wényán* was limited in most cases to members of the land-owning or merchant classes. This limited access no doubt served to enhance its prestige even further.

Other forms of written Chinese enjoyed little prestige, and were frequently deprecated by the literate elite. The most important of these non-Classical written languages was *báihuà*, the written vernacular, in which a rich and thriving popular literature existed. Although such literature was widely read and enjoyed, it was officially scorned by the literati. Before the time of the May Fourth Movement it was considered fit only to be a vehicle of popular entertainment, and totally unsuited for the expression of elevated and serious thought. Even lower on the scale of prestige were the written forms of local dialects, which were restricted to the recording of folklore materials and scripts for the local theater.

As with the written language, there was also a hierarchy of prestige relating to the varieties of spoken Chinese, although the lines were not drawn so sharply in this case. At the top of this hierarchy stood the dialect of the national capital, the center of imperial administration. As we have seen, an administrative lingua franca, *guānhuà* ('Mandarin') was based on the dialect of the capital. The capital dialect was the only dialect which enjoyed any sort of national currency; even though it was spoken only by a tiny minority of officials and merchants, it was a necessary tool to anyone who sought position and advancement within the imperial bureaucracy.

For the past six centuries (with only a few minor exceptions), Peking has been the capital of China. We know that during the Qing dynasty the Peking-based koine, *guānhuà*, was used extensively throughout the country. It is virtually certain that a similar situation prevailed in earlier dynasties when the capital was located elsewhere. In Chapter 2 we saw the importance of the dialect of Jīnlíng, the capital of the Southern dynasties, in the establishment of the phonological categories of the *Qièyùn* dictionary. During the Tang dynasty, the dialect of Chángān played a role similar to that played by the Peking dialect in later times. It is not unlikely that throughout most of Chinese history one regional form of Chinese has enjoyed a sort of pre-eminence as the elegant or prestigious form of Chinese. According to Zhōu Zǔmó (Zhōu and Wú 1956, x) even in the Chūnqiū period (770–476 BC) the dialect of Jìn, a feudal state located in the present province of Shānxī, provided the basis for just such a prestige language.

Somewhere between the dialect of the capital and the local dialects proper stood the dialects of various regional or provincial centers. Being centers of administration, education and commerce, important cities like Guǎngzhōu, Xiàmén and Sūzhōu also became centers of linguistic prestige. Their dialects were frequently learned by people living in outlying areas, and took on the role of regional koines, serving much the same function at the regional level as the capital dialect did at the national level. Even at the present time Cantonese (the dialect of Guǎngzhōu) is widely used and understood in much of Guǎngdōng province and in part of Guǎngxī province as well.

At the lowest end of the prestige scale were the purely local dialects which were the sole means of oral communication used by the great mass of the Chinese population. Since there was very little mobility either in the geographic or social sense in traditional China, most people rarely (if ever) left their native place, and consequently never felt the need to learn another form of Chinese.

The situation now found in China is quite different. The Classical language to all intents and purposes has passed from the scene. After 1920 the movement to replace the old literary language with a new, vernacular-based written language gained strength steadily. For a while the literary language continued to be used widely in journalism and in the bureaucracy, but in the late 1940s *báihuà* finally won out in these areas as well. At the present time the Classical literary language is used very little, and is more and more taking on a status similar to that held by Latin and Greek in the Western world. Most students get a smattering of it in middle school but rarely have occasion to use it in everyday life. Serious students of Chinese history or literature naturally are required to make a more thorough study of *wényán*, but even they mainly employ it as a tool for reading premodern texts and are rarely called upon to compose in it. In effect, all the functions which lent such a high degree of prestige to the literary language at the beginning of this century are now fulfilled by *báihuà*.

In practice, modern *báihuà* has replaced both *wényán* and the old vernacular written language, and can be considered the sole form of written Chinese at the present time.[2] It is the language taught in all Chinese primary and secondary schools (both in mainland China and in Táiwān) and is used in writing of all types – literary, journalistic, administrative, technical, academic and personal. It functions, in fact, exactly like any other modern standard written language, be it English, French, Russian or Japanese.

The spoken analogue of *báihuà* is *pǔtōnghuà*, earlier called *guóyǔ*. Unlike *guānhuà* in the Qing dynasty, which was mainly an administrative medium, *pǔtōnghuà* is a true national language, with official status and currency at all levels of society. Although its pronunciation and lexicon are codified in semi-official dictionaries, *pǔtōnghuà* is rarely spoken in its purely standard form outside the city of Peking and its environs. In the vast majority of cases, *pǔtōnghuà* represents a kind of *Umgangssprache*, a variety of speech that lies somewhere between the local dialect and the standard proper. In any given area there is a great deal of fluidity in the degree to which speakers succeed in approaching a standard *pǔtōnghuà*. Success depends on a number of factors: remoteness of the locality from cultural and educational centers, social and official station of the speaker, and the degree to which any given individual is called upon to communicate with outsiders in his daily routine.

Although *pǔtōnghuà* is now taught virtually everywhere in China, it is clear that there will be a closer approximation to the standard in heavily populated urban areas where there is an ample supply of teachers who themselves have a reasonably adequate command of the spoken standard, or where qualified teachers can be imported relatively easily. Likewise, the intelligentsia – the political cadre, teachers and technical personnel – are more likely to have a good command of *pǔtōnghuà* owing to their more frequent contact with outsiders and their easier access to travel. Peasants and most workers, on the other hand, have few opportunities to communicate with non-local people and their command of *pǔtōnghuà* is consequently weaker. It is probably also the case that even members of the intelligentsia employ a more dialectally colored lower register of *pǔtōnghuà* in certain social situations. The actual state of *pǔtōnghuà* in the various regions of China, little investigated at the present time, represents a rich field for future research.

The government actively promotes the teaching and use of *pǔtōnghuà*, but it does not forbid or even discourage the use of local dialects in everyday life, and in fact the dialects continue to show great vitality. In a city like Shànghǎi or Guǎngzhōu one rarely hears *pǔtōnghuà* spoken on the streets or in other public places; it is used in governmental and party meetings, schools, and on radio and television – but the local dialects still reign supreme in the home and most places of work. If this is the case in such large cosmopolitan centers, the relative strength of dialects in smaller cities and rural areas must be even greater. This is in fact the case in Táiwān, where, because of the massive immigration of main-landers after 1949, the position of the standard language is unusually strong for a non-Mandarin-speaking region. Here one finds widespread use of *pǔtōnghuà* (*guóyǔ*) in metropolitan areas like Táiběi, but in smaller towns and rural areas the Southern Mǐn and Kèjiā dialects are used almost exclusively, despite the fact that almost all people under forty possess at least a minimal working knowledge of the standard language. Thus, while great progress has been made in promot-ing *pǔtōnghuà* in the last thirty years, the position of the dialects has hardly been weakened as a result, and this state of affairs can be expect to remain fairly stable for the foreseeable future.

The city of Peking presents a unique situation with regard to its dialect. The Peking dialect is the dialect on which *pǔtōnghuà* is based. This does not mean, however, that the Peking dialect (*Běijīnghuà*) and *pǔtōnghuà* are identical; they are not. This is especially evident in the area of lexicon, less with regard to grammar. To give some idea of these differences, Table 10.1 lists twenty lexical items in the Peking dialect which would probably not be understood by speakers of *pǔtōnghuà* from other areas.

The teaching of *pǔtōnghuà*, which is an integral and important part of all

Table 10.1. Lexicon of Peking dialect and *pǔtōnghuà* compared

Peking dialect	*Pǔtōnghuà*	English
1. yémen	nánrén	'man'
2. niángrmen	nǔrén	'woman'
3. gūngmǔliǎ	fūfù	'husband and wife'
4. jīnr	jīntian	'today'
5. zuór	zuótian	'yesterday'
6. cāhēir	bàngwǎn	'dusk'
7. duózan	shénma shíhou	'when'
8. qūqin	qiūyǐn	'earthworm'
9. qūqur	xīshuài	'cricket'
10. dēi hàozi	zhuō lǎoshǔ	'catch a mouse'
11. jīzǐr	jīdàn	'egg'
12. nǎoguār	tóu	'head'
13. hālázi	kǒushǔi	'saliva'
14. chīmuhū	yǎnshǐ	'eye discharge'
15. néng	nóng	'pus'
16. zāngtǔ	lāji	'garbage'
17. qǔdēngr	huǒchái	'match (for lighting fires)'
18. bàngzi	yùmǐ	'corn (maize)'
19. cèi	sùi	'shatter'
20. kēijià	dǎjià	'fight'

primary and secondary education everywhere in China, has not only dramatically spread the knowledge and use of the standard language during the past thirty years, but has led to a leveling out of the peculiarities of dialectal vocabulary. More and more, local dialects are prone to adopt words from the standard language. It is likely, for example, that many of the words in the list given above are losing ground to their more general *pǔtōnghuà* equivalents, even among native Peking dialect speakers. Hú Míngyáng (1978) has described how the vocabulary of the Shànghǎi dialect has changed as a result of its sustained contact with *pǔtōnghuà*: the tendency is for words with a strong dialectal flavor to be eliminated in favor of more generally used terms found in *pǔtōnghuà* and written *báihuà*.[3]

The process whereby a standard language or koine exerts a strong influence on local dialects is, as we have suggested in Chapters 8 and 9, nothing new in Chinese linguistic history; it is in fact a leitmotiv that can be observed time and time again whenever a strong centralized authority imposes its rule over the country.

10.2 Diglossia, bidialectalism, bilingualism

The linguistic situation which existed in China prior to the May Fourth Movement fits Charles Ferguson's classic definition of diglossia (Ferguson 1964, 435) relatively well:

> DIGLOSSIA is a relatively stable language situation in which, in
> addition to the primary dialects of the language (which may include
> a standard or regional standards), there is a very divergent, highly
> codified (often grammatically more complex) superposed variety, the
> vehicle of a large and respected body of written literature, either of
> an earlier period or in another speech community, which is learned
> largely by formal education and is used for most written and formal
> spoken purposes but is not used by any sector of the community for
> ordinary conversation.

With only two reservations, this definition clearly fits the situation described
in the previous section for *wényán* and the popular spoken forms of Chinese (the
dialects). It is doubtful whether *wényán* was more complex grammatically than
most local dialects. For one thing, *wényán*, as we have pointed out, did not
properly speaking have a pronunciation of its own, but was read variously
depending on the native dialect of the person doing the reading; and in its mor-
phophonemics (which also varied according to the same conditions), it was probably usually rather less complex than the dialect on which its pronunciation was
based. And although it possessed a different set of grammatical function words
and employed somewhat different rules of word order, it would be difficult to
demonstrate that its syntax was any more complex than that of the spoken forms
of Chinese.

Unlike in most other diglossic situations, *wényán*, in its role as the higher and
more prestigious form of the language, was almost never used orally, for reasons
already explained. In other ways, the role of *wényán* in traditional China was
quite closely parallel to the role of Classical Arabic in Arabic-speaking countries
or the role of *katharévusa* in modern Greece.

Traditional diglossia has now been replaced with what Ferguson calls
"standard-with-dialects" (1964, 435). A standard differs from the higher literary
medium in diglossia in that it is actually used by a significant proportion of the
population as a medium of day-to-day communication. Note that it is not necessary that the standard in this sort of situation be absolutely identical to any one
regional or local dialect. In the Chinese case, standard *pǔtōnghuà* is not in fact
identical to any one local dialect in all its details, but in essentials and for most
practical purposes it can be considered the same as the Peking dialect. This
means that in the city of Peking there is a substantial population that uses the
standard as its ordinary medium of oral communication. In addition to this
rather considerable group, there are probably other groups found in various

other metropolitan centers who employ *pǔtōnghuà* as their main form of spoken Chinese. In the city of Táiběi, for example, large numbers of people under forty years of age speak only the local variety of *pǔtōnghuà*. Typically, these people are from families in which some dialectal variety of mainland Chinese is spoken, but even if they learned their own particular family dialect in infancy, in the course of growing up and especially as a result of their schooling, they have abandoned or forgotten these non-standard dialects and have switched to *pǔtōnghuà* as their sole means of oral communication. In some young families children learn *pǔtōnghuà* as their first language, and in effect become native speakers of this local variety of the standard language.

Táiběi also serves as an interesting example of what sort of process of development the standard language undergoes as its use spreads and takes root in areas remote from Peking. From a dialectal point of view, the population of Táiběi is very heterogeneous. A large part of the population speaks the indigenous Southern Mǐn dialect (*mǐnnánhuà*) as its native language, but a very sizable proportion of the Táiběi population is composed either of mainland immigrants or of the children and grandchildren of mainland immigrants who represent an extraordinary variety of dialectal backgrounds in which non-Mandarin, southern types probably predominate. The mainland population in Táiwān was originally associated with either the nationalist government or with the nationalist army, and many of them already possessed a basic working knowledge of *pǔtōnghuà* when they first arrived in Táiwān. Because of the presence of several mutually unintelligible dialects and the need for a common medium of oral communication, the government vigorously promoted the teaching and use of the standard language from the very outset in Táiwān. Although the official Peking-based pronunciation was advocated in theory, in fact very few teachers were able to reproduce this pronunciation correctly; the result was that the form of *pǔtōnghuà* which has actually taken root in Táiwān differs from the standard in a number of important ways. The most likely explanation for this (in addition to the inadequacies of teachers) is that it resulted from a kind of natural leveling process in a population of very disparate dialectal backgrounds. Phonologically, Táiwān *pǔtōnghuà* represents a kind of lowest common denominator of the many dialects that comprised its dialectal substratum. In vocabulary a similar process can be observed: many words which enjoy wide currency in Peking and other northern Mandarin dialects have been rejected in favor of words that have a greater currency in South China. A certain amount of southern (especially Mǐnnán) influence can also be detected in the grammatical system of Táiběi *pǔtōnghuà*. Despite these "non-standard" deviations, however, the *pǔtōnghuà* of Táiběi remains no more than a regional variety of the standard language, fully intelligible to speakers of other regional varieties as well as to speakers of the paradigmatic Peking standard.

Today Táiběi is a bidialectal city: both *pǔtōnghuà* and *mǐnnánhuà* are widely spoken in their own spheres. Many individuals are bidialectal and able to function in both spheres. At the present time this situation appears to be relatively stable, and is likely to continue to be so for some time to come.[4]

The linguistic situation of the city of Shànghǎi presents an interesting contrast to that of Táiběi. Here too the population is very heterogeneous, but the immigration which has brought about this heterogeneity has been more local in character. Hú Míngyáng (1978) estimates that two out of every three Shànghǎi inhabitants are in some sense outsiders; these new immigrants mostly come from the surrounding Wú-speaking regions of southern Jiāngsū and northern Zhèjiāng, whereas the number of non-Wú dialect speakers has been negligible. As a result the Shànghǎi Wú dialect has remained the only everyday means of oral communication, and *pǔtōnghuà*, while universally studied in school, has remained a second dialect, limited in its sphere of activity to communication with outsiders, schools, governmental functions, radio and television, and the like. It is interesting to note that the Shànghǎi dialect, like the *pǔtōnghuà* of Táiběi, has undergone a similar process of phonological and grammatical reduction.

From a multidialectal nation in which only a few members of the governing or commercial elite possessed a knowledge of more than one dialect, China is today rapidly becoming a bidialectal country. More and more people are learning and using *pǔtōnghuà* in a wide variety of activities; most of them continue to employ their local dialects in the family and in most social situations. It is also almost inevitable in a situation of this sort that the standard language will influence the local dialects, especially their vocabularies; in the long run, this should have the effect of bringing the dialects closer to one another provided the process is not impeded by some unforeseen factor. Will this lead eventually to the abandoning of dialects altogether in favor of a single standard or national *Umgangssprache*? It is of course impossible to say with any degree of certainty, but from what I have been able to observe, the incipient bidialectal situation in present-day China appears to be entering a relatively stable period; I suspect that the local dialects will continue to show a great deal of vitality and will be around for a long time to come.

The vast majority of the Chinese population, some 94 per cent, consists of speakers of some variety of Chinese. The remaining 6 per cent (over 60 million people at the present time) are speakers of more than fifty different, minority, non-Han languages. Some of these ethnolinguistic minorities are quite large, as Table 10.2 shows.

Table 10.2. Some ethnolinguistic minorities in China

Minority	Population[a]
Zhuang	12,190,000
Uygur	5,480,000
Miao	3,920,000
Tibetan	3,450,000
Mongol	2,660,000
Korean	1,680,000

[a] Population figures are based on *The peoples of China*, a map produced by the Cartographic Division of the National Geographic Society, 1980.

All of the groups listed here have their own non-Han languages possessing written forms, which are taught and used in schools. The teaching of standard Chinese is also promoted among the various minorities and the national language is widely used especially among cadres and students. In some regions where several minority languages are spoken in proximity to one another, knowledge of two or more minority languages is also common. For example, among the Xibe of the Ili region in Xīnjiāng, a Tungusic people who number approximately 20,000, many people are fluent in Uygur in addition to Standard Chinese (Lǐ 1979). As in the case of the Chinese dialects, the standard national language is a major source of influence on the minority languages. This is especially true in the area of lexicon, where new terms are frequently taken over from the standard language in their unadulterated Chinese guise.

In a few cases minority languages have exerted major influence on local varieties of Chinese. Some Chinese dialects in Qīnghǎi in northwestern China, for example, possess a number of features which reveal strong Tibetan inroads. A very interesting thing about this particular case is that the Tibetan influence is not limited to vocabulary but extends to grammar as well. Among the non-Chinese features these dialects have taken from Tibetan are SOV word order and the use of postpositions (Chéng 1980). This and similar examples of foreign influence on Chinese syntax are particularly interesting, since they demonstrate that Chinese may have been influenced by non-Han languages in the earlier course of its syntactic development.

10.3 Government language policy

Prior to the twentieth century, Chinese governments of the imperial period seem to have taken little notice of language problems. The sociolinguistic situation which prevailed for many centuries, wherein governmental business was carried out either in the written literary language or in the oral lingua franca based on the speech of the imperial capital, served the practical needs of the government quite well. When occasional difficulties arose, special, more or less ad hoc solutions were found. For example, in the eighteenth century, the Yōngzhèng emperor (reigned 1723–35) ordered the establishment of special schools for the teaching of *guānhuà* in Fújiàn and Guǎngdōng provinces because of the generally poor command of *guānhuà* exhibited by natives of these two provinces. Before China's traumatic encounter with Western culture after the Opium War in 1840–2, little attention was given to improving the educational level of the population as a whole, and consequently the awkward and difficult Chinese writing system was not viewed as a serious problem. Once the desirability of mass education and modernization along Western lines became evident, however, the problem of linguistic reform came to the forefront. By the early part of this century, it had become evident to several theorists of national reform that the linguistic situation in China was inadequate to meet the needs of a modern nation. The plethora of dialects, many of them more like separate languages than dialects of the same language, impeded communication among peoples from different parts of the country. *Wényán*, the common written language, was difficult to master and the literacy rate was abysmally low. It was clear that if China wanted to enter the ranks of modern nations, linguistic reform was essential.

Although the Qing government in its declining years took some steps to make the teaching of *guānhuà* obligatory in secondary schools, the measures were too late to have any real effect. It was during the republican period which lasted from 1912 until 1949 that the first significant steps towards implementing language reform took place. In 1912 the Commission for Unifying Reading Pronunciation (*Dúyīn Tǒngyī Huì*) was established by the Ministry of Education for the purpose of establishing a standard pronunciation for the words (characters) employed in the national language (*guóyǔ*); the members of the Commission were also charged with the task of devising a phonetic alphabet for use in promoting the national language. The Commission met in early 1913, and both of its assigned tasks were accomplished: a standard pronunciation which took into account features from several different northern dialects was agreed upon; a "national phonetic alphabet" (*guóyīn zìmǔ*) was devised; approved by the government in 1918, it was subsequently used widely in language instruction, and is still employed in the teaching of the national language in Táwān today. The *Guóyīn zìdiǎn*, a dictionary containing the standard pronunciation established by the Commission, was officially promulgated in 1919 (Liú 1925, 19ff). As indicated in Chapter 6, the pronunciation contained in this work was too artificial to gain widespread acceptance, and was subsequently replaced by a new standard based on the Peking dialect.

In 1919 the Preparatory Committee on the Unification of the National Language (*Guóyŭ Tŏngyī Chóubèihùi*) was set up by the Ministry of Education. This committee was charged with studying a wide range of problems relating to the national language (Liú 1925, 47ff). In 1923 a Lexicography Section for the National Language (*Guóyŭ Cídiăn Biānzuănchù*) was established as a part of the Committee's work; ultimately this group was responsible for the first sizable and authoritative dictionary of the national language, the *Guóyŭ cídiăn* in four volumes (see section 7.9).

The initiative in replacing *wényán* with *báihuà* was mainly taken by individuals associated with the May Fourth Movement and not by the government. In the early 1920s, however, the Ministry of Education did issue directives ordering the teaching of *báihuà* in the first two grades of primary school, thus legalizing the position of *báihuà* in the educational system. In government documents, commercial correspondence and certain types of journalism, however, *wényán* continued to hold its own well into the 1940s, and even beyond in some cases.

The War of Resistance against Japan and the subsequent civil war in China effectively impeded any important developments in the area of language reform. Another factor in slowing work in this area was conservative resistance on the parts of certain elements of society who viewed the integrity of the script and the literary language as indispensable elements of Chinese ethnic culture. On the whole, however, progress, though slow, was made during this early period.

In general, the communist government which took power in 1949 continued the linguistic policies of the former regime, expressing strong support for a single normalized national language based on the Peking dialect. The position of *báihuà* as the common written language was further strengthened, and the official use of *wényán* was curtailed altogether. Little official action on the language reform front was taken until the mid-1950s. Among the resolutions of the National Script Reform Congress (*Quánguó Wénzì Găigé Huìyì*) which met in October 1955 were suggestions concerning reform and simplification of the traditional logographic script, as well as suggestions about promoting the study of the national language, now officially called *pŭtōnghuà* 'the common language'. In 1956 the State Council issued an official directive ordering the teaching of *pŭtōnghuà* in schools beginning from the autumn of the same year; in addition, it contained broad instructions on how *pŭtōnghuà* was to be promoted in various areas of national life – the army, the Communist Youth League, broadcasting, journalism, industry, commerce, and translation and interpreting work. Among other practical measures mandated were the creation of a new phonetic alphabet and the compiling of a dictionary of the standard language. The policy outlined in this directive was actively implemented up until the inception of the Cultural Revolution (1966–76); during this period work on promoting *pǔtōnghuà* virtually ceased (Yú *et al.* 1979, 460).

Perhaps the most dramatic steps in language policy have been those concerned with the reform and simplification of the traditional script, long felt to be too complicated and difficult to learn. Reform of the writing system is the chief concern of the Committee on Script Reform (*Wénzì Gǎigé Wěiyuánhuì*) which is an organ of the State Council, the highest administrative organ in the People's Republic of China. The first major step in script reform took place in 1956 with the publication of a list of 515 characters, of which twenty-nine were to be abolished outright and the remainder simplified to some degree; most commonly simplification took the form of reducing the number of strokes in a given character, but in a few cases the components were changed more radically. In 1964, a further list of over 2,000 characters was promulgated; this list contained a number of simplified components (mostly based on cursive forms) which could be used in a large number of complex characters (Lehmann 1975, 46). In 1977, a list of 200 additional simplified characters was issued for trial use. A number of influential newspapers and journals began to use the new simplified forms; however, there was evidently a popular swell of negative reaction to the new reformed graphs. As a result of widespread criticism (and perhaps of other factors as well) the characters were suddenly withdrawn from use in the autumn of 1978 (Norman 1980, 494).

The future direction of script reform at the present time is somewhat unclear. Some further simplification is possible on a minor scale, but there is a widespread feeling that a period of stability and efforts toward greater standardization in the use of characters is now needed. One interesting problem under consideration is the possibility of somehow limiting the overall total of characters in use. As noted in Chapter 3, the average Chinese reader with a post-secondary education knows between 3,500 and 4,000 Chinese characters. Studies of large text samples and surveys of printers' stocks show that around 6,000 characters are in actual use at the present time. A comprehensive dictionary like the *Cíhǎi* contains on the order of 15,000 characters, but many of these are found only in the Classical literary language. A number of experiments carried out in the late 1970s indicate that by replacing low-frequency characters with homophonous forms, it is probably possible to produce a standard list of around 3,500 which will be adequate for writing the modern standard language (Guān and Tián 1981, 150). If such a curtailed inventory of graphs is indeed practicable, it will obviously greatly simplify problems of printing and computer processing of Chinese language materials. There is no indication, however, that the details of such a limited list of characters have been worked out, or that any such list will be put into force any time soon.

10.4 The fate of alphabetic writing in China

The Chinese language was an important item on the agenda of almost all reform-minded people in the early decades of this century. Dissatisfaction with the linguistic situation was so great that a few radical individuals advocated the abolition of Chinese altogether and its replacement with Esperanto (Sofronov 1979, 225). A more sober view held that the real problem was not the Chinese language itself but its complicated writing system. There was almost universal agreement that the cumbersome literary language had to go, and, as we have seen, the government, despite a certain amount of conservative opposition, eventually effected a transition from *wényán* to *báihuà* in the course of the 1920s and 1930s. The need for a common language was hardly controversial.

The question of the writing system evoked the most controversy. Even after the switch to *báihuà*, a Chinese student had to learn 3,500 to 4,000 complicated graphs in order to function as a literate person. Many felt that the learning of such a complex writing system, requiring many years and consuming such a large proportion of a student's school time, was an intolerable burden for the people of a modern nation. It is not surprising that almost all Western-oriented intellectuals in the early decades of the present century were in favor of abandoning the logographic script in favor of some sort of alphabetic writing. The advantages of such a switch were thought to be obvious: an alphabetic writing system can be mastered in a relatively short time and with relative ease; it is much easier to print; it can be written on a typewriter; it makes the learning of European languages simpler. But while there was wide agreement on the need to adopt an alphabetic writing system, the practical implementation of such a scheme was another matter.

The idea of writing Chinese in an alphabetic form was not new. In Chapter 2 we saw that the Mongols in the Yuan dynasty wrote Chinese in the 'Phags-pa alphabet. In the late Ming dynasty, Matteo Ricci, the famous Jesuit missionary, devised a scheme for romanizing Chinese intended mainly as an aid for Europeans in the learning of Chinese. In the nineteenth century, Christian missionaries devised a number of romanized writing systems for writing dialects, and some of them, like that for the Amoy dialect, were used widely among Christian converts as a practical means of writing their native dialect.

The first alphabetic writing system developed by a Chinese person for the

Chinese was the *guānhuà zìmǔ* ("Mandarin alphabet") of Wáng Zhào (1859–1933). Wáng modeled his alphabet on Japanese katakana (one of the two native Japanese syllabaries) which he learned during a two-year sojourn in Japan. The letters themselves were based on the components of Chinese characters. After returning to China in 1900, he taught his system in various parts of North China with some success, but its further development was cut short by a government ban in 1901 (Ní 1948).

A contemporary of Wáng's, Láo Nǎixuān (1843–1921) adapted the *guānhuà zìmǔ* for use in two Wú dialects, those of Níngbō and Sūzhōu. By doing this, he raised for the first time the issue that ultimately was most responsible for the failure of all alphabetic writing systems in China – namely, the notion that people should be introduced to literacy in their own local dialects. In Láo's view, learning to write in one's own native dialect was not only the sole practical way to teach the great masses of China to read and write, it was also the best and quickest way to promote the knowledge and use of a single national language, for once a person had a solid foundation in the alphabetic system of his own dialect, he would be able to learn the alphabetized form of the national language more easily. This also in essence was the line of argument taken by later promoters of alphabetic writing. For China this was a very radical idea indeed. Not only would it challenge the unique position of the 3,500-year-old writing system which had always served as the hallmark of Chinese cultural unity, it would for the first time create a linguistic polycentrism in which China would have more than one literary language. In place of a single nationwide written language there would be a multitude of written dialects. At one blow, such a proposal would destroy China's linguistic unity in both the historical and the geographic senses. It is not surprising, then, that from the very beginning there was strong opposition to proposals of this kind.

In the republican period, the cause of alphabetic writing took a course different from that advocated by Láo Nǎixuān. Instead of an independent way of writing that could be used for all of China's dialects, alphabetic writing came to be seen chiefly as an auxiliary device which could be used in teaching the national language; it would not replace the traditonal script, but would be used as a convenient pedagogic tool in the teaching of characters. It was ideas of this kind that were behind the creation of the *guóyīn zìmǔ* which, as we have seen, was officially adopted by the government in 1918. It is quite clear from its pronouncements that the government never intended the *guóyīn zìmǔ* to serve as an autonomous method of writing, but rather meant it to serve as a means of teaching correct pronunciation while the Chinese characters remained the sole officially sanctioned writing system. In 1930 the name of the system was officially changed to *zhùyīn fúhào* 'symbols for phonetic notation', in order to bring out more clearly the system's role as an auxiliary means of indicating the pronunciation of Chinese characters. *Zhùyīn fúhào* could be adapted to dialects, but only if simultaneously used in conjunction with an indication of the standard pronunciation. In the end *zhùyīn fúhào* was not a writing system but a set of phonetic symbols, rather along the lines of the IPA and other similar systems of transcription.

Many looked upon *zhùyīn fúhào* as a kind of unhappy compromise: it employed symbols derived from the traditional script, and in reality was not a real writing system at all; what China really needed was a thoroughly modern writing system, based on the Latin alphabet. The drawbacks of a logographic system were all too obvious: it was hard to learn, hard to write, hard to remember, and hard to print; in short, it was an outmoded and cumbersome nuisance, and the time had come to replace it with an adequate, up-to-date writing system. A majority of the liberal and leftist intellectuals in the 1920s were sympathetic to these or similar views. The committee which created *guóyǔ luómǎzì* was drawn from people espousing such ideas. *Guóyǔ luómǎzì* was the first Chinese system of latinization which obtained governmental approval. Unfortunately, the government never promoted its use actively, and in a few years after its creation it was clear that it had failed as a practical alternative to the traditional writing system and had come to be looked upon as a Westernized step-brother of *zhùyīn fúhào*.

It is sometimes said that *guóyǔ luómǎzì* failed because it was too hard to learn; the four tones were indicated by a set of rather complicated spelling rules which varied according to syllable structure. For example, the second tone was indicated by a suffixed *r* in syllables lacking a medial, but if a medial *-i-* was present, then the second tone was indicated by changing the *-i-* to *-y-*; if the syllable began with one of the sonorants (*m, n* or *l*), then no spelling change was necessary. It is no doubt true that a system of this type was more difficult to learn than systems which either left tones unmarked or indicated them with diacritics, but the difficulty is frequently exaggerated. As a writing system it was surely no more difficult than English or even Russian spelling for native speakers of those languages. Compared with English spelling it was in fact a great deal simpler. And, as Yuen Ren Chao has pointed out, this kind of tonal spelling, although complicated, "gives an individuality to the physiognomy of words, with which it is possible to associate meaning in a way not possible in the case of forms with tone-signs added as an afterthought" (1948a, 11). In the final analysis, *guóyǔ luómǎzì* failed not because of defects in the system itself, but because it never received the official support it would have required to succeed; perhaps more importantly, it was viewed by many as the product of a group of elitist enthusiasts, and lacked any real popular base of support. Subsequent history would show that these were precisely the problems that any alphabetic scheme for Chinese would face.

The alphabetization scheme known as *latinxua sin wenz* enjoyed considerably more success than did *guóyǔ luómǎzì*, for a time at least. This method of writing Chinese with the Latin alphabet was worked out in the USSR by a group of Chinese and Russian linguists. It was initially devised for promoting literacy among Chinese immigrant workers living in the Soviet Far East, principally in Vladivostok and Khabarovsk. *Latinxua* was actually used in teaching the Chinese population of this region to read and write, reportedly with great success (Sofronov 1979, 254). According to its supporters, this practical success proved beyond a doubt that Chinese written in the Latin alphabet was a totally viable system of writing for China.

Unlike *guóyǔ luómǎzì*, *latinxua* was not based on the Peking dialect, but took as its base a cross-section of northern dialects. This decision was no doubt influenced by the fact that a majority of the Chinese in the Soviet Far East were originally from Shāndōng and Manchuria, and spoke dialects which differed from that of Peking in a number of important respects. The most important difference between the two standards was the treatment of the so-called *jiān* ('sharp') and *tuán* ('round') initials (see section 8.6). In the Peking dialect there is no distinction between the two series of initials: both the Middle Chinese velars and dental sibilants have merged before high front vowels: MC *ki*>Peking *tɕi*, MC *tsi*>Peking *tɕi*. Many northern dialects, however, still retain this distinction under one guise or another; some Shāndōng dialects, for example, still retain a situation like that found in Middle Chinese, retaining velars before high front vowels. More common is the situation in which the velars have become prepalatals and the dental sibilants are retained unchanged: MC *ki*>*tɕi*, MC *tsi*>*tsi*. In *latinxua* the two series are distinguished by using velars for writing the *tuán* initials and dental sibilants for the *jiān* initials: thus Peking *tɕi* could be either *gi* or *zi*, depending on its etymological origin. This distinction, while convenient for speakers of dialects in which the *jiān/tuán* opposition was retained in some form, was difficult for speakers of dialects in which the two series had merged. A Peking native would have to learn to spell such words by rote, much as an English-speaking person has to remember the spelling of words like *rite* and *right*. It is interesting to speculate on why such a distinction was made. One possible reason is that the Chinese population of the Soviet Far East for whom the system was initially devised was largely made up of people from areas of North China, speaking dialects which by and large preserved the *jiān/tuán* distinction. Another factor may have been the influence of Qú Qiūbái and others of like mind who, as we saw in Chapter 6, opposed the Peking-based *guóyǔ* as a sort of elitist standard which was allegedly divorced from contemporary linguistic reality.

Did *latinxua* actually correspond to any one northern dialect? Although it is hard to be sure, it seems doubtful. It is much more likely that it was a compromise based on several northern dialects, much as the old *Guóyīn zìdiǎn* of 1919 was. In a sense, then, it was not really a standard at all; each individual would presumably read it according to his own dialectal habits, much in the same way that the logographic script was read in its countless different dialectal variants.

The feature of *latinxua* which in the long run made it most controversial was its lack of tonal markings; tones were indicated in only a few cases where serious ambiguity might result.[5] The feeling of its promoters was that the marking of tonal distinctions was an unnecessary complication which would only serve to make the learning of the system more difficult. Perhaps they were also influenced to some degree by the fact that stress accent is not indicated in Russian orthography even though it is phonemic. Making tone an integral and inseparable part of each syllable was considered an essential feature of *guóyǔ luómǎzì* by its framers; subsequently the question of whether or not tones should be indicated in Chinese alphabetic writing became one of the most hotly debated issues between the proponents of the two systems (cf. Chao 1948a, 11ff).

Latinxua was used by the Chinese in the USSR for about four years; in 1936 most of the Chinese in the Far East were repatriated and the Soviet experiment with latinized Chinese came to an end (Sofronov 1979, 255). In the meanwhile news of the Soviet efforts became known in China; *latinxua* quickly attracted a large number of supporters, particularly among leftist intellectuals. The famous writer Lǔ Xùn (1881–1936) soon became an ardent supporter of the system; he saw in it a new and highly effective method for educating China's illiterate masses. Realizing that to try to spread literacy solely in the northern-based form of *latinxua* would be well-nigh impossible in southern dialect areas, he advocated the creation of dialectal versions of *latinxua* and the teaching of literacy in the people's native dialects. Here we see once again the view first expressed by Láo Nǎixuān that if literacy were to be promoted by means of an alphabetic script, then dialectal writing systems would have to be created alongside that for the national language; to try to spread literacy in the southern dialect areas through the means of a phonetically written version of the standard language would be as difficult and ineffective as trying to teach Italians to read French or Spanish without first teaching them their own language. This view was widely accepted in the 1930s, and dialectal writing systems modeled on *latinxua* were created and tried out in several dialect areas.

Latinxua sin wenz was in its essentials the creation of Qú Qiūbái, one of the earliest leaders and members of the Chinese Communist Party, and from the very beginning this writing system had close links to the communist movement in China. There is abundant evidence that its use was promoted in areas under communist control, particularly in the border regions of Shǎnxī, Gānsù and Níngxià. In 1938 *sin wenz* winter schools were set up in this region for the purpose of instructing illiterate peasants and soldiers in the new script, and subsequently a newspaper and textbook in *latinxua* were published. At a series of conferences held in Yánān, the communist administrative center from 1937 until 1947, the role of *latinxua* in eradicating illiteracy was stressed. It is notable, however, that in the various pronouncements of this period a very moderate tone was taken: the new script was viewed as a powerful weapon in the fight against illiteracy, but it was not expected to replace the traditional character script overnight. The characters would continue to be used during a relatively long transition period before finally being phased out altogether. In the meantime they should be simplified to make them easier to learn (Ní 1948, 163ff; Sofronov 1979, 261ff). During the Yánān period, Máo Zédōng appears to have supported the aims of the *latinxua* movement; this can be seen from various declarations which he endorsed and from the fact that he was one of the members of the honorary directorate of the *Xīn Wénzì Xiéhuì* (Society for the New Script). His famous 1940 essay "On the new democracy" contained the subsequently much-quoted sentence, "The script, under certain conditions, must be reformed." Despite its vagueness, this statement was interpreted by some as an endorsement of the *latinxua* movement (Sofronov 1979, 263).

During this period there was little of the emphasis on dialectal scripts which had been so evident a part of the earlier propaganda in favor of *latinxua*. One reason for this is that the border regions surrounding Yánān were a part of the northern dialect area, and the standard form of *latinxua* was presumably quite adequate as a weapon in the battle against illiteracy there. It is also possible that the political leadership of that time already saw in dialectal writing schemes a potential for divisiveness and future political problems. Whatever the reasons, little is heard of this aspect of the *latinxua* movement after 1940.

In 1944 the latinization movement was officially curtailed in the communist-controlled areas on the pretext that there were insufficient trained cadres capable of teaching the system. It is more likely that, as the communists prepared to take power in a much wider territory, they had second thoughts about the rhetoric that surrounded the latinization movement; in order to obtain the maximum popular support, they withdrew support from a movement that deeply offended many supporters of the traditional writing system (Sofronov 1979, 264).

After the communist victory in 1949, the question of script reform remained unsolved. In the debates of this period, the supporters of the former *guóyǔ* movement came into conflict with the proponents of *latinxua* on a number of points. Both sides were in agreement concerning the desirability of alphabetic writing in China, and both agreed that the Latin alphabet was the best alphabet for this purpose. Disagreement arose concerning the dialectal basis of the writing system, and over the question whether tones should be indicated or not. Former supporters of the *guóyǔ* movement like Lí Jǐnxī favored the adoption of the Peking dialect as the basis of any alphabetic writing, while his opponents advocated a more broadly based *běifānghuà* ('northern speech'), presumably something like that used for *latinxua*. On the question of tones, Lí Jǐnxī, as one of the creators of *guóyǔ luómǎzì*, continued to insist on their importance in any system of alphabetic writing; the old advocates of *latinxua* stuck to their point of view that the marking of tones, either with diacritics or by spelling rules, was an unnecessary burden to inflict on illiterate learners (Lí 1957).

The early 1950s saw a thoroughgoing reevaluation of the language problem. Some of the conclusions that emerged from the debate were not what one might have expected. Most of the views espoused by the communists and other leftists in the 1930s and early 1940s were rejected, and the decision to replace the Chinese character script with alphabetic writing was put off until an undisclosed but apparently distant date. When the *pīnyīn* alphabetic scheme was promulgated in 1957, it was clearly for use as an auxiliary aid in the teaching of the standard language and not as a full-fledged autonomous writing system. Attention was turned to character simplification, a process that is still in progress at the present time. The Peking dialect was reaffirmed as the basis of the standard language, a decision reflected in subsequent dictionaries.

How do we explain this rather conservative turnabout? There is little question that political factors were in the forefront of all these decisions. The idea of alphabetic writing was simply too radical an idea from the point of view of national policy; not only would it have encountered immense resistance from those who still loved and defended the old script, but, for it to be practicable, the idea of dialectal scripts would have had to be adopted. It was no doubt clear to the political leadership that the linguistic polycentrism that would have resulted from several different dialectal writing systems bore in it dangerous seeds of political division as well. The decision to retain the Peking dialect as the basis of the standard language was merely the triumph of common sense over the impracticality of a system which lacked roots in a real, existing form of speech.

10.5 Present and future prospects

At the present time the position of the standard national language (*guóyǔ, pǔtōnghuà*) is firmly established and irreversible. At least this one issue of national language policy has come to a happy conclusion. Moreover, the position of the character script seems relatively stable, since any prospects of a system of alphabetic writing being put into effect in the foreseeable future are remote. Further simplification of the script in mainland China in the near future is possible, but it is likely to be on a relatively small scale; after that, prospects are for a long period of stability with regard to the writing system.

After a period of almost a century of controversy, the general outlines of China's linguistic future are emerging. China will remain a multidialectal and multilingual country, but the position of the national language will become progressively stronger; the dialects will probably remain important symbols of local identity while at the same time absorbing an ever-increasing number of forms from the standard language. Some of the larger minority languages like Mongolian, Uygur and Tibetan will most likely continue their own independent development.

The importance of language policy has obviously been downgraded since the end of the Cultural Revolution. The number of articles devoted to this subject in important journals is much smaller than it was in the 1950s. But even as the situation stabilizes, one can still detect a certain amount of malaise in writing devoted to linguistic policy and planning. China's priorities today are clearly economic and technological and not cultural or linguistic. It is only when language involves technology that it comes to the forefront of national concern. The chief problem in this area is how Chinese characters can be made to meet the needs of mechanization and computerization. Problems in this area have once more raised the question of alphabetic writing, albeit in a somewhat different form. Apparently few see any real hope for a wholesale switch to an alphabetic system (perhaps the model of Japan is suggestive here in more ways than one), but the clear advantages of such systems are universally acknowledged in certain technical areas like telecommunications and information retrieval. These considerations may well lead to wider use of alphabetic writing as an auxiliary system in these areas (Liú 1980).

Further reading

Barnes, Dayle 1974. Language planning in Mainland China: standardization. In Joshua A. Fishman (ed.), *Advances in language planning*. The Hague: Mouton. [A discussion of the problems of linguistic standardization in modern China.]

Lí, Jǐnxī 1934. *Guóyǔ yùndòng shǐgāng*. Shànghǎi: Shāngwù Yìnshūguǎn. [The standard history of the early *guóyǔ* movement.]

Lí, Jǐnxī 1957. *Wénzì gǎigé lùncóng*. Peking: Wénzì Gǎigé Chūbǎnshè. [A discussion of a wide range of language problems by one of China's leading linguists and language reformers.]

Milsky, Constantin 1973. New developments in language reform. *The China Quarterly* 53, 98–133. [An informative article concerning language policy in the People's Republic of China.]

Ní, Hǎishǔ 1948. *Zhōngguó pīnyīn wénzì yùndòngshǐ*. Shànghǎi: Shídài Shūbào Chūbǎnshè. [The best history of the alphabetization movement up until 1947.]

See also the list of suggested further readings at the end of Chapter 6.

NOTES

Chapter 1

1. Information concerning these languages is based on the following sources: Thai (Yates and Tryon 1970), Li (Ōuyáng and Zhèng 1980), Vietnamese (Thompson 1965), Khmei (Jacob 1968), Miao (Miao Language Team 1962), Yao (Yao Language Team 1962), Written Tibetan (Jäschke 1954), Yi (Chén 1963), Jingpo (Liú 1964), Malay (Lewis 1947), Rukai (Li 1973), Mongol (Dàobù 1964), Uygur (Zhū 1964), Korean (Park 1968) Information on the remaining languages is based on the author's personal knowledge.
2. Here, and in the remainder of this book, Middle Chinese is cited in F. K. Li's (1971) revised transcription of Bernhard Karlgren's reconstruction; in addition, non-distinctive diacritics are omitted. Old Chinese forms are given in Li's reconstruction (1971; 1976) Written Tibetan is from Jäschke 1881, written Burmese is taken from Benedict 1976 Bodo forms are from Bhat 1968, and Trung forms are from Luó 1942.
3. Unless otherwise indicated, modern standard Chinese words will be cited in the current official orthography employed in the People's Republic of China.

Chapter 2

1. Dobson (1959; 1962) divides Archaic (Old) Chinese into Early and Late periods Pulleyblank (1970) divides Middle Chinese into an Early and Late phase.
2. The Chinese terminology given here is that used by most modern Chinese linguists although it does not exactly represent that of any of the rhyme tables; cf. Luó 1956, 44.
3. F. K. Li, in his reconstruction of Old Chinese, leaves *píng* tone words unmarked (**njir* 'person'), designates *shǎng* tone words with a final *x* (**khagx* 'bitter') and *qù* tone words with a final *h* (**djangh* 'top'); *rù* tone words, since they are the only words ending in stops, are left unmarked. This system of tone marking is purely notational and is not intended to imply anything about the origin of tonal categories.
4. 'Phags-pa spellings are transliterated according to the scheme given in Poppe (1957) *Zhōngyuán yīnyùn* reconstructions are according to Dǒng Tónghé's (1954) system.

Chapter 3

1. I am greatly indebted to Professor Qiú Xīguī of Peking University for much of the information concerning the development of the Chinese script used in this chapter Professor Qiú lectured on this subject at the University of Washington in the winter term of 1983, and kindly made available to me a copy of his lecture notes. In addition he graciously consented to take time out of his busy schedule to read over a preliminary draft of this chapter; his corrections and suggestions were invaluable to me in the process of producing a final version. For the shortcomings and errors which remain, alone am responsible.

2. Attempts have been made in recent years greatly to extend the history of Chinese writing into the past. The chief evidence for this point of view consists of marks found on pottery unearthed at various neolithic sites. There is a very serious question, however, as to whether these markings can be considered writing in any real sense. See Qiú 1978.

3. Actually there is no way to be absolutely sure that the two words pronounced *shǒu* were homophonous at the time the script was formed; as far back as we are able to trace, however, they were pronounced identically.

4. In early texts such as the *Shījīng* (fifth century BC) *lái* still occurs in the sense of 'wheat', but this meaning did not survive into later stages of the language.

5. On Zhou bronzes, the primitive graph for *qí* is found with a phonetic consisting of a horizontal line above two parallel vertical lines; this phonetic, which is found below the original graph, has an OC reading **gjəg*. It is from this composite *xiéshēng* character that the modern graph is derived. Note that the use of *qí* as a modal particle is earlier than its use as a third person possessive pronoun (cf. sections 4.3, 4.5).

6. The forms on Table 3.2 are from Professor Qiú Xīguī's lecture notes.

7. Only one example of each graph is given for each period; actually there is a great deal of diversity in graphic form for each period of script development. For a more realistic impression of the variety of graphic forms, see Gāo 1980.

8. In works on calligraphy this classic form of *lìshū* is referred to as *bāfēn*.

9. This early form of cursive writing is referred to as *zhāngcǎo* 'regulated cursive' in works on Chinese calligraphy.

10. The *liùshū* classification in reality predates Xǔ Shèn, but its use in the *Shuōwén jiězì* served to make it the basis of later script analysis.

11. Lǐ Xiàodìng (1977: 41), basing himself on Zhū Jùnshēng's *Liùshū yàolüè*, indicates that of the characters in the *Shuōwén jiězì*, 81.2% are *xíngshēng* and 12.3% are *huìyì*; thus more than 93% of all the characters in Xǔ Shèn's time belonged to these two categories. Figures for the other categories are as follows: *xiàngxíng* 3.9%, *zhǐshì* 1.3%, *jiǎjiè* 1.2%, *zhuǎnzhù* 0.07%. (With the exception of the last figure for *zhuǎnzhù*, all the percentages have been rounded off to the nearest tenth.)

12. *Xíngshēng* characters are also frequently referred to as *xiéshēng* characters; see section 2.5.

13. The running script probably developed before *kǎishū* and in fact even influenced its development. It took its present form at about the same time as *kǎishū* reached maturity.

14. Perhaps this requirement is stated a little too absolutely. In actuality, the requirement that every word have its own graphic representation was applied only when the use of a single character to write two or more words tended to create confusion, or when the frequency of one of the words increased to the point that the need for an independent and unambiguous graphic form was felt.

15. Figures for various dictionaries are taken from Liú 1963, Zhào 1979 and Guān and Tián 1981.

16. The English word 'chopsticks' comes from Pidgin English, in which *chop chop* meant 'fast'; this shows that in the nineteenth century the relationship of *kuàizi* 'chopstick' and *kuài* 'fast' was still felt.

17. See also the comments on this topic in section 10.3.

18. This analysis of the principles used in script reform is based on Chén 1956.

Chapter 4
1. See Chou 1962, 22–3.
2. See, for example, *Analects* 5.3, and example (16) in this chapter.

3. There has been much controversy concerning the question of word classes in Classical Chinese. Such a great sinologist as Henri Maspero (1934) held that there were no word classes. Others, like Bernhard Karlgren (1961), have strongly upheld the opposite position. In point of fact, no-one has ever written a grammar either of Classical or of Modern Chinese without making some use of the notion of parts of speech. For an illuminating discussion of this problem, see Chao 1968, 496ff.

4. I have found especially useful the schemes proposed by Liú Jǐngnóng (1958) and S. E. Yakhontov (1965).

5. Each example is followed by a literal word-for-word translation as well as by a more idiomatic English translation. In the word-for-word version, the following abbreviations are employed: AUX auxiliary verb, CONJ marker of conjunction, NEG negative, NOM nominalizing particle, PCL particle, PNAME proper name, PREP preposition, PRF perfective marker, QUES question particle, SUB subordinative particle.

6. Yakhontov (1965) thinks that type A was used mainly by superiors speaking to inferiors, but this does not seem to be a widely held view. Lǚ Shūxiāng (1944) points out that in Postclassical literary texts, type B is used chiefly in dialogue, while type A is restricted to first-person narration.

7. For quite a different view, see Huáng Shèngzhāng 1963.

8. For some interesting explanations of possible differences among these locative prepositions, see Graham 1978 and Wén 1984.

9. Compare Emile Benveniste's (1971, 169) remarks concerning *avoir* in French: "*Avoir* has the construction of a transitive verb, but it is not a transitive. It is a pseudo-transitive. There can be no transitive relationship between the subject and object of *avoir* such that the motion might be assumed to pass over to the object and modify it."

10. See Lǚ (1944, §5.62). That *yǒu* and *wú* should be taken primarily as existential verbs and not as verbs expressing possession can be seen from the use of *yǒu* and *wú* as nouns meaning 'being' and 'non-being'. Cf. the sentence from the *Lǎozǐ: yǒu shēng yú wú* BEING BORN PREP NON-BEING 'being has its origin in non-being'.

11. A verb followed by the preposition *yú* and a personal object can be construed as a passive without *jiàn*: *zēng yú rén* 'be hated by (other) people'. For a recent study of passives in Classical Chinese, see Táng and Zhōu 1985.

12. In the case of verbal modifiers there is an ever-present danger of ambiguity; *shí kè*, for example, normally means 'someone who eats gratis at the table of a nobleman – an eating guest', but given the proper context, it could also mean 'to make a guest eat – to feed a guest' or possibly even 'to eat a guest'. Problems of this sort are generally more lexical than grammatical; nonetheless, this kind of ambiguity is very common in Classical Chinese, and represents one of the greatest problems encountered by learners.

Chapter 5

1. Liú Shìrú's (1956b, 97) explanation that it comes from a derived meaning of 'origin' or 'basis' seems rather forced to me.

2. It would appear that all third-person pronouns, including those of the Classical language, originate from demonstratives of one kind or another; similar developments are found in many other language families, including Indo-European and Altaic (Guō 1980).

3. It is of course possible that an example may be found in the future, but all the pre-Tang examples adduced so far are interpretable in the indefinite sense of 'others' or 'someone else'; see Táng 1980 and Guō 1980. For a discussion of *tā* in pre-Tang Buddhist translations, see Gurevich 1974.

4. *Nà*, the demonstrative, and *nǎ*, the interrogative, although written with the same character, should not be confused; *nǎ* 'how, where', etc., is attested much earlier than *nà* 'that'.

5. *Jǐ*, being a numeral, must of course be followed by a measure in the modern language.

6. Xiàmén *sim³ miʔ⁸*, as Zhāng Hùiyīng suggests, is almost certainly a dialectal variant of *shí wù*, the origin of standard *shénme*.

7. In the *Guǎngyùn*, the interrogative corresponding to *nǎ* has only a *píng* tone reading. The modern *shǎng* tone reading may have developed by analogy to *jǐ* 'how much' and *zěnme* 'how'. Some southern dialects have a *qù* tone in corresponding froms (Sūzhōu, Kèjiā).

8. It is also noteworthy that the morpheme for 'person' is used as a plural marker in several Mǐn dialects: Fúzhōu *nøiŋ²* 'person', *i¹ nøiŋ* 'they'. Lǚ Shūxiāng's tentative suggestion that *men* in some way derives from *bèi* (a frequent marker of plurality in pre-Tang texts) presents rather formidable phonological problems.

9. *Liǎo* does not occur in Classical texts. When it first makes its appearance in Han and Nanbeichao sources, it is most commonly found in the meaning of 'clear, bright, intelligent'; by extension it also means 'to understand'. The meaning 'to finish, come to an end' is a somewhat later development.

10. It is very hard to tell from texts written in Chinese characters when *liǎo* became atonic and was reduced to its modern form of *le*. The same holds true for all grammatical elements which lost their stress in the course of their development.

11. In the Fúzhōu dialect the word (Fúzhōu *tioʔ⁸* < MC *djak*) is still used as a preposition of location corresponding to *zài* in the standard language.

12. In the Classical language *céng* occurs in the meaning of 'unexpectedly, actually'; in this sense it often occurs *before* negatives. These two different uses of *céng* should not be confused.

13. Wáng Lì (1957) quotes in this regard the Russian example *deti – èto naše buduščee* 'children (this) are our hope'.

14. Gāo Míngkǎi (1957, 439) has observed that since *shì* is clearly a demonstrative in origin, *fēi* likewise may have developed from an earlier demonstrative. He suggested that *fēi* may be related to *bǐ* (MC *pjeː*) 'that'; if this is the case *fēi* originally would have meant something like 'that one (i.e., the other one), not this one' and from this developed its later negative function. It is interesting in this regard to note that the Mǐn, Kèjiā and Yuè dialects lack negatives with initial oral labials, as do the related Tibeto-Burman languages; this suggests that the *p-* negatives (see section 4.5) were an innovation in certain northern dialects of the Archaic period.

15. The tone of the Peking form is irregular; from a *rù* tone word with a sonorant initial, one should except a modern *qù* (fourth) tone reading. In the Jǐnán dialect in Shāndōng, which shares with Peking the same tonal derivation rules for *rù* tone words with voiced initials, the expected *qù* tone reading is found (Běijīng Dàxué 1964, 343).

16. To claim that *bié* derives from an earlier *biǎo* because *biǎo* is an impossible syllable in the phonological system of the Peking dialect is not cogent, since *béng*, which comes from a fusion of *búyòng*, is also an "impossible" syllable, but that has not prevented it from becoming firmly established in Peking speech.

17. *Bié* occurs textually at least as early as the Ming dynasty; *béng* seems to be a more recent development.

18. Since almost all premodern vernacular texts to some extent represent a mixture of literary and colloquial elements, *yú* has continued to be used alongside *zài* right down to the present time; it is consequently very difficult to say just when *yú* disappeared from the spoken language. The fact that it does not survive in any modern dialect known to us suggests that its demise was rather early.

19. In the modern Peking dialect both *jiào* and *ràng* are used to mean 'cause (someone to do something), allow (someone to do something)'.
20. In Gurevich and Zograf's chrestomathy (1982), for example, no mention is made of passives formed with *jiào* or *ràng* from the Nanbeichao through Ming dynasties in the survey of the grammatical features of the texts they studied.
21. For an excellent review of the problem, see Chu 1984. The most important articles relative to the Chinese word order controversy are Tai (1973), Li and Thompson (1974), Light (1979) and Mei Kuang (1980).

Chapter 6

1. A clear example of this usage is found in the preface to the Manchu–Chinese dictionary of 1768, the *Qīngwén huìshū*, where the term *guóyǔ* clearly refers to Manchu.
2. The earliest known use of the term *guóyǔ* is in reference to the Tabgach language in the Northern Wei dynasty (386–534); cf. Ligeti 1970.
3. At this period, it is likely that the choice of the term *guóyǔ* was influenced by the Japanese word *kokugo* 'national language' (Sofronov 1979, 94–5).
4. Qú was by no means alone in advocating the abolition of Chinese characters. Such non-Marxist scholars as Qián Xuántóng, Hú Shì, Fù Sīnián and Yuen Ren Chao all proposed or defended similar ideas at various times (Sofronov 1979, 231ff).
5. It is not certain where, when or by whom the term *pǔtōnghuà* was first coined, but it was employed by Qú Qiūbái as early as 1930 (Sofronov 1979, 251).
6. The initials are given in the official *pīnyīn* orthography followed by IPA values in brackets.
7. *Fān-àn* [fan ʁan] 'reverse a verdict' forms a minimal pair with *fā-nàn* [fʌ nan] 'to start a rebellion'. A minority of Peking speakers reportedly use [ŋ] in place of [ʁ] in syllables with 'zero' onset; others employ a glottal stop [ʔ], especially when the syllable in question is stressed or emphasized (Lǐ Róng 1963, 31; Chao 1968, 20).
8. The phonetic descriptions of the finals are mainly based on the work of Chao (1948a; 1968) and Lǐ Róng (1963). Certain details were provided to the author by Professor Yuen Ren Chao in a private communication.
9. The descriptions of tones given here are mostly based on Kratochvil 1968.
10. A few suffixes like *-zi* and *-le*, although they are historically derived from third-tone syllables, do not have the effect of raising a preceding third-tone syllable. From a synchronic point of view, they should be viewed as primary atonic morphemes, having lost all trace of their historical tonal origins.
11. Certain dialects spoken in northeastern Fújiàn form a striking exception to these observations. Dialects like those of Fúzhōu, Fúān and Níngdé all possess a set of complex sandhi rules which affect not only tones but the initials and finals as well.

Chapter 7

1. To obtain an idea of the range of work done in several post-structural schools, the reader is referred to the following representative pieces: W. Wang 1963; 1965; A. Y. Hashimoto 1969; 1971; Y. Li 1971; Li and Thompson 1973; 1974; Teng 1973; 1975; Tai 1975.
2. Most examples exemplifying grammatical points in this chapter will be given a word-for-word literal translation as well as a more free and idiomatic rendering. In the literal versions, dashes are used to join one or more English words that correspond to a single word in Chinese: e.g. *lǐfà* CUT-HAIR. The following abbreviations are used in the literal renderings: ACC 'accusative', DUR 'durative (aspect)', NEG 'negative', PCL 'particle', PERF 'perfective (aspect)', PREP 'preposition', QUES 'question (particle)'.

3. The syllable *de* serves to indicate an unusually large number of grammatical relationships in Chinese. In addition to the functions described here, the following important usages deserve mention:

    (a) marker of nominalization: *hóngde* 'RED *de* – red one, something red', *zhǔde* 'BOIL *de* – something boiled, boiled things', *bùdǒng yīngwén de* 'NEG-UNDERSTAND ENGLISH *de* – one who does not understand English'.

    (b) marker of adverbial modification: *kuàikuāirde pǎo* 'QUICK *de* RUN – run quickly', *fēichángde bùmǎnyì* 'EXCEEDING *de* DISSATISFIED – exceedingly dissatisfied'.

    (c) marker of potentiality with verbs: *chīde* 'EAT *de* – can eat, edible', *pǎodekuài* 'RUN *de* FAST – can run fast'

    The many functions of *de* are described in detail in several articles by Zhū Déxī (1961; 1966; 1978).

4. While it is doubtful that *cóng* can function as an independent verb in modern spoken Chinese, it occurs in a number of written expressions in the sense of 'to follow'.

5. For a recent study of this problem, see Coblin 1972.

6. The main reason why the *Kāngxī zìdiǎn* continues in use is the large number of characters it contains; its 47,053 characters are surpassed only by the *Jíyùn*, which contains 53,525 (Liú 1963). In the case of both dictionaries, the total number of graphs includes a high proportion of graphic variants of the same character.

7. Actually a great number of bilingual Manchu–Chinese dictionaries were produced during the Qing dynasty. Whether this native lexicographic work owed anything to the impetus of foreign lexicographic models is unclear.

8. A *zìdiǎn* is primarily a dictionary of individual characters with compounds and phrases given only for illustrative purposes; a *cídiǎn* is a dictionary of words, and includes both individual characters and words consisting of more than one syllable.

Chapter 8

1. The sources of data are the following: data on Shuāngfēng are from Yuán 1960; Jiànōu data are from my own field notes; information on the remaining dialects is all taken from *Hànyǔ fāngyán cíhùi* (Běijīng Dàxué 1964).

2. At the present time, few children are taught the traditional local reading pronunciation of characters, and they learn to read only in the standard language. The older reading pronunciations survive, however, in the learned or more elevated part of the dialect's lexicon. New terms are not borrowed from the standard language in their purely northern guise, but are converted morpheme by morpheme into the appropriate local reading pronunciation. In this way, the traditional reading pronunciations continue to survive, even though they are no longer taught in the schools.

3. I recognize of course that there is no exact method for measuring the differences between dialects and languages; the remarks here are impressionistic, and intended to give only a very general idea of how the Chinese "dialects" differ from one another.

4. Wēnzhōu forms are from Běijīng Dàxué 1964; Zhèróng forms are from my field notes.

5. In comparing dialects, Peking forms are cited in a broad phonetic transcription comparable to that used for other dialect forms; in other contexts, where no dialect comparisons are being made, Peking forms are cited in the standard *pīnyīn* orthography. Tones are given according to the etymological categories described in Table 2.12. Língbǎo forms are from Yang and Ching 1971; the remaining examples are all taken from Běijīng Dàxué 1964.

6. See Yuán 1960, 24ff.

7. Data are from Běijīng Dàxué 1962 and Yang and Ching 1971.

8. In all Mandarin dialects Middle Chinese *shǎng* tone words with voiced obstruent initials have merged with words in the *qù* category: MC *dzuâ:* 'sit' becomes Běijīng *tsuo*[5]. In Běijīng *yángrù* words with obstruent initials become tone 2, those with sonorant initials become tone 5; in Xīān *yángrù* words with obstruent initials become tone 2, those with sonorant initials tone 1.

9. Tonal values are given in Yuen Ren Chao's numerical notation as it is described in Chapter 7.

10. Under grammar we include such topics as the pronominal and negation systems.

11. All data are from Běijīng Dàxué 1964.

12. For example Wú dialects and most Gàn dialects distinguish *than*[5] 'to probe' and *than*[5] 'charcoal': Sūzhōu has *thɵ*[5] vs. *the*[5], Wēnzhōu has *thɵ*[5] vs. *tha*[5], and Nanchang *thɔn*[5] vs. *than*[5].

13. This remark is based on material elicited by the author from a speaker of the Qīngyúan dialect.

14. Shànghǎi data are from Sherard 1980.

15. Tone sandhi has been described for several Wú dialects: Shànghǎi (Sherard 1980), Sūzhōu (Yuán 1960), Dānyáng (Lǚ 1980b), Wēnlǐng (Lǐ Róng 1979), Yǒngkāng (Yuán 1960).

16. Data are from Chao 1928 and Běijīng Dàxué 1964.

17. Nánchāng forms are from Yáng 1969b; Línchuān forms are from Luó 1958; Fèngxīn forms are from Yú 1975; Jīxī forms are from Chao and Yang 1965.

18. Sources are as follows: Chéngbù: Yang 1974; Shuāngfēng: Yuán 1960; Běijīng Dàxué 1962; Shàoyáng: Yang 1974; Chángshā: Běijīng Dàxué 1962; 1964.

19. Dialect forms are from the following sources: Chéngbù and Qíyáng: Yang 1974; Shuāngfēng and Chángshā: Yuán 1960.

Chapter 9

1. Sources: Yuè: Hashimoto 1972; Kèjiā: MacIver 1926; Xiàmén: Douglas 1899.

2. An exception is the Zhōngshān word for 'lichee' *laai*[5] *ki*[1], where the second syllable has an MC reading *tśje* (Chan 1980, 203).

3. The Yuè forms were kindly supplied by Anne Yue-Hashimoto.

4. The Zhōngshān forms were kindly supplied by Marjorie Kit Man Chan.

5. This etymon is attested in the *Shuōwén* and in Guō Pú's commentary on the *Ěryǎ*; in the *Guǎngyùn* it is read *gjei*. Guō identifies the word as a Jiāngdōng or Southern form.

6. The sources used for Yuè dialects are the following: Guǎngzhōu: Hashimoto 1972; Yángjiāng: Běijīng Dàxué 1964; Zhōngshān: Chao 1948b; Chan 1980; Táishān: Chao 1951; Wong 1970; Téngxiàn: Yue 1979.

7. The tone of the Táishān first person plural is a "changed tone" with the value [21]. This tone is shown by an asterisk in this and subsequent examples.

8. Sources for Kèjiā data: Méixiàn: Běijīng Dàxué 1964; MacIver 1926; Hashimoto 1973; Hǎilù: Yang 1957; Huáyáng: Dǒng 1948b; Chángtīng: Pān 1963. Shātóujiǎo forms are quoted from O'Connor 1976.

9. The sources for Mǐn data are as follows: Fúzhōu: Běijīng Dàxué 1964; Chen and Norman 1965; Xiàmén: Běijīng Dàxué 1964; Bodman 1955; 1958; Cháozhōu: Běijīng Dàxué 1964; Jiēyáng: Choy 1976. Data on Chóngān, Fúān, Jiāngle, Jiànōu, Jiànyáng, Níngdé, Shàowǔ and Yǒngān are all from my own field notes.

10. In the case of Fúān and Fúzhōu, it is difficult to determine the etymological tone of the words for 'this' and 'that' since they are always bound and subject to tone sandhi.

11. For a full discussion of Mǐn tonal development, see Norman 1973.

12. Pǔchéng data are from my own field notes.

Chapter 10

1. There has been a consistent tendency toward a reduction of the number of discrete syllables in Chinese from ancient times down to the present, resulting in an ever greater number of homonyms; a large number of morphemes which were once distinct have now merged. This process is commonly thought to have led to a larger number of polysyllabic words in order to avoid ambiguity. Another result of the process has been that when one reads ancient or literary texts aloud, many words which were once phonologically distinct are now pronounced the same. Thus if one tries to "speak" *wényán* (which is based on a much earlier variety of Chinese), the high degree of homonymy makes it very difficult to understand; comprehension would also be complicated by the frequent use of abbreviated literary allusions which were an integral feature of *wényán* literary style.

2. There is even less writing in dialects now than there was in premodern times. For all practical purposes, dialectal writing is now a dead issue.

3. For a description of a similar process at work at the phonological level in the Nánjīng dialect, see Bào 1980.

4. This description of the sociolinguistic situation in Táiběi is based on the author's personal observations.

5. For example, *mǎi* 'to buy' and *mài* 'to sell' were distinguished by spelling the former *maai* and the latter *mai*.

REFERENCES

Allen, W. Sidney 1953. *Phonetics in ancient India*. London: Oxford University Press.
Bái Dízhōu and Yù Shìcháng 1954. Guānzhōng fāngyīn diàochá bàogào. *Yuyan zhuankan* 6. Peking: Zhongguo Kexueyuan.
Bào Míngwěi 1980. Liùshínián lái Nánjīng fāngyīn xiàng pǔtōnghuà kàolǒng qíngkuàng de kǎochá. *Zhongguo Yuwen* 4, 241–5.
Barnes Dayle 1974. Language planning in Mainland China: standardization. In Joshua A. Fishman (ed.), *Advances in language planning*. The Hague: Mouton.
Běijīng Dàxué 1962. *Hànyǔ fāngyīn zìhùi*. Peking: Wenzi Gaige Chubanshe.
Běijīng Dàxué 1964. *Hànyǔ fāngyán cíhùi*. Peking: Wenzi Gaige Chubanshe.
Benedict, Paul K. 1942. Thai, Kadai and Indonesian: a new alignment in Southeastern Asia. *American Anthropologist* 44, 576–601.
Benedict, Paul 1972. *Sino-Tibetan: a conspectus*. Contributing editor, James A. Matisoff. Cambridge: Cambridge University Press.
Benedict, Paul K. 1975. *Austro-Thai language and culture, with a glossary of roots*. New Haven: Human Relations Area Files Press.
Benedict, Paul K. 1976. Rhyming dictionary of Written Burmese. *Linguistics of the Tibeto-Burman area*, vol. 3, no. 1.
Benveniste, Emile 1971. *Problems in general linguistics*. Coral Gables: University of Miami Press. (Original title: *Problèmes de linguistique générale*. Paris: Gallimard, 1966.)
Bhat, D. N. Shankara 1968. *Boro vocabulary*. Poona: Deccan College Postgraduate and Research Institute.
Bodman, Nicholas 1955. *Spoken Amoy Hokkien*, vol. 1. Kuala Lumpur: Charles Grenier.
Bodman, Nicholas 1958. *Spoken Amoy Hokkien*, vol. 2. Kuala Lumpur: Charles Grenier.
Bodman, Nicholas 1980. Proto-Chinese and Sino-Tibetan: data towards establishing the nature of the relationship. In Frans Van Coetsem and Linda R. Waugh (eds.) *Contributions to historical linguistics: issues and materials*. Leiden: E. J. Brill.
Boltz, William G. 1986. Early Chinese writing. *World Archeology* 17, 420–36.
Chan, Marjorie Kit Man 1980. *Zhong-shan phonology: a synchronic and diachronic analysis of a Yue (Cantonese) dialect*. MA thesis, University of British Columbia.
Chang, Kun 1947. Miáo Yáo yǔ shēngdiào wèntí. *Bulletin of the Institute of History and Philology* 16, 93–110.
Chang, Kun 1953. On the tone system of the Miao-Yao languages. *Language* 29, 374–8.
Chang, Kun 1966. A comparative study of the Yao tone system. *Language* 42, 303–10.
Chao, Yuen Ren 1928. *Studies in the modern Wu-dialects*. Peking: Tsing-hua University.
Chao, Yuen Ren 1930. A system of tone letters. *Le Maître Phonétique*, troisième série, 30, 24–7. Reprinted in *Fangyan* 1980, 2, 81–3.
Chao, Yuen Ren 1941. Distinctions within Ancient Chinese. *Harvard Journal of Asiatic Studies* 5, 203–33.

Chao, Yuen Ren 1948a. *Mandarin primer.* Cambridge: Harvard University Press.

Chao, Yuen Ren 1948b. Zhōngshān fāngyán. *Bulletin of the Institute of History and Philology* 20, 49–73.

Chao, Yuen Ren 1951. Táishān yŭliào. *Bulletin of the Institute of History and Philology* 23, 25–76.

Chao, Yuen Ren 1967. Contrastive aspects of the Wu dialects. *Language* 43, 92–101.

Chao, Yuen Ren 1968. *A grammar of spoken Chinese.* Berkeley: University of California Press.

Chao, Yuen Ren and Yang, Lien Sheng 1947. *Concise dictionary of spoken Chinese.* Cambridge: Harvard University Press.

Chao, Yuen Ren and Yang Shih-feng. 1965. Jīxī língběi fāngyán. *Bulletin of the Institute of History and Philology* 36, 11–113.

Chao, Yuen Ren *et al.* 1948. *Húběi fāngyán diàochá bàogào.* Shanghai: Shangwu Yinshuguan.

Chén Guāngyáo 1956. *Jiănhuà hànzì zìtĭ shuōmíng.* Peking: Zhonghua Shuju.

Chen, Leo and Norman, Jerry 1965. *An introduction to the Foochow dialect.* San Francisco: San Francisco State College.

Chén Lĭ 1842. *Qièyùn Kăo.* Reprinted in Yīnyùnxué cóngshū. Taipei: Guangwen Shuju, 1966.

Chén Shílín 1963. Yíyŭ gàikuàng. *Zhongguo Yuwen* 4, 334–47.

Chén Yínkè 1936. Dōng Jìn Náncháo zhī Wúyŭ. *Bulletin of History and Philology* 7, 1–4.

Chéng Xiánghùi 1980. Qīnghǎi kǒuyŭ yŭfǎ sǎnlùn. *Zhongguo Yuwen* 2, 142–9.

Chou Fa-kao 1962. *Zhōngguó gŭdài yŭfǎ: gòucí biān.* Academia Sinica, Institute of History and Philology, monograph no. 39.

Choy, Chun-ming 1976. *A dictionary of the Chao-chou dialect (Cháoyŭ cíhùi).* Taipei: Sanmin Shuju.

Chu, Chauncey C. 1984. Hànyŭ de cíxù jí qí biànqiān. *Yuyan Yanjiu* 1, 127–51.

Coblin, Weldon South 1972. *An introductory study of textual and linguistic problems in Erhya.* PhD dissertation, University of Washington, Seattle.

Dàobù 1964. Měnggŭyŭ gàikuàng. *Zhongguo Yuwen* 3, 240–53.

Demiéville, P. 1950. Archaïsmes de prononciation en chinois vulgaire. *T'oung Pao* 40, 1–50.

Dīng Shēngshù 1953. Shì fŏudìngcí "fú" "bù". *Qingzhu Cai Yuanpei xiansheng liushiwusui lunwenji,* 967–96.

Dīng Shēngshù *et al.* 1963. *Xiàndài hànyŭ yŭfǎ jiănghuà.* Peking: Shangwu Yinshuguan.

Dobson, W. A. C. H. 1959. *Late Archaic Chinese.* Toronto: University of Toronto Press.

Dobson, W. A. C. H. 1962. *Early Archaic Chinese.* Toronto: University of Toronto Press.

Dŏng Tónghé 1948a. Shànggŭ yīnyùn biăogăo. *Bulletin of the Institute of History and Philology* 18, 1–249.

Dŏng Tónghé 1948b. Huáyáng liángshŭijĭng kèjiāhuà jìyīn. *Bulletin of the Institute of History and Philology* 19, 81–201.

Dŏng Tónghé 1954. *Zhōngguó yŭyīn shĭ.* Taipei: Zhonguo Wenhua Chuban Shiye She.

Douglas, Carstairs 1899. *Chinese–English dictionary of the vernacular or spoken language of Amoy.* London: Presbyterian Church of England.

Downer, G. B. 1959. Derivation by tone-change in Classical Chinese. *Bulletin of the School of Oriental and African Studies* 22, 258–90.

Downer, G. B. 1963. Chinese, Thai and Miao-Yao. In H. L. Shorto (ed.), *Linguistic comparison in South East Asia and the Pacific.* London: School of Oriental and African Studies.

Downer, G. B. 1967. Tone change and tone-shift in White Miao. *Bulletin of the School of Oriental and African Studies* 30, 589–99.

Downer, G. B. 1973. Strata of Chinese loanwords in the Mien dialect of Yao. *Asia Major* 18, 1–33.

Dragunov, Aleksandr A. 1930. The ḥP'ags-pa script and Ancient Mandarin. *Izvestija Akademii Nauk SSSR, Otdelenije Gumanitarnyx Nauk* 9, 627–47.

Dreher, John J. and Lee, Pao Chen 1966. *Instrumental investigation of single and paired Mandarin tonemes.* Douglas Paper 4156. Huntington Beach: Advanced Research Laboratory, Douglas Aircraft Company (research communication no. 13).

Egerod, Søren 1967. Dialectology. In Thomas Sebeok (ed.), *Current trends in linguistics,* vol. 2. The Hague: Mouton.

Ferguson, Charles A. 1964. Diglossia. In Dell Hymes (ed.), *Language in culture and society: a reader in linguistics and anthropology.* New York: Harper and Row.

Frei, Henri 1956. The ergative construction in Chinese, part 1. *Gengo Kenkyū* 31, 22–50.

Frei, Henri 1957. The ergative construction in Chinese, part 2. *Gengo Kenkyū* 32, 83–115.

Gāo Míng 1980. *Gǔ wénzì lèibiān.* Peking: Zhonghua Shuju.

Gāo Míngkǎi 1957. *Hànyǔ yǔfǎlùn.* Peking: Kexue Chubanshe.

Giles, Herbert A. 1912. *Chinese–English dictionary,* 2nd edn. Shanghai: Kelly and Walsh.

Graham, A. C. 1978. A post-verbal aspectual in Classical Chinese: the supposed preposition *hu. Bulletin of the School of Oriental and African Studies* 41, 314–42.

Greenberg, Joseph 1963. Some universals of grammar with particular reference to the ordering of meaningful elements. In Joseph Greenberg (ed.), *Universals of language.* Cambridge, Mass.: MIT Press.

Grottaers, Willem A. 1943. La géographie linguistique en Chine – necessité d'une nouvelle méthode pour l'étude linguistique du chinois. *Monumenta Serica* 8, 103–66.

Guān Ěrjiā and Tián Lín 1981. Rúhé shíxiàn hànzì biāozhǔnhuà. *Zhongguo Yuwen* 2, 147–53.

Guō Xīliáng 1980. Hànyǔ dìsān rénchēng dàicí de qǐyuán hé fāzhǎn. *Yǔyánxué lùncóng* 6, 64–93.

Gurevich, I. S. 1974. *Očerk grammatiki kitajskogo jazyka III–V vv.* Moscow: Nauka.

Gurevich, I. S. and Zograf, I. T. 1982. *Xrestomatija po istorii kitajskogo jazyka III–XV vv.* Moscow: Nauka.

Hartman, Lawton M. 1944. Segmental phonemes of the Peiping dialect. *Language* 20, 28–42.

Hashimoto, Anne Yue 1969. The verb 'to be' in modern Chinese. In John W. M. Verhaar (ed.), *The verb 'be' and its synonyms: Philosophical and grammatical studies,* part IV: *Twi, Modern Chinese, Arabic.* Foundations of language, supplementary series, vol. 9. Dordrecht: Reidel.

Hashimoto, Anne Yue 1971. Mandarin syntactic structures. *Unicorn* 8. Princeton: Chinese Linguistics Project.

Hashimoto, Mantaro 1967. The ḥP'ags-pa transcription of Chinese plosives. *Monumenta Serica* 26, 149–74.

Hashimoto, Mantaro 1969. Observations on the passive construction. *Unicorn* 5, 59–71.

Hashimoto, Mantaro 1973. *The Hakka dialect: A linguistic study of its phonology, syntax and lexicon.* Cambridge: Cambridge University Press.

Hashimoto, Oi-kan Yue 1972. *Phonology of Cantonese.* Cambridge: Cambridge University Press.

Haudricourt, André 1954a. De l'origine des tons en viêtnamien. *Journal Asiatique* 242, 68–82.

Haudricourt, André 1954b. Comment reconstruire le chinois archaïque. *Word* 10, 351–64.

Haudricourt, André 1954c. Introduction à la phonologie historique des langues miao-yao. *Bulletin de l'Ecole Française de l'Extrême Orient* 44, 555–76.

Haudricourt, André 1966. The limits and connections of Austroasiatic in the northeast.

In Norman Zide (ed.), *Studies in comparative Austroasiatic linguistics*. The Hague: Mouton.

Hirth, Friedrich and Rockhill, W. W. 1911. *Chau Ju-kua: his work on the Chinese and Arab trade in the twelfth and thirteenth centuries, entitled Chu-fan-chï.* St Petersburg: Printing Office of the Imperial Academy of Sciences. Reprinted by Cheng-wen Publishing Co., Taipei, 1970.

Hockett, Charles F. 1947. Peiping phonology. *Journal of the American Oriental Society* 67, 253–67.

Howie, John Marshall 1976. *Acoustical studies of Mandarin vowels and tones.* Cambridge: Cambridge University Press.

Hú Míngyáng 1978. Shànghǎihuà yìbǎinián lái de ruògān biànhuà. *Zhongguo Yuwen* 3, 199–205.

Huáng Shèngzhāng 1963. Gǔ hànyǔ de rénshēn dàicí yánjiū. *Zhongguo Yuwen* 6, 443–72.

Institute of Far Eastern Languages 1966. *Dictionary of spoken Chinese.* New Haven: Yale University Press.

Jacob, Judith 1968. *Introduction to Cambodian.* London: Oxford University Press.

Jäschke, H. A. 1881. *A Tibetan–English dictionary.* London. Reprinted by Routledge and Kegan Paul, London, 1965.

Jäschke, H. A. 1954. *Tibetan grammar.* New York: Ungar.

Jiāngsūshěng hé Shànghǎishì Fāngyán Diàochá Zhǐdǎozǔ 1960. *Jiāngsūshěng hé shànghǎishì fāngyán gàikuàng.* Nanjing: Jiangsu Renmin Chubanshe.

Karlgren, Bernhard 1915–26. *Etudes sur la phonologie chinoise. Archives d'études orientales*, vol. 15 (in 4 parts). Leiden: E. J. Brill; Uppsala: K. W. Appelberg.

Karlgren, Bernhard 1923. *Analytic dictionary of Chinese and Sino-Japanese.* Paris: Librairie Orientaliste Paul Geuthner.

Karlgren, Bernhard 1940. Grammata serica, script and phonetics in Chinese and Sino-Japanese. *Bulletin of the Museum of Far Eastern Antiquities* 12, 1–471.

Karlgren, Bernhard 1954. Compendium of phonetics in Ancient and Archaic Chinese. *Bulletin of the Museum of Far Eastern Antiquities* 26, 211–367.

Karlgren, Bernhard 1961. The parts of speech and the Chinese language. In *Language and Society: essays presented to Arthur M. Jensen on his seventieth birthday.* Copenhagen: Berlingske Bogtrykkerl.

Kennedy, George 1964. *Selected works of George A. Kennedy.* New Haven: Far Eastern Publications.

Kratochvil, Paul 1968. *The Chinese language today: features of an emerging standard.* London: Hutchinson University Library.

Laufer, Berthold 1919. Sino-Iranica: Chinese contributions to the history of civilization in ancient Iran. Field Museum of Natural History, Publication 201, Anthropological Series, vol. 15, no. 3. Chicago.

Lehmann, Winfred P. 1975. *Language and linguistics in the People's Republic of China.* Austin: University of Texas Press.

Lewis, M. B. 1947. *Malay.* London: English Universities Press.

Li, Charles N. and Thompson, Sandra A. 1973. Co-verbs in Mandarin Chinese: verbs or prepositions? *Journal of Chinese Linguistics* 2, 257–78.

Li, Charles N. and Thompson, Sandra A. 1974. An explanation of word order change SVO–SOV. *Foundations of Language* 12, 201–14.

Li, Fang-kuei 1937. Languages and dialects. *The Chinese yearbook.* Shanghai: Commercial Press.

Li, Fang-kuei 1971. Shànggǔyīn yánjiū. *Tsing Hua Journal of Chinese Studies, New Series* 9, 1–61.

Li, Fang-kuei 1976. Jǐge shànggǔ shēngmǔ wèntí. In Qián Sīliàng *et al.* (eds.), *Zǒngtǒng*

Jiǎng Gōng shìshì zhōunián jìniàn lùnwénjī. Taipei: Academia Sinica.

Li, Fang-kuei 1977. *A handbook of comparative Tai.* Oceanic Linguistics, Special Publication no. 15. Honolulu: The University Press of Hawaii.

Lí Jǐnxī 1934. *Guóyǔ yùndòngshǐ.* Shanghai: Shangwu Yinshuguan.

Lí Jǐnxī 1944. *Tóngguān xiànzhì.* Tongguan: Tongguan Xian Zhengfu.

Lí Jǐnxī 1957. *Wénzì gǎigé lùncóng.* Peking: Wenzi Gaige Chubanshe.

Li, Paul Jen-kuei 1973. *Rukai structure.* Institute of History and Philology, Special Publication no. 64. Taipei: Academia Sinica.

Lǐ Róng 1952. *Běijīng kǒuyǔ yǔfǎ.* Peking: Kaiming Shudian.

Lǐ Róng 1956. *Qièyùn yīnxì.* Yuyanxue zhuankan, no. 4. Peking: Kexue Chubanshe.

Lǐ Róng 1963. *Hànyǔ fāngyán diàochá shǒucè.* Peking: Kexue Chubanshe.

Lǐ Róng 1979. Wēnlǐng fāngyán de liándú biàndiào. *Fangyan* 1, 1–29.

Lǐ Shùlán 1979. Xībóyǔ gàikuàng. *Minzu Yuwen* 3, 221–32.

Lǐ Xiàodìng 1977. *Hànzì shǐhuà.* Taipei: Lianjing.

Lǐ Xíngjiàn 1958. "Shìshuō xīnyǔ" zhōng fùcí "dōu" hé "liǎo" yòngfǎ de bǐjiào. *Yuyanxue luncong* 2, 73–83.

Lǐ Xuéqín 1985. *Gǔ wénzìxué chūjiē.* Peking: Zhonghua Shuju.

Li, Ying Che 1971. Interaction of semantics and syntax in Chinese. *Journal of the Chinese Language Teachers' Association* 6, 58–78.

Ligeti, Louis 1970. Le tabghatch, un dialecte de la langue sien-pi. In L. Ligeti (ed.), *Mongolian Studies.* Amsterdam: Grüner.

Light, Timothy 1979. Word order and word order change in Chinese. *Journal of Chinese Linguistics* 7, 149–80.

Liú Fù 1925. *Les mouvements de la langue nationale en chine.* Paris: Société d'Editions "Les Belles Lettres".

Liú Jiān 1982. "Dà táng sānzàng qǔjīng shǐhuà" xiězuò shídài lícè. *Zhongguo Yuwen* 5, 371–80.

Liú Jǐngnóng 1958. *Hànyǔ wényán yǔfǎ.* Peking: Zhonghua Shuju.

Liú Lù 1964. *Jīngpōyǔ gàikuàng. Zhongguo Yuwen* 5, 407–17.

Liú Shìrú 1956a. Bèidòngshì de qǐyuán. *Yuwen Xuexi* 8, 32–3.

Liú Shìrú 1956b. *Wèi jìn nánběicháo liàngcí yánjiū.* Peking: Zhonghua Shuju.

Liú Yèqiū 1963. *Zhōngguó gǔdài de zìdiǎn.* Peking: Zhonghua Shuju.

Liú Zéxiān 1980. Tántán wénzì xiàndàihuà. *Zhongguo Yuwen* 2, 155–9.

Lù Zhìwěi 1946. Shì Zhōngyuán yīnyùn. *Yanjing Xuebao* 31, 35–70.

Lù Zhìwěi 1964. *Hànyǔ de gòucífǎ.* Peking: Kexue Chubanshe.

Lǚ Bìsōng 1980. Xiàndài hànyǔ yǔfǎ shǐhuà, 2. *Yuyan Jiaoxue yu Yanjiu* 3, 63–75.

Lǚ Shūxiāng 1940. Shì jǐngdé chuándēnglù zhōng 'zài', 'zhuó' èr zhùcí. In Lü 1955.

Lǚ Shūxiāng 1941. Lùn *wú* yǔ *wù.* In Lǚ 1955.

Lǚ Shūxiāng 1944. *Zhōngguó wénfǎ yàolüè.* Shanghai: Commercial Press. Reprinted Peking, 1982.

Lǚ Shūxiāng 1947. "Zhè" "nà" Kǎoyuán. Reprinted in Lǚ 1955.

Lǚ Shūxiāng 1955. *Hànyǔ yǔfǎ lùnwénjí.* Peking: Kexue Chubanshe.

Lǚ Shūxiāng 1980a. *Hànyǔ kǒuyǔ yǔfǎ.* Peking: Shangwu Yinshuguan. Translation of Y. R. Chao's *Grammar of spoken Chinese.*

Lǚ Shūxiāng 1980b. Dānyáng fāngyán de shēngdiào xìtǒng. *Fangyan* 2, 85–122.

Lǚ Shūxiāng et al. 1980. *Xiàndài hànyǔ bābǎicí.* Peking: Shangwu Yinshuguan.

Luó Chángpéi 1931. Zhī chè chéng niáng yīnzhí kǎo. *Bulletin of History and Philology* 3, 121–57.

Luó Chángpéi 1942. *The Trung language of Kung Shan.* Kunming.

Luó Chángpéi 1950. *Yǔyán yǔ wénhuà.* Peking: Beijing Daxue.

Luó Chángpéi 1956. *Hànyǔ yīnyùnxué dǎolùn.* Peking: Zhonghua Shuju.

Luó Chángpéi 1958. *Línchuān yīnxì.* Peking: Kexue Chubanshe.

Luó Chángpéi 1963. *Luó Chángpéi yǔyánxué lùnwén xuǎnjí.* Peking: Zhonghua Shuju.
Luó Chángpéi and Cài Měibiāo 1959. *Bāsībāzì yǔ yuándài hànyǔ.* Peking: Kexue Chubanshe.
Luó Xiānglín 1933. *Kèjiā yánjiū dǎolùn.* Canton: Shi-shan Library.
Lyons, John 1968. *Introduction to theoretical linguistics.* Cambridge: Cambridge University Press.
MacIver, D. 1926. *A Chinese–English dictionary, Hakka-dialect.* Shanghai: Presbyterian Mission Press.
Martin, Samuel E. 1953. The phonemes of Ancient Chinese. *Journal of the American Oriental Society,* supp. 16.
Martin, Samuel E. 1957. Problems of hierarchy and indeterminacy in Mandarin phonology. *Bulletin of the Institute of History and Philology* 29, 209–29.
Maspero, Henri 1912. Etudes sur la phonétique historique de la langue annamite. *Bulletin de l'Ecole Française de l'Extrême Orient* 12, 1–127.
Maspero, Henri 1934. La langue chinoise. Conférences de l'Institut de linguistique de l'Université de Paris, année 1933, *Revue des Cours et Conférences,* 481–502, 591–606.
Mathews, R. H. 1931. *Chinese–English dictionary.* Shanghai: China Inland Mission and Presbyterian Mission Press.
Matisoff, James A. 1970. Glottal dissimilation and the Lahu high-rising tone: a tonogenetic case study. *Journal of the American Oriental Society* 90, 13–44.
Matisoff, James A. 1972. *The Loloish tonal split revisited.* Research Monograph no. 7, Center for South and Southeast Asia Studies. Berkeley: University of California.
Matisoff, James A. 1978. *Variational semantics in Tibeto-Burman: the "organic" approach to linguistic comparison.* Philadelphia: Institute for the Study of Human Issues.
Medhurst, Walter H. 1842–3. *Chinese and English dictionary.* Batavia. Printed at Parapattan.
Mei, Kuang 1980. Is Modern Chinese really an SOV language? *Cahiers de Linguistique Asie Orientale* 7, 23–45.
Mei, Tsu-lin 1970. Tone and prosody in Middle Chinese and the origin of the rising tone. *Harvard Journal of Asiatic Studies* 30, 86–110.
Mei, Tsu-lin 1980. Sìshēng biéyì zhōng de shíjiān céngcì. *Zhongguo Yuwen* 6, 427–43.
Mei, Tsu-lin 1981a. Míngdài níngbōhuà de lái-zì hé xiàndài hànyǔ de "liǎo" zì. *Fangyan* 1, 66.
Mei, Tsu-lin 1981b. Xiàndài hànyǔ wánchéngmào jùshì hé cíwěi "le" de láiyuán. *Yuyan Yanjiu* 1, 65–77.
Miao Language Team 1962. Miáoyǔ gàikuàng. *Zhongguo Yuwen* 1, 28–37. English translation in Purnell 1972.
Miller, Roy Andrew 1967. *The Japanese language.* Chicago: The University of Chicago Press.
Miller, Roy Andrew 1971. *Japanese and the other Altaic languages.* Chicago: University of Chicago Press.
Miller, Roy Andrew 1975. The Far East. In T. A. Sebeok (ed.), *Current trends in linguistics,* vol. 13, *Historiography of Linguistics.* The Hague: Mouton.
Milsky, Constantin 1973. New developments in language reform. *The China Quarterly* 53, 98–133.
Morrison, Robert 1815–23. *A dictionary of the Chinese language, in three parts.* Macao: East India Company's Press. Reprinted 1865, Shanghai: London Mission Press.
Ní Hǎishǔ 1948. *Zhōngguó pīnyīn wénzì yùndòngshǐ.* Shanghai: Shidai Shubao Chubanshe.
Norman, Jerry 1973. Tonal development in Min. *Journal of Chinese Linguistics* 1, 222–38.
Norman, Jerry 1979. The verb *chí* – a note on Mǐn etymology. *Fangyan* 3, 179–81.
Norman, Jerry 1980. Linguistics. In Leo A. Orleans (ed.), *Science in Contemporary China.* Stanford: Stanford University Press.

Norman, Jerry and Mei, Tsu-lin 1976. The Austroasiatics in ancient South China: some lexical evidence. *Monumenta Serica* 32, 274–301.

O'Connor, Kevin A. 1976. Proto-Hakka. *Journal of Asian and African Studies* 11, 1–64.

Ohta Tatsuo 1958. *Chūgokugo rekishi bunpō*. Tokyo: Kōnan Shoten.

Oūyáng Juéyà and Zhèng Yíqīng 1980. *Líyǔ jiǎnzhì*. Peking: Minzu Chubanshe.

Pān Màodǐng *et al.* 1963. Fújiàn hànyǔ fāngyán fēnqū lüèshuō. *Zhongguo Yuwen* 6, 475–95.

Park, B. Nam 1968. *Korean basic course*. Washington: Foreign Service Institute.

Pinnow, Heinz-Jürgen 1959. *Versuch einer historischen Lautlehre der Kharia-Sprache*. Wiesbaden: Otto Harrassowitz.

Poppe, Nicholas 1957. *The Mongolian monuments in Ḥpʼags-pa script*. Wiesbaden: Otto Harrassowitz.

Poppe, Nicholas 1960. *Vergleichende Grammatik der altaischen Sprachen*, Teil 1, *Vergleichende Lautlehre*. Wiesbaden: Otto Harrassowitz.

Pulleyblank, E. G. 1962a. The consonantal system of Old Chinese. *Asia Major* 9, 58–144.

Pulleyblank, E. G. 1962b. The consonantal system of Old Chinese, part 2. *Asia Major* 9, 206–65.

Pulleyblank, E. G. 1970. Late Middle Chinese, part 1. *Asia Major* 15, 197–239.

Pulleyblank, E. G. 1971. Late Middle Chinese, part 2. *Asia Major* 16, 121–66.

Pulleyblank, E. G. 1978. The nature of the Middle Chinese tones and their development. *Journal of Chinese Linguistics* 6, 173–203.

Pulleyblank, E. G. 1979. Some examples of colloquial pronunciation from the Southern Liang dynasty (AD 502–556). In Wolfgang Bauer (ed.), *Studia Sino-Mongolica: Festschrift für Herbert Franke*. Wiesbaden: Franz Steiner.

Pulleyblank, E. G. 1984. *Middle Chinese: a study in historical phonology*. Vancouver: University of British Columbia Press.

Purnell, Herbert C. 1970. *Toward a reconstruction of Proto-Miao-Yao*. PhD dissertation, Cornell University.

Purnell, Herbert C. (ed.) 1972. *Miao and Yao linguistic studies: selected articles in English translation*. Ithaca: Cornell University.

Qián Xuán 1980. Qín Hàn bóshū jiǎndú zhōng de tōngjiǎzì. *Nanjing Shifan Xueyuan Xuebao* 3, 44–8.

Qiú Xīguī 1978. Hànzì xíngchéng wèntí de chūbù tànsuǒ. *Zhongguo Yuwen* 3, 162–71.

Ramstedt, G. J. 1952. *Einführung in die altaische Sprachwissenschaft*, 2: *Formenlehre*. Helsinki: Suomalais-Ugrilainen Seura.

Ramstedt, G. J. 1957. *Einführung in die altaische Sprachwissenschaft*, 1: *Lautlehre*. Helsinki: Suomalais-Ugrilainen Seura.

Sapir, Edward 1921. *Language*. New York: Harcourt, Brace & World.

Schaank, S. H. 1897–8. Ancient Chinese phonetics. *Tʼoung Pao* 8, 361–77, 457–86; 9, 28–57.

Sherard, Michael. 1980. *A synchronic phonology of modern colloquial Shanghai*. Computational analyses of Asian and African Languages, monograph series, no. 5. Tokyo: National Inter-University Research Institute of Asian and African Languages and Cultures.

Shorto, H. L. 1962. *A dictionary of modern spoken Mon*. London: Oxford University Press.

Shorto, H. L. (ed.) 1963. *Linguistic comparison in South East Asia and the Pacific. Collected papers in Oriental and African studies*. London: School of Oriental and African Studies.

Sofronov, M. V. 1979. *Kitajskij jazyk i kitajskoe obščestvo*. Moscow: Nauka.

Solheim, William G. 1964. Pottery and the Malayo-Polynesians. *Current Anthropology* 5, 360, 376–84.

Stimson, Hugh M. 1966. *The Jong Yuan In Yunn – a guide to Old Mandarin pronunciation*. New Haven: Far Eastern Publications.

Tai, James H. Y. 1973. Chinese as an SOV language. *Chicago Linguistic Society* 9, 659–70.
Tai, James H. Y. 1975. On two functions of place adverbials in Mandarin Chinese. *Journal of Chinese Linguistics* 3, 154–79.
Táng Yùmíng and Zhōu Xīfù 1985. Lùn Xiān-Qín Hànyǔ bèidòngshì de fāzhǎn. *Zhongguo Yuwen* 4, 281–5.
Táng Zuòfān 1980. Dìsān rénchēng dàicí "tā" de qǐyuán shídài. *Yuyanxue Luncong* 6, 55–63.
Teng, Shou-hsin 1973. Negations and aspects in Chinese. *Journal of Chinese Linguistics* 1, 14–27.
Teng, Shou-hsin 1975. *A semantic study of transitivity relations in Chinese*. Berkeley, Los Angeles and London: University of California Press.
Thompson, Laurence C. 1965. *A Vietnamese grammar*. Seattle: University of Washington Press.
Thompson, Laurence C. 1976. Proto-Viet-Muong phonology. In Philip N. Jenner *et al.* (eds.), *Austroasiatic Studies*, part 2. Honolulu: University Press of Hawaii.
Tōdō, Akiyasu 1957. *Chūgokugo on'inron*. Tokyo: Kōnan Shoin.
Volpicelli, M. Z. 1986. *Chinese phonology, an attempt to discover the sound of the ancient language, and to recover the lost rimes of China*. Shanghai: China Gazette.
Wang, Fred Fangyu 1966. *Mandarin Chinese dictionary, Chinese–English*. South Orange: Seton Hall University Press.
Wang, Fred Fangyu 1971. *Mandarin Chinese dictionary, English–Chinese*. South Orange: Seton Hall University Press.
Wáng Huán 1959. *Bǎzìjù hé bèizìjù*. Shanghai: Xin Zhishi Chubanshe.
Wáng Lì 1937. *Zhōngguó xiàndài yǔfǎ*. Chongqing: Shangwu Yinshuguan.
Wáng Lì 1957. *Hànyǔ shǐgǎo*. Peking: Kexue Chubanshe.
Wang, William S.-Y. 1963. Some syntactic rules for Mandarin. *Proceedings of the Ninth International Congress of Linguists*, 192–202.
Wang, William S.-Y. 1965. Two aspect markers in Mandarin. *Language* 41, 457–70.
Wang, William S.-Y. and Li Kung-pu 1967. Tone 3 in Pekinese. *Journal of Speech and Hearing* 10, 629–36.
War Department (USA) 1945. *Dictionary of spoken Chinese*. Washington, DC.
Wén Yòu 1984. "Yú" "yú" xīnlùn. *Zhongguo Yuyan Xuebao* 2, 44–8.
Whinnom, Keith 1965. The origin of European-based pidgins and creoles. *Orbis* 14, 509–27.
Whinnom, Keith 1971. Linguistic hybridization and the "special case" of pidgins and creoles. In Dell Hymes (ed.), *Pidginization and creolization of languages*. London: Cambridge University Press.
Williams, Samuel W. 1874. *A syllabic dictionary of the Chinese language*. Shanghai: American Presbyterian Mission Press.
Wong, James Poy 1970. *A study of the T'ai Shan (Hoi San) dialect*. Term paper for Chinese 299, spring term. San Francisco State College, San Francisco.
Xīnhuá Císhūshè 1953. *Xīnhuá zìdiǎn*. Peking: Remin Jiaoyu Chubanshe. (Since 1957, published by Shangwu Yinshuguan.)
Xióng Zhènghūi 1960. Guāngzé, Shàowǔ huà li de gǔ rùshēng zì. *Zhongguo Yuwen* 10, 310.
Xú Tōngqiāng and Yè Fēishēng 1979. "Wǔ-sì" yǐlái hànyǔ yǔfǎ yánjiū píngshù. *Zhongguo Yuwen* 3, 166–73.
Yakhontov, S. E. 1960. Fonetika kitajskogo jazyka v tysjačiletije do n.e. *Problemy Vostokovedenija* 6, 102–15. Translated by Jerry Norman in *Unicorn* 6 (1970), 52–75.
Yakhontov, S. E. 1965. *Drevnekitajskij Jazyk*. Moscow: Nauka.
Yang, Shih-feng 1957. *Táiwān Táoyuán Kèjiā fāngyán*. Institute of History and Philology Monograph, series A, no. 22. Taipei: Academia Sinica.
Yang, Shih-feng 1969a. *Yúnnán fāngyán diàochá bàogào*. Institute of History and Philology

of Academia Sinica, special publication no. 56. Taipei: Academia Sinica.

Yang, Shih-feng 1969b. Nánchāng yīnxì. *Bulletin of the Institute of History and Philology* 39, 152–204.

Yang, Shih-feng 1971. Jiāngxī fāngyán shēngdiào de diàolèi. *Bulletin of the Institute of History and Philology* 43, 403–32.

Yang, Shih-feng 1974. *Húnán fāngyán diàochá bàogào.* Institute of History and Philology of Academia Sinica, special publication no. 66. Taipei: Academia Sinica.

Yang, Shih-feng 1984. *Sìchuān fāngyán diàochá bàogào.* Institute of History and Philology of Academia Sinica, special publications no. 82. Taipei: Academia Sinica.

Yang, Shih-feng and Ching, Eugene 1971. The Ling Pao dialect. *The Tsing Hua Journal of Chinese Studies*, new series 9, 106–47.

Yao Language Team 1962. Yáozú yǔyán gàikuàng. *Zhongguo Yuwen* 3, 141–8. English translation in Purnell 1972.

Yates, Warren G. and Tryon, Absorn 1970. *Thai basic course.* Washington: Foreign Service Institute.

Yú Gēnyuán *et al.* 1979. Guānyú tūiguǎng pǔtōnghuà gōngzuò de jǐdiǎn rènshí. *Zhongguo Yuwen* 6, 459–63.

Yú Zhífū 1975. *Fèngxīn yīnxì.* Taipei: Yee Wen Publishing Co.

Yuán Jiāhuá 1960. *Hànyǔ fāngyán gàiyào.* Peking: Wenzi Gaige Chubanshe.

Yue, Anne O. 1979. *The Tengxian dialect of Chinese.* Computational Analyses of Asian and African Languages, Monograph Series, no. 3. Tokyo: National Inter-University Research Institute on Asian and African Languages and Cultures.

Zhāng Cháobǐng 1980. Máo Zédōng xuǎnjí yòng zì de zìshù, císhù àn yīnjié fēnbù qíngkuàng. *Zhongguo Yuwen* 3, 196–205.

Zhāng Hùiyīng 1982. Shì "shénme". *Zhongguo Yuwen* 4, 302–5.

Zhāng Hùiyīng 1984. "Hé" yǔ "héwù". *Fangyan* 4, 51–6.

Zhāng Qíngcháng 1978. Màntán hànyǔ zhōng de méngyǔ jiècí. *Zhongguo Yuwen* 3, 196–8.

Zhào Chéng 1979. *Zhōngguó gǔdài yùnshū.* Peking: Zhonghua Shuju.

Zhào Jīnmíng 1979. Dūnhuáng biànwén zhōng suǒ jiàn de "liǎo" hé "zhuó". *Zhongguo Yuwen* 1, 65–9.

Zhào Yīntáng 1936. *Zhōngyuán yīnyùn yánjiū.* Shanghai: Shangwu Yinshuguan.

Zhōngguó Dàcídiǎn Biānzuǎnchù 1936. *Guóyǔ cídiǎn.* Shanghai: Shangwu Yinshuguan.

Zhōngguó Shèhùi Kēxuéyuàn, Yǔyán Yánjiūsuǒ 1978. *Xiàndài hànyǔ cídiǎn.* Peking: Shangwu Yinshuguan.

Zhōu Zǔmó 1956. Cóng wénxué yǔyán de gàiniàn lùn hànyǔ de yǎyán, wényán, gǔwén děng wèntí. *Beijing Daxue Xuebao* 1, 127–35.

Zhōu Zǔmó 1966. Qièyùn de xìngzhì hé tāde yīnxì jīchǔ. In *Wènxué jí.* Peking: Zhonghua Shuju.

Zhōu Zǔmó and Wú Xiǎolíng 1956. *Fāngyán jiàojiàn jí tōngjiǎn.* Peking: Kexue Chubanshe.

Zhū Déxī 1961. Shuō "dì". *Zhongguo Yuwen* 12, 1–15.

Zhū Déxī 1966. Guānyú "shuō dì". *Zhongguo Yuwen* 1, 37–46.

Zhū Déxī 1978. "Dì" zì jiégòu hé pànduànjù. *Zhongguo Yuwen* 1, 23–7; 2, 104–9.

Zhū Jūyì 1956. *Yuánjù súyǔ fāngyán lìshì.* Shangwu Yinshuguan.

Zhù Mínchè 1958. Xiān qín liǎng hàn shíqī de dòngcí bǔyǔ. *Yuyanxue Luncong* 2, 17–30.

Zhù Mínchè 1982. Zhuāzǐ yǔlù zhōng "dì dǐ" de yǔfǎ zuòyòng. *Zhongguo Yuwen* 3, 193–7.

Zhū Zhìníng 1964. Wěiwúěryǔ gàikuàng. *Zhongguo Yuwen* 2, 153–71.

Zograf, E. T. 1962. *Očerk grammatiki srednekitajskogo jazyka.* Moscow: Vostočnye Literatury.

INDEX

ā-prefix, 113
a 'sentence particle', 150f.
a 'vocative particle', 158
ābhyantara, 31
ablative, 163
Academia Sinica, 188
Academy of Sciences, 178
action verbs, 164
active, 164
adjective, 92, 157
adverbial clauses, 164
adverbial modifiers, 105, 158
adverbs, 94, 127f., 158
adverbs of degree, 94
adverbs of scope, 94
agent, 161, 167
agent of passive verbs, 101, 129, 164
alphabetic writing in China, 257–63
Altaic languages, 6, 10, 12, 18, 20, 48
alveolar consonants, 139
ān 'what', 91
ăn 'I', 121
Analytic Dictionary, 44
analytic languages, 10; see also isolating languages
Ancient Chinese, see Middle Chinese
ā-nǐ 'you', 113
Annen, 53, 57
ā-nóng 'I', 113
apical vowels, 194, 201, 237
Arabic script, 74
Archaic Chinese, see Old Chinese
archaicisms, 179
ā-shúi, 'who', 113
aspect, 163f.
aspiration as a criterion for classification of Mǐn, 228–30
atonal syllables, 195; see also Weak stress
Austroasiatic, 7f., 18f., 54–6, 213, 231
Austronesian languages, 8
"auxiliary nouns", 174
auxiliary verbs, 92, 100f., 124f., 165f.

bā 'eight' (sandhi behavior), 150
bǎ 'instrumental preposition', 129, 130
bǎ 'pretransitive preposition', 131, 161
ba 'advisative particle', 158, 169, 170
bāfēn, 267 (c. 3, n. 8)

bāhya, 31
Bái Dízhōu, 188
Bǎi jiā xing, 50
Bái Jūyù, 113, 129
báihuà, 109, 134, 135, 136, 152, 176, 246, 247, 249, 255, 257
bèi 'passive marker', 102, 129, 164
bèi 'plural marker', 89, 120
Běijīng kǒuyǔ yúfǎ, 153
běn 'measure', 116
Benedict, Paul, 15
benefactive, 128
béng 'prohibitive', 127
Benveniste, Emile, 268 (c. 4, n. 9)
bǐ 'marker of temporal clauses', 107
bǐ 'that', 90
bì 'perfective marker', 123
-biān 'suffix for localizers', 117
-bian(r) 'suffix for localizers', 162
biànwén, 123
bidialectalism, 250–2
bié 'prohibitive', 127, 158, 165, 169f., 269 nn. 16, 17
bilabials: in Kèjiā, 211; in Middle Chinese, 211; in Mǐn, 211, 231
bilingual dictionaries, 172–6
bilingualism, 252f.
Bloomfield, Leonard, 152, 153
borrowing, see loanwords
bound, 154, 174
bronze inscriptions, 61
bronze script, 58, 64
bù 'negative', 76, 97, 126, 157, 158, 165, 168, 196
bù 'negator in potential compounds', 166
bù, sandhi behavior, 150
bù céng 'not yet', 124, 227
bù xū 'prohibitive', 126
bú yào 'prohibitive', 126, 165, 169f.
bú yòng 'prohibitive', 126
búbì 'doesn't have to', 165
bùcéng see bù céng
Buddhist texts, 111
bú-shì 'is not', 112
búyào see bú yào
búyòng 'doesn't have to', 165

Cantonese, 187, 191, 214f., 219, 246

283